D1061917

THE MINISTRY
OF HEALING

THE MINISTRY OF HEALING

VOLUME TWO

The History of the Alexian Brothers from 1789 to the Present

CHRISTOPHER J. KAUFFMAN

A CROSSROAD BOOK

The Seabury Press • New York

To my mother

Berenice O'Brien Kauffman Plimpton

and to the memory of my father

Daniel Emmanuel Kauffman

1978
The Seabury Press
815 Second Avenue
New York, N.Y. 10017

Copyright © 1978 by The Seabury Press, Inc. All rights re-
served. No part of this book may be reproduced, stored in a
retrieval system, or transmitted, in any form or by any means,
electronic, mechanical, photocopying, recording, or otherwise,
without the written permission of The Seabury Press.
Printed in the United States of America
Library of Congress Cataloging in Publication Data
Kauffman, Christopher J   1936-
Tamers of death.
"A crossroad book."
Vol. 2 has title: The ministry of healing.
Includes bibliographical references and index,
CONTENTS: v. 1. From 1300 to 1789.—v. 2. From 1789
to the present.
1. Alexian Brothers—History. I. Title.
BX2890.K38   271'.07   76-24469
ISBN 0-8164-0387-2

CONTENTS

PART THREE
STRUGGLE WITH MODERNITY, 1920–1970

PREFACE

When Brother Felix Bettendorf, c.f.a., and I first discussed the
need for a history of the Alexian Brothers I had no idea that I
would be embarking on such a pleasurable journey through
nearly seven hundred years of institutional, church, and cultural
history. Like all such journeys, this one has left a strong imprint
upon my understanding of the usable past, the contours of the
present, and the trends toward the future. In the process I have
learned a bit more of myself. I am grateful to Father John F.
Bannon, s.j., for introducing me to the Alexian Brothers.

The burdens of my historical travels were lightened by
Alexian Brothers, scholars, friends, and family. Superiors General Brothers Augustine Lohman, c.f.a., and Felix Bettendorf
c.f.a., graciously provided direction and support. The Alexian
Provincials, Brothers Ludger Göller, c.f.a., and Thomas Poier,
c.f.a., in Germany, Dominic Walsh, c.f.a., in England and
Ireland, Clements Aarts, c.f.a., in Belgium, and Brother Erhard
Flotzinger, Superior of the Alexians in Neuss and Siegburg, and
the American Provincials, Brothers Florian Eberle, c.f.a., and
Robert Wilde, c.f.a., provided warm hospitality for me and my
family during research visits to their archives. I am indebted to
Brother Damien Stayaert, c.f.a., of the Belgian Alexians, for
sharing with me his wealth of information and Alexiana, to
Brother Cornelius Kearney, c.f.a., of Twyford Abbey, London,
for his private archives and his oral history interviews, to Brother
Andrew McKenzie, c.f.a., for his charming anecdotes on Alexian past, and to Gregory Isenhart for his professional organization of the American Provincial Archives, for sharing with me
his notes and remembrances, and for his proofreading. Also
Brother Roy Godwin, c.f.a., the current American archivist, has
been very helpful. I am very grateful for Brother James Darby's

assistance in locating valuable documents in the current files of the American Province. Thanks to Brother Innocent Doonan, C.F.A., I was able to chat with his old friend, Father James J. Mertz, S.J., who played a historic role in the American Province. So many Brothers have aided me on my exploration of Alexian past and so warmly extended their hospitality that each of them is lodged somewhere in this book.

Many colleagues and friends have made helpful suggestions and criticisms, particularly Professors José M. Sanchez and Frederick Cowie of St. Louis University. Professor George Hickenlooper of McKendree College kindly made available his scholarly, editorial, and linguistic skills. His editorial criticism and his help with difficult German, Flemish, and French texts were invaluable. Besides helping me with German texts, Dr. Benjamin Shearer, a historian of ideas, was a responsive sounding board during many discussions on methodology and organization. Special thanks to Mrs. MollyLu Vonland, an expert typist, for patiently deciphering my handwriting and the convuluted way in which the manuscript developed.

Tamers of Death, the first volume of this study, was dedicated to my wife, Helen. Because she has been part of the taming process of everything I have written, her presence permeates this book. "How many pages did you write today, Daddy?" was uttered many times over the past three years. Loving thanks to Jane, Christopher, and Kathryn Ann for inspiriting me with the joy and the wonderment of youth.

INTRODUCTION

The introduction to volume one, *Tamers of Death*, involved the author in a lengthy self-exploration of his relationship to the religious-cultural problem of the late medieval world, as well as an exploration of the methodology that allowed him to develop his theses. Because his cast of characters was for the most part oral folk mendicants, many of his hypotheses regarding the motivating spirit of the early Alexians reached the level of theses only through analogical and inferential reasoning.

To introduce volume two requires no such lengthy self-exploration. As a participant in the modern world with an abundance of documentary evidence, the historian of the modern Alexians shares much, historically, with his cast of characters. As a student-participant in a culture influenced by the French Revolution and the major nineteenth-century isms (i.e., liberalism, capitalism, industrialism, secularism, socialism, nationalism and imperialism), he can immerse himself in those documents that reveal the impact of these trends upon the Alexian Brothers with the confidence of passing from hypotheses to theses with relative ease. However, self-reflection must be persistent if he is to avoid viewing the past through the lens of bias, prejudice, and hindsight. Also, because volume two is organically tied to hypotheses and theses of volume one, the writer is required to state explicitly the philosophical and theological content forming the ground of volume one. In the premodern world the profound events of life and death were ordered by religious symbol and ritual. By analogy and inference one may penetrate the world-view of late medieval people and, more particularly, discern the charism of the original Alexian Brothers. A fivefold conclusion was based upon this ground.

1

These oral-culture mendicants lived out of the New Testament, which converted them into apostles of Jesus; their mendicant life in urban squalor was implicitly grounded in the sacred, i.e., they lived their poverty in quasi-mystical terms as embodiments of Jesus; the specific calling, their charism, was gradually discerned as being one of ministry to the "outsider," the plague victim, the insane, to whom they brought sacramental ritual and symbol at bedside and graveside: after 175 years on the borderline (somewhere between the monastery and the parish) they institutionalized themselves into a religious order to preserve their tradition and to guarantee their future.[1]

Volume two is the story of the Alexian Brothers' passage to the modern world. A continuum of modernity stretches from the Renaissance to the present. Because it involves every facet of culture and because aspects of tradition persist to the present, the continuum is multilinear and is entwined with nonmodern vestiges of the past as well as antimodern trends and movements of the present. Indeed, the modernization process is characterized by dialectical tensions.

One must distinguish between modern attitudes and the modernization process. King Louis XIV of France was a traditionalist who strongly influenced the development of the modern state, whereas Henry Thoreau possessed a deeply modern notion of individualism but escaped the modern world. The modernization process is most easily appreciated by juxtaposing traditional agrarian society with urban industrial society; a peasant uprising with the French Revolution, religious myth, symbol, and ritual with secular analytical thought; political structure of feudalism with that of the national state; and, in general, the folk life in the fields and in the workshop with complex technological life in megalopolis. Between 1789 and the present the Alexian Brothers went from medieval community to modern statelike governance structures, from nonliterate working-class custodial nurses to sophisticated middle-class nurses with scientific and technological training, and from hospice to asylum and general hospital. As they evolved into a modern nursing congregation they reflected portions of the evolution of the church. This volume rests upon a threefold thesis: the Alexian Brothers developed their medieval charism into modern communal and ministerial forms in defense of traditional world Catholicism; as these forms evolved along divergent lines in each province, the

Brothers gradually adopted modern professional attitudes, e.g., toleration of pluralism, drive for individual fulfillment, analytical perspective toward life's problems vis-à-vis mysteries; since Vatican II they have experienced profound tensions as they grope to integrate the communal, prayer, and ministerial lives according to the spirit of Vatican II and the charism of their anonymous founders, within and outside their centuries-old hospital structure.

Part one, 1789–1865, opens when the Alexians were floundering between a world of ritual and symbol and closes when they had become absorbed into the antimodern spirit so characteristic of the papacy of Pius IX. During this period the Aachen Alexians evolved from a tiny family steeped in the abuses of poverty and directionless in a confusing milieu to a papal congregation with a well-designed constitution, which tightly regulated their communal, prayer, and ministerial lives, and with a thriving asylum ministry that was in the vanguard of the modern healing ministry of the mentally ill.

Part two, 1865–1920, is the story of their expansion to America and England. Because of the congregation's deeply standardized and centralized authority structures, the German Alexian imprint was heavy upon the divergent characters of the two non-German provinces. However, the general-hospital ministry of the American Province deeply affected its development. Though still under the authority of the German Motherhouse, the U.S. Province Americanized and modernized along its own lines. A low rate of vocations, the English legal and social barriers against male nurses, and poor economic conditions prevented the English Province from developing along modern lines. Until well into the twentieth century it remained an enclave of German Alexian tradition.

Part three, 1920–1970, is arranged around the topics of depression, totalitarianism, war, accelerated pace of social change, and Vatican Council II. By 1920 the institutionalization of the Alexian asylums and hospitals is in the forefront of their story; from 1920 to the present the modernization process, spurred by the catalyst of war, continues to have a strong impact upon the Brothers' institutions and, ultimately, their way of life. The congregation possessed a modern state-like authority structure through which the Brothers could manage their large institutions and still remain aloof from the secular world. However, as their hospitals progressed, the need for professionally trained Brothers brought them into closer relations with the laity. Vatican II engendered a radical reexamination of the role of the religious in the modern world; most of the proposals led to a breakdown of the dichotomy between the cloister and main street. In the immediate post-Vatican II period the Alexian Brothers drastically departed from the ideals of the nineteenth century: centralization gave way to subsidiarity; provincial diversity rather than uniformity became cardinal; the self-fulfillment of the individual Brother blended with the traditional esprit de corps; a groping for new directions in spirituality replaced the traditional emphasis on devotional exercises; in short, as in most religious orders, a new theology of the religious life, new authority structures, new movements in spirituality and in ministry characterize the Alexian Brothers, particularly those within the American Province.

Part three is integrated by the climax of the modernization process. Though one must struggle against hindsight's tendency to narrate the past through the perspective of the present, one is compelled by the complexity and the vast amount of evidence to organize the material along those lines which form a continuum from the past to the present. The modernization-process theme is merely a mechanical device for discovering and ordering historical truth.

The concluding chapter deals with the entire congregation as it was directed by the Vatican Council II fathers to embark on renewal and adaptation to the modern world. The epilogue, 1970–1977, is a brief summary of recent major events as they reflect trends in the congregation and in society. Though the making of the modern Alexian Brothers is the theme of this volume, it is predicated on the ironic fact that to be a thoroughly modern Alexian Brother one must discern and repattern the persistent strands of one's traditional charism.

PART ONE

✢

DESINTEGRATION, REFORM, AND REVIVAL, 1789-1865

1

Eighteenth-Century
Church and Society

I

The Alexian Brothers have lingered in the shadows of ecclesiastical history. Though their nursing homes and large hospitals have housed tens of thousands of patients over the past century, few appreciate the richness of their past. Even in Aachen, where they dwell on Alexianergraben, knowledge of the Brothers' origins and their contribution to the general welfare of the city for nearly seven centuries is limited to local-history enthusiasts. Indeed, even the Brothers themselves lack a full awareness of their past; the practical demands of nursing and the founderless obscurity of their origins prevent many from pursuing the historian's quest. Brother Bernhard Giergen of the Cologne Alexians and Brother Ignatius Wiegers of the Aachen community prove to have been exceptions.[1] Unfortunately the history of their houses has not been widely disseminated.

Readers of volume one will recall the themes woven into the narrative. The Lollard and Brot-Beghard founding Brothers were lay mendicants who had chosen a middle path between the monastery and the parish.[2] They preferred to dwell on the anonymous limits of the ecclesiastical structure where they gradually concentrated their ministry on serving those on the limits of society: the dying, the dead, and the plague sufferers. Their heroic response to the victims of the Black Death (1348–1350) marked their services as vital to the towns of the Rhineland,

7

Westphalia, and the Low Countries, which were ever in danger of pestilence. Within a century they had expanded to dozens of houses, each of which entered into a contractual agreement with the town "welfare establishments." During this period they were harassed by papal and diocesan inquisitors because their Beghard-Lollard identity was mistakenly associated with other lay mendicants who preached a hard anticlerical line and distorted mysticism to form a rationale for amoral anarchy. The Brothers' friends in city government and later in the parishes and diocesan chanceries successfully sought papal protection for them. Expansion and harassment urged the disparate Cellite houses to form a common consciousness and organization.

The next step, that of acquiring the status of a religious order, was motivated not only by their need for recognition and their projection of permanence but also by the then dominant climate of spirituality, the *Devotio Moderna,* and by the current reform spirit embodied in John Busch and Nicholas of Cusa.[3] Deeply disturbed by the decline of monasticism, these reformers stressed the need for a strict observance of religious vows and the monastic rules. These practical and spiritual considerations necessitated obtaining the status of a religious order. In 1472, after nearly two hundred years of self-styled mendicant existence, the Brothers received papal approval as lay conventuals in a religious institute under the monastic rule of St. Augustine.

The shift from Beghard-Lollard communalism to the institutionalization of the Cellite congregation did not mark a drastic break with their original spirit. The founding Brothers pursued the *vita apostolica*[4] by immersing themselves in those gospel streams that stressed Jesus the helper and healer of the poor and afflicted. Like the *pauperes Christi* groups, which had been spawned by the awakening of the laity during the previous two centuries, the early Brothers identified voluntary poverty and their ministry to the dying and the dead as sacramental invocations of Jesus. Situated on the limits of ecclesiastical and secular society, their nursing and burial response to the plague victims was the clearest manifestation of their charism. Infused with the sacrament of poverty, these folk mendicants were apostolic servants who brought ritual and symbol to diseased exiles.

Their general ministry to the dying and the dead marked them as tamers of death; their specific calling—to minister to the plague victim and later to the insane—marked them as passage brothers. Their sacramental witness was viaticum for the plagued and the insane who were cast out from society, exiles who could only wait for the liberation of death.

Beghards and Lollards viewed their roles in the church not as officials in the institution but as servants. When they became a religious order with an institutional structure they routinized their prayer day and developed an authority system. Yet they were rather more a confederation of small families than a large unitary society. Their living tradition of mendicancy, communalism, and ministry (infused with the *Imitation of Christ* spirituality of the *Devotio Moderna*) maintained their original charism. The late medieval Cellite worked hard and long hours, but he did not distinguish between work and his religious witness. He was not institutionalized in the modern sense in which his prayer time and work time were tightly compartmentalized and dichotomized. Though the Alexians' (i.e., Cellites of the Middle Ages) way of life, their gift, their sacrament-witness and their general character expressed by the terms *tamers of death* and *passage brothers* were refined during the late medieval period, the evolution of culture from the waning of the Middle Ages to the rise of the modern period did not profoundly influence the Brothers' unique character. Until the French Revolution threatened them with extinction, the Brothers remained a medieval enclave.

Indeed, if one could follow the Brothers on their daily routes through Cologne or Aachen or Antwerp, once through a late-medieval day and again through a late-eighteenth-century day, one would probably be struck by the continuity of their activities. Each time one would see the Cellites ministering to sickbed and graveside. A closer view of the Brothers would reveal their bent postures and calloused hands, the marks of hard work in the funeral processions and the cemeteries. The late medieval and early modern Brothers were drawn from the "little people" nurtured on hard work, who daily struggled for subsistence, and who explained the events of birth and death, of a joy and sadness in terms of the divine drama of Providence. The

death motif would dominate both scenes including common religious symbols, the Cellite habit, and the passage rituals for the
dying and the dead. Yet the two-dimensional nature of the pictures could mislead one to conclude that the Cellites had been
dwelling in timelessness for nearly five hundred years.

A different pair of scenes, depicting daily life within the Cellite houses, would convey a contrary impression. We have specific documents containing these vivid contrasts. John Busch's
fifteenth-century "portrait" of the Cellites stressed their stringent asceticism, their many hours in prayer, and their strong
sense of detachment.[5] Brother Hendrik Kerkhoff (in his introduction to the 1711 Cellite Rule for the Brabant Province)
painted a very bleak picture of the Brothers' life, stressing the
need for a strict observance of the rule, urging superiors not to
spare the rod, and endorsing rules for the Brothers' behavior,
which were long on punishment and short on trust.[6] The gentle
tones and soft colors on Busch's canvas, in contrast to the authoritarian blacks and whites of Brother Hendrik's, portray the
changes that had occurred. Busch may have added his own romantic coloration to the Brothers' way of life but, because he
was well known for his authoritarian approach to monastic reform, his credibility is strong. Brother Hendrik was also a reformer who appears to have been driven to extremes by what
he considered the Brothers' flagrant abuses of the religious life.
Documents evidencing the general abuses of poverty add credibility to Brother Hendrik's witness.

In urging the need for reform Brother Hendrik stressed a
return to the purity of the Cellite foundations. The Rule of 1711
was, therefore, a recapitulation of tradition implying that old law
was good law.[7] This conservative position reveals a major difference between the medieval and early modern Cellites; the
latter possessed a historical consciousness. When the medieval
Brothers absorbed the principles of the *Devotio Moderna* they
were apparently conscious of the need to structure their prayer
day to guarantee a closer contemplative harmony between their
lives and the life of Christ. Their historical consciousness, which
was limited to the time span from Beghard origins to the mid-
fifteenth century (roughly 150 years), was extremely primitive
by modern standards. Their oral-culture perspective situated

10

them in a timeless sphere in which the spoken word was capable of invoking the reality of the past rather than an idea of the past. When Brother Hendrik made his written plea for a return to the pure foundations of the Cellites he revealed an idea of the past as distinct from the present; he had a conceptualized frame of reference for deviations from tradition and the proper course for reform. The contrasting view of the two portraits by John Busch and Brother Hendrik leads to the conclusion that there were vast differences between the medieval and the early modern Alexian.

The eighteenth-century Cellites were not just more worldly but were also conscious of their secular departures from the past. Brother Hendrik's comments, the break between Aachen and Cologne in the early eighteenth century, and the Aachen constitution of 1763 all indicate abuses of poverty and the need for reform.[8] Yet the documents fail to illustrate specific abuses. Judging from the number of wealthy pensioners residing in the houses and the number of valuable religious and art objects there, one concludes that the Brothers were courting the rich. Income from the funerals in Aachen brought in enough money to allow the community to lend considerable sums of cash during the mid-eighteenth century. In Cologne and Aachen the Brothers owned a goodly amount of income-producing property.[9] The correlation between their degree of prosperity and the apparent decline in their religious life is impossible to chart. One may, however, draw some fairly strong inferences by examining the trends of eighteenth-century ecclesiastical and secular societies and by contrasting the Alexians with other monastic communities.

II

Eighteenth-century Europe may be best understood by the notion of the unity of opposites. In many areas, such as France, modern states with their sophisticated bureaucracy were situated at the apex of feudal social structures, where the nobility and the church dwelt in privilege and peasants and curates dwelt in ignorance, relative poverty, and frequent exploitation. Merchant enclaves dominated the affairs of towns, nations, and empires. At the same time much of the land was tied up in feudal tenure, labor was harnessed to the guilds, and a great deal of potential capital was spent on luxuries rather than invested in banking, trade, and industry.

In France and part of Germany, the Roman Catholic Church of the eighteenth century was ensconced in the Ancien Régime where it presumed its privileges and censored the "dangerous" expressions of reason, which were frequently riddled with anti-clericalism. Choosing to ignore the obvious contradiction of a well-educated, sophisticated, and wealthy hierarchy ruling over an ignorant, primitive, and poor clergy, the eighteenth-century papacy dissolved the Jesuits, its traditional intellectual and po-litical palace guards. The story of the suppression of the Jesuits is pregnant with those trends thematic to mid-eighteenth-cen-tury church and society. The Society of Jesus was, in a sense, a major casualty of the predominantly political battle between the "enlightened despots" and traditional corporate bodies, which hampered the expansion of the state's absolute power.

The Cellites were remote bystanders in such dramas, but they were subjected to the religious and secular trends that shaped the conflict over the Jesuits. The secular sentiments of the pa-pacy were circulating on the diocesan level: the struggle for wealth and power by both the Jesuits and their clerical enemies affected many smaller religious communities. Critics of the Jes-uits also lashed out at the "parasitical" character of all religious orders, and the ambitions of enlightened despots within the hierarchy of church and state directly affected the Cellites of Cologne, Aachen, and Antwerp.

Catholicism in the Rhineland reflected the general eigh-teenth-century conflict between tradition and reform. Popular piety expressed itself in medieval forms, the veneration of relics and local patron saints, mass pilgrimages, and many religious holidays. The church self-consciously nourished the medieval simplicity of the laity. One bishop advocated the abolition of all rural schools and all but a few within the towns because "a knowledge of reading and writing is usually the main source for the poison of heresy. . . . The illiterate section . . . of the peo-ple preserves its Catholic faith as a matter of course."[10]

While many bishops favored an ignorant laity they themselves were frequently lax in performing their duties. For example, when an apostolic nuncio visited a small town in the Cologne archdiocese, he noted 16,000 persons who had not been confirmed.[11] Pluralism and absenteeism, abuses harking back to the Middle Ages, were not uncommon. For example, in 1763 Klemens Wenceslaus, the fifth son of the Polish king Augustus, was simultaneously appointed bishop of Münster, of Paderborn, and of Hildesheim.[12]

Reform Catholicism, representing the Enlightenment in society, was attempting to drive a wedge into traditional attitudes and practices in Germany. Abbot Johann Ignaz von Felbiger vigorously supported popular education by introducing a new catechism and fresh instructional techniques to form a critical-thinking laity.[13] Some ecclesiastical states ruled by bishops introduced toleration edicts and attempted to curb the superstitious excesses of pilgrimages and the veneration of saints. Reform Catholicism was a diverse movement with many of its proponents motivated by the political ambition to rationalize the church rather than an ambition to purify her rich tradition. The effects of the reforms were also mixed; in 1785 when the archbishop of Mainz introduced German singing into the liturgy, he was confronted with mob protests provoked by the fear that "Lutheranism was on the march."[14]

The most controversial reformer, whose heretical theories were borrowed by both devout Catholics and despotic princes, was Nikolaus von Hontheim, suffragan bishop of Trier, a city where the Cellites were located. In 1763 Hontheim, under the pseudonym Justinus Febronious, published a scholarly yet polemical treatise on the constitution of the church. Influenced by Gallicanism, Jansenism, and Enlightenment theories on natural law, Hontheim advocated a separation of the legislative and executive powers of the church, with the Pope as chief executive following the directives of his legislature, the Council of Bishops. Though Hontheim supported the primacy of Rome, his antimonarchical proposals virtually divested the papacy of supremacy. The center of corruption was the Roman Curia, which he said was responsible not only for tyrannizing the dioceses but also for the schism with the Eastern church and for preventing the reunion of Protestants with the church. He advocated the "reestablishment" of national churches under the secular arm of the state. Because only a prince possessed the authority to legalize church law, he should be its sovereign.

Hontheim presumed the Pope and his court to be tyrannical and, like Voltaire, he presumed the secular prince to be enlightened. When a second edition of Febronious's writing reached the papacy in the fall of 1769, the Pope instructed the archbishop of Trier "to stifle that poisonous and pestilential abortion before it sees the light of day."[15] However, the archbishop of Mainz, along with his counterparts in Cologne and Trier, showed their Febronian colors when they approved a document penned by Febronious and other sympathetic scholars. Besides lashing out at the Roman Curia as a bureaucratic obstruction between bishops and the Holy See, the document called for the restoration of the bishops' autonomy, the abolition of church taxes, and the restoration of the emperor's authority to reform the church and rid her of abuses and scandals. Many of Febronious's ideas were incorporated into the reform agenda of the most ambitious Enlightenment ruler, Joseph II, the nominal Holy Roman Emperor.[16]

Though the Cellites of Cologne and Aachen dwelt in Free Cities, autonomous political units within the empire, the Cellites of Antwerp were under Emperor Joseph II, ruler of the Austrian Netherlands. Austrian Febronianism, or Josephism, was expressed in a series of reforms intended to transform the church into an agency of the state. Joseph dissolved all papal prerogatives: all papal and diocesan decrees must have the state's prior approval before promulgation; the state was to control the appointment of bishops; the church lands were subject to taxation, and state seminaries replaced those of the local dioceses. Joseph reflected the era's critical stance toward traditional piety when he imposed regulations on the frequency of religious holidays, festivals, and the use of relics.[17]

The Enlightenment influence was most apparent in Emperor Joseph's views on the monastic life. In 1781 (1783 in the Netherlands) all contemplative orders were dissolved in accord with the then current notions of social utility; they were declared "completely useless to religion, the state, and their neighbors."[18] Over eight hundred monasteries and convents were suppressed.

14

Because the Cellites were committed to the "socially useful" nursing apostolate, they were not affected by these decrees. However, their future was placed in doubt by laws prohibiting the profession of perpetual vows and placing the acceptance of novices under the authority of the state.

Joseph's religious and political reforms touched off a series of reactions ranging from a lay protest against the state's encroachments on popular piety to the papacy's strong appeal on behalf of its traditional privilege. Pius VI even journeyed to Vienna (March 1782) to make a personal plea to the emperor. Greeted with warm applause by the Viennese people and cold obstinacy by Joseph II, Pius failed in his mission to revive the papacy's privileged position in the empire. Within a year the emperor and the Pope signed a concordat confirming the state's authority virtually to control all episcopal appointments. Though the Austrian state appeared to have gained enormous strength during this period, many of Joseph's enlightened reforms were poorly funded, badly administered, and the cause of deep resentment, particularly in the Austrian Netherlands.

The political and religious reforms were aimed at establishing rationalized political and ecclesiastical structures in the Netherlands but, instead, they provoked political and church leaders to form an anti-Austrian coalition, which rapidly fomented revolution. Two years prior to the storming of the Bastille in Paris, the "Belgian" revolutionaries proclaimed their independence. Though the emperor's troops soon subjugated the Netherlands, neither side could claim a secure victory as the events in Paris rapidly threatened the security of throne and altar throughout Western Europe.

The story of the suppression of the Jesuits and the rise of Febronianism and Josephism illustrates the weaknesses of the church on both the diocesan and papal levels. The church suffered from poor leadership, a preoccupation with past battles with Protestantism, a fragmented structure more grounded in secular than spiritual concerns, and a ministerial character chained to routine. There were few eighteenth-century saints, and only a few new religious orders, e.g., Redemptorists and Passionists. The Cellites, like most religious orders, reflected the general ills besetting the eighteenth-century church. They

15

lacked visionary leadership; their structure was fragmented; their spirituality and their ministry did not demonstrate charism but only past routines. Thus, when they conflicted with the modern state in the form of the French Revolutionary governments in Cologne, Aachen, and Antwerp, they were nearly extinguished. The sources of their vulnerability as well as their perseverance are explained by recalling some of the major events and chief characteristics of the eighteenth-century Cellites.

Far from representing the Catholic *Aufklärung,* the Alexians appear as clear manifestations of the persistence of the traditional world. Like the original "municipal" Beghards and Lollards, the eighteenth-century Cellites were almost completely dependent upon the towns. The Protestant Reformation and the religious wars had so fractured the order that the Brothers were without a centralized structure, a superior general, and their traditional privileges as a papally exempt institute. Though two eighteenth-century popes had confirmed these privileges, by the eve of the French Revolution the Cellites were virtually a diocesan religious congregation.

The Aachen Brothers, who had rebelled against their provincial in the 1720s, were a de jure diocesan congregation. In 1763 their ordinary, the bishop of Liège, imposed upon them a new rule but the Aachen Brothers "were not consulted."[19] In the introduction to that rule, an anonymous Brother wrote:

> There were many abuses in the various houses which resulted in separation. However, had the Bishop's commissar endeavored to correct the abuses it might not have been necessary to force the new constitution upon us. We, also, are at fault. Had the Provincial's visitations, and the Chapter's, taken different action for correcting abuses, things might have been different. Finally, it might be said that all this occurred because of a failure to observe the Rule and Constitutions, resulting in a so-called "constitution" being forced upon us.[20]

The remorseful references to abuses and the alternative ways they may have been remedied indicate that the Brothers were disappointed with the lack of leadership on the diocesan and provincial levels. Their former Cologne provincial, Brother Peter von Efferen, had alienated the Aachen community by his abuses of authority and by "his scandalous life."[21] Even before the Aachen house had rebelled, the Provincial Chapter of 1710 considered the issue of "raising the discipline of the order"[22] with no apparent success. Only after they had noted the failures of their superiors did the anonymous Brothers admit their guilt in deviating from the rule. The precise nature of their abuses went undocumented, but there is ample evidence that the Brothers were courting the rich and were preoccupied with expanding their wealth. Yet there were countervailing factors to the abuses among the Cellites. In spite of the decline in observance of the rule in the seventeenth century, the Brothers responded heroically to the plague of 1665–1666. Even beyond the French Revolution the townspeople identified the Brothers' houses as refuges for wayward priests, "bad boys," the feeble-minded, and the insane.[23] The Brothers, conscious of the abuses, had sought reform from above and regeneration from below, while lay people reiterated their consistent trust in the Cellite ministry to the outsider. One concludes, therefore, that the decline of the Cellites was on a relatively minor scale. There is no evidence of bizarre scandal or gross behavior among the communities. Just as the Brothers could point to no saintly heroes during their peak periods, so there were no villains in their days of decline.

From its origins Cellite spirituality had been eclectic. Beguine-Eckhartian mysticism blended with *pauperes Christi* mendicancy and communalism, and an identification with Jesus the helper and healer formed the original Cellite spirit. Their original communal spirituality had given way to an individualism reflected in their emphasis on personal sanctification and mental prayer. The schedule for prayers that John Busch recorded in the late fifteenth century, and which was regulated by the 1686 constitution, indicates the deeply monastic character of the Brothers: at midnight, rise for Matins and an hour of prayer, at four o'clock (between four and five o'clock in the winter) mental prayer and Mass. The remaining hours at prayer were not specified according to time, but chapter XII of the 1686 constitution states:

> The office of the Holy Cross is to be said in the oratories at Matins and at Vespers 10 Our Fathers and Holy Marys are also said, but at

the other hours of the office, 7 Our Fathers and Hail Marys are said. Once a week the Brothers shall say 15 Our Fathers and Hail Marys, and the Psalms Miserere and De Profundis.[24]

In addition to following this relatively ascetic prayer day, the Brothers were to abide by rigid fast and abstinence rules, such as total abstinence from meat during Advent. When a Brother died, the confreres of his house were to take the penance, i.e., to scourge themselves. Because the Brothers had such an active nursing and burial apostolate, tensions between their monastic and ministerial duties appear to have been unavoidable. While other active orders such as the Hospitallers of St. John of God required an annual Ignatian retreat of eight days, the Cellites had no opportunity to break away from the daily conflicts between monastic and ministerial duties. Indeed the tendency seems to have been to become so immersed in ministry as to transform it into routine work. Perhaps this was the way abuses crept into the community. An overemphasis on their active apostolate may have resulted in a disregard of poverty and a general decline in the observance of the rule. The general secularism on the ascendancy in the eighteenth century may have seeped into the Cellite way of life, contributing to a spirit of religious apathy. Yet, as one recalls that their houses were still popularly considered refuges for outsiders, particularly the insane, one is led to conclude that much of their traditional religious world-view must have still been viably demonstrated. On the eve of the French Revolution, when the tensions of Western European society were ready to burst forth in a tidal wave of change, the Cellites were experiencing analogous tensions. They possessed a fragmented medieval authority structure which, like the secular political structure, precluded efficient reform. Just as the papacy, much of the episcopacy, and many religious orders traded their medieval ideals for political and economic status, so the Cellites traded their *pauperes Christi* idealism for economic advantage.

2

The Decline of the Alexians

in the Era of

the French Revolution

I

It is not surprising that the church was deeply involved in the complex social, economic, and political origins of the French Revolution, enmeshed as she was in the traditional social structure with many economic privileges protected by the state. Anticlericalism was endemic among the revolutionaries and as the revolution drifted to the extreme left (1792–1795), this anticlericalism reached its peak of intensity. During the early moderate phase (1789–1792) when there was an attempt to forge a compromise between the prerogatives of the monarchy and the "rights of men," the French church, traditionally under the arm of the monarchy (Gallicanism), was controlled by revolutionaries under the influence of the Deist and atheistic writers of the Enlightenment. By a series of acts the National Assembly stripped the church of all its property and autonomy. In February 1790 it dissolved most of the monasteries and congregations (in 1768 a royal commission had closed over a thousand communities).[1] Teaching and nursing communities were permitted to carry on their work, but their members were no longer bound by monastic vows. On July 12, 1790, the National Assembly enacted the Civil Constitution of the Clergy, which reorganized the church along rationalist and democratic lines, fixed salaries of all clerical grades, and imposed reforms curtailing absenteeism and pluralism. Gallicanism reached its climax as the church became an agency of the French state juridically, though neither spiritually nor symbolically separated from Rome. Just as the papacy struggled against Febronionism and Josephism, so Pius VI condemned the Civil Constitution of the Clergy. Those clergy who followed the Pope by refusing to take the required oath to the constitution were branded as nonjuring clergymen at first; as the poor economic situation, the outbreak of war, and the disloyalty of the king gave credibility to the anticlerical radicals, religious garb was enough to brand one a traitor to liberty, equality, and fraternity. In October 1793 the Convention that in effect ruled France from 1792 to 1795 de-Christianized the calendar, substituting the first year of the republic for the birth of Christ as the year one. Months were named according to the cycles of nature as the cult of civil religion replaced all traditional trappings of the sacred.[2] Churches were stripped of their valuables and in November 1793 a woman was crowned Goddess of Reason in Notre Dame Cathedral.

By the spring of 1794 only about 150 parishes in France were open for the celebration of Mass. Between the fall of Robespierre and the rise of Napoleon (1794–1799) the church gradually regained some public respect, though there was a period of renewed persecution in 1797–1798. Napoleon, believing that religion was necessary to cement the loyalties of the people to the state, pursued a policy of peace with the church, which ultimately led to the Concordat of 1801. Pius VII and Napoleon struck a compromise: the Civil Constitution was virtually abolished but the confiscated church property remained in secular hands; Napoleon had the authority to appoint bishops, but the Pope invested them with canonical authority; the state paid salaries to the clergy, but the church was guaranteed freedom of public worship. In general the rupture with Rome was healed and the traditional powers of the French state's supervision of the church were expanded and refined.[3] Though Napoleon was the immediate victor the concordat's long-range effect was to strengthen the papacy's influence in France. Without their pre-revolutionary feudal privileges and land, French bishops became almost entirely dependent upon the papacy.

II

The Cellites of the Austrian Netherlands were the first Brothers to experience the impact of revolution. Because revolutionary ferment originated in opposition to the decrees of Joseph II, the church was associated with anti-Hapsburg protest. Though the cause for independence gained a temporary victory in 1787, in June 1789 Austrian troops forced the Netherlands to submit to the throne in Vienna. However, events in Paris greatly affected the neighbors to the north; news of the storming of the Bastille resulted in demonstrations in Tirlemont, Tournai, Louvain, and Diest, where the Cellites had been living for centuries. With Joseph II preoccupied with the status quo in a Europe threatened by the French Revolution, the army of the independence movement in the Netherlands successfully drove out the Austrian troops, culminating in a declaration of independence on January 11, 1790. The coalition between the anti-Josephist church and the Enlightenment leadership composed of intellectuals, industrialists, and many town politicians disintegrated as soon as it became evident that the landed aristocracy and the church supported a return to the pre-Joseph era during which time these two groups dominated provincial government. The enlightened element rallied around the liberal Flemish lawyer François Vonck. The Vonckists wished to establish a more centralized and democratic government through which reforms aimed at the demise of the traditional privileges of the church and aristocracy could be initiated. Their enemies, the Statists, had the upper hand with the people. The vast majority of ordinary people, led by their bishops and clergymen, lashed out at the Vonckists as enemies of church and state.[4] Adrien de

Meeus describes the role of the church in protecting Belgium from the liberals:

> On the pretext of an alleged plot to assassinate [their leaders] . . . the Statists assembled thousands of peasantry armed with pitchforks and rifles in Brussels, under the leadership of priests on horseback. In the Churches the Capuchins openly preached that it was pleasing to God to kill a Vonckist. . . . [The] peasantry was organized under the leadership of armed monks who demanded a crusade, while wearing swords and crossbelts beneath their cowls, as they shouted for blood. The capital was forcibly occupied by 20,000 of them, and the October riots in Paris sparked the same excesses in Brussels.[5]

Given De Meeus's rather liberal interpretation of events, it is nevertheless evident that the Brussels crowd was directed "backward" to support throne and altar while the crowd in Paris was pushing events in a leftward direction. Floris Prims notes that during this period of Statist domination the Cellites of Antwerp were compelled to take in political prisoners who were, no doubt, liberal-Vonckist sympathizers. Though Austria once again suppressed Belgian independence in December 1790, the revolutionary momentum in Paris ultimately determined Belgium's fate.

As the French Revolution moved to the left and the European war widened (1792–1794), French nationalism evolved from a relatively benign force to one of militant expansionism. During the first phase of the war (December 1792) Aachen was occupied by the French army. Determined to impose (through elections) a "revolutionary government" upon the town, the French command met with continuous resistance by the townspeople who realized that such a revolutionary government would ultimately have led to the French annexation of Aachen. In February 1793, with the Austrian troops pressing for the recapture of the city, Aachen citizens cried out, "Our religion is being profaned. . . . We are [asked] to become the enemy of the Emperor and the Empire. It were better for us to die on the spot. Death is better. We prefer death. . . ."[6]

The Austrians defeated the French at the battle of Aldenhoven (March 1) and forced the French to evacuate Aachen. In the process, the Austrians were assisted by many citizens who fired at the fleeing French troops from the windows of their homes. Sick and wounded French soldiers who had been quartered in their homes were turned out to the streets. Though French loyalists successfully rescued these victims, the incident illustrates the anti-French sentiment in Aachen, which drove Robespierre to promise that upon recapture the city would suffer plunder and conflagration.[7] However, by the time General Jourdan reconquered Aachen (September 23, 1794) Robespierre had been a victim of his major political weapon, the guillotine, and the city was spared his vengeful wrath.

Military occupation of Aachen and Cologne brought economic depression. With prices controlled by and for the French government commerce suffered. Army provisions were virtually extorted from the Aachen sellers. Even a French envoy was surprised by the degree of economic oppression of the city, as if the occupying army were there solely for personal gain.[8] By a series of laws the French Government established procedures for the army to seize and transport to Paris all valuable art treasures found in the occupying territories. Accordingly, all thirty-eight porphyry columns of Aachen Cathedral, seven of which were supports for Charlemagne's tomb valued at 300,000 livres, were sent to Paris. Such plundering of culture led to the seizure of the rich church and religious order libraries in Cologne as well as most of its art collections, including its prized stamp collection.[9]

When the French government carved the occupied territory north of the Mosel River into administrative districts, Aachen was designated as the headquarters for the Central Administration. In late December 1794 a 25-million-livre "general contribution" was imposed upon the area, 5 million of which was to be contributed from the Aachen district. Early the following year the Cellites on Alexianergraben were compelled to hand over to the government all their money. While the Alexians of Aachen and Cologne were coping with these indignities at the hands of their conquerors, the Antwerp Alexians became French citizens when on October 11, 1795, Belgium was annexed to France. During the preceding period of occupation (June 1794–October 1795) the Antwerp Cellites were also compelled to give up all their money. Prims reports that during that period three Brothers, along with other religious, were taken as hostages; and immediately after the annexation the Brothers' house was used as a prison for political offenders, including many French priests who had refused to take the oath to the Civil Constitution of the Clergy.[10]

On October 20, 1796 the Cellites of Antwerp were informed that their property was to be secularized and the community dissolved.[11] Though the Cellite superior, Brother Gummarius Beldens, rented a house in the Hopland area (far from the center of Antwerp) for his confreres and their mentally ill patients, he did protest the dissolution order on the grounds that nursing orders were exempt from the law.[12] The sale of their property was postponed, but the Brothers were nevertheless forced to evacuate their house on January 17, 1797, and to dress in secular garb within twenty-four hours. On November 12, 1798 Brother Gummarius was arrested and imprisoned until he could be deported.[13] Perhaps this action was in retaliation for his protest; but after the Cellite property was sold (February and March 1799) we note that he was back with his community. By design rather than coincidence Brother Gummarius repurchased the Cellite monastery under the title Hasuert and Co. (his brother-in-law's firm), and on July 5, 1800, two Brothers returned to their home. In August 1801 the city government finally recognized the legality of the Cellite community and promised it their protection:

> . . . that the Alexians have always been associated with hospitals and houses of charity for the true object of their institution . . . , that they had infirmaries for plague victims; that the insane were nursed in their hospitals; that they are under the surveillance and immediate authority of the magistrates.[14]

This story of persecution and ultimate recognition of the Brothers closely follows the French government's relationship with the church. In 1797, when they were forced to evacuate their house, the dominant political faction in Paris was bitterly anticlerical. By 1801 Napoleon was consolidating his authority and negotiating the Concordat with the papacy. Like the church in general, the Antwerp Cellites remained unmolested after 1801, but their possessions had been greatly reduced (their seven houses adjacent to the monastery were sold), their traditional burial privileges were dissolved because such services had been contracted out to a private undertaking firm, and the Black Sisters (called the Cellitenen in Germany) had recently decided to nurse sick males. Thus, the Brothers' income was entirely dependent upon pensions received from their mentally ill patients. We know of at least three Brothers who left the community during the critical years 1797–1798, but we have no evidence of their motives.[15] Perhaps they were swept up in the political movements of the day or were merely afraid to remain religious during a period of persecution. Though nursing congregations were officially tolerated, aspirants were discouraged by laws forbidding the profession of perpetual vows.

Brother Gummarius must have been a very adept superior. Not only did he have the foresight to provide for the community and their patients during a crisis but he also managed to keep the community intact. Superior of the Antwerp house (1795–51828), he was elected provincial of all the Brabant Brothers in 1810.[16] Such strong leadership was particularly necessary during critical times when survival was the crucial issue. No doubt the Antwerp community was discouraged by the secularist policies of the French government and by the contraction of their community and their ministries.

III

The ancient city of Aachen had always possessed special political privileges allowing it to be virtually autonomous, but with French occupation in 1794 this self-determination ended, never to be revived. In 1802 Aachen was absorbed, along with most of the Rhineland, into France. Like the Antwerp Brothers, the Aachen Alexians were led by a strong superior, Brother John Porten, who guided the community (except for a three-year interval) from 1779 to 1806.[17] Immediately prior to the French Revolution, the Aachen Brothers were very prosperous. Brother John added to their wealth; between 1782 and 1788 he built four homes (three along Alexianergraben), which brought the total to twelve.[18]

The first hardship imposed upon them by the French army

was the billeting of fifty to sixty soldiers and the exacting of forced cash contributions.[19] By a law issued on September 1, 1796, all monastic property was to be seized, but Pater John, supported by many physicians, successfully appealed for exemption from seizure as well as from the billeting of soldiers and the payment of contributions.[20] The French government of 1797–1798, motivated by anticlericalism and a desperate need to finance its war effort, passed a law dissolving seminaries and religious congregations in the recently occupied territories of France. In 1798, the Aachen Brothers were forced to provide the following inventory of their property.

Estimate of the institution	6,000 livres
Estimate of the rented houses	7,725 livres
Rent receipts	516 livres
Copper church goods: value	66 livres
Tin church goods: value	2 livres
Iron chandeliers (4)	3 livres
Chasubles (6), Cope (1), Albs (4), Altar cloths (6)	91 livres
In the house: 4 copper chandeliers, 6 cooking pots and 4 iron pans	66 livres
Large paintings (7), chairs (24), tables (12), Bedsteads (6), Old cupboards (3), Clocks (2)	119 livres
Linens for the boarders	228 livres[21]

By a decree of February 9, 1798 religious orders were prohibited from professing perpetual vows and accepting novices. In 1802, after their goods and property had been placed under the supervision of the Hospital Commission, they could accept novices with the permission of that agency.[22] In that year Aachen was designated as a diocese with authority over Cologne and much of the former diocese of Liège (the district of Liège was, with the other provinces of Belgium, absorbed by the French in 1795). The first bishop, Marc Anthony Berdolet, confirmed the election of Brother John as superior in 1803, but when Brother John died in 1806 a replacement was not elected until 1818, though the Brothers did request the bishop to preside at an election in 1809.[23] Without a superior and without affiliation with either the German or the Belgian Province the Aachen Brothers floundered, their religious life deteriorated, and their numbers diminished. Moreover, according to an 1802 law they were forbidden to wear religious garb on the streets. Besides, the government regulated their care for the mentally ill, i.e., nursing the sick in their homes and burying the dead, and also instructed them to take in unmanageable boys.[24] With so few Brothers these many tasks imposed a heavy burden. Indeed, some aspects of the traditional ministries must have suffered from neglect. Because they were deprived of leadership and autonomy, the Aachen Cellites could easily conclude that they had become merely quasi-officals of the Hospital Commission. In 1810 one French official played upon the Brothers' vulnerability by offering them an annual pension of 500 francs if they would leave the religious life.[25] Within two years eight of the Brothers left the house. By this time the Aachen diocese was administered by John Camus who, because of a conflict between the papacy and Napoleon, never received the staff and crozier of a bishop from the Pope. Both he and his predecessor seem to have felt little compunction to fill the spiritual vacuum of the Cellites.

At the end of the Napoleonic period, three members of the Aachen community, Brothers Werner Schweren, Bernard Gerhards, and Anton Starz, and a handful of mentally ill patients formed a tiny witness to the over four hundred years of Alexian tradition in Aachen.[26] Of all the Cellite houses, few seemed so close to extinction. Without a superior, provincial, or effective diocesan authority, this small Aachen community was soon to experience a phenomenal revival, one that ultimately led it to expand within Germany and into Belgium, the United States, and England.

IV

The story of the Cologne Alexians on the Lungengasse follows the pattern of the Aachen community. Cologne and Aachen were governed under the same secularization laws and by the same ecclesiastical officials. The Cologne Lugenbrüder were compelled to "contribute" to the French army, to billet soldiers, to wear secular dress on the streets, to be under the hospital adminsitration, and to house unruly boys, and they were prohibited from accepting novices. Though they suffered many indignities, the Alexians were the only male religious order in Cologne exempt from the dissolution laws. They carried on their traditional ministries, nursing the sick in their homes, burying the dead and providing a home for the mentally ill. During this period these many tasks appear to have placed a heavy strain on the community. For example, in 1802 Brother Heinrich Krapoll, the superior, complained to the municipal authorities that the community's revenue was dwindling because of the low fees for caring for the sick and the low pensions paid by the mentally ill, and because many respectable families were now burying their dead without the services of the Brothers.[27] Again in 1810, after they had opened their own cemetery, the Alexians asked the Hospital Commission to relieve them of their duties of carrying the bodies of the poor to the parish churches on the basis that there were too few Brothers and not enough income for their needs. On October 25, 1810 the commision decided in favor of the Cellites' request, an action that terminated a tradition dating from the fifteenth century.[28]

According to a report of November 28, 1809, drawn up by the Hospital Commission, the Cologne community included fourteen Brothers—twelve professed and two novices (who entered only with the permission of the commission). Their ages ranged from twenty-four to fifty-nine. Among the fourteen only one was unable to care for the sick. The Brothers nursed sixteen patients scattered throughout the city.[29] Their total annual income was 12,000 francs: 3,200 from real estate and capital, 800 from nursing and burial fees, and 7,800 from the mentally ill pensioners' payments for room and board.[30] Since the average pensioner paid 500 francs, the Brothers cared for roughly eighteen mentally ill men. Because part of the property was on the right bank of the Rhine—that area not incorporated into the French state—it was confiscated. In addition to this loss of income the Brothers received no rent from the city and state occupation of their property. Thus their expenditures exceeded their income by 540 francs per year. In contrast to the Antwerp Brothers who lost seven houses, and the Aachen community which had dwindled to three Brothers, the Cologne house was prosperous. However, Brother Bernhard points out that the general morale of the Lungenbrüder was very low. Rather than finding prosperity and a preoccupation with their economic status as the insidious causes for the general decline, Brother Bernhard places the blame on the secularist climate of church and society.[31]

The adminstrator of the Aachen diocese (which encompassed Cologne), Bishop Camus, was apparently alerted to the need to regulate the religious life of the Cologne Alexians. On July 30, 1813, he provided the Brothers with new statutes and a rule. Though the Cologne Alexians had such a rule for centuries, one which was revised in 1686, Camus was probably entirely unaware of the Cellite traditions as he referred to them as Frères de la Miséricorde—Brothers of Mercy.[32] The bishop's views on the religious life reflected the Enlightement notions of individualism and the role of the state in the administration of all charitable organizations. A superior and his assistant were to be elected for five-year terms by a majority of the Bishops' Council in the presence of a representative from the Hospital Commission. Novices were to be accepted into the community only in the presence of the bishop or his representative and a municipal official. A copy of the document testifying to the acceptance of a novice was to be registered in the mayor's office.[33]

The individualistic character of the rule was revealed in that statue regulating the property of the Brothers. Each Alexian had full rights to his property and income, including the right to decide on the proper use of his funds. In spiritual matters the Brothers were entirely under the authority of the bishop and in secular matters entirely under the authority of the head of the Hospital Commission. In effect the Cologne Alexians were a diocesan congregation of laymen who were municipal nurses and pallbearers, each of whom possessed full rights to the disposition of his property and income.[34] The traditional Alexian stress on poverty and communalism was totally undermined. Four years prior to the introduction of these statutes, Napoleon's government precluded the true profession of the vows of poverty by decreeing that all religious maintain full individual property rights. Camus's statutes did not remain in effect long; in January 1814 the Rhineland was liberated by the allied troops and Camus fled to Paris.

The Cellites of Cologne, Aachen, and Antwerp were confronted with forces that challenged their very raison d'être.

From the revolutionaries' point of view the Alexians were allowed to survive because they were socially useful. Like most religious during the revolutionary period, the Brothers passed through a crisis of identity. Though they were probably unaware of the full implications of the many changes in society, they were obviously conscious of their absorption into the French nation and of the secularization laws affecting the privileges and structure of the entire church and of their own status.

Before the revolution the Alexians were conscious of the abuses that had crept into their way of life. With the expansion of their property came the distractions (or attractions) attached to the management of real estate and capital. In contrast to the large holdings of the major religious orders, theirs was a "small business" indeed. Yet their prosperity seems to have insidiously worked its way into their religious consciousness. Perhaps because their ministries were not as noticeably vital or as necessary to the common good of the cities, business could easily dominate their religious concerns. So long as the towns remained small, twelve Brothers or so could visibly contribute to the common good. With the growth of population and the emergence of a secular cosmopolitan climate, the Brothers' ministry to the dying and the dead became considered increasingly as a secular work, rather than Christian witness at sickbed and graveside. The care of the insane could also be viewed as income work.

When they were confronted with the revolutionary situation, that which was implicit became explicit. Many Brothers left the cloister; there was an urgent concern over the loss of property; leaders adept at management made forthright pleas for the economic common good and general stability of the Brothers, but not one came forth on a religious issue; the townspeople appear to have been relatively unconcerned with the fate of the Alexians; and the Brothers' religious and secular autonomy was dissolved as they became members of diocesan institutes and virtually city nurses. The most profound effect of the revolution was that the French state and its burgeoning bureaucracy, armed with the duty to regulate the health and welfare of the nation, greatly extended the secularization of burial duties. Though the Brothers remained funeral people, they were no longer medieval tamers of death.

30

3

Spiritual Rebirth

I

The Congress of Vienna, entrusted with redrawing the map of Europe after the defeat of Napoleon, was infused with reviving the principles of legitimacy and balance of power. Strong buffer states were formed on France's borders as insurance against potential aggressiveness. Prussia absorbed most of the Rhineland, including Aachen and Cologne; the Kingdom of the Netherlands absorbed what is now Belgium. The Cellites of Aachen, Cologne, and Antwerp once again came under foreign jurisdiction, but more importantly the Catholic Church in these cities, still sensitive to the crusading call of the Counter-Reformation, was compelled to dwell in Protestant-dominated states.

In the Netherlands the church once again formed an alliance with liberal groups, this time in opposition to the Dutch king William I. Though the church was traditionalist by character and ultramontane by allegiance, the Belgian church joined the struggle for constitutional liberty as a means of achieving independence from Protestant political authority. When in 1830 liberal nationalist insurgents successfully revolted against King William's government and established an independent Belgian state based upon the principles of constitutional monarchy, the church-liberal coalition broke down as there was no longer a common enemy. However, by this time liberal Catholicism, which aimed at a reconciliation between the church and modern pluralistic society, was gradually becoming influential. Later in the century social Catholicism became a third force in the Belgian church, one that sought the reconciliation of capital and labor.[1]

Though this is an oversimplified sketch of the various trends within the Belgian church, it does highlight some of the major characteristics of the dynamic century, 1815–1914. If one would view the century from the vantage point of the papacy, there appears to have been a hundred years' war between medieval Christendom and the modern secular pluralistic world, one not fully terminated until Vatican II. The ultramontane position resembled that of the Counter-Reformation church in that it was a defense of religious hegemony against the heretical doctrines of the French Revolution. A series of popes, culminating with Pius IX, battled against what they viewed to be the disintegrating forces of Christian (Catholic) civilization, i.e., the separation of church and state in Catholic nations, freedom of press, speech and assembly, and any ideas associated with the cause of pluralistic constitutional government. However, the eighteenth-century enemies, Febronianism and Josephism, were also declared anathema when they were promoted by antidemocratic figures such as Napoleon III (1851–1870) and Otto von Bismarck. Though in hindsight the papacy's defense of its temporal power appears anachronistic, one may easily understand the vigor of its defense when one recalls the stringent anticlericalism of many leading liberals, the bloody shirt of Jacobin anti-Catholicism and the *Realpolitik* of some leading liberals and conservatives ever in pursuit of state hegemony over church. The papacy's "antimodern" policies up to Leo XIII were consistent, but its diplomacy with each national church was flexible to suit local conditions. For example, it theoretically opposed Catholicism's accommodation with liberalism, but it reluctantly accepted the Belgian church's accommodation with a liberal constitutional government, particularly because the church was placed in a privileged position—independent yet subsidized. This situation illustrates another characteristic of nineteenth-century church history, i.e., because the major isms of the 1815–1870 era (liberalism, conservatism, nationalism, industrialism, and socialism) assumed different forms according to economic, social, political, and national conditions throughout Europe, the church's response to those isms in individual nations assumed a variety of forms. For example, French liberal anticlericalism provoked an impassioned conservatism among most leading French ecclesiastics, whereas liberalism was a minor challenge to the church in Germany. Indeed, in first half of the nineteenth century, the major thrust of the German church was in response not to a liberal but to the deeply conservative chancellor, Otto von Bismarck, who waged a brief but impassioned battle against Catholicism. Though the Cellites were not political activists, Bismarck's *Kulturkampf* did profoundly affect their history.

The most dramatic series of social changes occurred as a result of the industrial revolution. The factory system, the appearance of urban industrial masses characterized by rootlessness, squalor, and powerlessness, and the accelerated pace of social and cultural change drastically altered the landscape of Western Europe. Because the effects of the industrial and French revolutions occurred simultaneously, the consciousness of the proletariat gradually expanded into a social and economic interpretation of the "rights of man," which led to an increasingly intense revolution of rising expectations.[2]

Because the Brothers responded to many victims of industrialism, because many Brothers were drawn from rural and urban working-class families, and because the Cellites nursed the psychological casualties of industrial society, there is a strong relationship between the Industrial Revolution and the history of the Brothers.

II

Of the three Cellite communities the Antwerp Brothers were in the most depressed condition in 1815. Owing to a division in the monastery there were two Alexian communities in Antwerp.[3] Increasing indebtedness resulting from their meager income (their traditional burial privileges were contracted out to a private undertaking firm) forced Brother Gummarius to sell the Cellites' property, a decision that polarized the community. Brother Gummarius and six of the eldest Brothers accepted the hospitality of a wealthy nobleman, while five Brothers under Brother Peter Verheyen moved into a house on Jesustraat.[4] The two communities also divided the patients.[5] In 1816, each community was seeking legal recognition from the new political authorities representing the Dutch government. In 1821 the statues of both communities were approved and ultimately they achieved reconciliation as both decided to form one community in the house in Jesustraat.[6]

After Brother Gummarius's death in 1828 a gap appears in their history until 1848, eleven years after Belgium's successful struggle for independence, when the Brothers purchased the property they had rented on Jesustraat, allowing them to enlarge the hospice-asylum. No doubt they shared the general prosperity of both the Belgian church and society. Between 1839 and 1846 the number of Belgians in religious orders increased from 4,791 to almost 12,000.[7] In 1853 the Brothers cared for thirty mentally ill patients.[8] Perhaps because of the growth of the community and the trends in care for the mentally ill toward a pastoral setting for asylums, the Brothers decided to move from Antwerp to one of the small towns in its environs, Boechout, in 1876.[9] Though this story of the Antwerp Brothers has many missing chapters, one may conclude that during the period 1815–1870 they went from near collapse to a prosperous condition in which the number of Brothers and patients steadily grew.

The entire community of Belgian Alexians were living under statutes (along with the Rule of St. Augustine) that were first printed in 1711 and republished in 1862.[10] Because these statutes were actually a compilation of tradition, the Belgian Cellites were grounded in a very ancient rule. That general trend of the nineteenth-century church to preserve tradition against the attacks of the secular world appears to have been manifested in the Brothers' preservation of traditional customs. They even republished the stringent 1711 letter of Brother Hendrik Kerkloff, which urged the Brothers to live according to the letter of the law. Brother Hendrik, a firm advocate of the maxim "old law is good law" vowed by the "blood of Jesus Christ" to enforce the statutes with such vigor that one surmises there was a wholesale breakdown in law and order in the early eighteenth century.[11] The mid-nineteenth-century Brothers could easily recall the decline of the Cellites during the French Revolution and Naploeonic period as evidence of the effects of lack of discipline. Unlike the Aachen and Cologne Brothers who were granted new statutes in 1763 and 1813 respectively, the Brabant Brothers remained under the traditional customs. Hence there was no immediate cause prompting them to draw up a new rule. The general asceticism of the 1711 statutes probably struck them as a timeless feature of the religious life.

The Belgian Cellites of 1862 were, however, quite different from their 1711 predecessors. They were no longer primarily tamers of death whose ministerial lives were grounded in funeral rites but, rather, were generally limited to their role as Passage Brothers who cared for the mentally ill. With the nineteenth-century development of the asylum, the treatment of the insane shifted from a prison style to "civilized" rational methods of control that stressed paternalism and a limited freedom for the patient on a reward-punishment basis. The Brothers' ministry, therefore, tended to be expressed in pragmatic rather than traditional religious terms. As this tendency gained momentum the Cellites evolved further along the lines of modern Alexians. Though the Brothers were evolving into modern nurses of the mentally ill, their asylum existence did not contain the potential tensions between an active ministry and an ascetic religious life. Thus their 1711 statues, which were extremely "monastic" in the asceticism of their cloister life, were suitable to their remoteness from the secular worlds in asylums, a condition that reinforced the preservation of tradition in a rapidly changing society.

III

In 1815 the Alexians of Cologne and Aachen became subjects of the Hohenzollern monarch Frederick William III (1797–1840). Under Frederick the Great (1740–1786) Prussia had become a great power in Europe and an efficiently administered state in Germany. Frederick's policy toward the Catholic Church was guided by the traditional Erastian principle which allowed him to govern the Lutheran Church and by his motivation to enlarge the role of the state in the entire modernization of Prussia. These principles were later embodied in the Code of Common Law (1794) through which the state was empowered to regulate the entire institutional life of the church. The appointment of bishops, the establishment of new parishes, the calendar of religious holidays, the flow of all ecclesiastical communication, including the relationship with Rome, came under the control and direction of the Prussian state. In 1808 two new departments in the Ministry of Home Affairs—Religious and Educational—were established to deal with all Catholic matters.[12] The Alexians had a dual relationship with the state: they were under both the health and the religious-affairs authorities. Because the Cellites had experienced the French bureaucracy for nearly twenty years, they were somewhat prepared for the centralized control of the Prussian government in Berlin. One should recall that in 1809 the Cologne Alexians numbered twelve professed Brothers and two novices, that they cared for fifteen sick men scattered throughout the city, that their mentally ill pensioners numbered about twelve to fifteen, and that in 1810 their pallbearer duty for the poor was terminated.[13] Their religious life had been severly affected by the civil authority's prohibition of perpetual vows, its control over the entrance of novices, and its stipulation that each Brother maintain the right to private property.[14] Thus when Prussia assumed sovereignty over Cologne, the Alexian community had devolved into a sort of secular institute.

During the Napoleonic period the Cologne house developed a sizable deficit. The numbers of pensioners who provided the bulk of its income had greatly declined; income from rental property had not yielded profitable interest; income had been reduced by the seizure of their rental property on the right bank of the Rhine.[15] In the spring of 1814 the Brothers sought a financial remedy from the Hospital Commision, but the bureaucratic shift from French to Prussian rule obstructed any immediate response. After a long delay the Prussian authority finally responded in January 1816 with permission for the Brothers to raise their burial fees for the wealthy as well as those fees for in-home nursing, both of which had not been altered since the late fifteenth century.[16]

36

The Prussian Ministry for Home Affairs, which had authority over all religious houses, declared (1815) that the Alexians of Cologne—referred to in the generic as *barmherzige Brüder*—Brothers of Mercy—were permitted to remain intact, with the provisions that the government had the authority to inspect their house and that novices could be accepted only with its approval.[17] Because Prussia and the Vatican had yet to negotiate a settlement on which appointment of an ordinary of the newly revived Archdiocese of Cologne could be based, there was a total vacuum of episcopal authority in the Rhineland from 1814 to 1825. Thus the civil authorities communicated directly with the Alexians on matters that would have been normally channeled through diocesan offices. One such communication involved the issue of the very raison d'être of the Cologne Brothers. In 1817 the lord lieutenant of the Rhine Province, von Ingersleben, inquired as to the function and purpose of the Alexian community. The Poverty Commission (which was linked to the Hospital Commission in 1818) responded by stating that its duty was to care for the sick and bury the dead. Von Ingersleben replied that though these were worthy works in themselves, they appeared to him to be obsolete for both church and state. Because the Brothers' burial services had been replaced by gravediggers and because the sick of the city could be cared for by others, and pensioners cared for in hospitals, he concluded that their traditional work was an anachronism. In a town of 53,000 people twelve Brothers could be more efficiently serving society in a new capacity. He noted that since there was only one professed Brother who had legal rights to all property of the community, he should be joined to another religious nursing order. If the remaining eleven who did not wear religious garb desired to continue nursing outside their house, then they should be given a special uniform and a competent cleric as leader, one who would direct them to care for the sick as a charity rather than as a business. The monastery could be made into an institution for punishing wayward priests or a nursing home for the care of poor, old, or handicapped clerics.[18]

From the vantage point of the Prussian bureaucrat the Brothers were floundering between the medieval and modern worlds—unless there was a plague, they performed little that could be called socially useful. Yet Von Ingersleben noted that the Alexians needed to be instructed on the charitable rather than the business basis of nursing, implying that they were too affected by modern secularized notions of their work. Ironically the French, and later the Prussian, state indirectly encouraged the Alexians to become modern. They attached the Brothers to modern bureaucracies, prohibited the profession of vows, and promoted the right of private property, thereby undermining their medieval communalism and traditional asceticism, and transforming their concept of service from that of ministry to one of work.

In 1825 the Prussian government and the Vatican finally reached agreement in a concordat that gave Berlin a strong role in church affairs. The state maintained the *regium placet,* the king's right to approve all church documents. Though elections of bishops were theoretically free, the state could easily interfere in the process. The state supervised the examination of seminary students, even though only five Prussian officals were Catholic. Indeed, Catholics were excluded from many state offices, even professorships in the universities. Though the state paid the salaries of the bishops and clergy, members of religious orders who came under the Poverty Administration such as the Alexians, were not included in the concordat.[19] However, as of 1817 the Poverty Commission in Cologne directed the city to subsidize the Brothers proportional to the amount of their annual deficit.[20]

On April 21, 1825, Ferdinand August von Spiegel took up residence as archbishop of Cologne. At this point there were twelve Brothers, five pensioners, a house priest, and four servants living in the Alexian house on the Lungengasse.[21] On August 6, 1825, the city Poverty Commission proposed that since the Alexians were not observing the principles of religious life they should move to a hospital where they could more easily follow the life of dedicated nurses. The archbishop, who apparently was amenable to the Prussian authorities, agreed to the proposal. His vicar general reported, however, that the Alexians were not grounded in a constitution, and that Brother Wendlin was the only Alexian in vows. Subsequently the archbishop placed Pastor Geistmann of Holy Apostles Church, known for his work with the sick and the poor, as their spiritual director and provided the Brothers with a rule. Dated February 6, 1826 this rule received the approval of the minister of culture and the interior, thanks to King Frederick William III's cabinet order of October 9, 1826, with the stipulation that after ten years the archbishop would revise the rule.[22]

According to the first two statutes the Alexian spiritual life was placed under the authority of the archbishop and their material welfare under the Poverty Administration. They were to profess the vows of chastity and obedience, and if in the future the state permitted life vows, they were directed to profess the vow of poverty. Before a candidate entered his novitiate year, he had to be approved by the diocesan authorities who were to refer him either directly or through his superior to the Poverty Administration in order that a contract might be drawn up stipulating which possessions the candidate could bring into the community. A representative of the Poverty Administration was to be present on the occasion of the candidate's entrance into the novitiate as well as the profession of vows, which occurred after five years. Both diocesan and state officals were to be present at the election (by secret ballot) of the pater and his assistants, who served three-year terms of office. Upon the advice of the Poverty Administration the archbishop either approved or vetoed the election. All decisions regarding finances and the acceptance of pensioners were to be made in consultation with the Poverty Administration. Each Brother maintained full property right over all his goods, but was allowed to keep only one-third of his nursing fees or any other payment, turning the remainder over to the community.[23]

An elected Brother-Director—who could also hold the office of pater—was to be responsible for the management of property and income of the community, abide by the budgetary procedures of the Poverty Administration, seek the latter's permission for all important business ventures, and present an annual financial report in triplicate to be audited by the Poverty Administration.[24] The civil authority's prominent role in the entire management of the Alexian house stemmed from the period of French occupation when the Cologne Brothers were placed under the Hospital Commission. Archbishop von Spiegel's deference to the civil authorities was vividly expressed in the 1826 rule for the Alexians. Though it may have been considered as a sign of the ordinary's concern for the general welfare of the

Brothers, it subjected them to a set of rules which formed a binding legal contract between the Alexians and the Prussian government. Later in the century when the Brothers attempted to gain independent status, they were confronted by a bitter thirty-year struggle with both the Cologne Poverty Administration and the government in Berlin.

Archbishop von Spiegel's new statutes did not form a canonical rule for the religious life but, rather, a rule for a specific institute. The Brothers maintained the Augustinian rule, and since there is no evidence to the contrary it appears that their traditional prayer day was still ordered by the office of the Holy Cross. The Cologne Brothers' attitudes toward their religious life is undocumented, but nine of the twelve Brothers accepted the new rule and on March 8, 1826, a large crowd gathered in the Alexian Chapel to witness the profession of vows. With many civic and church dignitaries present, Pastor Geistmann, their spiritual director (visitator), presided over the ceremony in which the nine Brothers garbed themselves in the holy habit. Pastor Geistmann's homily stressed the significance of the vows and the rich tradition of the Cologne Brothers. He recalled their courageous plague ministry, their privileges from the Holy See, and the historic relationship between the diocese and the Brothers, one that had culminated in Archbishop von Spiegel's reforms intended to bring the Alexians closer to their calling in accord with the spirit of the times. The vow formula contained the explicit statement of obedience "to the Most Reverend Archbishop," indicating that the Cologne Alexians were a diocesan congregation.[25]

The first challenge to the Brothers under their new rule occurred when both the archbishop and the Poverty Administration decided to move them from their houses on the Lungengasse and Neumarkt to the city hospital where their social utility could be more thoroughly exploited. However, the Brothers refused to be absorbed into a large institution and after negotiation they agreed to leave their home, founded by Brot-Beghards in the early fourteenth century, and move to a vacant monastery (owned by the city) near the parish church of St. Mauritius.[26] Interestingly, the Brot-Beghards first settled in the cemetery of St. Mauritius before moving to the Lungengasse.

Though the Brothers were able to maintain their traditional

community life in their own home, the Poverty Administration did not suffer a loss from the bargain, as the Brothers paid 15,500 talers according to a contract of July 17 (the feast day of St. Alexius) in 1829. Since they recieved only 8,600 talers for the old house, this left them with a 6,900-taler deficit, which they paid off by 1830.[27] Besides their new house with its three-acre garden, they owned three other pieces of arable land in the vicinity of Cologne, providing them with their own agricultural produce.[28] Had the Brothers not protested the proposed move, their traditional identity would have gradually melded with that of the civil nurses at the large city hospital. With their new house they could carry on one of their traditional ministries, the care of the feeble-minded and insane.

According to the last will and testament of their chaplain who died in 1837, the Brothers' fine spirit had been expressed in the charitable hospitality afforded to him over the years. Because he was so honored he left them many of his valuable possessions, such as two gold crosses and other works of religious art.[29] Under the leadership of Brother Alexius Kürfgen and Pastor Geistmann the Cologne Alexians experienced continous growth in numbers and spirit. Though they underwent many tedious conflicts with adjacent property owners, in 1858 they added a new wing to the house, thus enabling them to have a brewery, bakery, and laundry below and rooms for more pensioners above.[30] Thus the Cologne Alexians reflect the general nineteenth-century trend of the entire Alexian family, i.e., the gradual development of large institutions for the care of the mentally ill.

IV

When Prussia absorbed the Rhineland in 1815 the Aachen community was without a pater and had dwindled to merely three Brothers. The community was legally recognized by Frederick William III in 1816, and since the Berlin government maintained the French welfare system, the Alexians maintained their official ties.[31] The Aachen diocese, established during the period of French occupation, was under the direction of Vicar

General Fonk. Though the Poverty Administration interfered in the election of pater and the acceptances of novices, the Alexians in 1818 successfully appealed only to the vicar general for approval of the election of Brother Bernhard Gerhards as pater and Brother Werner Schweren as sub-pater and for permission for seven candidates to enter the novititate.[32] During that same year the Great Powers of Europe met in Aachen to consider the status of occupied France. The Austrian emperor, Francis I, stayed in a home adjacent to the Brothers and attended Mass in the Brothers' chapel. A painting entitled "Franz I, Emperor of Austria, hearing Holy Mass in the Alexian Chruch . . . at Aachen, 1818" memorialized the occasion. Upon his departure from Aachen the emperor donated 1,000 franks to the Brothers, which they spent on a carved-wood Communion rail bearing the Hapsburg coat of arms.[33] The year 1818 is of marked significance for the Aachen Brothers: they were growing in numbers and wealth and they once again were under the leadership of a pater. Yet their image among the people had deteriorated over the years; like the Cologne Brothers, the Aachen Alexians were accused of working only for profit.

Within a few years the Poverty Administration became increasingly active in its control of the Brothers' income and property. For example, in 1823 it established the sum of 239 francs as the annual payment to be made from the community's income to each Brother to cover the cost of his clothing and maintenance.[34] It decreed that the community could not exceed twelve Brothers. As in Cologne the administration passed judgment on the suitability of candidates for the novitiate and elected superiors. In 1825 it vetoed the election of Brother William Koepp as pater "because of a lack of mature age, experience and reserve," whereupon the Brothers elected the former pater, Brother Werner Schweren, one of the three Brothers to survive the Napoleonic period.[35]

The Prussian-papal concordat dissolved the diocese of Aachen and placed the city within the archdiocese of Cologne. Shortly after his ascension to the episcopal seat (1825), Archbishop von Spiegel directed Father Matthias Claessen, who was provost of Aachen Cathedral, to be his commissioner over the Alexian Brothers. Claessen reported to the archbishop that the religious life of the Brothers was poor.[36] A year after von Spiegel had introduced the 1826 statutes for the Cologne Brothers, he appealed to the Prussian government and the Aachen Poverty Administration for their approval to introduce them as a rule for the Aachen Brothers. However, the Aachen Brothers rejected the statutes.[37]

Brother Ignatius Wiegers reports that the Aachen Alexians rejected the statutes because they gave excessive authority to the Poverty Administration with which the Brothers had been feuding for years.[38] However, Father Claessen wrote to von Spiegel that the Brothers were incapable of orderly self-government: "They are neither instructed nor unified enough for a free government . . . considering their feeble condition and their situation with their money, I find giving the Brothers greater autonomy a highly doubtful proposition."[39] He also wrote that the Brothers' religious life had greatly deteriorated; in the past they received the Sacrament every two weeks but in 1827 only every six weeks. According to Claessen, only three or four Brothers possessed the genuine spirit of the order and manifested a religious inclination in their vocation.[40] Though he strongly favored the introduction of the Cologne statutes for the Aachen Brothers, particularly those which regulated their finances, he informed von Spiegel that, because the Aachen citizens were so bound by the tradition of having the Alexians bury their dead, the statutes should be changed to include their traditional ministry (the first draft of the statutes referred to the Brothers' work as exclusively nursing).[41] Though Claessen did not mention the reason the Brothers rejected the statutes, one may surmise that because of their poor religious spirit they were struggling against further encroachments by the Poverty Administration not merely for religious but also for financial reasons. The Poverty Administration may have been a harsh master motivated by rigid fiscal principles, yet it may also have expected members of a religious order to be more concerned with charity than with profit.

Claessen and the Brothers did achieve a compromise when in 1828 the community accepted Claessen's proposal to appoint a chaplain for the Brothers.[42] Archbishop von Spiegel followed with an eleven-paragraph directive concerning the chaplain's duties. On December 22, 1829, twelve Brothers and Father H. Beys signed a contract specifying their mutual obligations.[43] In spite of these developments conditions within the community did not noticeably improve. In 1833 Claessen threatened to expel three Brothers who were not following their calling as nursing Brothers of charity. Claessen noted that they were unwilling to nurse because they received no payment for that service. He considered that to be a violation of their calling, particularly since the Poverty Administration provided a suitable cash allotment for each Brother.[44]

Claessen, in his annual report of 1834, proposed that because the pater's reform efforts had been unsuccessful, private cash privileges should be abolished. This proposal so polarized the community that Claessen demanded that the ill-disciplined Brothers be expelled from the community.[45] On March 6, 1835, the archbishop requested Father Müller, a member of the Cathedral Chapter, to investigate the situation in the Alexian house. Müller reported that the Brothers "were wholly lacking in monastic sentiment" and "completely rude in their manners."[46] He also said that the Brothers were motivated by cash profits rather than by the spiritual ideals of their vocation. Müller therefore agreed with the recommendations of von Spiegel that the Brothers regulate their lives in accord with the spirit of poverty (the perpetual vow of poverty was still not legally recognized) by placing all their income in a communal fund. Five Brothers accepted this proposal, while the six dissenters were expelled from the community with the Poverty Administration's approval and with their full dowry.[47] Claessen stated that these six were expelled because they "stubbornly refuse to obey and do not wish to accept the vow of poverty according to the modification of the times and show a lack of Religious spirit by their conduct—and among them is also the Sub-Pater."[48] To compensate the community for the loss of six Brothers, the Poverty Administration hired several lay nurses until new novices entered the community.[49]

The way was now clear for the introduction of the Cologne statutes, which took place on September 21, 1835. The statutes were identical to those under which the Cologne Brothers lived, except that the Aachen community was not allowed to elect its own financial director and the Poverty Administration was directed to keep a key to the community's money chest. The Brothers continued to be paid wages but deposited them in a communal fund rather than maintaining individual cash; spending was regulated by the superior. The only spiritual innovation contained in the statutes was the mandate that the Brothers receive the Sacrament once a week.[50]

The reformation of the Aachen Alexians paralleled the revival of German Catholicism. In 1837, two years after Archbishop von Spiegel imposed the Cologne statutes upon the Aachen Brothers, the German church, particularly in the Rhineland, was engulfed in a bitter controversy with the Prussian state, one which led to the intense politicization of German Catholics. The archbishop of Cologne, Clemens August von Droste-Vischering, who had succeeded von Spiegel in 1836, was, unlike his predecessor, unable to compromise the church's position on mixed marriages. He publicized the papal decree demanding guarantees that the children of mixed marriages be reared as Catholics. Because Prussian law stipulated that the religion of such children was to be determined by the religion of the father, the state retaliated by arresting the archbishop on November 20, 1837. Catholics throughout Germany rose in condemnation of the Prussian government. Johann Joseph von Görres, a leading figure in the Catholic intellectual revival in Munich (1776–1848), wrote a stirring pamphlet, *Athanasius*, in which he depicted Clemens Augustus as the defender of Catholic culture against the Prussian heretics.[51] The controversy was not resolved until the death of King Frederick William III in 1840. His successor, Frederick William IV, pursued a course of compromise with the papacy. Clemens Augustus was released from prison; he maintained his archbishopric of Cologne but the diocese was administered by a coadjutor. The new monarch also established a permanent embassy in Rome, abolished all restrictions on official church communication between Rome and Prussia, created a new agency for Catholic affairs, and donated funds for the completion of Cologne Cathedral. These broad conciliatory measures illustrate the changed political atmosphere within the German Catholic Church. Indeed, 1837 was a turning point in the history of the German Church. Alexander Dru remarks:

This first trial of strength on the religious question aroused the feeling of Catholics throughout Germany, and they became conscious of the need for solidarity. . . . This triumphant demonstration of Catholic solidarity in the cause of the "freedom" of the Church drew it more decisively than before into the arena of religion and politics. . . . The Cologne Affair is the moment when Catholics in Germany, becoming conscious of their strength, first sided against Prussia and began to take the idea of a "Greater Germany" seriously. The myth of the Holy Roman Empire of the German nation was romantically attractive and provided an emotional escape from the idea of the hegemony of Prussia.[52]

It is a twist of irony that in 1837, the year of the Cologne affair, John Peter Brock received the Alexian habit and soon became a major reformer, one who struggled against the hegemony of the Prussian civil authorities over the life and ministry of the Alexian Brothers in Aachen. Born into a middle-class Cologne family in 1813, Brock received a relatively good education before he was apprenticed to a master goldsmith. The latter stated, "I hereby testify that John Peter Brock worked for me as a goldsmith and during the time showed himself faithful and diligent, so that I can recommend him to everyone."[53] Brother Dominic Brock immediately gained the confidence of his confreres; he was elected sub-pater in 1838 and pater in 1844.

Though there were German Catholic Romantics who stressed the fundamental unity of altar and crown, the German Catholic revival primarily expressed itself in those Romantic terms which placed the church in relationship to the entire web of culture through which it could revitalize itself by the new sensibilities in philosophy, theology, art, science, and history, free of the battles in the political arena. Two major figures in the German Catholic Renaissance, Bishops Sailer and von Ketteler, were to the general revival in spirituality and social justice what Dominic Brock was to the particular revival of Alexian prayer and ministerial life.

Prominent among the progenitors of the Catholic revival in Germany was John Michael Sailer (1751—1832), who became bishop of Ratisbon. "It was Sailer who led the way out of the wilderness of the old world and, starting from the renewal of personal religion, prepared the way for a full understanding of the Church."[54] Sailer represents the reaction against the Counter-

Reformation's stress upon the institutional church and its rationalized defense of orthodoxy as well as the movement to reform the church within. He also studied the mystics of the late Middle Ages and translated Thomas à Kempis's *Imitation of Christ*, a pursuit that characterized the Romantics' urge to integrate religion and culture.[55] Sailer's revival of the late medieval mystics was paralleled by Brother Dominic Brock's revival of the late medieval Alexian spirit, which had been nurtured by the streams of mystical spirituality from Meister Eckhart to Thomas à Kempis.

Emmanuel von Ketteler (1811–1877) represents the social conscience of the living church in its struggle with the dynamics of industrial capitalism, which by the 1840s was threatening to unravel the traditional social fabric in the Rhineland, Saxony, Upper Silesia, and the Ruhr Valley. Though German factory workers and urban artisans were better off in the German states than in other parts of Europe, the sympathetic reaction among sections of the intelligentsia to the plight of the propertyless was swelling during the 1830s and '40s. The great French social critic, Félicité de Lammenais, whose ideas on democracy and social justice marked him a dangerous radical in the politically conservative French church, found much support among the German Catholic leaders. Franz von Baader (1765–1841) collaborated with Lammennais during the early thirties. Von Baader, in *Evolutionism and Revolutionism*, lashed out at capitalistic individualism: "No Christian may declare: this property, this right, this office are mine, to handle as I please; for in reality these are God's gifts and tasks . . . and a Christian may therefore handle them only as it pleases God. . . . "[56] Emmanuel von Ketteler was not directly influenced by von Baader but followed much of the same line of social reform. In 1848, two years before he was appointed bishop of Mainz, Ketteler was elected to the Frankfort Assembly. Triggered by the February Revolution in France, revolutionary activity exploded throughout the German and Austrian states in 1848. Social and economic unrest (famine and unemployment) articulated by students and liberal-democratic intellectuals broke out in the form of militant protests demanding constitutional government and the right to work. Karl Marx returned to his native Germany, where he edited the

Neue Rheinische Zeitung in which he urged the workers to join the struggle for democracy. In December 1848, while Marx was publishing his radical views in Cologne, Ketteler delivered his Advent sermons in Mainz Cathedral on "The Great Social Issues of our Time," in which he condemned the individualistic ethic of capitalism. "In its doctrine on the concept of property the Catholic Church has nothing in common with the ideas on property rights that are generally current in the world, according to which man regards himself as the absolute master of the things he owns. . . . This false doctrine that property confers strict rights is a perpetual sin against nature."[57] Ketteler ultimately designed social reform strategies that might fit into the loosely defined category of "Christian socialism."

Though Dominic Brock may not have been familiar with Ketteler's theories, the social activism of the day—embodied in Ketteler—was clearly expressed in Brock's leadership of the Aachen Alexians. Almost immediately after he became pater, Brother Dominic sent Brothers to nurse the sick at the Maria City Hospital in Aachen. By 1848 the Alexian visitator, Wilhelm Dilschneider, reported to the archbishop of Cologne, Johannes von Geissel, that the Brothers' spiritual life had greatly improved. They were observing monastic silence and receiving the Sacrament frequently.[58] Brother Dominic was deeply concerned with rekindling the spirit that had animated the original Alexians, that character which we would refer to today as "the Alexian charism." When cholera struck the city in 1849 the Brothers responded with selflessness, illustrating that their traditional character—the ministry to the outsider—had indeed been revived.[59]

Brother Dominic personified the renewal of Alexian spirituality and ministry; the next step in renewal was to ground the community in the vow of poverty. The Prussian government, following the principle established by the French during the occupation of the Rhineland, had prohibited profession of perpetual vows and had established the contractual relationship between the Poverty Administration and the Brothers whereby the latter were salaried employees of the civil authorities. The Prussian monarch, Frederick William IV, who was a conservative flying liberal colors, summoned in 1847 an assembly of representatives appointed by the various Prussian states rather than popularly elected. Frederick William quickly dissolved this united *Landtag* when it challenged his traditional prerogative of power. A sense of rising expectations was therefore frustrated, only to be revived when in February 1848 there were ignited in Paris the flames of revolution, which within a month spread to Berlin. Frederick once again wore the garb of liberalism and ultimately accommodated the Prussian government to the popular demands for constitutional rule by evolving a political system with the trappings of democracy but with the authority of the monarchy intact.[60]

In Article 12 of an 1850 charter, Frederick William granted the Catholic Church autonomy, a legal provision upon which the Aachen Brothers appealed for the right to govern themselves free from the Poverty Administration.[61] Though the state authorities did not relinquish control over the Alexian budget, even after the mediation of Archbishop von Geissel, they did achieve the right to govern themselves internally (i.e., accept novices and elect superiors) and their responsibility to the Poverty Administration was limited to a quarterly audit of their budget.[62] Brother Dominic was reelected superior in 1853 and, as Vicar Dilschneider reported to his archbishop, "the Religious spirit of the Aachen House has notably improved under the nine-year guidance of Pater Dominic."[63]

The rising action of the reform drama, directed by Brother Dominic, reached its climax in November 1853 when, after some hesitation, Archbishop von Geissel approved his request for the Alexian community's profession of the principal perpetual vows: poverty, chastity, and obedience. On March 14, 1854, six Brothers stood before the altar in the Alexian Chapel and made the following profession:

> I, Brother N.S. vow and promise to God, to the ever Blessed Virgin Mary, Mother of God, to the Most Rev. Archbishop of Cologne, to the Pater of this House, and to his legitimate successors, into the hands and in presence of the Rev. Archbishop's Commissary [Vicar Dilschneider] Chastity, to possess nothing as property, and Obedience, according to the rule of St. Augustine and according to the privileges and Statutes of the Cellites, until death.[64]

During the ceremony one novice professed five-year vows according to formula and a postulant and two temporarily professed Brothers promised to profess perpetual vows upon a mandate from their archbishop.[65] Eighteen years had passed since Father Claessen had ejected six Brothers for their general disregard for the spirit of poverty. By his profound renewal efforts Pater Dominic may be considered the founder of the modern Aachen Alexians. The revival of Aachen Alexian spirituality and ministry was soon followed by an elaborate codification of their entire way of life.

In 1856 Pater Dominic asked Brother Clement Wallrath and the superior of the Aachen Jesuits, Nicholas Schleiniger, to draw up a new constitution. Three years later it was completed and confirmed by Archbishop von Geissel on October 15, 1859.[65] Because a lengthy discussion of this document, which was revised in 1870, is included in the following chapter, suffice it for now to point out that it is the foundation of the modern Alexian character.

The Antwerp and Cologne Cellites also developed along modern lines, but they remained tied to their diocesan authorities. On the other hand, the Aachen Alexians' expansion ultimately led them to break from their local moorings and rise to the status of a papal congregation. The original impetus toward religious renewal came from Dominic Brock but it was Brother Clement Wallrath who had the foresight and courage to refine the modern character of the Alexians and confidently embark on new paths leading to the United States and Great Britain.

4

The Asylum Brothers

The revival of the traditional Alexian spirit occurred as the Brothers' ministerial focus shifted from the medieval hospice and cemetery to large asylums and general hospitals. When the Cellites were medieval "Tamers of Death" they spontaneously responded to those passengers on a Ship of Fools (*Narrenschiff*) and those madmen imprisoned in towers of the city gates (*Narrentürmer*). In a sense they became Passage Brothers for those whom society had exiled. For the late medieval man the *Narrenschiff* may have symbolized not only exile from the town but an "absolute passage" to the unknown world from which he came, that imaginary world populated by all sorts of fantasy creatures who influenced human behavior. Ironically, the madman was portrayed as a prisoner amid the freedom of the waters. An identical irony was present in the *Narrentürmer* in which the mad were imprisoned within the "threshold of the city."[1]

The medieval Cellites in Aachen and Antwerp and other towns lived near the walls. When the plague victim replaced the leper as the major infected exile the Cellites nursed and buried the exile beyond the town walls. In the late sixteenth and seventeenth centuries Cellite houses replaced the *Narrentürmer* as refuges for the insane. Though the Nijmegen and Braunschweig Cellite houses developed into large confinement institutions (*Dolhuis*—madhouse) in the late sixteenth century,[2] the Cologne, Aachen, and Antwerp houses were small hospices for all sorts of exiles—unruly boys, priests in need of moral reform, as well as the mentally ill.[3] For example, during the period of the French Revolution each house cared for an average of a dozen mentally ill patients.

During the eighteenth century the prevalent attitudes toward the insane underwent a change. Instead of viewing the insane as animals to be disciplined and brutalized into righteous moral behavior, they were seen as victims of illness. Though confinement was still considered a necessary protection for both the insane and the sane, the modern asylum of the nineteenth century literally liberated the insane from their chains.[4] Yet, in a real sense the asylum was still an island of unreason, an orderly world of disordered persons whom society stigmatized as outsiders. The other-world of demons has been declared superstitious by the enlightened men of the Age of Reason. But by the very fact that the mentally ill were regarded beyond the pale of reason, they were treated as objects to be observed and controlled rather than as full human members of civilized (rational) society. Though humanitarianism prevailed in many asylums, the we-they dichotomy was fundamental to society's "progressive" views of the treatment of the insane.[5]

From the mid-eighteenth century the Aachen Alexians could accept mentally ill pensioners only upon the approval of city authorities. In his history of the Aachen community, Brother Ignatius Wiegers included some interesting documents relating to this aspect of the Brothers' ministry. One consignment notice of September 21, 1769, states: ". . . it is permitted to the widow, Jean Devoux of Vervier . . . upon proper request and the presentation of reliable documents, to put her mentally ill son into the trust of the Alexian Brothers."[6] The following quotation from a 1776 document illustrates the popular pre-asylum attitude as it stressed the immoral rather than the irrational nature of mental illness: ". . . the permission is hereby granted, based on appropriate presentation, to confine the mentally weak John Nicolassen Jansen in the local Alexian convent for *correction*" (italics added).[7] Just as the *Narrentuürmer* had housed both criminals and the insane, so did the Alexian house (June 28, 1792): "The wife of Mathias Cruetzer herewith duly notifies that her husband is dissolute and of very bad behavior . . . and that he may still squander her property completely and that she finds herself compelled to have him confined for correction for some time in the Alexian convent. This upon request to be granted and to be helpful with a firm hand."[8]

During the period of French occupation the prison character of the Brothers' house was underlined: "Since according to the report of 25 Nivose [January 15, 1795] of the police officer . . . Dautzenberg, the supervision of the delinquents confined in the local criminal prison is no longer sufficiently secure, but general security absolutely demands the close and strict supervision of the confined Deutz, the supreme judge hereby decrees that he be temporarily kept in prison confinement at the Alexians, however, without any relaxation of criminal procedure and under the close vigilance of the police."[9]

By 1820 the official views of the Alexian house had shifted from a *Narrentürmer* to an asylum.

To the board of directors of the local Alexian Institution:
I hereby authorize you to admit the mentally deranged Mathias Joseph Hambuechel of Horbach, who by order of the administration . . . , will be brought to the insane asylum [*Irrenanstalt*] entrusted to your care.[10]

In the 1830s there were twenty-five to thirty patients living with the Brothers on the Alexianergraben. Gradually the Alexians had become known as *Irrenpfleger*, or nurses for the insane. When the Aachen Alexians professed vows in 1854 there were nine Brothers, one novice, and one postulant. In 1858 they had expanded to twenty Brothers who cared for fifty patients in Aachen and had established a new foundation in München-Gladbach. The new Alexian house was originally founded by three Aachen Brothers who had refused to profess vows and live a life of communal poverty.[11] Apparently they were motivated by the desire to remain religious, but according to the then recent innovation that they would be salaried as any city nurse. Their attempt was frustrated, however, as the cardinal of Cologne would not recognize their convent as an official Alexian house but instead offered it to the Aachen Brothers. His vicar general wrote to Pater Dominic Brock on September 25, 1856: ". . . if the convent at Aachen with its board of directors plans on erecting a Branch-House in München-Gladbach, and should also desire this having the means for it in hand, His Eminence would look forward to the proposition advanced having the agreement of both sides."[11]

On September 5, 1857, three Aachen Brothers moved into a tiny four-room house in München-Gladbach. The cardinal had approved the venture on a temporary basis with the understanding that the Brothers would limit their activity to home nursing. Though Brother Dominic supported the foundation, it was Brother Clement Wallrath who was the project's major promoter. Under the rector, Brother Aloys Speck, the tiny Alexian community suffered great difficulties in initiating the new mission. There was little demand for unknown nurses to care for patients in their home. With no income and no extra cash flowing from Aachen, the München-Gladbach house was on the point of closing when Brother Clement made a visit to decide its future. He wrote:

> In deep sorrow and discouragement I went there and found Brothers in a desperate situation. They had no means at all, no money and no supplies. Brother Alexius, who wanted to make an attempt at collecting alms, just returned and said that everywhere the police were on his heels. It would have been too dangerous for him to make further attempts and hence he had returned. In two weeks time he had collected only 18 marks. And so all seemed desperate. I found only one man full of trust in God and with firm reliance on the help of the Mother of God—Brother Rector Aloys Speck. . . . I remained about two weeks but nowhere could a ray of hope be seen. I myself had to believe in abandoning the place since there was no other alternative. And thus the first Sunday of October had arrived on which the Church celebrates the feast of "Mary of Victory." When the afternoon devotions were over and the people had left the church, we repaired to the crypt of the Cathedral, knelt before the miraculous picture of the Blessed Mother in fervent prayer for assistance. Finally our confidence increased so that we intoned the song: Arise Christians, come one and all, etc., Maria Victoria! We sang with such enthusiasm as if we had already been heard. Thereupon we went to our table to eat the little we had. We had hardly been seated when the door bell rang. The Brother who had answered the call was informed that someone was wanted to nurse a prominent sick person. It was the first such request since the Brothers had been in München-Gladbach. Brother Rector, a pious, zealous and saintly Religious himself went to the sick person.

And behold, the help of the Mother of God of the Rosary! Brother
Aloys had not mentioned our domestic needs and yet the family
sent baskets of bread, coffee, rice, etc.; in short, a large supply of
victuals. How happy it made us all! And from that moment we have
never been in need of anything. . . . And still the incredulous world
says there are no miracles!—Well, is this not a miracle! Indeed, the
Blessed Mother and St. Joseph are the real founders of our convent.
Had Mary not helped us within a week we would have given up.
Not only would this foundation have gone on the rocks, but we
would also have been intimidated and disheartened for the future
from ever again attempting to establish a Branch House.[12]

Once the Brothers were accepted by the townspeople they
gained the confidence to strike out on their own, making un-
solicited house calls, nursing the poor and, according to their
ancient mendicant tradition, begging alms from the wealthy to
distribute to the poor. In 1858 one wealthy patient donated
nearly four acres of land upon which the Brothers soon built a
new home and a chapel financed through begging. Upon its
completion in 1859 Brothers Bonaventure Thelen and Mathias
Speuser joined the three founding Brothers to form what became a very viable Alexian house in München-Gladbach.[13]

By another twist of irony the Aachen Brothers established a
house in the industrial city of Krefeld where a self-styled religious community of men had established a house beset with all
sorts of difficulties. They ultimately turned to the Aachen
Alexians for affiliation and to assume ownership of their house.
No sooner had Clement Wallrath, with the advice and consent
of his council, signed the contract for ownership of the house
and for the future investiture of the Krefeld men into the Alexian community, when the latter refused to become Alexians
and demanded a large payment for the house and for their labor
in building it, which came to 9,000 marks. Burdened with this
debt, Brother Clement appointed München-Gladbach's first
rector, Brother Aloys Speck, to be superior of the Krefeld community. Like its sister foundation in München-Gladbach, the
Krefeld Alexians immediately suffered hard times. Their poor
financial situation was compounded by the city's economic
recession; its silk industry, dependent upon the American market, was extremely depressed during the American Civil War.[14]

After a visit to Krefeld during which he discovered that the

Brothers' attempts at begging had been to no avail, Brother Clement went to Father Dilschneider, the cardinal's commissary in Aachen, appealing for permission to beg throughout Germany. Father Dilschneider immediately acceded to his request by writing a testimonial on the life and work of the Brothers and their need to establish a permanent residence to serve Krefeld. The cardinal endorsed the fund drive after Brother Clement, not without great difficulty, convinced the dean in Krefeld that the Brothers would not collect alms in the city.[15] Indeed it was Catholic Bavaria where the Brothers concentrated their collecting efforts. In November 1861 Ludwig granted Brother Albert Engeln authority to beg in Bavaria so that the Alexian Brothers could "meet the expenses for the building of a House for the sick and insane at Krefeld."[16] By the following spring they had paid off their debts and opened the Krefeld house to patients, who soon numbered around thirty.

The Alexians in Krefeld earned an excellent reputation, one which led to a second foundation in the city in 1862. In the early period of industrialism many craftsmen formed Benevolent or Friendly societies which, through subscriptions, provided sick benefits and funeral expenses. The Workers Benevolent Society in Krefeld had established a hospital but decided to appeal to the Aachen community to send two Brothers and an aspirant to assume control of the administration and care of the sick.[17] Pater Clement (he had been elected pater in 1860) and his council accepted the offer, stating that their sole motivation was that upon which their congregation was based, "The practice of Love of neighbor and not a consideration of any pecuniary profit but only to see that no financial losses accrue by it."[18] Hence the General Council asked that no salary be given to the three Brothers other than the Benevolent Society providing their board and a modest clothing allowance.[19] A year and a half after the Brothers moved into the hospital a public report stated that in 1864, 262 patients had been nursed in the hospital, 763 in their homes, and that 13 had died.[20] Noting a surplus in the treasury the report concluded, "The good outcome of the present year we certainly owe primarily to the circumstance that since a year and a half ago, the administration and care of the sick had been in the hands of the venerable Alexian Brothers who combine the greatest possible economy with painstaking care of the sick."[21] In the meantime the other Alexian community in Krefeld bought and moved into a new house (November 1863) on a twenty-five-acre plot of ground, formerly the site of a popular shooting gallery.[22] Though the move entailed a heavy financial burden and a sizable risk, Pater Clement Wallrath appears to have thrived on risky ventures. The München-Gladbach and Krefeld foundations were at best tenuous projects which elicited Pater Clement's continuous support. In order to finance these works the Aachen community initiated a broad fund-raising effort throughout the German states and even into Holland and Belgium.[23] Brother Dominic Brock appears to have been the charismatic source of the religious revival of the Aachen Alexians. Pater Clement was the practical architect who extended and fashioned new foundations; he was a shrewd businessman who brokered all sorts of deals and a religious superior who vigorously demonstrated his belief in the providential guidance of the Aachen Alexian Brothers.

Pater Clement was also concerned with maintaining the Brothers' diversified ministry—general and psychiatric hospital work, home nursing, and burial of the dead. In 1803, following a decree by the government of France, Aachen was compelled to establish a cemetery outside the city and burials in city churches and churchyards were prohibited. The new cemetery was under the city administration, which delegated supervisory and custodial authority to laymen.[24] By 1857 conditions had so deteriorated, particularly in the house where the bodies were prepared for burial, that the city administration appealed to Pater Dominic to assign Brothers to care for the cemetery. Of the opinion that such work would interfere with nursing, Pater Dominic rejected the offer in spite of Brother Clement's eagerness to pursue the project.[25] On November 26, 1862, Brother—now Pater—Clement successfully negotiated a contract with the city.[26] Three Brothers established a community on the cemetery grounds where the duties included, besides the general care of the graves, watching and preparing the bodies for burial. Hence the general revival of the Aachen Alexians was accompanied by a revival of the *Seelenbrüder* (Soul Brother) service. Though modern notions of death had replaced medieval attitudes, the folk spirit lingered on among many groups in society. A local liberal newspaper even welcomed the Brothers:

> We can break the gratifying news that a universally long cherished desire has been finally verified in the fact that in the past few days the supervision and the care of the Catholic cemetery and mausoleum have been entrusted to the local Alexian Brothers. This arrangement warrants the best for the future. If . . . the city officials will endeavor even more to further the work of charity of the pious Brothers materially, then our cemetery will soon get that order and those advantages which it has so painfully been deprived of so long.[27]

Pater Clement appears to have been so concerned with the general expansion, diversification, and modernization of the Aachen community that it must have come as no surprise to his confreres when he announced plans to redecorate and enlarge the asylum on Alexianergraben. As a result of his leadership the asylum grew from roughly a fifty-bed institution to 182 beds within twenty years.

The renovation of the asylum on Alexianergraben ran contrary to the trend in psychiatric treatment, which stressed a pastoral setting for the patients, thus allowing them the maximum amount of fresh air and exercise.[28] Aware of this trend, Pater Clement seemed to be waiting for an opportunity to move to the countryside. He even announced to the Poverty Administration (November 1865) that he might sell the city asylum in order to finance a new and larger asylum. The foundation of a house in Chicago interrupted his plans, but by another ironic coincidence the Aachen Brothers soon found themselves in a favorable position for the building of a new asylum in the countryside. Because the Aachen city asylum, developed during the 1830s, was in great need of repair and because of the new direction in treatment, the Prussian government ordered the city to construct a new facility in a rural setting. While the city was searching for a site, Pater Clement, urged on by the competition, bought twenty-eight acres containing farm buildings suitable for conversion into a temporary asylum. In 1866 twenty-six patients from the Brothers' city asylum moved into their new quarters in a rural area adjacent to the city. With shrewd business acumen Pater Clement, realizing that the Brothers and the

Poverty Administration had mutual interests, successfully negotiated a contract (August 10, 1871) whereby all mentally ill
males under the authority of the administration would be sent
to Mariabrunn, the new asylum, with an annual allotment for
their general care. After negotiating an 18,000-mark loan and
after visiting asylums in Germany and other countries, Pater
Clement initiated construction of an asylum (300 to 400 beds)
according to his own design. A year later (August 1868), the first
wing was completed and seventy patients from the Motherhouse
on Alexianergraben moved into the new asylum, Mariabrunn.
Within a few weeks forty-five patients from the city asylum
moved into the Brothers' vacant hospital on Alexianergraben.[29]

The 1860s was a period of profound significance in the history
of the Aachen Alexians. They had expanded into Westphalia
(München-Gladbach and Krefeld), established two houses in
the United States (Chicago and St. Louis), and built a modern
mental hospital near Aachen. This extraordinary decade was
dominated by Pater Clement Wallrath. Indeed, he embodied
the modern Alexian spirit. He sensed that the medieval Alexian
family-hospice had become anachronistic by the nineteenth century, that if the Brothers were to have an impact in a rapidly
expanding industrial society they had to develop large institutions to serve society's mental casualties, and that the Brothers
must not be tied to local houses but be willing to go anywhere
they were called. Hence, when Prussia went to war in 1864,
1866, and 1870, Pater Clement sent Brothers to nurse on the
battlefield.[30] When he needed funds to finance expansion he
sent Brothers throughout Germany and neighboring states to
beg. The medieval Brothers begged "Bread for the Love of
God" ("Brot durch Gott") throughout the towns of the Rhineland and the Low Countries. Pater Clement's Brothers were
modern fund raisers who solicited not for immediate personal
relief of hunger but for long-range development of large institutions to serve thousands in need of mental care. Though Pater
Clement was the embodiment of the modern, he also possessed
a strong sense of tradition.

Pater Clement seems to have had a keen appreciation of nineteenth-century trends in psychiatry. The predominant school of
thought among German doctors of the mentally ill considered

the illness physiological, to be exact, a form of brain disease. Though this was a narrow approach by today's standards, it did symbolize the victory of medicine over theology. Gregory Zillboorg noted that treatment "outside the humanization of hospitals and the use of drugs, baths and electricity [created] little discussion."[31] The German doctors were so bound to the physiological basis of mental illness that Sigmund Freud's mentor, Theodor Meynert, attributed psychoses to "changes within the circulatory system."[32] Because treatment on this basis was so limited, hospital management was the major concern within the asylum. Yet hospital management included separating patients according to symptomatic categories which led to a refined systematic order within the asylum.[33]

> The creative genius of the German psychiatrist seems to have risen to the needs of his day with more than creditable efficiency and dispatch. The work of non-restraint [working with unchained patients] alone—a matter of struggle, contention and bureaucratic obstacles in many parts of France and England—was carried out in the greater part of Germany almost without difficulty. . . . The German hospital became an institution for treatment and research work almost within one generation. Nowhere in the world during the middle part of the century was so much research done in psychiatry as in Germany.[34]

According to a circular of the Prussian minister of Public Worship, Instruction, and Medicine, there were three classifications for asylums—cure, mixed, and care—with each subdivided into public and private asylums. Because the Alexian asylums were called *Irrenanstalten*—institutions for the insane—they were probably classified as mixed rather than private, as private *Pflegenanstalten*—care-institution—or private *Heilanstalten*—cure-institution. Institutional care of the mentally ill expanded rapidly in the latter half of the nineteenth century. In 1852 there were nineteen private asylums in Prussia; in 1872 there were forty-eight, and in 1886 the number reached eighty-six.[35] Henry C. Burdett noted in his book, *Hospitals and Asylums of the World*, published in 1891, that "the largest [asylum] is that of the Alexianer Brethren in Aix-la-Chapelle [Aachen], with 310 beds."[36] All private asylums were licensed by the Prussians and inspected by the Prussian authorities frequently without prior notice. The

Brothers cared for mentally ill men and for children suffering from congenital retardation. The contract between the Alexians and the Poverty Administration by which the Brothers accepted patients who were wards of the civil authority prevented the Alexian asylums from becoming a refuge for the upper classes. Though the Brothers maintained their religious motivation they were instructed to abide by rigid rules of civility. In the constitution of 1870 (a revision of Pater Clement's 1859 statutes), the following rules for the "care of the insane" illustrate the ideals of religious civility of the Alexian Brothers.

1. Every Brother should look upon the insane who are entrusted to his care, as beings whose unusually helpless condition claims a greater share of Christian charity, and for whose security and welfare he must labor to the best of his power, for the love of God, whose image they still retain in their souls.

2. In order that a Brother may fulfill his duties toward the insane in a proper manner, he should know how to govern himself. In presence of the insane he should never suffer himself to be carried away by impatience, anger, fear or other disorderly movements of the soul, but should always preserve a uniform tranquility of mind, and exteriorly show himself stern or pleasant, as circumstances shall require. That he may do this more easily, let him reflect that whatever, in the conduct of these unfortunate beings, might provoke him to anger, should be looked upon as merely a manifestation of their disease; and hence that, even if they break out into violent bursts of passion, or into furious complaints and calumnies, nay, even should they attack him, their guardian, with treacherous tricks or open violence, he should look upon all this as the conduct of men who are not responsible for it.

3. Every Brother should make it a constant rule to treat the insane with kindness and love, for the more gentle he shows himself, the greater will be his merit before God. It is never allowed to lay violent hands on an insane person. It is sufficiently plain that the Brothers are allowed to defend themselves, provided they observe due moderation in their defence, from the attacks of furious madmen; but in this case they must intend nothing more than to deprive such persons, and that with all gentleness, of the power of doing injury.

4. Every insane person should be treated with that care and civility which are due to his estate and condition, just as though he were of sound mind. Abusive expressions, such as fool, silly, crackbrained, madman, should never be heard from the lips of a Brother.

5. When the insane persons give vent to foolish or delirious language, or when they are disturbed by strange phantoms of the imag-

ination, the Brother should endeavor to quiet them with kind words; he should beware of enraging them still more by contradictions, and if he sees that he cannot pacify them with words of kindness, he should be silent.

6. The Brothers should keep a watchful eye upon their patients day and night, lest the latter should hurt themselves or others, or injure and destroy their clothing, bedding, food, etc.

7. With regard to food, linen, occupation, recreation and medicines, the Brothers should comply strictly with the orders of the physician, and, at every visit, they should give him an accurate account of whatever they have observed in the patients.

8. When food is put into the cell of those who are furiously mad and violent, the Brother should see that they eat, and observe the quantity which they eat.

9. He should attend with particular care to such as refuse all nourishment for a considerable time, especially when they manifest an intention to starve themselves. In such cases, he should refer the matter to the Rector, who should obtain the personal aid of the physician.

10. It is a rule to be observed with regard to all insane persons, that they shall get possession of no utensils or instruments with which they may injure themselves or others; or at least such things must be given only with great discretion, and while the patients are properly watched.

11. The taking of medicines should never be left entirely to the patient, but the Brother should watch that the remedies be taken, or administer them with his own hands.

12. When a Brother notices that any of the patients under his charge has disappeared, he should inform the Rector, whose duty it is to see that necessary measures be taken.

13. It is the duty of the Rector to provide that insane persons be never left to themselves, but that a Brother be always with them and watch over them.

14. The strictest care should be had over such insane persons as are led by blind instinct to the commission of indecent actions. They should be prevented, as much as possible, from doing such things, and especially from drawing others to the same by their example.[37]

Pater Clement Wallrath has been viewed as the chief exponent of expansion and as the major developer of Prussia's largest private asylum. He was also responsible for the reorganization of the Aachen Alexians, placing them on a modern constitutional footing. It has been previously mentioned that Pater Clement co-authored the statutes of 1859; at the General Chapter of February 1870 representatives from the Aachen Alexian houses approved the revised statutes of 1859. In September 1870 Pater Clement journeyed to Rome where he had a private audience with Pope Pius IX; he returned with the news that he had achieved his goals, the Aachen Brothers had been restored to their medieval status as a papal (exempt) congregation.[38] In October the General Council organized the various Aachen Alexian houses into three provinces. The first province included Mariabrunn, the Aachen cemetery and the Motherhouse on Alexianergraben; the second München-Gladbach, the houses in Krefeld, and the Kaiserwerth community (a home where the Brothers nursed sick and retired priests from 1870 to 1875); and the third included the houses in Chicago and St. Louis. The three Brothers provincial were Dominic Brock in Aachen, Albert Engeln in München-Gladbach, and Paul Pollig in Chicago.[39]

According to the Statutes of 1870 the Papal Congregation of Cellites, or Alexian Brothers, maintained the traditional religious life with relatively modern authority structures and ministerial expression. The stated aim of the congregation, "the sanctification of the Brothers, and the active exercise of charity toward the neighbor"[40] was a traditional formula for an active religious life. However, the following ways in which charity was practiced stressed the institutionalization of their ministry.

> 1. In undertaking the care of sick persons of the male sex, without distinction as to religion; of the poor and forsaken as well as the rich, in private houses as well as in houses of the Congregation, and in public hospitals.
> 2. In directing institutions for the insane, the feeble, or other destitute persons of the male sex, whether such institutions be connected with houses of the Congregation, or otherwise entrusted to its charge.
> 3. In burying the dead, especially in times of pestilence. Where circumstances render it advisable, the Brothers also undertake the care and management of cemeteries.[41]

Since the Reformation the Cellites have never discriminated against non-Catholics in their nursing apostolate. Whereas nursing in homes was a traditional mode of their charity, nursing in public hospitals and directing instituions illustrated the shift from medieval Cellite hospice to modern hospital work. In an 1866 cholera epidemic in Aachen the Alexians nursed and buried the dead of pestilence, but in general their burial ministry was gradually relegated to a minor role.[42] Professional nursing work was also evident in their rules for the admission of postulants and novices. Besides prior instruction in "the truths of our holy religion" the candidate was expected to be skilled in the "rudimentary elements of education."[43] The development from postulant to final profession (a six-year process) was directed by a number of procedures guaranteeing the spiritual maturity of the Brother. A two-thirds vote of all the professed Brothers in the province was required before perpetual simple vows could be professed. The vow formula was identical to that contained in the Cologne statutes with the exception that within a papal congregation the rector-general replaced the ordinary as the ultimate superior. In simple vows the professed still had dominion of his property but was not entitled to administer or use such property, whereas in solemn vows the religious himself had no such dominion or use.

The authority structure of the congregation was a drastic break from tradition. The earliest constitution designated the positions of local superior, provincial and rector-general as elected offices. The 1870 statutes called for an election of the rector-general and his four assistants (every five years at a General Chapter) who in turn appointed Provincials who appointed local superiors.[44] Since local and provincial superiors could be reappointed for another three-year term and the rector-general for even a third term in rare circumstances, the governing apparatus was extremely centralized, with the possibility of relatively few remaining in authority for a long period of time. Because each Brother at the Motherhouse and the appointed provincials and house rectors were ex-officio delegates to the General Chapter they easily outnumbered the elected delegates chosen from each house, further illustrating the centralized character of the congregation. Indeed, the statutes explicitly state that the congregation was "ruled by one Rector-General who is called Father";[45] provincials and rectors were his eyes and arms on the local levels. The rector-general was directed to consult with his four assistants (the General Council) on all major matters and make a general report to the Holy See every three years.

The Jesuit co-author of the 1859 statutes (codified again in

1870) appears to have been very influential in the design of the authority structures. The Alexian Brothers were juridically members of a congregation rather than a local community or province. The ancient principles of subsidiarity and *stabilitas loci* which were embedded in tradition were replaced with a highly modern centralized system of governance. The medieval Cellites resembled Benedictine communities, the modern Alexian congregation the Society of Jesus. Centralization also characterized the trends in church and state authorities. The year before Pius IX granted the Alexians the status of a papal congregation, Vatican Council I proclaimed the Pope infallible, symbolizing not only the ancient primacy of Rome but also confirming the monarchical principle of church authority. In 1871 the centralization of Germany culminated in the creation of the German Empire. In a sense the consolidation of sovereign authority in the papacy was Pius's way of protecting the traditional prerogatives of the church in what many considered to be a hostile society. Pater Clement's concern that all authority be consolidated in the rector-general originated in a similar motivation. He could look back to the time of the French Revolution and note how the Alexian way of life had suffered grave decline. If the temptations of the modern world were to be successfully combated, a modern centralized system had to be imposed upon the Brothers. The practical considerations of maintaining large hospitals and providing for a staff skilled in medical and management procedures also encouraged Pater Clement to rationalize the authority structure along modern lines.

For an active religious community the Alexian rules governing spirituality and religious deportment were very monastic. Brothers were instructed to recite the office of the Holy Cross daily, meditate for three-quarters of an hour, attend Mass ("with either vocal or mental prayer"), and recite the "third part of the Rosary" and the Litany of the Blessed Virgin; evening prayers were to be in common from the prayer book of Saint Alphonsus. For the first time annual eight-day retreats were required, as were ten-day retreats before receiving the habit and professing vows. Weekly confession and Holy Communion on every Sunday and feast days of obligation were mandatory. Spiritual reading, attendance at bi-monthly conferences of spiritual instruction, preferably by a regular (religious order) priest and Friday fasting were also expected.[46] "Now and then, of his own accord, every Brother should ask his Superior to impose some penance upon him."[47]

The Brothers' day was minutely regulated on a relatively ascetic basis.

Daily Distribution of Time

To the end that, in every Community, that well-regulated order, without which the religious spirit cannot long exist, may reign through all the exercises, corporal as well as spiritual, and that thus self-will may be entirely excluded, and every entrance to idleness closed, the following daily order shall be strictly observed by all the Brothers, whenever they are not hindered by the duties of their vocation.

They rise in the morning at about half past four o'clock. At a quarter before five, they go to choir and they recite the morning prayers, and then the office of the holy Cross, as far as None, inclusively.

At half-past five, they assist at the Holy Sacrifice of the Mass.

At six o'clock, they take breakfast, during which there is spiritual reading.

At half-past six, the domestic occupations begin.

At a quarter before eleven, the examen of conscience is made.

At eleven domestic occupations again. (Dinner for the patients under their charge.)

At twelve o'clock, dinner for the Brothers, during which spiritual reading is made. After dinner, all go to the chapel, reciting the psalm "Miserere" on the way, and make a short visit to the Blessed Sacrament.

At one o'clock, recreation. With permission of the Superior, a short repose may be taken.

At two, a visit to the Blessed Sacrament, and the recitation of the Seven Penitential Psalms, if time permits the saying of these optional prayers.

At half-past two, domestic occupations.

At half-past five, Vespers and Compline of the Holy Cross; also the Beads and the Litany of the Holy Name of Jesus.

At six o'clock, domestic occupations.

At seven, supper with spiritual reading; after which, visit to the Blessed Sacrament, as at noon.

At half-past seven, common recreation.

At half-past eight, night prayers are said in common in the chapel. Then follow the examen of conscience and the preparation for the morning meditation.

At nine o'clock, all retire to rest.[48]

This highly structured schedule resulted primarily from the nature of the hospital schedule.

The chapter entitled "Additional Rules for Preserving and Promoting the Religious Spirit of the Congregation" abounded with advice on self-mortification and obedience to superiors. Correspondence with the secular world was severely censored, as all incoming and outgoing mail was first read by the house superior. Twice a year the Brothers were to write the rector-general so that the latter would be made aware of individual concerns and thoughts on the general welfare of the congregation.[49] Since such correspondence was confidential, this provision contains a significant pastoral theme. Considering that the abuse of poverty had been endemic in the immediate pre-reform period, reflections on this vow stressed the ascetic character of the Alexian way of life:

> 8.   The common life must be observed in its perfection; and hence poverty, as a guardian and most firm bulwark of religion, must be loved and maintained in its purity and integrity. All should sometimes feel its effects; they should not use anything as their own, and must be ready to beg from door to door when obedience or necessity shall require it. Their diet, apparel and lodging shall be such as become the poor of Christ.[50]

Poverty was also stressed in the rooms of the Brothers where "simplicity should reign, and the poverty of Jesus Christ should shine. Wherefore, these rooms should be furnished with the following articles only: a bedstead with a straw sack, and other things necessary for sleeping; two chairs and a small table, with a drawer for necessary articles of linen; a crucifix and a few pictures, for example: of the Blessed Virgin, their patron saint, St. Alexius, St. Augustine, and St. John of God."[51]

Community life was relegated to the formal recreation period. Many statutes prohibited idle conversation, visiting others' rooms, leaving the house without a companion, and making friendships with lay people. Numerous offenses were categorized into five groups, according to the seriousness of the crimes, with penances including recitation of prayers, fasting on bread and water for three days, and expulsion from the congregation. As a check upon harsh superiors, severe punishment could be imposed only with the provincial or the rector-general's consent. The following are samples from five categories of offenses, or "defects": "Breaches of religious decorum in the presence of others. Sullenness, or want of sociability—abuse of a Superior or a Brother, in the presence of seculars. Intriguing before an election of the Rector-General and his Assistants, for the purposes of directing the votes upon this or that person. Rebellion against legitimate ecclesiastical authority."[52]

Many "defects" among the fifty listed appear in hindsight to be petty. To place them in their historical context one may recall that many groups in society were anxious to exploit scandalous clerical or religious behavior.

The rules regulating the Brothers' nursing and burial apostolate evinced a general concern for their religious duties, virtuous moral behavior, and professional nursing qualities. When a patient was critically ill they were urged to "take care that the sick man be fortified with the Sacraments."[53] When a patient was dying the Brothers were instructed to be pastoral ministers: "especially when the agony lasts very long [the Brother] should comfort him with pious words, and help him with prayer."[54]

With the recent nursing services during the Austro-Prussian War (1866) fresh in mind, their rules included a chapter on "The Care of Sick and Wounded in Camps and Military Hospitals." Led by a superior, six to ten Brothers constituted a band for camp-nursing service. "None should be chosen for this arduous duty but those Brothers who, by their prudent judgment and strength of mind, and also by their dexterity in bandaging wounds and the like, have shown a peculiar fitness for it."[55] They were urged to assist army chaplains, give good example, not complain, and "avoid the immoderate use of spirituous liquors."[56]

The rule for Funeral Services is worth quoting in full because it provides insights into the ways in which the Brothers viewed their most ancient ministry as well as into the social history of the period.

FUNERAL SERVICES

1. The Brothers are bound in duty to render whatever services their Superiors may require, in laying out, transporting and burying corpses.

2. Hence, when called upon, they must be mindful of the primitive and peculiar end of the Congregation, and paying no regard to the wordly circumstances of the deceased person, or to the nature

of the sickness which destroyed him, they must remove the clothing from the corpse and prepare it for the burial; and in time of pestilential diseases their zeal in attending to such duties should be the greater, as then the majority of mankind has a greater horror of performing such work of mercy.

3. When they enter a house, just before a funeral, for the purpose of carrying the corpse, they should take no refreshment there.

4. They should carry or accompany the corpse to the cemetery, with religious modesty.

5. At funerals, mindful of the words of the apostle, "Weeping with those who weep," they should avoid whatever would betray a heart destitute of pity or compassion.

6. As soon as they return home from a funeral, they should hand over to the Superior, for the benefit of the Community, whatever they may have received for their services, whether it be money, clothing or anything else.

7. When about to close the coffin, they should again satisfy themselves that the person is really dead, abstaining, however, from any removal of the clothing, and judging only by the appearance of the face and the smell.

8. They should put the corpse into the hearse with becoming decency, and take it out again in the cemetery.

9. But if the Brothers have charge of the cemetery, they must conform to the ecclesiastical laws.

10. They must be very watchful that the corpses be not robbed, or profaned in any way.

11. Corpses delivered to them in the cemetery should be placed in the dead-house, and should not be interred, until evident signs of corruption have appeared.

12. They must be most scrupulous in observing all the regulations prescribed by law, to prevent the burial of persons who are still alive.

13. When the slightest doubt exists as to the presence of real signs of corruption, the corpse should be exposed in an open coffin, decently covered, and the strictest watch should be kept over it, until every doubt has vanished.

14. The Brothers who have charge of a cemetery, should receive the relatives of the dead with compassionate kindness, and be most ready to answer all their inquiries; being, at the same time, extremely on their guard againt allowing to such persons anything contrary to the rules of the cemetery.

15. When persons of the other sex visit the cemetery, the Brothers must be very careful not to admit them into the interior of the house, but must carry on all necessary conversation with them in a parlor near the entrance of the house, and furnished with a glass door.

16. For Rectors of Cemeteries, none should be chosen but vir-

tuous, prudent, and experienced men, who also possess sufficient cultivation to enable them to deal properly with persons of every class.[57]

The foundations laid in the rule were so firm that fifty-four years after its promulgation there were 529 Brothers in eighteen houses located in Germany, Belgium, Switzerland, England, Ireland, and the United States.

The original medieval Cellites were founderless and anonymous; documented heroes and saints were not a part of their ranks. A remnant of medieval culture, the Cellites nearly perished during the crisis of the French Revolution. Brothers Dominic Brock and Clement Wallrath were extraordinary religious who, in the Cellite tradition of quiet anonymity, rewove the remnant to fit the patterns of modern society.

PART TWO

✚

INTERNATIONAL FOUNDATIONS, 1865-1920

ALEXIAN FOUNDATIONS, 1850–1914

1850   1875   1900   1914

German Provinces

- (ca. 1330) Aachen Motherhouse
- 1857 München-Gladbach
- 1863 Krefeld Asylum
- 1867–1875 Mariabrunn
- 1875 Henri Chapelle
- 1878–1896 Mariaberg
- 1885 Lierre (origins 1430)
- 1887 Haus Kannen
- 1888–1908 Köln-Lindenthal
- 1897 Maria House
- 1905 Ensen
- 1911 Krefeld, Maria Hilf

American Province

- 1866 Chicago, Ill.
- 1869 St. Louis, Mo.
- 1879 Oshkosh, Wisc.
- 1893 Elizabeth, N.J.

English Province

- 1875 Moston Cemetery, Manchester
- 1879 St. Mary's Home, Manchester
- 1883 Cemetery, Middlesbrough to 1904
- 1889 Sacred Heart Home to 1904
- 1902 Twyford Abbey, London

5

From Aachen to Chicago

I

The first American Alexian house originated from a cluster of causes. Pater Clement was first alerted to the need for a mission to the United States by a priest who was residing at the Aachen house. The Franciscan Sisters of Aachen, who had established houses in the United States, also encouraged the venture. With the termination of the Civil War and with the advantage of sending a Brother along with the Sisters who were scheduled to leave for the States in December 1865, Pater Clement, with the approval of his General Council, initiated the American project.[1] On December 12, 1865 Brother Bonaventure Thelen was officially appointed superior, "Rector of America," with the qualification that the General Council might recall him at any time. From the outset the council was concerned about the potential separatism of such a distant foundation. According to the December 12 document appointing him rector, Brother Bonaventure acknowledged his primary loyalty to the General Council:

> . . . he solemnly declares that whatever he will found, arrange, buy, or otherwise acquire in America or in some other part of the world for himself and his successors will be done only in the name of the General Council and its successors . . . that all shall be done in the name of the entire Congregation of the Alexian Brothers and that he will never separate these new foundations without the consent of the General Council in Europe nor detach them from it.[2]

Brother Bonaventure, who was born in a small town near Trier (November 17, 1825), entered the congregation in December 1856, after which he served in Krefeld, München-Gladbach, and on the battlefield during the Danish war.[3] He appears to have possessed those qualities that characterize the ideal pioneer, a rugged sense of confidence and independence and a keen determination to accomplish his task. Pater Clement was by nature and by design a strong authority figure, determined to hold all the reins, and may have been a bit ambivalent about this pioneer Alexian. As Bonaventure's former novice master, Clement commented:

> Brother Bonaventure really aspired to perfection in his own way, but thought he was called especially to those deeds which he himself had realized to be good and proper by personal reflection. What he thus found to be good and salutary he strove to achieve with sacrifice and self-denial. But if that what he thought was perfect, would, if done, actually prove to be harmful, it was difficult to dissuade him, even for his superiors, unless the latter expressed their opinion in the form of a direct command in which case, he would obey, but would still maintain that his opinion was correct.[4]

Idealism, self-denial, and a relentless determination to pursue what he thought was right are attributes applicable to both Brothers Bonaventure and Clement. However, Pater Clement's ambivalence ultimately gave way to total confidence when Brother Bonaventure reported to him that during an eight-day retreat (May 1865) he had received a call from God to be a missionary. Recognizing Brother Bonaventure's vocation as providential, Pater Clement chose him as the founder of the American Province.[5] Brother Ignatius Wiegers reported that Brother Bonaventure "accepted the offer with great joy and enthusiasm but requested that he be commanded to go because . . . he thought a formal command was the will of God."[6] Though he was a tough-minded independent missionary, his deep sense of the religious life urged him to suppress his own will in deference to the will of God expressed through his superior. Though by nature a pioneer type, he was primarily an Alexian minister dedicated to serve the outsiders in the New World. On December 12, 1865, Brother Bonaventure, in the company of the Franciscan Sisters, began his long journey. He carried with him letters of recommendations from local church notables as well as the following letter of introduction written by Pater Clement.

Since the undersigned canonically elected and by the Diocesan Ordinary approved Superior of the Alexian Brothers, who for more than 400 years have been nursing the sick and burying the dead, had learned to know that an establishment of such Brothers was earnestly desired in the U.S.A. in order to devote their vocational works of charity to the helpless Faithful there, he hereby gives his beloved fellow Brother Bonaventure, called Hubert Thelen in the world, the commission to betake himself to these parts, in order there to negotiate with the most Rev. Bishops and Rev. Pastors the establishment of a Religious House for said purpose at a suitable place. He promises, when necessity requires it, to send still more Brothers, Members of the Order, to him to assist him, and he takes the liberty of recommending the above named Brother Bonaventure as an honest, judicious and pious man, to all concerned with great assurance in the Lord.[7]

J. J. Thompson, who wrote a history of the Chicago diocese, noted that Brother Bonaventure suffered shipwreck, during which time he lost his papers. "As a result of this he was looked upon as a swindler until, finally, he received new papers through the Archbishop of Cologne."[8] After such an ominous beginning Brother Bonaventure landed in New York on January 2, 1866, and soon made his way to Cincinnati, where the Aachen Franciscan Sisters were located. Unable to elicit a positive response for an Alexian house in Cincinnati, Brother Bonaventure took the advice of the Franciscan Sisters and made his way to Milwaukee. Because a group of Sisters had recently built a hospital in his diocese, Archbishop John Martin Henni opposed Brother Bonaventure's proposal to initiate an Alexian health-care facility.[9]

Frustrated with the bleak prospects in Milwaukee, he ventured to Quincy, Illinois, a Mississippi River town still without a hospital. He first stopped over in Chicago and visited with the German Redemptorists, who successfully urged him to try St. Louis. Though Archbishop Kenrick approved Brother Bonaventure's plans, the lonely Alexian did not find a suitable site for a hospital, nor did he see any signs for a promising future. After eight days in St. Louis he traveled to Quincy only to reexperience the set of discouraging circumstances that had

75

characterized his mission from the outset.[10] He had come through the most German-populated section of the country, forming the triangle Cincinnati-Milwaukee-St. Louis, but had not really settled down long enough to establish the network of contacts among the German community so necessary to the foundation of a hospital.

Nearly drained of finances and self-confidence, Brother Bonaventure returned to Chicago. Unable to find lodging with the Redemptorists, he was befriended by the Jesuits. Bishop Duggan, having refused him permission to collect alms for a hospital on two previous occasions, surprisingly gave his approval on March 31, 1866, under the title "Reception of the Order of St. Alexius":

> Brother Bonaventure, professed member of the order of St. Alexius, founded for the benefit of the aged, the poor and sick, being commissioned by his Superiors to travel to America, in order to extend the beneficial labours of his order also to this country,— upon his request, to establish a new foundation of this time-honoured religious association in this diocese and to found an hospital in the City, receives hereby our most cordial reception and most generous permission.[11]

The friendship between Brother Bonaventure and Redemptorist Father Joseph Muller, who had been instrumental in gaining this response from the bishop, represents the spirit of the close relationships that developed between the two religious communities (until very recently the Brothers were the official pallbearers for deceased Redemptorists in Chicago). However, the Benedictines, who had charge of the relatively affluent German Parish of St. Joseph's, were hosts to Brother Bonaventure on his first fund drive, one which netted a mere $4.50.[12]

Brother Ignatius Wiegers points out that the Alexian pioneer was riddled with doubt, anxiety, and indecision.[13] If this view is accurate, then Brother Bonaventure must have had very fragile illusions regarding the ease with which one could establish an Alexian hospital in America. Within three months he had traveled to five different cities, had settled in Chicago, had been cordially received by two bishops, and had begun a fund drive. Though the immediate future did not appear all that promising, he had nevertheless accomplished something in a short time.

To one who had visions of America as the land of limitless opportunity and instant success, disillusionment could have easily led to doubt and anxiety. Perhaps his high ideals rather than illusions compelled him to wonder about the viability of his mission. Motivated by a deeply religious experience, he may have been led by the hardships of the three months to doubt the integrity of his retreat experience of the previous year. As a religious in a foreign land without the props of community he was particularly vulnerable to self-doubt. Just as his perseverance was wearing thin, his situation took a sudden reversal. By the beginning of June 1866 he had collected enough funds to erect a small frame house on diocesan property at Dearborn and Schiller streets. The only other Catholic hospital was maintained by the Sisters of Mercy, located at the corner of Calumet Avenue and Twenty-sixth Street. The first Alexian hospital was actually an infirmary with a bed capacity for six patients, while Mercy Hospital was enlarging its capacity to three hundred beds.[14]

Brother Bonaventure moved into the hospital on June 12, 1866, and immediately went in search of patients. As if he were a medieval Brot-Beghard in fourteenth-century Aachen, Brother Bonaventure found his first patient on the street and carried him back to the new hospital.[15]

On June 15 Peter Bernhart, a German immigrant from Massilon, Ohio, became the first novice to enter from the United States. The following day Brother Paul Pollig and Novice Ambrose arrived from Aachen to form the first Alexian community in America. A week later the Alexian Brothers became intimately tied to the life of the Chicago diocese when Bishop Duggan consecrated their chapel and hospital.[16]

However, the Chicago community did not immediately accept the Alexian Brothers. Male nursing orders possessed a rich tradition in the Catholic nations of Europe, but they were virtually unknown in England and the United States. However, after the Brothers became known among the German-American community and after their thoroughly professional approach to medicine was established, the biases began to break down. The immediate breakthrough occurred when the Brothers expressed their original charism, ministry to the diseased outsider; on July 21, 1866, the first case in what became a cholera epidemic was

77

reported.[17] By the end of November 1866, the Brothers had two physicians on their staff and two additional Brothers; Leonard Jansen and Postulant Martin had arrived from Aachen. Though the hospital cared for non-cholera patients as well (there was a temporary cholera hospital established by the city) there appears to have been a causal relationship between the Alexian response to the outsider and the general acceptance by members of all nationalities and religious denominations. Indeed, they soon outgrew their tiny hospital.[18]

Brother Bonaventure had hoped to build a larger facility on the Dearborn Street property, but the diocese was unwilling either to donate or to sell the lot. Eventually he found a suitable site on the corner of Franklin and Market streets, a 250-by-204-foot lot with a sale price of $10,000. The seller, W. B. Ogden, arranged a four-year payment period at 6 percent interest and graciously donated $1,000 to the Brothers.[19] The generosity of Ogden, a non-Catholic, illustrates the growing appreciation of the Brothers by a cross-section of Chicago society. W. B. Ogden had accumulated a fortune from a variety of investments; he was a partner with Cyrus McCormick during the late forties and subsequently invested in railways, real estate, and banking. He served on the Chicago Sanitary Commission, was a charter member of the Chicago Historical Society, and a trustee of the University of Chicago.[20] Within a year and a half the Brothers had made one valuable friend among Chicago's brahmins.

With accommodations for seventy patients, the new hospital was ready for occupancy in September 1868. The solemn dedication ceremony took place with the vicar general presiding and with German and Irish bands playing.

The modernity of their German hospital training was an important asset to the Chicago Brothers. From their origin they were required to publish detailed annual reports collating the religious affiliation, nationality, occupation, and disease of every patient who entered their hospital. The General Council in Aachen also demanded a semiannual financial report. Because the Brothers of the original Chicago community were trained in Aachen, they were well aware of the need to establish corporation status for the hospital, not merely to limit the liability of the individual Brothers but also to safeguard their independence from city or church encroachment. On March 30, 1869, the State of Illinois granted corporate right to "The Alexian Brothers of Chicago." Those who formed the corporation were listed according to their surnames: Hubert Thelen, Mathias Pollig, Peter Bernhart, Johannes Schwipperich, Heinrich Garsonn, and Nicholas Schyns. Section 2 of the Act of Incorporation defined the "object and purpose" of the corporation as the

> religious improvement of its brothers and an active exercise of Charity, particularly in times of war, the gratuitous nursing and taking care of the wounded Soldier on the battle field, the gratuitous burial of the dead in times of epidemics, the establishing, and conducting of hospitals, the nursing of sick male persons, and the nursing and taking care of idiots and lunatics of the male sex.[21]

The Chicago Brothers were obviously prepared to import the entire array of Alexian ministries from Germany. The foregoing list was not arranged according to any set of priorities. Perhaps they wished to express their sense of loyalty to America by placing their wartime services first. To substantiate this notion it was stipulated in another section of the act that "no person shall be a member of this corporation unless he be a citizen of the United States or have declared his intention to become such under the laws of Congress."[22] One should also note that they did not include cemetery work but, rather, limited their burial ministry to the victims of epidemics. The use of the plural, hospitals, and the reference to their traditional ministry to the mentally ill indicate their hope to expand throughout the United States. As a not-for-profit charitable corporation the Brothers' real estate and personal property up to $100,000 was granted tax-free status.[23] Though still a very small community in charge of a moderate-sized hospital, the Alexians had achieved full canonical and civil rights and privileges, which marked them permanent ministers to the people of Chicago.

II

Brother Bonaventure, encouraged by Archbishop Kenrick's 1866 welcome, wrote to him again in 1869 seeking permission for a St. Louis foundation. On September 1 Archbishop Kenrick urged the Catholics of St. Louis to support the Brothers in their endeavor to build a hospital.[24] When Brothers Bonaventure, Paul, and Alexius arrived in St. Louis two weeks later, they must have been struck by the dynamic pace of the great river city. The archdiocesan vicar general, Monsignor Henry Muehlsiepen, hosted the Brothers in his home until they found a suitable house for themselves.[25] Monsignor Muehlsiepen, a Rhinelander who may have known the Brothers during his youth in Cologne and Essen, was appointed vicar general of all the German, Polish, and Bohemian Catholics of the archdiocese.[26] September 21, a week after they left Chicago, the Brothers purchased the old Simons Mansion, located on five acres at Carondelet and Osage streets. James Lucas, a wealthy railroad and banking magnate, sold them the property for $25,000 ($2,000 down and the balance to be paid in four years at 7 percent interest). Like his counterpart in Chicago, W. B. Ogden, Lucas donated $1,000 which the Brothers combined with a $1,000 donation from the Chicago Alexian Corporation to form the down payment.[27] Brother Paul Pollig wrote of those first days in their new residence:

> When we took over the new place on which there was a neat little house our entire belongings consisted of a tea pot, a wash basin and $23,000 in debt. Brother Rector [Bonaventure] had brought $1,000 along from Chicago and the seller had immediately donated $1,000. A poor woman, Caroline Hoppen, donated the first bread and the most necessary kitchen utensils. Her husband, Clement Hoppen, was the first companion when we went out collecting alms. May God bless him and may St. Joseph be his constant companion to heaven![28]

On December 8, 1869 Monsignor Muehlsiepen blessed the house and chapel (which was built as a donation by a German-American carpenter) and dedicated the hospital to St. Joseph. The Brothers successfully gained legal status when, on March 19, 1870, the St. Louis "charter" was granted. It was similar to that of the Chicago corporation's statement of "object and purpose," with the exceptions that St. Louis listed hospitals for the care of the sick, idiots, and lunatics and ended with the care of wounded soldiers in wartime and it entirely omitted the traditional burial ministry for "victims of epidemics."[29] Missouri's laws were more liberal than those of Illinois; the Chicago corporation's tax-free status was limited to $100,000 in total corporate wealth, while St. Louis was allowed a $500,000 limit.[30]

After begging from door to door, the Alexians of St. Louis gradually transformed their house into a hospital. On April 12, 1870, they admitted their first patient, Father Strombergen. Because the Alexians were to become the unofficial nurses of the St. Louis clergy, it was very appropriate that their first patient was a priest. Brothers Paul Pollig, Alexius Bernhart and Aloysius Schyns, the St. Louis founding Alexians, had made a relatively easy assimilation into the bustling St. Louis community. With two foundations in America, the General Council in Aachen transformed their status from mission houses to a full province.

The establishment of the American Province was preceded by what appears to have been a heated conflict between Pater Clement Wallrath and Brother Bonaventure. To assume a $23,000 debt for St. Louis before the Chicago debt was liquidated ran contrary to Brother Clement's fiscal sensibilities. He also thought it unwise to break up a relatively small community in Chicago in order to staff the St. Louis hospital. Large debts compelled the American Brothers to spend an undue amount of their time collecting alms; Brother Clement considered this dangerous because it brought the Brothers into an unbalanced contact with the world and threatened to undermine the orderly world of the religious life.[31]

A juridical issue also separated the American pioneer from his superior. Brother Bonaventure considered the American houses subservient to their local ordinaries rather than to the archbishop of Cologne. (Papal exemption was granted four years later, in 1870.) Because Brother Clement interpreted Bonaventure's position as portending the eventual separation of the American houses from the Motherhouse, he urged the American Brothers to maintain their loyalty to the congregation's constitutions and warned them not to consider separation. This conflict, which predated the foundation of the St. Louis hospital, appears to have been the major cause for the General Council's appeal to Rome for permission to establish an American Province.[32]

In October 1869 Rome approved the creation of an American Province with the qualification that as soon as possible the province be expanded to three houses. Hence the appeal must have been made immediately upon receiving news of the new St. Louis house. On October 17, 1869, the General Council formally imposed provincial status upon the two American houses and ordered Brother Bonaventure to return to the Motherhouse. Though the cause for the American founder's fall from grace was his expansionist view of the Alexian role in the United States (which Aachen seems to have interpreted as secessionist), Brother Bonaventure's position was, ironically, endorsed by the papacy's insistence that the American Province should expand to three houses.[33]

Brother Albert Engeln was appointed first provincial of the American Alexians. In a letter in which Rector-General Clement introduced Brother Albert, he urged the American Brothers to accept their new provincial as the general's "other self" and reminded them that the foundation of the new province was the result of the blessings derived from the 600-year Alexian tradition in the service of the church. As if he were publicly reprimanding those Brothers who were "Americanizers," eager for expansion and changes suitable to the New World, Brother Clement strongly defended his conservative leadership:

> Hence, it would be more than presumption, it would be . . . pride, if any member would wish to direct the order otherwise according to his own head and short-sighted spirit. All of us . . . would protest against this, we would say to such a party: We have no need of you; we shall adhere to the past; we want no innovations! An existence of 600 years gives us sufficient guarantee that the spirit and the vocational activity of the Brothers based on the old constitutions are good.[34]

With only four temporary professed Brothers recruited from America, the innovators must have been fully professed Aachen-trained Brothers. The phrase "according to his own head and short-sighted spirit" closely resembles Pater Clement's earlier remark on Brother Bonaventure's character: ". . . it is difficult to dissuade him [Bonaventure], even for his Superiors, unless the latter expressed their opinion in the form of a direct command in which case he would obey, but would still maintain that his opinion was correct.[35]

For an understanding of the conflict between Brothers Bonaventure and Clement, we have relied upon Brother Ignatius's undocumented narrative of the events which culminated in Brother Bonaventure's recall from America. One incident not included concerns a letter from Brother Clement dated June 12, 1869, introducing Brother Peter Verheyen as his representative to the Brothers in America. Brother Peter was specifically directed to ascertain the wishes and needs of the Chicago Brothers (the St. Louis house had yet to be established) and to report back to the rector-general all he had learned from his visit particularly the "order of the day and spirituality" of the American community.[36] Brother Peter, who was novice master in Aachen, had served with Brother Bonaventure and Brother Paul Pollig as a battlefield nurse during the Danish War (Prussia and Austria vs. Denmark). Without any documentation related to Brother Peter's visit, other than the introductory letter, one must rely totally upon inference for a reconstruction of the events. One such inferential line of reasoning leads to the conclusion that Brother Bonaventure resented Brother Peter as an intruder who symbolized the rector-general's distrust of his leadership in Chicago. If Brother Bonaventure was the headstrong individual so clearly portrayed in Brother Clement's remarks on his character, then the American pioneer may have frankly stated his opposition to such intrusion. The complexity of this entire story is compounded by another document, the official statement (October 7, 1869) establishing the American Province, which was signed by Brother Peter Verheyen and two Brothers from America, Paul Pollig and Stanislaus Schwipperich.[37] Brothers Paul and Stanislaus could have returned to Aachen with Brother Peter, or the document could have been sent to them for their signature. Because the others who signed the statement were Brothers located in Germany, because the Aachen seal was imprinted next to their signatures, and because immediately below the signatures was written Brother Clement's appointment (made on the same date) of Brother Albert as the first American provincial, it seems logical to assume that Brothers Paul and Stanislaus did return with Brother Peter.[38] However, it must have been an emergency journey, since Brother Paul had just established the St. Louis house twenty-two days before the historic October 17 date, and this required a very speedy journey by 1869 transportation standards. Whether or not the American Brothers were actually present in Aachen, their signatures were solicited; whereas, if Brother Bonaventure's was, it was refused. The founder of the American Province returned to the Motherhouse under a cloud of suspicion. Though he laid a strong foundation for the Alexian Province in the New World his superior apparently thought he was attempting too much too soon.

6

Expansion and Conflict in America

In three short years the Alexian presence in the United States had evolved from a mission outpost to an established province that included two relatively large hospitals. Though its founder had been removed from the scene, the dramatic tensions between the Motherhouse and the frontier province persisted for the next ten years. In a very real sense the character of the American Province was the product of this tension between the Old and New Worlds.

When Brother Provincial Albert Engeln arrived in Chicago in the fall of 1869, he knew little of the American Province, and was unaccustomed to the Chicago climate. It was the latter which caused him the most trouble; in July 1870, just nine months after he was appointed provincial, poor health compelled Brother Albert to resign and return home. Brother Leonard Jansen was appointed temporary administrator of the province until the General Council decided on a permanent replacement. Brother Paul Pollig, who had been replaced by Brother Stanislaus Schwipperich on January 25, 1870, as rector in St. Louis, and who had returned to the Motherhouse, was appointed provincial of the American Province, rector of the Chicago house, and novice master of the province.[1] Brother Paul was among the first Alexians to be assigned to assist Brother

Bonaventure in Chicago. He was the co-founder of the St. Louis house who, one may recall, appears to have had an idyllic view of the rigors of mission life. Shortly after he became provincial he underwent a test of his leadership and human endurance in the great Chicago fire.

At 8:45 P.M. on October 8, 1871, the O'Leary barn at 137 DeKoven Street caught fire and within thirty minutes the flames had spread throughout the block with such ferocity that they were completely out of control. Though O'Leary's cow has been the legendary culprit, the exact cause of the first spark remains unknown. The Alexian hospital on Market and Franklin streets was engulfed in flames around 4:00 P.M. on October 9.[2] A reporter for the Chicago Times described the fire as it threatened to wipe out the vicinity in which the Brothers were located:

> As early as twelve o'clock, the air of the extreme South Division was hot with the fierce breath of the conflagration. The gale blew savagely, and upon its wings were borne pelting cinders, black driving smoke, blazing bits of timber, and glowing coals. These swept in a torrid rain over the river, drifting upon house-tops, and drying the wooden buildings along the southern terminus of Market, Franklin, Monroe and Madison Streets still closer to the combustion point for which they were already too well prepared.[3]

Though their patients were removed to safety, the Brothers' hospital was entirely destroyed at an estimated loss of $100,000.[4] However, the sacristan salvaged the sacred vessels and the vestments by burying them in the ground before the fire devoured the property. After the fire a makeshift dormitory was constructed along the wall where the sick were housed. On January 22, 1872, Brother Paul Pollig appealed to the General Council for permission to negotiate a $15,000 loan to rebuild the hospital.[5] The General Council's reply is undocumented but, according to a letter dated December 3, 1872, permission was granted for a $12,000 loan.[6]

The third hospital in Chicago was designed by the architect Otto H. Matz. Born in Berlin in 1830, he was a prominent Chicago architect who in his mid-twenties designed the Union Depot "at the foot of South Water Street, the most prominent building in Chicago at that time."[7] The new hospital was a magnificent chateaulike structure—116 feet long, 71 feet wide, and 46 feet high—with space for 150 to 175 patients. In contrast to the old hospital, which had housed 75 patients, the new structure was planned with the phenomenal growth of Chicago in mind. Brother Paul appears to have been an energetic, foresighted developer who was willing to venture deep into debt to enlarge the Alexian presence in Chicago. Bishop Thomas Foley presided at dedication ceremonies on Pentecost Sunday 1873. Three thousand people were in attendance, representing parishes from the North and South sides, and four bands provided entertainment. Father Karlstaedter delivered the sermon on the steps of the new hospital, concluding with the words:

> And you, merciful Brothers, now that the blessing of the Church has descended upon the Institution, consecrate your whole life, all the faculties of body and soul to such an exalted vocation. Be grateful for it, for it is the Church who opens unto you an unlimited field of activity. Show that even in the 19th century the spirit of Christianity has not died, that there are still hearts that sacrifice themselves. Show the world that the Church hates no one but nurses both the faithful and the Unbelieving with the same charity.
>
> May this Institution unfurl the Catholic banner of Charity; may it be an ornament of the great prospering city of Chicago, a glory of Christian Civilization; an outstanding testimony to Religion and to the Church in the U.S.A.[8]

Brother Paul was very anxious to have Pater Clement visit the American Province. Though the latter did write toward the end of 1872 that he planned to attend the ceremony during which Brothers Alexius and Aloysius were to profess their perpetual vows the following spring, the church-state struggle in Germany prevented him from traveling during the crisis.[9] On May 28, 1873, Brothers Dominic Brock, Albert Engeln, and Alphonse Houben wrote to Brother Paul sympathizing with his many requests for Pater Clement to visit America. They stated that they and Pater Clement would like to journey to the United States but the political situation in Germany precluded a journey; then they asked Brother Paul to stop requesting such visitations.[10]

Provincial Paul Pollig's new Chicago hospital was a reflection of his progressive-expansionist views not only on the Chicago Alexians but on St. Louis as well. The day after the dedication of the house and chapel on Franklin and Market, Coadjutor-Bishop Patrick J. Ryan laid the cornerstone for a new St. Louis

Alexian hospital building, which was to be joined to the old edifice. As if to stress the Americanness of Alexian Brothers, the new structure was dedicated by Bishop Ryan on July 4.[11] Brother Peter Verheyen, the St. Louis rector, was the major fund raiser for the new hospital, which was a two-story building containing all the modern features—pharmacy, operating rooms, private and ward patient accommodations, as well as recreation and chapter rooms for the Brothers on the first floor and quarters (cells) for them in the attic. Following the lead of Brother Paul, Brother Peter spared no expense in constructing an impressive health-care facility on a fiscal base heavy with debt. The Chicago Alexian Corporation was $50,000 in debt; the St. Louis debt was $42,000. On May 19, 1873, the General Council in Aachen permitted the St. Louis Alexian Corporation to borrow $20,000.[12] By accumulating a $92,000 total debt the American Province, i.e. provincial, Brother Paul Pollig, was tacitly violating his superior's wishes. However, the total St. Louis debt far exceeded that figure, implying that Brother Paul's many requests for Pater Clement to visit America were prompted by his conviction that the rector-general would approve such indebtedness after he directly experienced conditions in Chicago and St. Louis.

Because Pater Clement was obliged to send a three-year report to Rome, he announced on May 1, 1874 (by letter), that Brother Leonard Jansen would be making an inspection of the American Province.[13] Just as Brother Peter Verheyen's 1869 inspection was immediately followed by the recall of Brother Bonaventure, Brother Leonard's was followed by the removal of Brother Paul from his office as provincial. In a letter dated July 25, 1874 Pater Clement stated that since Brother Paul's term of office had expired, his replacement was Brother Leonard Jansen.[14] Pater Clement referred to chapter 6, no. 3 of the rule book, designating a three-year term for a provincial and stipulating that the rector-general possesses the authority to depose a provincial for "weighty reasons."[15] Since Brother Paul was first appointed provincial in 1870, an 1874 expiration date contradicted the three-year term unless in 1873 Pater Clement reappointed him on some innovative provisional basis not included in the constitutions. Hence Brother Paul was more than likely deposed from office. Pater Clement's next two letters to the American Brothers verify this conclusion. In a letter of July 29, 1874, he specifically directed the Brothers to shift their obedience from Brother Paul to Brother Leonard, a directive which, if contained in an ordinary appointment of a new provincial, would have been unnecessary. Pater Clement concluded by stating his hopes for peace and unity among the Brothers in the difficulties that lay ahead.[16] On August 3, 1874, Pater Clement admitted that he did indeed depose Brother Paul when he ordered the American Brothers to obey the new provincial despite the fact that Brother Paul's term had not expired.[17] During Brother Leonard's visitation to the two American houses he must have uncovered not only the debt-authority issue but also the controversial ramifications of Brother Paul's style of leadership among the American Brothers. As if Pater Clement were directly responding to a report from Brother Leonard, he instructed the latter to call a Provincial Chapter particularly for the consideration of twelve points related to the entire Alexian way of life in America.[18] He seems to have been convinced that religious life in America was easily undermined and that Brother Paul's leadership had led to a decline in moral discipline. For example, he specifically forbade the Brothers to visit taverns, implying that such a practice was widespread.[19]

There is a vacuum of documentary evidence as to the activities of Brother Paul for the three years following his fall from grace. On the other hand, Brother Bonaventure, within two years after he received a "no confidence" notice from his superior, did achieve the trust of the General Chapter (1871) and was elected second assistant to the rector-general.[20] Relations between Bonaventure and Clement had been strained to the breaking point during the 1869 authority conflict. Because the two men were strong-willed, tensions from the previous conflict must have been, at best, a potential source of further conflict within the General Council and, at worst, an actual obstruction to the formation of unanimity on the council. When issues concerning the American Province were up for consideration, heated disputes between Bonaventure and Clement could have easily erupted. Tensions must have been exacerbated by the presence of the first American provincial (Brother Bonaventure's replacement), Brother Albert, on the council. Brother Bonaventure may have also resented Brothers Paul Pollig and Peter Verheyen; the former had been Brother Clement's visitator to America immediately prior to his recall to Aachen, while both Brothers had signed the document recording the establishment of the American Province, a document which subsequently led to Pater Clement's appointment of Brother Albert rather than Brother Bonaventure as the first American provincial.

Regardless of the basis for and content of the disputes between Brothers Bonaventure and Clement they reached crisis proportion sometime in early 1873. Though the rising action and climax to this dramatic clash remain undocumented, it is certain that Brother Bonaventure appealed to the archbishop of Cologne to consider specific charges that he listed against Pater Clement. Unfortunately, the only extant document about the case is a letter from the archbishop (dated April 21, 1873) to Father De Roth of St. Foilen's Parish in Aachen in which he encouraged De Roth to seek a reconciliation between Bonaventure and Clement. He stated that after considering the accusation against the superior, the reports (of Brother Clement Wallrath and Father De Roth) and the charges against the superior of the congregation were without foundation, and that even had they been true they were not of sufficient gravity to warrant action on his part.[21] Unless one concludes that there was an obvious rupture between Brother Bonaventure and Clement, one is left with too many unknowns to draw any specific inferences from this one document. The conflict could have originated in a personality clash entirely unrelated to the American Province.

Two other facts add some substance to an otherwise shadowy story: first, the fact that official documents signed by members of the General Council did not include Brother Bonaventure's signature after May 28, 1873, a month after the archbishop's adjudication letter; second, the fact that his term as assistant was to have ended in 1876, and thus he either resigned or was removed from the General Council; furthermore, a reconciliation did ultimately occur, for on April 3, 1877, Pater Clement appointed Brother Bonaventure as his official inspector to the American Province, an appointment implicitly grounded in trust.[22] To set the chronology straight one should recall that Brother Bonaventure's accusations occurred in 1873, a year before Brother Paul was removed from office, and his appointment as inspector occurred in 1877, three years after Brother Leonard Jansen had replaced Brother Paul. Brother Peter Verheyen, the St. Louis superior whose views were apparently in accord with Paul's, was also removed from office in 1874. Eventually they returned to Aachen. Brother Paul remained in Germany, while Brother Peter was sent to Manchester, England. Hence during that period three leading figures in the foundation and expansion of the American Province had no impact upon its development. Each of them, either explicitly or implicitly, had questioned Pater Clement's judgment of the direction of the American Alexians. The three Brothers who were removed from authority in America seem to have shared the point of view that deep indebtedness was a risk worthy of the need to develop quality hospitals.

Shortly after Pater Clement appointed Brother Leonard as Paul's replacement (1874), he ordered him to call a Provincial Chapter which was to assume the task of writing provincial statutes and bylaws. After passing through the Provincial Chapter, these statutes were altered by a committee of the General Chapter—chaired by Pater Clement—and were finally approved by the entire General Chapter on May 23, 1876.[23]

Though many of these statutes concerned the Brothers' hospital work in America, a topic which will be considered later, the final section of the first provincial constitution seems to have been derived from the conflicts between the Motherhouse and provincial leaders. The article entitled "About leaving house" warns against the dangers of collecting, i.e., begging or soliciting funds. Only the "old and trustworthy Brothers" should be assigned to perform the task. In a sense the statute directed the formation of "professional" fund raisers, as it stated that they should "not be readily removed from office, in order that . . . they may become acquainted with businessmen."[24] (In 1874, after Brother Peter was removed from the rectorship of the St. Louis community, an incident of financial mismanagement due to his apparent naïveté was uncovered.) Since collecting frequently required prolonged absence from the community, the constitution stipulated a maximum period of three months for collectors to be on the road.[25] As if to condemn what had become a customary practice for the Chicago and St. Louis Brothers to host a dedication party, one rule stated: "The Brothers are not allowed to frequent public festivities, much less arrange such themselves."[26]

Unlike the German Brothers who, because they were living in predominantly Catholic towns, could wear their religious habits on the street, the American Brothers were forced to devise a proper attire for outside the hospital. American informality may have crept into the German-American Alexian communities requiring a detailed rule for such attire. "For use in winter: black pantaloons, a black frock-coat, with turned down collar, a black vest, closely buttoned, and a black, broad, and stiff felt hat. In summer they are allowed to wear a light black sack-cloth and a lighter black hat."[27]

The chain of command, from the rector and his house consultors to the provincial and his consultors, was rigidly applied to the decision-making process on costs for building construction, repairs, redesigning the grounds and the contracting of debts.[28] The congregation's statutes included the provision that a provincial might not "undertake anything of great importance and extraordinary expense, such as the buying of immovable property, without the prior authorization from the Rector General."[29]

Pater Clement's views were strongly imprinted on these statutes, which appear as a codification of German customs upon the American Province. The proscription of festivities, the urgings of caution regarding collection of alms, the imposition of austere religious garb, and the mandate for strict accountability to superiors through the chain of command were all directives which seem to have been motivated by the need to guarantee law and order for the American Brothers ever threatened by the dangerously antireligious texture of frontier existence. Pater Clement could have easily feared that the American Province would ultimately write its declaration of independence, that American democracy would break down the Brothers' sense of obedience to authority, and that American informality would breed a disrespect for the traditional decorum of the religious.

In the 1860s, '70s, and '80s rumors spread throughout Germany of the many Catholics in America who had lost their faith. In 1865 the St. Joseph's Society in Aachen was linked to a major effort to preserve the faith and German customs among emigrants to the United States.[30] No doubt such rumors served to exaggerate Pater Clement's fears. In 1873 Otto von Bismarck initiated the *Kulturkampf*—culture struggle—against the Catholic Church. Though another chapter includes a detailed discussion of this church-state conflict, one should note the strong atmosphere of acrimony in Germany during that period when Pater Clement was experiencing difficulties with the American Province.

A year after the American statutes were approved, Brother Paul Pollig made a dramatic entrance into the center stage of Alexian history where, according to the available documentation, he repudiated Pater Clement's authority. Because he traveled to America against the expressed will of his rector-general, the General Council unanimously voted on September 9, 1877, to dismiss Brother Paul (secular name, Mathias) from the congregation. By order of Pater Clement he was to be given civilian clothes for work and a suit for Sunday dress, those things he brought with him upon entering the order, and fifty Prussian thalers.[31] Mathias Pollig wrote that he had begged for his passage money, as if that would have put him in good stead,[32] but Pater Clement must have been furious with such news, since that was begging for individual rather than congregational needs.

When Paul arrived in America the situation in the province was already polarized; however, the tensions did not originate with Paul but, rather, with Brother Bonaventure, who had been appointed visitator for the United States Province in April 1877. It appears ironic that the major problem which Bonaventure was sent to resolve was the heavy indebtedness incurred by the hasty expansion under Paul, a policy he had also pursued as the founding Brother in the United States. Yet Bonaventure was elected assistant to the rector-general at the 1876 chapter. After seven years in Aachen and after the province had become permanently cemented to the congregation, Bonaventure had apparently regained Clement's trust.

On April 3, 1877, Bonaventure was granted all the powers of

visitator in lieu of Pater Clement, who was unable to leave Aachen at that time "due to the situation [threat of renewed church-state struggles] in Germany."[34] The visitation was the regular three-year tour of the province prescribed by the statutes. Pater Clement also notified the American provincial, Brother Leonard, that Bonaventure was "to remain in America until recalled by the General Rector."[34]

In a June 18, 1877, letter from Pater Clement to Brothers Bonaventure and Leonard, the rector-general congratulated the United States provincial "for stemming the tide of materialism in the American Province" and also urged Brother Bonaventure to remain longer in America "to help, study, observe, guide" and report back to his superior when he returned to Aachen.[35] Clement ordered the implementation of specific regulations to improve the spiritual and material welfare of the province: he urged the Brothers to bring the crucifix to patients' rooms for morning and evening prayer, to abide by fasting and other regulations, and to prepare breakfast as in Europe.[36] Concerning the poor financial situation in the St. Louis house, which had grown worse, Pater Clement placed a moratorium on all new building and renovation until the debts were paid off.[37] The most significant order stipulated that because of many complaints from the Brothers, house and provincial decisions were to be made in consultation with councilors and, in the case of provincial decision, within the council and in the presence of the visitator, i.e., Brother Bonaventure.[38] Obviously Brother Leonard had gained a reputation as a tyrant, which may have been a causal factor in the financial deterioration of the province.

During the remainder of the summer of '77 tensions between the visitator and the provincial reached the breaking point. The issue of indebtedness was a minor point of conflict in contrast to a bitter personality struggle. Though Pater Clement explicitly endorsed the broad powers of his visitator, Brother Leonard resisted Brother Bonaventure's interference.[39] Finally on October 6 Brother Bonaventure cabled to his pater, "Danger rings. I must suspend Leonard or come back."[40] Brother Leonard refused to step down and was ultimately supported by Pater Clement, who reappointed him provincial on October 16 and ordered Brother Bonaventure to return to Aachen.[41] However, apparently the pater rescinded the recall order; the Provincial Council minutes of November 14 reveal a continuously polarized situation, one exacerbated by Brother Bonaventure's presence. "Due to Brother Bonaventure's declaration that Brothers with 5-year vows can participate in decision making, and the clarification from Aachen that they may not, and due also to Brother Bonaventure's declaration that Brother Leonard's term of office had expired, and another clarification that it had not" the council was unable to make certain decisions related to the pater's orders of June 18. [42] The Bonaventure-Leonard conflict was ultimately resolved with the latter as permanent provincial and Bonaventure back in Aachen. Though the documents specifying these decisions have been lost, others reveal that Bonaventure did eventually return to Germany and that Pater Clement continued to trust Leonard's leadership, displayed by the way in which he handled Paul Pollig.

During Brother Bonaventure's visitation the Paul controversy was included in the general conflict between the visitator-commissar and Brother Leonard. The documentary evidence on the Paul Pollig story is very incomplete; the following narrative has many gaps. Yet, because the Paul-congregation conflict was crucial to the evolution of the American Province's character, the story, in spite of its gaps, deserves as full narration as possible. One fact is certain: Paul never wanted to leave the congregation. "Yesterday, Paul came and declared to me that he did not want to leave the Order," wrote Brother Leonard to his pater on November 15, 1877. In an undated letter to Brother Leonard, Paul exclaimed, "I long to live as a Brother and to die in our Congregation." [43] In December 1877 Paul visited Leonard and complained of the injustice of his dismissal. According to Brother Leonard, he couldn't imagine what he had done to warrant such treatment. Brother Leonard admonished him to reflect upon all he had said and done against the congregation. [44] By this time Paul had somehow convinced Brother Aloysius Schyns, the St. Louis rector, to write a letter of recommendation stating that Paul was an Alexian in good standing with the congregation. [45] Throughout the winter and spring of 1877–1878 Paul made use of this letter to raise financial and moral support for the establishment of an Alexian institution under his direction.

He apparently received much encouragement, for in the summer of 1878 he traveled to Rome where he appealed to the Sacred Congregation of Religious for permission to found an American Alexian house independent of the Motherhouse in Aachen.[46] Paul never received such permission, but since there were many Alexian houses in Belgium and Germany which had never been incorporated into the Aachen Alexian Congregation, ample precedent supported Paul's plan.[47]

Paul returned to America in the autumn of 1878 with plans to establish Alexian institutions. He had received encouragement in New York City and in Wisconsin. In October of that year Leonard wrote to Pater Clement that Paul was to build an institution in New York. "I want to put a stop to Mathias Pollig's plans. He can no longer go collecting here."[48] In the October 19 issue of the New York *Freeman's Journal*, in an article entitled "A Pernicious Blunder" the author severely criticized the Alexian Brothers for their treatment of Brother Paul, particularly Brother Leonard's opposition to his New York venture:

> When "Brothers" get into a snarl, they make a great mistake in trying to use the *Freeman's Journal*.
> A "Brother Leonard," reputed Superior of a community called "Alexian Brothers," wrote us a note, that we published, last week, saying that one "Brother Paulus" late of theirs, had been "*expelled* from their Brotherhood more than a year ago." It is not *true*! Unless "Brother Aloysius," Superior in St. Louis, has been telling falsehoods.
> We have seen a letter, of Brother Aloysius, of St. Louis, dated November 5, 1877—*inside* of a year, praising "Brother Paulus," as a wonderful "Brother!" "Brother Paul" has not a *rag* to show that he is any "Brother."
> . . . But "Brother Leonard," has stated to us what seems not true—and we wish these *quarrelling Brothers* to understand that they come on dangerous ground when they—any of them—try to fool the *Freeman's Journal*. This "Brother Paul" has *not*—he says—been making any collections in New York—having been very peremptorily and properly *snubbed* by Cardinal McCloskey.
> We are exceedingly indignant at the impudence of the Superior of these "Alexian Brothers"—who has misled us! The *falsehood* is printed on its face! His "Brother Paul," may, or may not be an untrusty person. But, however unworthy, it is *not* true that he was *expelled*, from whatever there is of this "Alexian," over a year ago.
> "Brothers!" No more "Alexians" for us![49]

Brother Leonard wrote a response to this article, which the New York *Freeman's Journal* and the *Catholic Register* did not publish; he sent it to the *Western Watchman*, a Catholic publication housed in St. Louis. Dated November 21, 1878, Brother Leonard's letter was a rejoinder to both the *Journal* and Paul.[50] He told the editor that he regretted "arousing [his] indignation or ruffling [his] equanimity" but that the editor had been misled by letters from Paul. He then stated "the true facts of the case."[51]

> The ex-Brother Paul has been formally expelled by our Superior General from the order of the Alexian Brothers. . . . Moreover I can safely assert that any letter of recommendation, whether obtained from lay or ecclesiastical persons, of a subsequent date to the month of July 1877, was fictitious or procured under false pretenses. To my knowledge he has obtained two three [*sic*] such letters from ecclesiastical authorities wilfully concealing his real character from them, and the fact of his expulsion from the Order. I presume you would brand this mode of procedure imposition. Hence, Brother Paul is not to be believed when he informs you that he made no collections of means of funds under the cover of our name, thus palming himself off to the public, as an Alexian Brother in good standing whereas he is not. . . . He has sought permission from a certain prelate but the good and prudent Bishop discovered the ruse in time. . . . I have to defend and protect our Brotherhood by honorable legitimate means, against a fraud, as well as against injustice and public censures.[52]

Brother Leonard's defense was apparently an explanation of his interference in Paul's plans to establish an Alexian institution in the New York City diocese. He explained to his pater (November 22, 1878): "I've prevented Paul's establishment in New York because this Cardinal had actually given the permission. Two Redemptorist Priests whom Paul had led astray were with him at the Cardinal's [office]. If the Cardinal had given the permission to establish an institution other than Alexian then it wouldn't have made any difference."[53]

Paul was determined to remain an Alexian Brother; as long as neither he nor Pater Clement sought a dispensation from his vows Paul was still canonically an Alexian Brother. Brother Leonard urged his pater "to procure a dispensation" because he had been advised that if a bishop did accept Paul he could legitimately "found as many Alexian [institutions] as he wishes entirely independent of us but with our name."[54] He noted that Paul had received some support from Bishop Krautbauer of Green Bay, Wisconsin, but that he had successfully "hindered the Bishop's taking in Paul."[55] Leonard also told Clement that "everyone knows that the Alexian Brothers were planning to found a hospital in Oshkosh,"[56] which meant that Paul was close to the bishop.

Bishop Krautbauer had merely been delayed by Leonard's intervention; on August 8, 1879, the bishop announced that Brother Paul had recently established a hospital in Oshkosh, which was to be used for priests unable to fulfill their vocations.[58] Because the Oshkosh Alexians did eventually nurse alcoholic priests, perhaps the origin of the hospital was related to this specific calling. In an August 16th letter Brother Cunibert reported to Pater Clement that Paul received the bishop's permission to establish a house in Oshkosh under the Alexian name as well as permission to wear the traditional habit.[58] Obviously Bishop Krautbauer had been informed that Paul had not been dispensed from his vows, which provided the bishop with a canonical basis for his action.

Pater Clement appears to have responded positively to the Oshkosh project. Clement may have been motivated by the papacy's 1869 approval of the Alexian American Province containing the stipulation that a third house be established as soon as possible. Hence on January 24, 1879, he gave his permission for the province to take control of the Oshkosh house. Exactly one month later (February 24) Bishop Krautbauer turned over to the Alexians their new Wisconsin home. It must have been a rather elaborate ceremony, as Leonard later wrote there was a public demonstration in favor of the Brothers as well as newspaper articles noting that the Oshkosh institution "would be a branch of the well-known and highly praised Alexian hospital in Chicago."[59] Indeed the Chicago corporation did own the property until the Oshkosh Hospital incorporated itself according to the Wisconsin laws.

The Brother Paul issue was not so easily resolved. He was told to write a letter to the rector-general seeking approval for his reentrance into the congregation. Leonard's correspondence with Pater Clement provides no information on Paul's attitude nor that of the rector-general.[60] He does mention Bishop Krautbauer's disillusionment with Paul: "He told us Paul lied to him."[61] Leonard, who had been struggling with the Paul situation for two years, was obviously cool to the possibility of Paul's Alexian renewal. As if he thought Paul would be received back into the congregation, Leonard said, "I don't believe he should be in one of these [American] houses.,"[62] but, rather, be sent to one of the European houses. Leonard's last extant remark on Paul is extremely enigmatic. On March 26, 1880, he wrote to Pater Clement: "Your letter to Mr. Pollig has been read. Since I can't wish for any other Provincial to fight with him, I wrote Cunibert that he should invoke the name of God that he find another place to save his soul."[63] Brother Ignatius Wiegers reported that Brother Paul was "readmitted into the community as a member," implying that he remained at Oshkosh.[64] He also quoted a letter from Brother Clement to Brother Stanislaus (the first rector in Oshkosh) in which the pater urged all the Brothers there "to be filled with enthusiasm by the vocation" in order to persevere through crises.[65] Concluded Brother Ignatius: "But, alas Brother Paul Pollig was not permeated with such a disposition. A half year after his readmission to the community, he left it a second time and then settled in Chicago as a secular nurse."[66]

Paul Pollig's postdismissal life appears enigmatic at best. He seems to have expressed deep loyalties to the Alexian way of life but interpreted it in his own terms, which were greatly affected by the American scene. Paul's efforts to found his own American Alexian house, which reached temporary success in Oshkosh, must have struck Pater Clement as proof of the dangerous temptations of the American scene and reinforced his determination that only by rigid enforcement of the Old World traditions and customs would Alexians be able to retain their vocations in the New World. Paul's apparently charming personality, which appears to have reached its most effective expression on the fund-raising trail, and his view of the future of the Alexians in America, ran contrary to a rigid interpretation of Old World customs and statutes.

With the crucial distinction that Brother Bonaventure persisted as an Alexian, Paul and the founder of the Alexian mission in America shared many characteristics. In contrast to the views of Clement and Leonard, Bonaventure and Paul responded to the challenge of the frontier by accommodating the Alexian traditions to what they perceived as the needs of the American scene; Clement and Leonard represented Alexian resistance to what they viewed as the pernicious trends of the New World. In each conflict the resistance position, supported by many German Catholics who vigorously worked to protect the souls of immigrants to the United States, prevailed. Within the extremely centralized authority structure there was little room for dissent.

In 1882, when Paul was "out in the world" and Brother Bonaventure was in England, the reformist trend in America continued. A small group of young Brothers in St. Louis, supported by the vicar-general of the archdiocese, Monsignor Muehlsiepen, advocated many constitutional changes of which the most significant was a proposal to allow the American Brothers to elect their superiors.[67] Pater Clement was so disturbed by such a display of dissent that he wrote Monsignor Muehlsiepen a lengthy letter in which he clearly enunciated the traditionally strict interpretation of the constitution. To quash dissent Pater Clement had ordered all Brothers in perpetual vows "to sign a document in which they pledged . . . never to criticize the holy rules, or they would be held in contempt."[68] Pater Clement implied that Muehlsiepen had encouraged the St. Louis reformers to oppose such a loyalty oath. His attack upon American individualism was followed by a bitter denunciation of those who advocated democratic reform. He rejected any constitutional adaptation "to accommodate to America."[69] Stressing the need for unity and order within an international religious congregation, Pater Clement stated that "the spirit of the Order may not and cannot be bound to the peculiarities of a country."[70] His notion of spirit was not what today's Alexian would identify as charism; it was, rather, the general attitude of dedication, respect, service, and loyalty to the congregation, which was grounded in the constitution. To violate six centuries of tradition in order to accommodate to a minority reform movement in America struck him as a sacrilege.[71]

The St. Louis reformers not only embodied American individualism and democracy but informality as well. They had registered a protest with their provincial, Brother Leonard, against his order requiring them to wear full clerical garb on public streets. They were supported by Muehlsiepen and Archbishop Kenrick. In his letter to Muehlsiepen, Pater Clement defended the provincial, reminded the vicar-general of how religious garb protects Brothers from "possible excesses" in the secular world, and urged him to admonish the dissenters and to direct them to a proper spirit of loyalty toward authority and love of their rules.[72]

It would be a mistake to project modern sensibilities upon the dissenters and view Pater Clement as a downright ogre. He had a very elevated notion of the Alexian calling to a life of sanctity, which he considered to be grounded in respect for authority and tradition. When he entered the order in the mid-nineteenth century the Aachen house had just experienced a revival of asceticism after decades of corruption. His authorship of the 1859 statutes, his leadership in expanding the Aachen community throughout the Rhineland and Westphalia and into the United States and England, and his successful efforts to restore the ancient papal congregation status for the Aachen Alexian Congregation were accomplishments which he saw undermined by American dissenters. Until Brothers Dominic Brock and Clement Wallrath arrived on the scene, the Aachen house was like any other Alexian house, directly under its archbishop. With Dominic's inspiration and Clement's direction, the Alexians gained international stature as modern nurses and ascetically charitable brothers. We must also recall that Clement's perspective of the religious life was affected by his experiences with the advance of secularism, particularly in the forms of the *Kulturkampf.* No doubt this battle of cultures was interpreted not merely in terms of a local church-state conflict but as illustrative of a culture crisis; the entire church was besieged by modern secularism and anticlericalism. In this light his notion of the traditional Alexian authority structure is very understandable; he viewed the Alexian survival in the antireligious modern world as intimately tied with obedience to Alexian transcultural principles of the religious life.

Brothers Bonaventure and Paul seem to have represented a very moderate accommodation to America, while the St. Louis dissenters were explicit in their introduction of American elective principles into the Alexian statutes. Pater Clement and his successors were able to maintain the centralized authority structures until the post-Vatican II period. Though the American Province was legally anchored to Aachen it gradually became Americanized socially: just as the third-generation German immigrant assimilated into the mainstream of American society, so the third-generation Alexian Brother became more American. Yet their German heritage continued to express itself in their drive to provide modern, efficient health care within a spirit of quiet inconspicuousness.

7

The Consolidation

of the American Province

I

The Old World-New World dialectic did not include conflicts over the quality of Alexian Brothers' health care for the American Province. Indeed, had Brothers Paul and Bonaventure been present at the Provincial or General chapters concerned with the codification of statutes for the American Province, they certainly would have agreed with those principles encouraging modern efficient hospitals. These statutes placed the corporate management of the province in the hands of the Directory, of which the provincial was president and his three consultors were vice president, secretary, and treasurer of each of the corporations. In those houses where the provincial did not reside, the rector was "acting" president accountable to the provincial.[1] Each hospital formed a corporation under the Directory and was obliged to meet in January of each year for the purpose of submitting all the books and accounts. All the institutions were to be renamed "Alexian Brothers' Hospital"; the Chicago institution had been the Immaculate Conception Hospital, while the one in St. Louis was St. Joseph's. Immaculate Conception became the name of the province, but in official correspondence it was referred to merely on a chronological basis as the Third Province.[2]

The statutes codified the proper procedures for running an

Alexian hospital, ranging from admissions to release. The Brothers admitted any male person "not incurably sick unless suffering with a contagious disease [regardless of] class, nationality, religion, race or color."[3] Only in exceptional situations would they accept the incurably sick, the crippled, or the aged.[4] Needy patients were cared for without charge, but those not in need were asked to pay weekly "in advance" a sum in accord with their treatment.[5] A written agreement was required of all those patients who wished to make the hospital their home for life, for which the amount of payment was arrived at by considering the circumstances of each case.[6] Since the Brothers did not care for the aged, these lifetime patients were mentally ill persons.

The rules regulating the patient's stay in the hospital were recorded in such detail that little was left in doubt. Upon receiving a patient the porter was required to ascertain the patient's financial circumstances and the nature of his illness, then report to the chief infirmian, who would decide which division was suitable for treating the illness. By a special order of Pater Clement (November 17, 1877), each American hospital was to include the following divisions: internal and external wards, eye and ear facilities, "nervous and brain diseases," and if necessary a division for "private sickness."[7] Each ward should have two doctors—an acting physician and his assistant—as well as a consulting physician "so that we have the necessary medical assistance at all times."[8]

The meal schedule of each hospital was regulated in detail. "The kitchen shall be furnished and conducted in the German style."[9] The hours of the meals and the types of food served at each were standard.[10] The rules were so all-embracing that they even stipulated the specific type of reading material in the recreation room. Regimentation and standardization were the pillars of efficient modern Alexian hospitals. However, these statutes should not be considered illustrative of German authoritarianism but of forming a practice for the young Brothers pursuing their hospital apprenticeship. Though the Brothers published annual public reports from the origin of each hospital, the earliest extant document is an 1886 report of the Chicago hospital. However, Ruth Meier's privately published history, *The Alexian Brothers in Oshkosh*, contains a copy of an 1881 report.[11]

The product of Brother Paul Pollig's efforts to establish a new Alexian institution, the Oshkosh hospital was placed under the direction of Brother Stanislaus. When the Brothers arrived some anti-Catholic sentiment had been expressed, but in general the booming lumber town was gratified finally to have its own general hospital.[12] Indeed, signs of public favor appeared very early; in October 1879, seven months before the formal opening of the hospital, the Brothers raised $1,085.10 at a fair.[13] Of the three United States Alexian hospitals, Oshkosh, because of its pioneering status, was the least modern, with space for only twenty-five patients. The founding Brothers (Stanislaus, Vincent, Hospitius, and Aloysius) were trained in modern facilities and gradually their Alexian expertise transformed the old mansion into a highly respected hospital. At the Open House celebration on May 9 (or 10), 1880, the Brothers hosted the public, and three days later they accepted their first patient, Henry Grim, a twenty-four-year-old clerk, who was suffering from a "brain fever."[14] The first report, dated January 6, 1881, indicated that during the first seven months (May to December) the Brothers cared for twenty-five patients (according to the standardized Alexian form listing the religion, occupation, marital status, and type of illness of each patient). The types of illness were either internal or external; there was no patient listed as mentally ill.

The following financial report illustrates their priorities in outflow: building maintenance, repairs, and payment of debts. Their income illustrates how much they depended upon fundraising activities and how little they depended on payments from patients. One should note that the Brothers took in boarders, perhaps handicapped priests, and that they did some nursing in homes, a customary Alexian service deriving from their fourteenth-century origins.

Collections [proceeds from begging]	$ 626.28
Nursing private patients and in the hospital	118.50
Vegetables sold	15.34
Presents to the Brothers	24.26
Board from different boarders	160.45
Money borrowed from Chicago	1,374.00
Strawberry festival	70.00
From the fair	1,085.10
TOTAL	$3,473.93

Expenses

Linen, etc.	$ 54.27
Groceries	202.38
Light and heat	31.34
Clothing material	15.58
Medicine and instruments	12.57
Tobacco and spirits	33.76
Building and repairs	1,649.97
Furniture and cleaning mat'ls.	67.18
Library and chapel	20.60
Traveling expenses and diverse	102.68
Presents and wages paid	113.24
Interest paid	457.25
Debts paid	500.00
TOTAL	$3,260.82

Cash on hand first day of January, 1881, $223.07.[15]

Despite the apparent success of the Alexians' first several months at Oshkosh, Brother Stanislaus wrote to Pater Clement seeking advice on the possible dissolution of the Oshkosh house. We have no evidence of the contents of Stanislaus's letter other than Pater Clement's reply, which merely provides information on the proper procedures for a petition for dissolution from the Provincial Council through the General Council to the Holy See. Were such a petition to materialize, Pater Clement doubted the Vatican's confirmation because the Holy See, in granting permission to establish the American Province, explicitly stated that permission was conditional upon the foundation of a third Alexian house as soon as possible. Pater Clement noted that he personally found it difficult to make such a decision.[16] In another letter Pater Clement urged Brother Stanislaus to persevere in the new foundation. Illustrative of Clement's stress upon the religious ideals he wrote:

> A splendid work of Mercy can be made of Oshkosh if only the right Religious, zealous for the honor of God and the Holy Church, are at hand. To be sure, sacrifices must be made by the Brothers; they must not have regard for their conveniences, but must be filled with enthusiasm by their vocation.[17]

Regardless of the causes of the disillusionment with the Oshkosh endeavor, the Brothers persevered. When Brother Stanislaus was appointed provincial on April 1, 1882, Brother Clemens

Marnach succeeded him as rector. Perhaps Stanislaus continued to harbor doubts regarding Oshkosh's viability since, according to a September 25, 1883, letter from an official of the Baltimore diocese, the provincial had requested permission of the archbishop to accept a piece of property with the intention of erecting an institution there.[18] Though the Brothers never followed through on this request, the fact remains that there was temporarily the intention to establish the Alexian presence in Baltimore, a plan which, because of the manpower situation (roughly fifty brothers at the time) would have necessitated the closing of Oshkosh. By 1884 it was evident that the Brothers' presence in Oshkosh was permanent. They purchased an additional six and a half acres at a cost of $3,000 which, according to a letter (November 1, 1884) from Pater Clement, was to be funded from the excess cash of the two other Alexian hospitals.[19] In that same year the Brothers expanded their hospital from twenty-five to forty beds. On January 4, 1885, Pater Clement wrote to Brother Stanislaus that he agreed with the provincial; the order should accept a piece of Oshkosh property donated by Bishop Krautbauer of Green Bay.[20] With additions to the hospital and grounds the Oshkosh institution altered its character from a general hospital to "the Alexian Brothers' Asylum for Insane, Idiotic and Nervous."

Without specific documentary evidence one may infer that the need for such an asylum, particularly for physically and mentally handicapped priests, seems to have been greater than the need for a general hospital. After 1891, when Sisters of the Sorrowful Mother established a general hospital in Oshkosh which accepted male and female patients but not the mentally ill, the Brothers' asylum assumed permanence.[21] However, the asylum was not exclusively for the mentally ill, nor limited to the clergy; the Brothers accepted retired men as pensioners and helpless aged men were cared for from the late nineteenth century until the dissolution of the asylum in 1965. By 1898 the hospital had been enlarged to accommodate sixty patients; in that year twenty-seven mentally ill and twenty-two physically ill were nursed by nine Brothers.[22]

The Oshkosh asylum was more in touch with the ancient Alexian tradition of care for the mentally ill than the other foundations in America. Though the St. Louis hospital developed a psychiatric division, it remained a general hospital. Oshkosh's asylum character gradually isolated the Brothers from the general public. Their patients had few visitors; the public's phobia of the mentally ill further contributed to isolation; the around-the-clock demands of their patients and the maintenance of the building required an extraordinary amount of work. In time, they cared for alcoholic priests and there grew a secretive tone to the atmosphere, as if the Brothers were protecting the public from scandalous clergy. By caring for the mentally ill and the alcoholic priest, the Oshkosh Brothers were adding to modern nursing techniques their traditional charism, that specialized ministry to the outsider.

II

In the 1885 edition of a multivolume *History of Chicago*, the author, Alfred T. Andreas, included a brief historical account of the Alexian presence in Chicago. He was grossly misinformed about the general history of the Brothers ("The order of Alexian Brothers was founded by Saint Alexius of Rome in honor of San Juan de Dios de Hispana . . . who lived in the 13th Century.")[23] but he seems to have had a good grasp of the story of the American Brothers. "The fraternity exact payment from those who are able to pay, but receive the poor gratis, making no distinction on account of religious belief, or irreligious unbelief, of a prospective patient."[24] Though he criticized the Brothers' tradition of excluding females from their hospital, a practice which he said, stemmed "from monastic dogmatism partaking of misogyny,"[25] he nevertheless concluded, "But to those who obtain access to their hospitals and asylums, the Alexian Brothers prove kind, gentle, scrupulously careful nurses, and many poor, afflicted men have reason to bless this benevolent and philanthropic organization."[26] No doubt some of his remarks had elicited criticism from Brothers and friends, for in his 1886 edition Andreas allowed Brother Provincial Stanislaus to write the account of the Alexians in Chicago, which included the following:

108

Year ending Dec. 31	1873	1874	1875	1876
Patients remaining	—	35	36	34
Patients admitted	338	384	462	513
Discharged cured	276	317	390	415
Discharged improved	—	—	46	52
Discharged unimproved	—	—	12	21
Died	27	31	50	59
Remaining	35	36	34	46
Single	—	—	—	—
Married	—	—	—	—
Widowers	—	—	—	—
Charity patients				
Pay patients (in full or part)	160	—	—	—

1877	1878	1879	1880	1881	1882	1883	1884	1885
46	42	50	62	71	71	81	80	83
462	479	762	829	936	975	1,055	1,133	—
356	402	285	274	632	649	730	787	—
85	47	252	274	166	153	188	188	—
33	24	42	43	52	66	43	35	—
34	48	71	74	86	97	105	120	—
42	50	62	71	71	81	80	83	—
—	273	459	571	656	726	781	793	—
—	190	202	232	245	252	290	326	—
—	58	51	88	106	68	65	94	—
—	307	409	556	599	623	719	780	—
—	214	403	335	408	423	417	433	—

The new hospital, constructed in 1873, contained "all the modern improvements" with room for over one hundred patients. The percentage of free patients ranged from 60 to 70 percent of the total admitted. Because the Brothers received no salary and did virtually all of the work—administration, fund raising, nursing, and maintenance—the low costs of running the hospital allowed them to carry so many charity patients. The average daily cost per patient in 1884 was fifty-eight cents. The medical staff included one consulting and two attending physicians, four surgeons, a pathologist, and a resident physician.

The outpatient dispensary, which provided treatment for men and women, was open two hours each day: "Poor patients, who come suitably recommended, get medical and surgical help free of charge."[28] Though the hospital was entirely private, the city police patrol wagons brought emergency patients to the hospital. In 1885 they transported 116 such patients to the Brothers.[29]

The annual public reports were models of accountability. Besides including those categories found in the Oshkosh report of 1880, the Chicago publication contained the diagnosis of every patient according to the general categories of Surgical and Medical Diseases. Under the latter come such local diseases as eight kinds of fevers, seven types of rheumatism, and nineteen other local diseases with numerous types in each, for example, twenty kinds of diseases of the nervous system and nine of the brain. The German influence was paramount throughout the report, but was most evidenced by the treatment of melancholia and alcoholism as a disease of the nervous system, and insanity as a brain disease.[30] The Brothers' open policy toward patients of all religious or nonreligious persuasions was quite apparent in the report for 1885 in which the religion of the patients was listed: 669 Catholics, 526 Protestants, and 26 Hebrews.[31] One newspaper reporter commented on the ecumenical character of the Brothers' Chicago hospital: "Any sick person who desires the solaces of his religion can send for any representative of his faith . . . whether they be a Protestant preacher or a Catholic priest, a Jewish rabbi or a deacon of the Mormon Church."[32] The patients in 1885 represented 146 different occupations, from actors to wagon builders.[33] According to an unidentified newspaper cutting (ca. 1890s):

> . . . one of the most eminent physicians on the North Side commented on the atmosphere of the Alexian Brothers Hospital: "It is above all the poor man's hospital. It is a place where the tramp and the homeless, the poor laborer and the artisan always find the door open. It is the most unalloyed charity of any hospital in the city. On the bitter cold nights of winter a small army of tramps is served with soup in the basement and provided with shelter if there is room. No one can realize what a simple and unaffected charity it is without seeing it. All are treated alike. A man is never sent to the poorhouse unless he is crowded out by one who needs his bed more

than he does. So far as kindness and regard for the comfort of each patient are concerned absolutely no distinction is made. Although by accident many men of means find their way to the rooms of the hospital they receive the same uniform, unaffected, simple, charitable treatment accorded the charity patients and no more."[34]

Another undated newspaper cutting (ca. 1880) verified the Chicago Alexians' response to the poor: "Healthy persons in pecuniary distress, who call at their hospital, are fed. Especially during times of business crisis this benevolence of the Brothers is greatly made use of by people of all classes."[35] The *Chicago Pilot* (ca. September 1879) also stressed the "unaffected" manner by which the Brothers served the poor: "They do their work in a quiet way and encompassed by humility, they serve God and His poor."[36] Their traditional charism of ministering to the outsider derived from their *pauperes Christi* origins and so permeated Alexian life that the Brothers strongly identified with the poor, thereby developing an "unaffected" posture toward all in need.

Another strong Alexian feature, which is characteristic of both traditional and modern Alexians, was their deep sense of dedicated hard work within a genuine spirit of social equality, as the eminent physician from the North Side stated.

Harmony always exists in the ranks of the brothers. A brother may be holding the highest position in the order this year and be in the kitchen next year. Each man is expected to keep to his place, do his work faithfully, and it comes to most who live long enough to occupy all positions. Nothing can exemplify the unobtrusive and modest quality of this charity better than to say that for years the brothers have taken charge of what are called patrol-wagon cases of the whole North Side as well as most of the Northwest section without ever asking what part of the appropriation the county devotes to the care of its poor unfortunates should come to them.[37]

The Alexian élan appears to have been so pervasive within their hospitals that the entire medical staff was touched by it.

Money can hardly buy luxuries within the hospital walls, because the word "luxury" is not in the brothers' vocabulary. The medical men who have devoted years of their lives to the service of this institution without pay and without even the eclat that comes of being connected with large hospitals (because the work is so unobtrusive that it attracts little attention) eventually become permeated with the spirit that prevails throughout the institution, and year after year this work becomes a work of love as well as a duty to humanity.[38]

Though the Chicago hospital was extremely cosmopolitan (twenty nationalites were represented among the patients in 1885), it bore heavily the German imprint.[39] The earlier-mentioned statutes regulating Alexian institutions were composed by Germans; the meals were prepared according to German culinary customs; the Brothers' official reports to Aachen as well as all corporation and house council minutes were written in German; German was the first language of most of the Brothers; the medical staff were mostly German or of German descent; as one newspaper reporter stated, "The whole institution wears the stamp of a decided German character."[40] The provincials, and the vast majority of their councilors, from 1869 to 1920, were Aachen-trained Brothers. Hence it was very natural for the American Province to maintain its German character and tie itself to the various German-American associations which, during the 1880–1910 period, were springing up throughout the German triangle—Cincinnati-Milwaukee-St. Louis. In the hospital field "German" was synonymous with the most progressive modern medical care. The German-American press, even one newspaper from as far west as San Francisco, sang the highest praises of the Alexianerbrüder.[41] Fund-raising events such as fairs and concerts with a German flavor were frequently featured in the German-American press.

The typical day of the Alexian Brother began at 4:30 A.M. with prayers and Mass. At 6:00 A.M. the day's work commenced. In 1888 there were fifteen Brothers who nursed and maintained the Chicago hospital with its 100-patient capacity. They served meals at 7:00 A.M., 11:00 A.M., and 6:00 P.M., made beds or bathed patients, accepted and dismissed patients, assisted doctors, managed labs and the pharmacy, and manned the dispensary as well as the laundry and boiler room. The *Tribune* reported (article undated): "The service of the Alexian Brothers is very severe and fatiguing. On an average day they are engaged in their calling during seventeen hours out of twenty-four, and an undisturbed night is unknown to the Alexian. No wonder, therefore, that very few reach their 40th year."[42]

With the Alexians' stringent style of life in mind, the *Catholic Record* placed the Alexian Brothers as the most ascetic religious order after the Trappists and the Franciscans.[43] Though their severe day was ingrained in the Brothers during their novitiate, because they were always either paying off old debts or assuming new ones for the continuous improvement of the institutions, hard work was an economic necessity particularly if patient costs were to be kept at a minimum and charity at a maximum. Despite the amount of charity cases they kept from the city hospital rolls, the city and county did not distribute funds to them.

The Chicago hospital consistently admitted more patients each year. In 1894 the Brothers cared for 1,814 persons, 344 of whom were emergency cases brought to the hospital by city police patrol wagons and ambulances. The original 1872 structure was enlarged, with a new wing in 1878 and an additional floor in 1880, another wing in 1888, and the grounds enlarged by the purchase of a tract of land in 1892. Though 1894 was an excellent year in terms of the numbers treated by the Brothers, they experienced a strong shock when, in the fall of '94, the Northwestern Elevated Railroad Company announced its intention to build a railway line right through the front yard of the hospital. On November 25 the General Council in Aachen instructed Brother Aloysius Schyns to establish a "Railway Committee" to negotiate with the company. If it failed to convince the company to alter its plans, then the committee was to negotiate the sale of the property at its full value plus the cost of relocation.[44] After almost a year of negotiation, which included threats of court action by the company, the Northwest Railway Co. bought the property for $200,000 in cash and allowed the hospital to remain in operation rent free until the completion of a new institution, which was two and a half years later.

Brother Aloysius, who had been in the United States Province since 1867, made a rather bold move when he purchased property far north of the city center, a 596-by-269-foot lot bounded by Belden Avenue and Huber Street and by Racine Avenue and Herndon Street. On October 4, 1896, a large procession began from the vicinity of the Redemptorist church, St. Michael's, and paraded to the building site where Archbishop Patrick A. Feehan, assisted by twenty-four priests, laid the cornerstone.[45] In the spring of 1898 the new hospital, which cost nearly $250,000, was ready for occupancy. Richard E. Schmidt, the architect, had visited hospitals throughout the country before making the final design. The result of his efforts was an exceptionally modern hospital with a capacity of over three hundred patients. Schmidt wrote an elaborate description of the hospital in which he stressed that the function of the building determined much of its form:

> The whole structure will consist of a group of five distinct but connected buildings, each for the use of a separate department; the front building for administration and private patients, the east for the large wards, the north is the "Brothers House," and the west which will not be built at present, is to be used for the care of patients afflicted with nervous troubles. In the center of all is the chapel. There are two wings, one for operating, the other to isolate certain patients.[46]

In 1961 Dr. Alexander Horowitz, who had interned at the Brothers' new hospital in 1901, recalled his experiences with the Alexians. His favorite was Brother Ambrose Nussbaum, a character of legendary proportions who kept the patients' record of payment. He noted that Brother Ambrose used a secret code for marking a charity patient to make sure that the patient received the same consideration as a paying patient.[47] Dr. Horowitz remembered one occasion in which he was called by Brother Ambrose to care for a tramp who had pneumonia. Realizing that the hospital was full, Brother Ambrose made room for the tramp by having a convalescent paying patient give up his bed.[48]

Dr. Horowitz was deeply impressed with the clinical knowledge of the Brothers, their personal concern for patients, and the general spirit of service that prevailed throughout their thoroughly modern hospital.[49] He recalled that after Brother Remigius Kochaneck (later provincial in England) had stayed with a critically ill patient for an entire week, the patient experienced a full recovery.[50] In contrast he also remembered an experience with a novice who, when confronted with a choice between answering a patient's or the chapel's bell, went into the chapel. Some years later Dr. Horowitz asked the Alexians' rector-general whether he had acted properly when he seriously reprimanded the young novice. The rector-general replied, "Doctor, our salvation lies first in taking good care of our patients and then in going to Chapel. Yes, you did exactly right."[51]

By the time of the Golden Jubilee Year of the Alexian presence in Chicago—1916—the Brothers could look back with pride upon their phenomenal impact upon the city. During those fifty years they nursed 101,663 patients, 35,082 of whom were full charity cases and 15,200 partial charity patients.[52] In 1916 there were approximately forty professed Brothers working at the hospital assisted by over twenty novices, many of whom attended the Alexian nursing school located on the grounds of the Belden Avenue hospital. During that period in which the Alexians' hospitals evolved from Brother Bonaventure's mission infirmary on Shiller Street to the ultra-modern hospital on Belden Avenue, the city of Chicago evolved from a frontier town into a modern metropolis. To the south the St. Louis Alexians developed their hospital along somewhat different lines.

III

Before the foundation at Oshkosh the American Province was concerned with the establishment of a third foundation in accord with the Vatican's specific directives. According to a contract dated April 17, 1872, the bishop of St. Joseph, Missouri, John J. Hogan, entered into an agreement with the Alexian Brothers of St. Louis in which the bishop granted nearly eleven acres to the Brothers for the "keep, ornament, and repair" of a Catholic cemetery.[53] Brother Paul Pollig, who was provincial at the time, signed the contract, but other than an old photo of the Brothers' St. Joseph house, all relevant documents have been lost. Apparently the Brothers remained there for only a year or so. Though their cemetery ministry was thriving in Aachen and became the original rationale for their first foundation in England, generally their hospital ministry was of much greater significance.

We know of another American venture (which never became a foundation) through a letter, dated November 16, 1874, from Pater Clement Wallrath to Brother Provincial Leonard Jansen in which the rector-general denied the provincial's request for permission to take over an orphanage at an unspecified location. Pater Clement interpreted the Alexian constitutions along strict-constructionist lines; if orphanage work was not cited as one of the prescribed works of the Alexians then it was forbidden to pursue such an endeavor unless the orphanage housed the mentally ill.[54]

The St. Louis Brothers were the first to restructure their general hospital to accommodate the mentally ill. Economic consideration blended with this traditional Alexian ministerial response to the mentally ill. Ever since the rectorship of Brother Peter Verheyen (1871–1874), the St. Louis hospital had accumulated a large debt. Because psychiatric patients were generally full-payment and long-range residents of the hospital, the new department promised to ease the burden of indebtedness. Like most cities of the day, St. Louis desperately needed mental-health-care facilities. The following account, published in 1878, illustrated this need:

> We speak of the insane as we speak of a class, the bond, the free, the high, the low, the rich, the poor. The imbeciles and cripples, and the poverty-stricken of every class, are brought to the city by one and two by the railroads [sic]. The traveling expenses are paid by the counties and municipalities to save the cost of their maintenance, by imposing on the great city as a charge. Hence, St. Louis receives, and is consequently credited with having, a heavy percentage of insane in proportion to its population.[55]

When the Provincial Council met in St. Louis on November 1, 1878, it decided that the Alexian hospital there would not be turned into a mental hospital.[56] However, a few months later (January 12, 1879) the St. Louis House Council resolved that the old hospital would indeed become a mental institution, which would provide additional income to decrease the corporation's indebtedness.[57] On January 21, 1879, the Provincial Council confirmed this decision, allocating $300 for the necessary building alterations.[58] It also decided to establish a mental institution in or near Chicago at a cost of $5,000 to $6,000.[59] The latter never materialized, but the St. Louis project did.

On March 10, 1879, the Provincial Council agreed that the St. Louis asylum would be guided by fifteen rules.[60] It decided to establish a separate administration accountable to the St. Louis rector.[61] All income generated by the asylum was to be used to decrease the debt of the St. Louis hospital. Though the cost of care was to be judged according to the needs of the patient, a minimum charge of $7 per quarter-year was placed on all ward patients and a $10 fee for all private-room patients.[62] However, if the ward patient did not demand much care or supervision or if he could contribute his work skills to the institution, then he could be charged less than $7.[63] All violent measures for patient control, such as locks and chains, handcuffs, and straitjackets, were strictly forbidden. If a patient suffered a "seizure" he was to be placed in a "security room" until the agitation subsided.[64] In short, the care for the mentally ill was to be according to a strict enforcement of those rules and principles for humane and charitable care stipulated in the Alexian constitutions which codified the Alexian concern for the mentally ill outsider.

An undated newspaper cutting reported that the new department of mental and nervous diseases was located in the old building of the hospital complex and was open for public inspection. "The neighborhood is healthy and no ponds are to be seen where malaria fills the atmosphere. The Brothers are experienced nurses and are eminently qualified to take charge of the insane."[65] Under the direction of Dr. Charles Hughes, the former superintendent of the "State Lunatic Asylum," and Dr. F. J. Lutz, the psychiatric department assumed a sort of autonomy, as it was called the Misericordia Hospital.[66] Another undated cutting, one from a German-American newspaper, contained an advertisement—"Misericordia INSANE ASYLUM unter Leitung der Alexianer Brüder, Jefferson Avenue and Osage Str. St. Louis, Mo."—under an impressive panoramic photograph of the hospital and grounds.[67] One reporter paid a glowing tribute to the heroism of the Brothers who cared for the insane:

> Not even relations wish to care for them once reason has left them—
> they manage to get them out of the house as soon as possible. . . .
> Yes, when their friends and relatives have forsaken them, they find
> in the good Brother a father and mother. This part of their vocation,
> in our judgment, requires a more heroic charity, and a much greater

sacrifice, because it is more contrary to human nature to wait on those who are bereft of their reason, than upon those who are corporally infirm. . . . The quietness and love with which the patients see themselves treated, have a gentle and beneficial influence upon them. The religious, who is bound by vow to overcome himself, must be able with meekness to render the most excitable service. He must patiently submit to abuse of all kinds, depending more upon his example than on his deeds; for the weak minded have a natural desire to be treated well.[68]

The traditional Alexian charism to the exiled was unaccustomed to such an exaggerated display of public appreciation. It is as if this reporter were deeply touched not only by the Alexian ministries but by the quiet mode of charity when he stated, "Who of us knew that they were engaged in all branches of human suffering and sorrow? The vocation of these Brothers is certainly a beautiful, a grand one, and a heroism is theirs that all must admire."[69]

Though the Misericordia Asylum title was dropped sometime in the early 1880s, the psychiatric department gradually became a very prominent sector of the hospital. As they gained a reputation for the care of alcoholics, many dioceses identified the Brothers as nurses for priests stricken with the disease. The St. Louis Archdiocese was particularly dependent upon the Alexians for this ministry, which was not widely available in the United States. Although it is impossible to say just exactly when this ministry to exiled priests began in St. Louis, readers of volume one will recall documents revealing that the Alexians of Cologne cared for "bad" priests in the eighteenth century, a ministry which, given the stigma of scandal, was in full accord with the Alexian charism to the outsider.[70] However, the care for the alcoholic had progressed parallel to the care for the insane. The trend in German psychiatric care, stressing all mental illness as brain disease, was clearly evident in the "application for admission into the Insane Department of the Alexian Brothers Hospital."[71] One such application was filled out on May 3, 1888, by a physician and friends and/or family of a patient suffering from chronic alcoholism. The man was a Protestant, a widower, forty-six years of age, and in answer to "pecuniary circumstances" the response was "none." Besides the normal questions concerning age, occupation, etc. there were seventeen questions related to the cause, symptomatic behavior, and prior treatment of the patient's condition. One question was particularly relevant to this man's condition: Is the patient intemperately addicted to the use of liquor, opium or tobacco, etc.?[72] There was no sign of moral disapprobation associated with alcoholism which, like many mental disorders, was considered to be a physiologically rooted disease.

The development of the psychiatric department gradually strengthened the financial condition of the hospital. When the Oshkosh Brothers needed money in 1880 the St. Louis Brothers contributed $1,000 which, according to Pater Clement's directive, was in excess of their financial needs. However, as one Brother's comments indicate, the hospital became a financial success only by the hard work of the Brothers.

> The order had not much money. Brothers purchased supplies for the hospital sometimes meal by meal, and sometimes the Brothers were not quite certain whether they themselves would eat. The patients, however, were not neglected. The Brothers did the laundry, taking care of this work in the wee hours of the morning so that it should not interfere with their regular duties in direct nursing of the sick. However, they were not discouraged; it appears that they really took pleasure in the hardships necessary to the success of their undertaking, and certain it is that their enthusiasm carried them over all the rough places so that they eventually could look upon a successfully launched hospital in St. Louis.[73]

Because of the many requests for admission of mental patients, on June 4, 1883, the Brothers decided to add another eighteen rooms at a total cost of $3,000.[74] Again, in December of 1884 they built a recreation room for the mentally ill, at a cost of $4,000.[75] The financial improvement and the increasing demand for admissions to both the asylum and the general hospital prompted the Brothers to plan an addition to their facilities on Carondelet (later South Broadway) on January 27, 1888.[76] The House Council sought permission from the Provincial Council for a new wing, which would be at least partially dedicated to asylum patients. On May 2, 1889, plans for the new eastern wing were approved and in October 1890 Father H. van der Sanden, chancellor of the archdiocese, presided at its solemn dedication.[77] Though the new wing, built at the cost of $5,000, was designed for medical and surgical patients, the additional space allowed the hospital to provide more beds for alcoholics and the mentally ill.

In 1892 the St. Louis Brothers cared for 1,600 patients, 837 of whom paid full rates, 364 part, and 399 were full charity patients.[78] It is not surprising that 806 patients were German immigrants; parts of South St. Louis are still predominantly German.[79]

The St. Louis House Council minutes from 1900 to 1914 abound with decisions to make capital improvements on the facilities, such as a new $40,000 boiler system, walls to enclose the gardens, and particularly acquisition of the latest X-ray, sterilization, and other med-tech equipment.[80] The St. Louis and Chicago Brothers obviously shared the same Alexian spirit, work ethic, and drive for modernization. However, the St. Louis house possessed its own character. Because psychiatric and alcoholic nursing played such a significant role, the St. Louis hospital had permanent patients who demanded special care and attention. Indeed many St. Louisians still mistakenly consider the Alexian Brothers' hospital as an asylum. Another feature of the St. Louis house was its free dispensary. Established shortly after the 1909 affiliation with St. Louis University's Medical School, the dispensary opened in October 1910.[81] The Brothers had purchased the home of John Padberg adjacent to their property and thoroughly renovated it to suit the needs of a clinic.[82] With the St. Louis population rapidly growing (1900 to 1910, from 575,328 to 687,025), many poor immigrants were in need of free health care: 1911–19,373 treatements; 1914–18,680 treatements to 2,844 persons; 1915–21,168 treatments to 3,438 persons.[83] Women and children were treated only at the clinic. Though the Chicago hospital also had a dispensary, the St. Louis free clinic appears to have been more active.

The Brothers' reputation for modernization, efficiency, and fine physician and nursing staffs ultimately led to an affiliation with St. Louis University's School of Medicine. John C. Burke, s. J., regent of the Medical School, initiated the cooperative venture, and on November 7, 1909, the House Council agreed to the affiliative scheme on an experimental basis.[84] Because the scheme was mutually beneficial—training for students and an enlarged staff for the institution—the affiliation became permanent the following year with the establishment of a joint council. Public accountability had been a persistent characteristic of the entire province from its origin. Annual reports were originally placed in the newspapers, but on January 17, 1887, the St. Louis Brothers decided to publish 1,000 copies of their '86 report at a cost of $35.[85] The free dispensary and the affiliation with St. Louis University strengthened the Alexian ties to the community. In 1918 they became charter members of both the archdiocesan Central Bureau of Catholic Charities and Kindred Activities and the Catholic Hospital Association of the United States and Canada.[86] Hence when the St. Louis hospital celebrated its Golden Jubilee in 1919 the Brothers could recall with pride those pioneering days when Brothers Paul Pollig and Alexius Bernhart moved into the Simons Mansion, $23,000 in debt and begging from door to door. The twenty-five Brothers who celebrated the Golden Jubilee had no doubt heard many tales of those frontier days, but it must have been difficult for them to appreciate fully that pioneer life while they were nursing the physically and mentally ill in one of St. Louis's most modern hospitals.

IV

Until 1892 the American Province was limited to the midwest: Oshkosh, Chicago, and St. Louis. With the rise in vocations and the stable financial condition, the American provincial, Brother Ignatius Mickenberg, sought to fulfill a long-cherished hope of establishing an Alexian house along the eastern seaboard, preferably near the New York harbor, convenient for the Brothers' transatlantic journeys. Through the efforts of Brother Joseph Marx, who was on a fund-raising tour in the east in 1891, the Alexians interested Bishop W. Michael Wiggers, ordinary of the Newark diocese, in a project for a new hospital. After preliminary negotiations in the spring of 1892, Bishop Wiggers became so committed to the project that he offered the Brothers a valuable piece of land in Elizabeth, New Jersey. Armed with the General Council's permission to accept the offer, the provincial and his two consultors traveled to Elizabeth to inspect the property. On July 16, 1892, after notifying the rector-general of their favorable impression, they received a cable from Aachen: "ACCEPT."[87] Bishop Wiggers, whose parents were from Westphalia, may have heard of the Alexian work in Germany. His concern for the sick, which may have originated with his own bouts with sickness as a youth, was a strong drive in promoting this pastoral dimension of his diocese. On October 3, 1892, Brothers Constantine Schaider, Joseph Marx, and Aloysius Schyns moved into a small frame house on East Jersey Street and they awaited the groundbreaking of their new hospital. Elizabeth was a small city (population 40,000 to 50,000) located about eight miles from Newark and thirteen miles from New York City. The Catholic population was divided into five parishes; the Brothers provided the city with its first Catholic hospital.[88]

On June 11, 1893, Bishop Wiggers laid the cornerstone for the new hospital. Brother Aloysius Schyns, who had supervised the building of the new wing in St. Louis and later the new Chicago hospital, worked with the architect. Brother Constantine, an expert carpenter, helped with some of the construction and built the three altars for the chapel. Brother Joseph was the chief fund raiser, and succeeded in collecting many donations including all the necessary devotional and liturgical furnishings for the chapel. The financial report of January 31, 1894, listed the expenditure of $46,847.02 for the new hospital, which was paid from a total loan of $51,300.[89] Other loans were required, and at the end of 1894 the total indebtedness reached $109,415.04.[90] On June 6, 1894, the Elizabeth Alexians admitted their first patient, John Holland, who "suffered from a nervous condition."[91] With a bed capacity of around forty patients, the new hospital housed a total of one hundred patients during its first six months.[92] Of that figure seventy-two were full charity cases.[93] Before moving into the hospital the Brothers nursed patients in their home on Jersey Street. With only one other hospital in the city, Elizabeth General, and given Elizabeth's large Catholic immigrant population, the Alexian hospital flourished. In 1895 the Brothers cared for 354 patients, 233 of whom were nonpaying patients;[94] in 1896 of 453 patients 339 were charity cases.[95] As early as 1895 both Union County and the city of Elizabeth subsidized the hospital according to the number of charity patients treated by the Brothers. In 1895 this amounted to $1,000 and $925.06 from county and city, respectively.[96] Since the combined subsidies came to nearly 20 percent of the income of the hospital, they provided strong support.

Annual reports for the first decade indicate that the hospital was operating at nearly 100 percent capacity. To meet the increasing demand for beds the Brothers, under the direction of Brother Cajetan Theisen, added a new wing in 1906–1907 at a cost of $35,000.[97] With the additional space the annual number of patients treated rose from an average of 525 to well over 1,000. In 1907, 1,101 men were admitted, 203 of whom were full-paying patients; of a total income of $37,588.92 for 1907, patients' charges amounted to $10,714.15.[98] The total indebtedness from the Brothers' two major building projects was nearly $17,000 in 1907.[99] A major expense for that year illustrates the Brothers' concern with maintaining a modern health facility; they paid $2,112.21 for furnishing a new operating room and for a new X-ray machine.[100] The Elizabeth *Evening Times* reported before the 1906 addition and improvements were made: "When the additions are made to the hospital in the line of the new operating room, it will be one of the finest equipped hospitals of its kind in the State and, in fact the entire country."[101]

Brother Cajetan Theisen, who presided as rector for six (nonconsecutive) terms during the period 1901–1931, left a strong imprint upon the character of the house. During this time the people of Elizabeth became so familiar with the hospital that they referred to it not by its formal name, Alexian Brothers' Hospital, but rather the Brothers' Hospital. Indeed today one may still hear of a patient staying with the Brothers. Of the four hospitals in the Province, the Elizabeth foundation has been recognized by the Brothers as the one most rooted in the community.

The town's loyalty expressed itself in strong financial support of the hospital. In 1916 voluntary donations totaled $2,529.12, while the Ladies Auxiliary raised $1,710.[102] That same year the city granted $4,000 and the county $9,000 which, when combined with all other fund-raising activities, came to nearly half of the Brothers' yearly income.[103] In the late 1890s the Brothers cared for roughly 500 patients a year; in 1916 that figure climbed to 1,480, only 268 of whom were full-paying patients.[104] The average daily fee per person in 1916 was $1.18, while the average daily cost of maintenance was $1.98 per person. The heavy patient load made the year "a very strenuous one, [as] . . . many patients had to be refused admission. . . . Taken all in all the Hospital was taxed to its utmost capacity . . . but has met the congestion with much skill and when patients had to be refused admission it was for only one or two days."[105]

There were seventeen Brothers employed in the Hospital assisted by twenty-nine orderlies and other workers. The Elizabeth Dispensary "for the poor" treated 4,157 persons. According to Brother Alban Bauer's report, the Brothers fed only 523 unemployed laborers in 1916 as compared to 1,241 the previous year.[106] Though unemployment fell off considerably, prices rose to the point where food and general provisions were $9,000 above the 1915 figure. "The Hospital did not increase its prices to the public, and hopes it won't have to resort to this either, expecting that the time will soon come, when prices on foodstuff and material . . . are on the decline again."[107]

The X-ray department was particularly busy during 1916, processing 2,157 X-rays of which 1,029 were dental. "The method of examining teeth with the aid of the x-ray, was only recently established in the Hospital, but how readily the dentists of Elizabeth and neighboring towns and cities appreciated the fact of its establishment here, and the value they received the report shows, in the number of patients sent to the Brothers for this kind of work."[108]

The Brothers' ambulance service was in the hands of Brother Prosper Ridel. He lived for over fifty years at the Elizabeth house and became a legendary figure in his own lifetime. A native of New York City, Brother Prosper entered the order in 1895 and within a few years was recognized as an extremely gregarious person. The Brothers still did some home nursing then and because of his pleasing personality Brother Prosper became a popular nurse throughout the city. In 1916 he was

"Solicitor of Contributions" besides being the head ambulance driver well known for his emergency work in the city. He broke in fourteen teams of horses and when the auto was introduced, he drove it until the early 1940s.[109] Indeed, his ambulance was one of the first to reach the site of the Hindenburg dirigible disaster at Lakehurst, New Jersey, in 1937.

Though each of the Brothers' communities developed distinctive characteristics, they all shared the Alexian drive to develop a blend of personal and modern health-care institutions. Their personalistic spirit was expressed not only in the bedside manner so highly priased by Dr. Horowitz but in the many ways in which the Brothers' attitude permeated the entire hospital. The Brothers nursed, fed, and bathed the patients as well as attending to every aspect of the hospital's physical plant. Each hospital possessed in varying degrees a mini-farm adjacent to the institution. Because the Brothers represented so many trades and because the Alexians strove for full self-sufficiency, their institutions were analogous to a medieval manor in which the Brothers were servants to the lords, the patients.

8

From Aachen to Manchester

Like so many major developments in Alexian history, the expansion into England originated not by design but by accident—or Providence in the guise of coincidence. The English Catholic Church, officially reconstituted within diocesan structures in 1850, experienced rapid growth from the flow of Irish immigrants to cities such as Liverpool and Manchester as well as from an impressive number of conversions. Without a large native clergy, the new dioceses recruited priests from the Continent and during the *Kulturkampf* eagerly welcomed Germany's exiled clergy. A Father Saffenrueter, pastor of St. James Church in the Pendleton area of Manchester, was a native of Aachen who introduced the Alexian Brothers to his bishop, Herbert Vaughan.[1] Appointed to the bishopric of Salford (actually Manchester, but the diocese was entitled Salford in deference to the Anglican dioceses of Manchester), Bishop Vaughan was just forty years old when he was installed as ordinary of a diocese teeming with Irish Catholics who had gravitated to the bustling industrial city. The young bishop, who was born into an old Catholic Gloucestershire family, presided with what appeared to be aristocratic aloofness. "Slim of figure, his fearless blue eyes, aquiline nose, and firm set mouth, made him in appearance an ideal Sir Galahad, setting forth in quest of the Holy Grail."[2] Prior to becoming bishop he had founded the Mill Hill Fathers and had bought *The Tablet*, a Catholic journal that he edited.

Shortly after his installation as ordinary of Salford, Bishop Vaughan laid plans for the development of the diocese's first Catholic cemetery. Having had prior experiences with the Alexian cemetery ministry in Aachen, Father Saffenrueter urged his bishop to consider the Aachen Brothers for the tasks of managing and caring for the cemetery.[3] To provide the diocese with clergy and religious, Bishop Vaughan was very dependent upon his recruitment efforts on the Continent. As his biographer remarks, "The breaking out of the *Kulturkampf* in Germany enabled him to obtain the services of a little band of zealous helpers from the country, who for some years did work in the diocese of Salford which is still greatly remembered."[4] After visiting the Brothers' cemetery in Aachen, Bishop Vaughan met with Pater Clement and urged him to establish an Alexian house in Manchester. With the *Kulturkampf* uppermost in his mind, Pater Clement was favorably disposed.

Notifying the bishop of his positive interest in the project, Pater Clement asked him to place the proposal in writing for the General Council's consideration.[5] When Bishop Vaughan wrote to the rector-general in April 1875, the proposal had expanded to include a request for both cemetery and nursing Brothers.

> We have two needs. The greater and more urgent need would be the establishment of an asylum for the mentally ill, especially for the middle and lower classes. We have none of this type in the whole of England. Every effort that experienced Brothers would make to supply this lack, would certainly receive the approval of the Bishops of England. . . . The other need is one of Religious, who by their presence, their Rule, their accomplishments and piety would further devotion for the dead and would arouse respect for the memory of the deceased . . . [as] Protestantism thwarts these ideas. It means much to me to have the assistance of a Brotherhood to care properly for the services in the first Catholic cemetery in the large city of Manchester.[6]

Bishop Vaughan's anti-Protestant remark may be explained by the common theological notion among Protestants that denied purgatory and the efficacy of prayers for the dead.

In June 1875 when Brothers Peter Verheyen, Cyril Kranepohl, and Gerard Teubensel arrived in Manchester, they were led to a large fourteen-acre plot of ground on Moston Hill over-looking the smoke-choked industrial city. Bishop Vaughan's decision to seek high ground for the cemetery was prompted by a disastrous flood in 1872, which so inundated the area near the municipal cemetery that "the dead were uprooted . . . [and coffins] were carried down the stream and dashed to pieces against embankments, embrasures and bridges."[7] With these horrors in mind Bishop Vaughan appointed a Cemetery Board which held its first meeting on July 23, 1873. The establishment of a diocesan cemetery was extremely significant to the thousands of Manchester Catholics. In the 1840s they were dependent upon the good grace of Protestant clergymen for permission to bury their dead in their churchyards. Thomas Curley writes: "Many curious customs arose in consequence. It was usual to take some small quantity of the soil or grave from the precincts of the [Catholic] church and throw it on the coffin, as it was being lowered in the grave, our Catholic people thereby consoling themselves that their dear departed ones had some holy ground in their Protestant graves."[8]

On August 1, 1875, between the time that the Alexians had made their first preparatory visit and their assumption of a permanent residence, Bishop Vaughan solemnly consecrated St. Joseph's Catholic Cemetery in Moston Lane, Manchester. In his pastoral letter commemorating the consecration Bishop Vaughan elaborated on the canonical basis of the cemetery:

> A cemetery, like a Church, in order to be solemnly consecrated to God must be the absolute freehold of the Church. Otherwise, it may be blessed as a place of internment, but cannot be consecrated. The Catholics of Manchester and Salford now possess a Cemetery of their own, in which their mortal remains may rest after death in ground solemnly consecrated to Almighty God. It is appropriately dedicated to the great patriarch, St. Joseph, under his title of "Patron of a Happy Death."[9]

In accord with the language and sentiment of the Catholic-Romantic ethos, Bishop Vaughan admonished all to give "Love and Succour For the Dead." With the rhetoric of deep compassion he wrote:

> Alas, alas, O shame! The Dead remember the living but the living forget the Dead. Thoughtlessly and heartlessly they leave those

whom they loved in life without help after death, they leave them for years and generations to pay in their own person the last farthing of awful retribution in that dread, patient, silent, suffering realm of the Divine Justice.[10]

After setting forth the traditional Catholic theology of death, he introduced the work of the Alexian Brothers, who for over five hundred years had been religious participants in the taming of death.

> For the benefit, therefore, of the dying and of the deceased, and to stir up the faith and the charity of the living towards the departed, an Order or Religious Congregation of Brothers has been founded in the Church, whose duty it is to nurse the sick, to lay out the dead, to bury them, and to pray for them.
> A branch of this order has been established at St. Joseph's Cemetery. The Brothers will cheerfully perform these religious [acts] of charity, as far as they may be able, for the Catholics who call for their services, they will take charge of the cemetery, and above all will daily offer up public prayers in the chapel, especially for those who sleep within the precincts of S. Joseph's Cemetery. A Chaplain has also been appointed, and the adorable sacrifice of the Mass will be offered during the week at the Privileged Altar in the Cemetery Chapel over the remains of the holy Martyrs.[11]

It was only in a footnote that Bishop Vaughan named this congregation of Brothers. Instead of calling them the Alexian Brothers or Cellites, he gave them what he may have considered a more dignified title, "The Brothers of St. Alexius," one which they wore for decades. Also included in the footnote of his pastoral letter was a reference to the Brothers' ministries; they "nurse the sick, and lay out, and bury the dead." Bishop Vaughan pointed out that though the Brothers nursed the sick "without charge . . . it is customary that those who can afford it should give them an alms according to their means."[12]

The three Brothers were provided with a house on the cemetery grounds, and were responsible for the maintenance of the grounds and attendance at the funeral and burial services held in the cemetery chapel built the year after they arrived. Responsible to the Cemetery Board, the Alexian community was paid one pound sterling per week as well as any profits derived from the decoration of the graves.[13]

Though the cemetery was a large portion of the social fabric of Catholic Manchester and though the Brothers were generally well respected by the clergy and laity of the diocese, the three Alexians at St. Joseph's were certainly on the fringes of the secular and religious life of Manchester. Of the three Brothers, only Brother Peter Verheyen had experience outside Germany. He was rector of the St. Louis house from 1871 to 1874.[14] Whereas the American houses were strongly sustained by the German-American neighborhoods of Chicago and St. Louis, the Manchester Brothers living on the edge of a graveyard were compelled to lead a relatively insular life. They had been trained to view the modern world as a threat to their vocations but they had also been led to believe that they would dwell in a large community attached to an institution. Perhaps individually the Brothers of St. Joseph's were grateful for the challenges of such a mission, but the Alexian witness in Manchester in comparison to the frontier hospitals in America was remote from the life of the city.

Brother Rector Peter Verheyen was unable or unwilling to cope with the mission situation. Sometime between his arrival in Manchester in the summer of 1875 and September 7, 1877, Brother Peter grossly violated the statutes, for on that latter date he was dismissed from the congregation.

On October 7 Brother Leonard Jansen wrote to Pater Clement the sad news of Peter's death.[15] According to the letter Brother Leonard was informed that Peter had been drinking heavily and committed suicide while on board a ship destined for the United States.[16] With only the dismissal notice and this letter as documentary evidence, the one certain conclusion is that Peter did not long survive the conditions in Manchester.

From the outset the Alexians had viewed their cemetery mission as one aspect of their general ministry in England. They and Bishop Vaughan had projected the establishment of a private asylum for middle- and lower-class mental patients. Three years after they arrived in Manchester the Alexians found a suitable location for such an asylum. In late 1878 Brother Celestine Mohnen, Brother Pater's replacement, wrote to Brother Pius Welter, provincial of the first province, seeking his aid to "induce the Pater" to purchase a large house with substantial land just ten minutes from the Moston Cemetery. "It is situated on an elevation, looks like a castle, surrounded by grounds and a vegetable garden. Moreover a fish pond and hot house are on the grounds. . . . The House has twenty rooms and there is another house to the side of it which could serve for the isolation of the very sick. I venture to say dear Brother Provincial that if our Pater were here and saw this house, he would buy it at once."[17] Brother Celestine's enthusiasm had a positive effect upon the General Council, as on February 6, 1879, the latter agreed to purchase the property and authorized Pater Clement to negotiate a suitable price. Because both the pater and the Manchester Brothers were unfamiliar with the legal entanglements in real estate they relied upon Father Saffenrueter to be their agent. He encountered several problems involving the various mortgages on the property and the legality of a religious community as a property owner. The final purchase contract called for five Alexian Brothers under their Christian (vis-à-vis their religious) names to pay £1,630 for the house and property; £180 was paid on the closure of the contract (April 10, 1879) and the balance, £850, was paid the following year. Because a foreign religious order could not own property in England, the ownership was in the name of the five Brothers, two of whom had recently arrived from Aachen.[18]

With only five Brothers, divided between the cemetery and the new house, the Alexians welcomed additional support from America. On March 28, 1879, before the final contract was signed, Pater Clement wrote to Brother Leonard Jansen notifying him of the new house in Manchester. Because the five Brothers "need to beg" as well as do all the work in the two foundations the pater asked the American provincial to send two English-speaking Brothers, of his own choosing, to the Manchester house, Mariaheim, i.e., Mary's House.[19]

The plans to establish an asylum were frustrated by the state's moratorium on licensing private asylums. In the early nineteenth century social conditions resulting from industrialization had effected a rise in the incidence of mentally ill in the workhouses and houses of correction. This situation encouraged the pattern of placing these mentally ill in private "madhouses." Gradually, enlightened opinion effected a series of laws regulating the licensing of private madhouses and ultimately the establishment of county asylums.[20] The Lunatics Act of 1845 established a Board of Commissioners on Lunacy, which was decidedly in favor of county vis-à-vis private madhouses that putatively trafficked in lunacy for a profit. Lord Ashley, a leading spokesman for the reformers, stated in 1859, "I feel strongly that the whole system of private asylums is utterly abominable and indefensible."[21] Yet public asylums could not be built rapidly enough to keep pace with the rising demand, so private asylums continued as a social necessity. Bishop Vaughan's remarks on the need for the middle and working classes were certainly accurate. The public asylum housed paupers but there was a strong need for institutions to house the mentally ill among the educated classes, some of whom chose to reside in private asylums on the Continent in order to escape the local inspectors of the private asylums, who were likely to spread the "scandal" of the local notables' lunacy.[22] The high cost of asylum care, the result of the progress in humane treatment in private institutions without subsidy, as well as the licensing problem, made it virtually impossible for a group like the Alexian Brothers to operate a private asylum.[23] Refused a license for the care of the mentally ill and, as German male nurses, unqualified to establish a general hospital, the Brothers at St. Mary's Home attended to the needs of elderly men, particularly the senile. With a cemetery and a twenty-bed hospice the Brothers in Britain departed from the late nineteenth-century trend toward large Alexian institutions. Though they may have been self-conscious of their meager beginnings, the Manchester Brothers were actually pursuing a ministerial life more in accord with the earliest Cellite traditions than their modern confrères in Germany and America.

In May 1882 Brother Bonaventure Thelen arrived in Manchester. He was placed as rector of St. Mary's Home and novice master. Founder of the American Province, a controversial visitator there during the first phase of the Paul crisis, Brother Bonaventure had held posts on the General Council and had been rector in Krefeld before his assignment to England. His first novice, an Irishman, Michael McGill, assumed the religious name Brother Camillus, and like his novice master was destined to play a variety of leadership roles within the congregation.

The earliest extant House Council minutes, those for September 28, 1882, note that the original plan to found and manage a hospital had been frustrated but that it still should be kept in mind for the future. The councillors discussed the need to hire a solicitor who could instruct them in British law and, in exceptional circumstances, speak for the community.[24] They also discussed the need to incorporate themselves, a legal issue that ultimately reached fruition in the foundation of the Manchester Joint-Share Company. News of the Brothers' cemetery ministry circulated among the hierarchy of England. On April 3 Bishop Richard Lacy of the Middlesbrough diocese wrote to the rector of St. Mary's Home requesting him to establish an Alexian house on the grounds of that diocese's new cemetery. Pater Clement recalled the situation: "The conditions were so favorable, the Bishop pleaded so urgently . . . and was so hopeful, that we could but not consider the offer more closely."[25] After Brothers Cyril Kranepohl and Leonard Jansen had explored the Middlesbrough situation and negotiated with the bishop, the Alexians decided to assume the care of the new cemetery located in Yorkshire far north of the Manchester houses. St. Mary's Council minutes for February 15, 1884, recorded the foundation of the third English house at Middlesbrough: "three Brothers are working there as of this date."[26] Besides caring for the cemetery the Brothers also did home nursing, a ministry which eventually led them to seek a site where they could develop a hospice comparable to St. Mary's Home.

German Brothers engaged in cemetery and nursing ministries did not elicit many vocations. Pater Clement was compelled, therefore, to staff the three houses with Brothers from the American and German provinces. In late 1884 one Brother from America, Brother Andreas, had apparently refused to be transferred to Manchester, invoking the principle of conscience, i.e., England endangered his soul. On January 15, 1885, Pater Clement wrote a long letter to Brother Andreas which not only illustrates the rector-general's attitudes toward the recalcitrant Brother but also those toward the ideal Alexian spirit.[27] Opening his letter with an essay on the vow of obedience. Pater Clement accused Brother Andreas of being infected with the secular spirit of individualism. The transfer to England "will not harm your soul but strengthen it through obedience."[28] As an indictment of the American character of lawlessness, Pater Clement observed, "Here in Germany obedience is held in higher esteem than what I experience with you. I have never encountered such twaddle as goes on there [U.S.A.]."[29] He illustrated the German sense of obedience by informing Brother Andreas that three German Brothers were notified of their transfer to England on January 6 and departed two days later without question. "That's what I call obedience."[30] One of these Brothers was the pater's nephew, Brother Albert Wallrath. "If I send my own nephew there it couldn't be all that bad."[31] The pater considered England a far better place than America, as it was a "highly civilized land where the people have long obeyed the law."[32] He portrayed the Alexian houses in rather idyllic terms: "three well disciplined monasteries, two quiet cemeteries and a hospital [sic] with beautiful buildings and gardens"[33] which accomodate sixty to seventy patients. He extolled the virtues of Brother Bonaventure, "who also knows America very well," as well as the other "pious obedient Brothers who will provide you with a good example."[34] Brother Andreas must have projected begging as his primary responsibility in Manchester, a notion which the pater said was "idle prattle."[35] Pater Clement was so confident of the wisdom in transferring Brother Andreas that he said, "If you are sick you will be healed and if you are distressed you will be undistressed."[36] He closed the letter with a warning that if Brother Andreas did not leave for England within eight days then the full force of the statutes would be applied, i.e., he would not be recognized as a Brother, he could not vote, eat at table, or receive the sacraments. "Unconditional obedience is required of all Brothers; an order without obedience is a body without a head, in other words a caricature."[37] Brother Andreas did obey, for some time later the St. Mary's House Council minutes revealed his presence in Middlesbrough.

The establishment of a third house prompted Pater Clement to consolidate the communities into a province. Though this did not officially occur until 1884, Brother Leonard Jansen signed the House Council minutes of March 1884 as provincial rector.[38] He had been provincial in America (1874–1881) and had been stationed at the Motherhouse since 1881. During the two previous years he had been visitator there. Brother Leonard established his provincialate at St. Mary's Home. Brother Bonaventure was one of his councillors and remained as novice master. Perhaps their intense rivalry during 1876–1877 when Bonaventure was visitator and Leonard was the American provincial haunted their relationship during their years together in England. However, it was Brother Cyrillus Kranepohl, appointed provincial in December 1885, who experienced a deep conflict with Brother Bonaventure. From his remarks it seems that Brother Bonaventure remained rector of St. Mary's during Brother Leonard's tenure as provincial. On December 2, 1885, Brother Cyrillus noted in the Minute Book that he and Brother Bonaventure had "many stormy meetings" during which the latter apparently challenged the judgment of the provincial.[39] Brother Cyrillus did not specify the contents of these conflicts but, rather, stated that "in charity best to forget this";[40] one may infer that the tensions were derived from their conflicting views on fiscal priorities. From Brother Cyrillus's comments on the debt-ridden character of the St. Mary's Home when he took office, it appears that he considered Brother Bonaventure either a spendthrift or a careless manager; "when I arrived I found £50 in the treasury and unpaid bills totaling about £100. There was a £360 building debt; St. Mary's Home was only partially furnished; the greenhouse had collapsed; £50 was needed to repair the heater and bandages, beds and furniture were in short supply."[41] What a dismal picture in contrast to the one Pater Clement projected for Brother Andreas some eleven months earlier! The day after Brother Cyrillus noted these dismal conditions, Brother Bonaventure was transferred to Middlesbrough.[42] In 1886 he was transferred to Germany where he was made the first rector of Mariaberg, a position he held until 1889 when he became provincial of the Second German Province.

The Alexians' first decade in England was a profound test of the Brothers' endurance of mission life. In contrast to their large German and American institutions the houses in England were attached to two cemeteries and a small home for elderly men. Like the medieval Cellites the Alexians in England were on the fringe of ecclesiastical and secular society. With only a handful of German Brothers attending graves and caring for men within the tombstone shadows the Brothers formed a tiny enclave within the English Catholic Church. Though they begged door to door and nursed in the homes of clergymen and laymen their institutional impact upon the social landscape was barely visible.

9

Expansion and Conflict

in England

The development of the English Province, hampered by legal, economic, ethnic, and religious obstacles, was very gradual. Brother Cyrillus, one of the founding Brothers at Moston Cemetery, inherited the chronic economic and manpower problems so endemic to the early history of the province. Though Brothers Leonard and Bonaventure were no longer on the scene, personality conflicts continued to disturb Brother Cyrillus. Middlesbrough became a constant source of distressing tension. Though documentary evidence is sketchy the Middlesbrough incidents apparently originated with Pater Quirinus's appointment of his predecessor's nephew, Brother Albert Wallrath, as rector of the Middlesbrough house. In May 1888 Provincial Rector Cyrillus noted in the Minute Book that Brother Albert was making difficulties for his pater and his provincial because "he simply wants everything to go his way" and that he "grumbled" at the rules.[1] In early 1889 Brother Cyrillus recorded a series of incidents that ultimately led to the establishment of a new Alexian hospice in Middlesbrough. Brother Albert's behavior elicited an extraordinary visitation by Assistant Rector General Brother Leonard Jansen "to quiet things down."[2] The Albert issue had apparently polarized the community to the point where Brother Leonard assumed the office of rector. At this point the foundation of the hospice became an issue. Brother Cyrillus responded to Brother Leonard's request for money to be placed in purchase of property for the new hospice by stating that the province's cash was entirely tied up in St. Mary's Home.[3] He went on to say that Brothers Albert and Stanislaus surreptitiously intercepted Brother Cyrillus's letter and made the contents public, "causing great consternation."[4] Evidently the Albert-Cyrillus conflict was based on the new house issue with Brother Albert the expansionist and Brother Cyrillus the fiscally conservative opponent armed with provincial authority. Hence perhaps it was Brother Albert who alerted Aachen to the situation and, upon the arrival of Brother Leonard, was successful in achieving the pater's support for the project. To the consternation of Brother Cyrillus and without his consultation, the Alexians purchased a stately mansion in a spacious suburb of Middlesbrough for £2,000, a sum which Brother Cyrillus noted "had to be paid for . . . ourselves."[5] Named Sacred Heart Home, the new house continued to be a source of irritation for Provincial Brother Cyrillus. Pater Quirinus appointed Brother Amadeus Harderer, the once reluctant Brother whose "disobedience" had elicited the ire of Pater Clement, as the first rector of Sacred Heart Home. According to the embittered provincial, Brother Amadeus was of the same independent stripe as Brother Albert.[6] In Brother Cyrillus's notes Brother Amadeus was appointed rector not by the Provincial Council but by the pater, a process which led Brother Amadeus to consider himself accountable directly to Aachen rather than to the English provincialate.[7] Brother Cyrillus was more than miffed by Amadeus's independent ways; his notes reveal him as a very isolated provincial. The Middlesbrough crisis was resolved toward the end of 1889 when Brother Amadeus was replaced by Brother Gerard Teubensel.

In December 1888, prior to the surfacing of the Middlesbrough crisis, the Provincial Council decided, probably at the request of Provincial Brother Cyrillus, to appoint the latter as rector of St. Joseph's Cemetery and Brother Eusebius Klütermann as rector of St. Mary's Home.[8] Brother Albert Wallrath was also removed from Sacred Heart Home. Thus, by the end of 1889 the personalities involved in the controversial foundation of the new Middlesbrough house were no longer situated there. In 1890 Brother Bonaventure returned to Manchester as Pater Quirinus's official visitator to the province. Though his report is not extant, there is a curious notation written along the side of the page where Brother Cyrillus had noted "the many stormy sessions" between himself and Bonaventure: "In March 1890 when Brother Bonaventure visited England he asked to be pardoned at which time I asked him to pardon me."[9] Reconciled with Brother Bonaventure and located at the Moston Cemetery, Brother Cyrillus seems to have delegated much of the responsibility to Brother Eusebius, who was primarily concerned with the development of St. Mary's Home, the most problematic Alexian institution in England.

The financial situation at St. Mary's Home had become acute by February 1889.[10] The House Council agreed that the origin of the problem was the large number of indigent patients. "We no longer have first or second class patients. . . . In the three or four years we had them we got along fine."[11] The council presented the reasons for this trend: first, the location of the home was ill-suited for the care of the aged, convalescents, etc.; second, in order to compensate for the deficit budget the Brothers were compelled to beg rather than concern themselves with upgrading the home. In order to make ends meet the Brothers had to care for forty or fifty patients paying ten shillings per week. To reverse the trends the council decided to limit admissions to those third-class patients (ward patients) who could pay ten shillings and to place an advertisement in the newspaper notifying the public that the home included facilities for first- and second-class patients.[12]

St. Mary's Home admitted epileptics on the grounds that their disease was not a mental illness. According to the provincial minutes of September 8, 1889, the Brothers encountered a legal problem in their care of such patients.[13] The Manchester police brought an epileptic to the home who was in a severe seizure. A judge responsible for declaring the man mentally ill asked the Brothers if they had a license to operate a mental institution. The Brothers explained their interpretation of the disease as physical and that they did not operate a mental institution "but a nursing institution [*Pflegeanstalt*]," in which the patients had a right to come and go freely.[14] "When they leave the home they are their own lord and master not responsible to us."[15] Since the Brothers had twelve epileptic patients and since they had always intended to establish a mental institution they appealed to the appropriate government commission for a license to operate a mental hospital.[16]

The movement to prohibit further licensing of private asylums had by this time succeeded. Hence the commissioners wrote that "according to Statute 556 concerning the mentally ill no more licences will be given to houses for the mentally ill; therefore it is impossible to give it to the Alexian Brothers for their home."[17] The House Council minutes noted that because of the law the "Brothers should be very careful about admitting epileptics."[18] However, they were still uncertain about the legality; "we now await more visits from the commission."[19] Though there is no extant evidence on how this problem was resolved, an October 1, 1889, notation indicates that the St. Mary's financial situation improved: "collecting [begging] go well."[20]

Between 1888 and 1897 the province developed slowly. The following illustrates an almost glacial-paced progress: 1888: nine Brothers in St. Mary's Home cared for a daily average of thirty-five men; five Brothers at the Manchester cemetery serviced 1,200 funerals; three Brothers at the Middlesbrough Cemetery serviced 400 funerals. 1897: nineteen Brothers, novices, and aspirants at St. Mary's Home cared for a daily average of thirty-four men; five Brothers at the Manchester Cemetery serviced 2,100 funerals; seven Brothers at Middlesbrough serviced 450 funerals at the cemetery and cared for ten men at Sacred Heart Home.[21]

Brother Cyrillus Kranepohl was provincial during this period characterized by personality conflicts, manpower shortages, restricted budgets, and the rigors of mission life for German Catholic Brothers in a predominantly Protestant British society. On October 27, 1891, Brother Eusebius Klütermann replaced Brother Cyrillus as provincial, with the latter appointed first provincial councillor.[22] The Brothers seem to have been aware that in order to rectify their poor financial and vocational situation they must become more conspicuous, i.e., advertise St. Mary's Home.

publish brochures on the various ministries of the Brothers, and enlarge both Sacred Heart and St. Mary's Homes. At the February 1, 1892, Provincial Council meeting plans were made to add a wing to Sacred Heart Home and purchase additional property adjacent to St. Mary's Home.[23] To accommodate Irish and English vocations, an English Prayer Book was approved on March 11, 1894.[24] The first extant document illustrating the trend to publicize the presence of the Brothers took the form of an album on St. Joseph's Cemetery. Intended to publicize both the cemetery and the Alexian ministry, the album stressed the Brothers' heritage as "tamers of death." That portion dedicated to the Brothers opened with a direct quote from Bishop Vaughan's pastoral letter in which he introduced the Alexians to the church in Manchester.[25] In addition the album stressed the heroic character of the Alexians' Black-Death origins.

> An Order of men devoted with such ardour to the relief of suffering humanity, and who shrank from neither pestilence nor death in the performance of their good works, could not fail to win the affection and admiration of Christian people. The Order spread rapidly, and soon founded branches in different countries, where they continued their excellent work.[26]

In 1898 the Brothers enlarged Sacred Heart Home and were seriously considering establishing a house in London. The new wing of Sacred Heart Home cost £4,300 but it did expand the home's capacity from ten to forty boarders.[27] Upon completion of the wing the Alexians published a brochure which, because it describes the aims and objectives of the Brothers' ministries in such fine Victorian prose, is worth quoting at length.[28] The introduction to the Alexian ministry to the aging included an insightful commentary on the needs of the elderly within an industrial society as well as a tribute to the sensitivity of the late Victorian social conscience:

THE ALEXIAN BROTHERS,
SACRED HEART HOME,
OAKLEIGH VILLA, LINTHORPE, NEAR MIDDLESBROUGH.

In these closing days of the Nineteenth Century, nothing is so striking to the general observer, as the immense amount of money and care expended on various charitable works. Philanthropists seem to vie with each other in their desires to find some new sort

141

of Institution, for the benefit of their suffering fellow-creatures. Consequently, we see springing up—especially in busy commercial centres—Hospitals, Infirmaries, Convalescent Homes, Nursing Institutions and such like. These, no doubt, meet a great want among the working-class population, but unfortunately they are, at the best, only of a local character and influence, and the help they afford is but temporary. But outside these classes requiring occasional help, there is a large number for whom very little provision has been made in this country. Take for instance the retired professional men, or the tradesmen, weary with the din and strife of business, where are they to find a home in which to spend their declining years? And those unfortunate men—young or old—who through paralysis or some other awful form of physical infirmity are unable to help themselves, and are a constant burden of care and anxiety to their relatives. What provision has been made for them? The care of such people brings no worldly honour or emolument, it can only be done by those who "love their neighbours as themselves." Happily, the Church has provided the world with persons who give themselves up to such heroic work, as that undertaken by the Alexian Brothers, who nurse the sick, take care of the aged and the helpless, and offer a peaceful retreat to those who desire to spend their remaining days in peace and comfort.[29]

The Alexians' interest in establishing a house in the vicinity of London was noted by Archbishop Vaughan who, in 1892, replaced Cardinal Manning as head of the English Catholic hierarchy. In the autumn of 1898 the Provincial Council discussed establishing a hospice for alcoholics at Buntingford, thirty-two miles from Liverpool Railway Station in London. Inquiring about the qualifications for obtaining a license for such an institution, the Brothers discovered that according to British law the superintendent and physician of an institution for alcoholics must be English born.[30] On April 11, 1899, the Provincial Council discussed a letter from Pater Quirinius Bank in which the latter said that the law precluded the German Alexians in England establishing the hospice. The council agreed and decided to notify Archbishop Vaughan of this decision.

In the summer of 1899 a Dr. Loffan of Caskel, Ireland, wrote to Provincial Rector Eusebius notifying him that if the Brothers were interested in establishing a hospice for alcoholics he had a house for rent.[31] Later that year, after Brother Bernhard Kleppel, who had served in the American Province, had been appointed provincial, Pater Quirinius urged him to "tread carefully in this matter."[32] Without further evidence on this Irish project one may infer that the Brothers found the offer too risky. It is a twist of irony that some seventy years later the Brothers established a hostel for alcoholics in Limerick, one which has attracted widespread interest and appears to have an appeal to young men seeking a challenging religious life. No doubt the Brothers must have seriously considered the 1899 project, for Ireland would have been a wealthy source of vocations. Indeed, with the establishment of the first Alexian house in Ireland in 1927, Irish vocations to the congregation increased dramatically.

The search for a London site persisted through Brother Bernhard's brief two-year tenure of office (1898–1900) and when Brother Eusebius once again became provincial the pace of the search was intensified. The costly addition to the Sacred Heart Home in Middlesbrough did not improve the financial condition of the province. The home was never full to capacity due to its unappealing location in a damp climate far to the north and near the sea. Apparently the decision to sell Sacred Heart Home coincided with the discovery of a suitable site for an Alexian nursing home near London. On March 12, 1902, the congregation purchased a stately house, attached to a nineteen-acre estate (at a cost of £9,000), which since the early nineteenth century has been called Twyford Abbey. Located in West Twyford near Ealing, Twyford Abbey has a rich history. Brother Cornelius Kearney, C.F.A., a member of the Alexian community at the abbey, has authored *The History of the District and Manor House of West Twyford* in which he traced the district back to the Domesday Book (1085–1086) and the manor back to at least the mid-thirteenth century when it was noted as a fief of the bishop of London and supportive of one of the prebendary stalls at St. Paul's Cathedral.[33] Its present architectural motif was derived from an early nineteenth-century revival of medieval forms, though portions of the old manor house and stables were incorporated into the neo-Gothic structure.

According to restrictive covenants placed upon the Twyford Abbey estate in 1898 a "noxious factory or a lunatic asylum or a fever hospital" could not be established on the property.[34] Hence, even if the Brothers had succeeded in obtaining a permit for an asylum or a hospice for alcoholics they could not have settled at Twyford Abbey. Though there is no evidence of neighborhood resistance to the establishment of a nursing home there, controversy arose over the possession of St. Mary's Anglican Church which was a part of the estate purchased by the Alexians.[35] The church with its graveyard had not been under Catholic auspices since the Reformation. Apparently the Brothers' lawyer who negotiated the purchase of the property had not considered the legal implication of a Catholic religious order owning a church that was an advowson (i.e., the right of presenting a benefice or installing the vicar) of the Anglican bishop of London. Perhaps the oversight derived from the fact that the church was not in use in 1902. St. Mary's Church, noted in 1927 as the smallest in the diocese, was claimed by the bishop of London in 1903, and in 1907 he won his case before the Ecclesiastical Commissioners of the Church of England.[36] Because the legal issue over the church was brought to the fore immediately after the Brothers arrived at Twyford Abbey they adapted an old conservatory for their chapel.[37]

By mid-April 1902, a month after the purchase of the estate, the six Brothers and their patients from Middlesbrough and five Brothers from Manchester settled Twyford Abbey.[38] The house could accommodate only twelve to fifteen patients but the provincialiate and novitiate were also lodged at Twyford Abbey. Brother Brendan Weston recalled the early years at the abbey: "At the time I joined [the Congregation], Twyford Abbey, in 1905, had a community of ten brothers and two novices, and eleven patients. Altogether there were twenty brothers in the whole Sacred Heart Province. These were made up of fifteen Germans and five English and Irish."[39] The latter comment illustrates the predominantly German character of the province, which by this time was thirty years old.

John O'Keefe, maintenance man at Twyford Abbey for over forty-two years, provided posterity with his impressions of leading figures in the Alexian community. Provincial Rector Brother Eusebius (1900–1909) "was the silent man, with the head always wobbling, but ever industrious, gentle, yet exerting authority, kind yet austere in demeanor, wise, without laudation, lenient yet exacting in all concerning the rules."[40] In contrast Brother Camillus McGill, the first native vocation, struck

O'Keefe as "the fiery, the impetuous, the hasty, the impatient, the man of moods and tense: yet the kind, the lovable, the generous, the confiding, the forgiving, the just."[41]

A historical anecdote has been circulating through the province for decades, one which reveals the cultural gap between the German Alexians and Anglo-Irish society and how Brother Camillus played the envoy role to bridge that gap. It seems that when Brother Camillus was in the novitiate (1882–1884), Alexian begging in Manchester was not bringing in enough revenue. It was therefore decided to seek the bishop's permission to release Brother Camillus from the rules governing the novitiate so that he could accompany the Brothers to Ireland where he could be their spokesman in their begging efforts. With the bishop's permission Novice Camillus and two German Brothers set off for Ireland. When they arrived in Dublin they had but a half-crown—2 shillings, 6 pence—among them. Apparently they were successful at begging and Brother Camillus thus established himself as a valuable resource for the province.[42]

In 1888, just six years after he entered the community, Brother Camillus was the first consultor to the provincial, Brother Cyrillus Kranepohl. The latter remarked in the Provincial Minute Book for December 3, 1888, that Brother Camillus was "a very sensible young man. I had more or less every day, a consultation with him especially as I found him not in any way prejudicial, but every matter, which was put before him he looked upon, calm and indifferent; he helped me a great deal, in my difficult position as Provincial. God bless him."[43] In 1891 Brother Camillus became rector of St. Joseph's Cemetery for a six-year term. After various other positions he was appointed novice master in 1907 but held the position for only one year. In 1909, while engaged in a private nursing assignment in county Waterford, Ireland, Brother Camillus wrote to the recently appointed provincial, Brother Remigius, regarding the latter's interest in pursuing an appropriate school for training the Brothers in nursing.

From the contents of this letter it appears that Brothers Remigius and Camillus were the first ardent spokesmen for modernization. Brother Camillus urged his provincial to visit various hospitals in Ireland for firsthand experience with training facilities.[44] Brother Camillus favored having the Alexians locate in

Dublin. "The Dublin 'Hall Mark' on a certificate will in my opinion bear [sic] more weight, besides being preferable owing to the greater number of cases taken in, hence more experience in a given time. Dublin training will be looked upon as geniune, whereas training in a provincial town like Cork may be termed inferior or counterfeit." In August 1909 Brother Camillus once again reported to Brother Remigius on training facilities in Ireland and England. After visiting Dublin Catholic hospitals run by Sisters of Mercy, Brother Camillus related his frustrating experience. At the Mater Misericordia he was told, "Such training [of Brothers] here is out of the question. Start as we have done and train yourselves."[45] Indeed the Brothers had trained themselves but without a certificate recognized by the British authorities they could never establish a hospital. The other hospitals were not so opposed but offered no encouragement.[46] Spokesmen for some Protestant hospitals in England as well as the "Temperance Male Nurse Cooperation at Manchester" told him they "were unacquainted with any hospital for the training of male nurses."[47]

Brother Camillus then shared "other bits of inconsiderate information" with his Provincial: ". . . female nurses in Hospitals are entirely opposed to male nurses taking up the work. They raise every difficulty so much that even those men who offered to endow a ward in some Hospital, specially for the training of men could not find anyone to accept their offer."[48] After relating so many disappointing experiences, Brother Camillus concluded with the remark, "The American scheme (if prudently handled) is not beneath consideration."[49] With only this rather cryptic statement one may infer that an interprovincial arrangement for training English-Province Brothers in America had been proposed. Though such an experiment would have drained the province of manpower, it would have provided many long-range benefits. However, the English Province did not embark on such a venture until the 1930s. In the meantime the Alexians in England were impelled to limit their ministries to retirement homes and cemeteries.

In February 1910 the provincial wrote to Brother Camillus at St. Mary's Home exploring the possibility of appointing him rector there. Camillus's reply (the provincial's letter has been lost) reveals his "fiery" temperament: "Your rough letter pleases me very much. . . . Had I been dealt with so openly before, the phantom of roughness would have long since disappeared. St. Mary's Rectorship is no sinecure and you will find few to make grand promises. I shall however go farther than ever I thought I should for any office."[50] Three days later, when he was stationed at Ampleforth Abbey in Yorkshire where he was doing private nursing, Brother Camillus replied to another letter from the provincial. Brother Remigius must have told him of opposition to his appointment as rector of St. Mary's: ". . . don't think that I feel . . . annoyed or upset, personally I should rather rejoice but this is not sufficient reason why I should shirk my responsibility—if you deem it advisable to make the appointment after you have investigated the objections of my opponents Bros. Eusebius, Quirinus, and one or two others who are doubtless influenced by personal motives."[51] He admitted that he was "impulsive" but hoped that it would never develop into "roughness."[52]

Brother Camillus was definitely a progressive Alexian in the sense that he was driven to persist in improving or modernizing the Brothers' institutions in England. "Whoever is put in charge of St. Mary's will I hope change it from a convict settlement into a Nursing Home, by degrees, say for instance for the special treatment of Rheumatism; arrangements for this can be effected at a slight cost."[53] He suggested that the home's physician could establish a "surgery" (his own clinic) for outpatients on St. Mary's grounds. Brother Camillus considered these changes a "stepping stone to our starting a private hospital here on a small scale thus qualifying our Brothers for more extensive work elsewhere and in a congenial atmosphere."[54] Because of its location on the edge of a working-class neighborhood and its reputation as a home for derelicts rather than a hospital, St. Mary's had always been considered an albatross by many Brothers. Brother Camillus was hoping to relieve the province of this burden, but that would have required a "time when the spirit of indecision will (let us hope) be less prevalent than it is at present."[55] In the meantime he hoped to establish a training facility at the home. Provincial Rector Remigius considered such proposals the product of Brother Camillus's impulsive character; six days later the latter wrote to the former informing him that "It is of course understood that I shall take no steps without obtaining your approval and even then go slowly on as a radical change is not advisable."[56]

His strategy for establishing a male-nurse training facility included, besides the home's physician developing a surgery, inserting two advertisements in newspapers. He suggested the following to Brother Remigius: "Male attendants required to nurse patients in their homes must be thoroughly qualified, good character essential, apply giving references and full particulars to Alexian Brothers Nursing Institute Newton Heath Manchester."[57] The other was aimed at attracting patients for the institute. The projected result of such advertisements "will make us known and give confidence besides giving our own members an opportunity of improving." His long-range plan was to "select a suitable locality" for the Alexian Brothers Nursing Institute and "take proper steps to sell St. Mary's (if necessary) without asking a farmer to buy it or telling everyone that it is useless and only fit for giving away."[58]

Perhaps such advertisements did appear, but the earliest extant item is from the diocesan monthly *The Harvest*, for August 1913. Rather than stressing the nursing institute character, it was under the title "St. Mary's Home, Manchester: A Haven of Rest."[59] It included references not to St. Mary's *Home* but to St. Mary's *Hall* as if the Brothers were consciously endeavoring to raise the character of the home's image from its traditional "convict settlement" to the status of a stately residence:

Situated on a high elevation, and yet within the area governed by the Manchester City Council, and consequently close to one of the greatest centres of industrial activity in the world, stands St. Mary's Hall, Newton Heath, the abode of the Alexian Brothers. Here for a modest sum of from 12s. 6d. to £2 per week, gentlemen may be accommodated. It may be information to many to hear of this. Gentlemen who may be somewhat "run down" in health, and desire quiet restful surroundings in which to recuperate, can find here all they desire. Others who have retired from business and are seeking some Home or Institution where they could be well looked after, and as Catholics have all the consolations and benefits of religion in the evening of their days, have in St. Mary's Hall their ideal. Then again there are many afflicted with some crippling physical ailment or other disability, and oftentimes a source of anxiety and constant burden to themselves and their relations and friends. Such persons may receive the kind attention and solicitude of the good Brothers, whose vocation has been, under God, to minister to the wants of the afflicted. A visit to St. Mary's Hall would convince anyone of the utility of such a Catholic Home. The buildings are spacious, well lighted, and heated throughout, and possess all the latest sanitary and domestic appliances.[60]

Since Brother Camillus was superior of St. Mary's when this appeared, it seems that attempts to found a male-nursing institute had failed and that the struggle to elevate St. Mary's to a financial success was a persistent concern. Two years later an advertisement in article form appeared in *The Harvest*.[61] Brother Camillus copied parts of the seventeen-year-old brochure on Sacred Heart Home, Middlesbrough, added some commentary on St. Mary's Home, and inserted it in the magazine. Previously quoted in full, the brochure was aimed at "the professional man, or the tradesman, weary with the din and strife of business," who were in need of a "home in which to spend their declining years."[62] Brother Camillus's specific comments on St. Mary's indicate his impact upon the modernization of the home. "Several improvements have been made lately, including new heating apparatus, new system of electric light, etc. For home comforts, St. Mary's cannot be surpassed by any of its kind."[63] According to the article, the home appears to have become a financial success. "For some time back applications have been so numerous that rooms have to be secured in advance."[64] Reflecting the then recently initiated trend in providing for constructive leisure for pensioners in such homes, the article referred to the "variety of games and hobbies available."[65] There was also an appeal to those who would work at "different trades . . . by way of pastime," for which one could receive a "reduction in terms for services rendered."[66] The article concluded with a comment linking the Brothers' ministries to their medieval origins: "Here then the noble work [of the Alexian Brothers] is carried on with the same spirit of humility, charity, and unabated zeal for the relief of the afflicted, which was so conspicuous in the early days of the Order."[67]

Brother Camillus's fiery temperament had been a source of

friction at St. Mary's. He wrote to Brother Remigius: ". . . you keep on harping about my treatment and guidance of the Brothers, and hint at neglect, rudeness, harshness, want of consideration, violation of fraternal charity, etc. etc. . . . I know you are sincere with me and therefore I shall take all your exhortations in good part with the hope that the preaching from Twyford will be followed up with the practice of fraternal charity."[68] In spite of the fact that he considered his rectorship of St. Mary's as an "unenviable position,"[69] he persisted in the office until 1919, when he was assigned to Twyford Abbey as a provincial councillor.

Brother Camillus's experiences as related in his letters and implied in his advertisements in *The Harvest* provide a singular witness to the character of the Sacred Heart Province. Though his vision was obviously influenced by his "impetuous" personality, he was very bright and alert, dedicated to modernizing the province and to breaking through those limitations imposed by its relatively impoverished condition, by its German-Catholic enclave character, and by British society's biases against male nursing. His provincial seems to have had some reservations with his modernizing schemes, but by keeping him in office he indicated his trust in Brother Camillus's keen leadership abilities.

Stately Twyford Abbey evolved along lines characterized by the brochure on the Middlesbrough house; it appealed to professional men as a pastoral retreat within a short train ride from the smog-choked London. In 1910 there were forty patients and eleven Brothers living at Twyford Abbey. Some of the Brothers worked on the abbey farm raising produce and tending the livestock, poultry, and beehives.[70] In 1912 one observer remarked on the Brothers' character and their ministry.

> They are devoted to the nursing of the sick, the nervous, the paralyzed, and sometimes the eccentric. The Brothers wait on the boarders like military orderlies, and attend them with the greatest assiduity, the sick and the infirm, each one in his own room away from friction of any kind. Members of the best families in the land are sometimes to be found in these houses. Creed, or religion or rank, makes no difference. When one sees a sturdy old Protestant complacently jibing a simple-minded lay brother attending him, one seems to forget that there ever existed a Smithfield or a Battle of the Boyne.[71]

Though this depiction appears rather romantic it does verify the Brothers' sense of service and the cosmopolitan social composition of the abbey's residents.

The relationship between Twyford Abbey and the Westminster diocese was generally cordial but limited to offical communications regarding chaplains' and diocesanwide functions. One exception to this rule concerned the Brothers' care for priests with alcoholic or other mental problems. The superiors at Twyford received numerous letters from the bishop of Ripon (i.e., Liverpool) relating to their care for sick clergymen. Occasionally conflicts between the Brothers and their priest residents developed as the latters' priest status could lead them to be rather obstreperous and patronizing to the lay Brother. For example, on June 24, 1912, the vicar general of the Westminster diocese wrote to Brother Rector Columcille McGuiness, who is still known for his sense of humor, reprimanding him for sending away one of his diocesan priests "without previous notice to the Cardinal or myself."[72] On behalf of the cardinal he ordered Brother Columcille to readmit the priest "without delay."[73] He was also perturbed to discover "that priests from other Dioceses, who are addicted to drink are received at the Abbey without our knowledge and permission."[74]

The significance of this incident lies not in its specific detail but, rather, in the way it illumines the general trend in historic Alexian relationship with the ecclesiastical structure. The St. Louis, Oshkosh, and other American hospitals as well as St. Mary's and Twyford Abbey in England serviced many dioceses by providing a quiet refuge for alcoholic priests. This illustrates the persistence of the Alexian response to the outsider, the refuge character of the Alexian houses far from the center of ecclesiastical action, and the mutual trust formed by the spirit of confidentiality between the chanceries and Alexian cloisters. Caring for priests was never an easy task for Alexian Brothers; it was, however, a strong expression of their ancient charism.

The story of the Alexian Brothers in World War I will be told in the final portion of this 1870–1920 history. It should be noted here that the predominance of German citizens within the community engendered suspicions among their British neighbors, particularly at Twyford Abbey. Four German Brothers were imprisoned and Twyford Abbey experienced anti-German demonstrations. Direct communication between Aachen and Twyford Abbey was severed; neutral America (till 1917) was the only link with the congregation.

Provincial Brother Remigius was an elderly German who guided the Alexians during the war years. However, in 1918 Brother Gilbert Holmes, an Englishman, was appointed provincial, a sign that the Alexians in England had reached maturity as well as a sign that the Aachen Motherhouse was aware of the need for English leadership to heal whatever divisions may have occurred as a result of wartime hostility. The character of the province was still heavily influenced by German tradition. Though the Brothers possessed an English Prayer Book their daily schedule was the same as that of their confreres in Germany and America, even though their hospice work was entirely different from that of either the asylum or the general hospital. German founding Brothers formed a Catholic ethnic enclave in British Protestant society. British law and traditional biases against male nurses prevented the province from establishing either modern asylums or modern hospitals. Limited to cemetery and hospice work, the Brothers did not form that strong institutional character necessary to attract many young aspiring religious to consider their congregation as the means for mediating their vocations. Though Brothers such as Camillus McGill and Remigius did represent the modernization trend, the Alexians in England formed the exception to the general modernization rule. As small communities engaged in burial and hospice ministries they more closely resembled the traditional Cellites than the modern Alexians.

10

The *Kulturkampf* and Expansion in Germany

Through its centralized authority structure the Aachen Motherhouse dominated the personality and character of the entire congregation. The reform spirit of Brother Dominic Brock's leadership during the mid-1850s cannot be overemphasized. The revival of perpetual vows, particularly the vow of poverty, was a profound turning point in the history of the Aachen Alexians. Imbued with a strong sense of the austere ground for the religious life and an equally strong fear of the insidious return of the secularist character of the early nineteenth century, the Aachen Motherhouse closely regulated the lives of the Brothers. Though the Alexian leaders abhorred the advance of modern materialism, they vigorously pursued the establishment of modern asylums and hospitals. The new constitution, which was considered to be a codification of tradition, was actually a very modern document reflecting Jesuitlike, highly depersonalized and centralized authority structures rather than the traditional Alexian familial character.

Confident of the principles for the religious life and of their thriving nursing apostolate, the Aachen Alexians attracted a large number of German vocations allowing them to continue to expand within the Rhineland and Westphalia. Though they successfully straddled the traditional and modern worlds, during

153

the *Kulturkampf* their existence as a religious order was placed in jeopardy. The immediate cause of this anti-Catholic policy was Chancellor Otto von Bismarck's determination to cement all German loyalties to the state in Berlin. As a Protestant member of the state Lutheran Church, he was suspicious of all Roman Catholics. For a variety of reasons many German Catholic groups struck him as potential enemies of the new Prussianized German state. Many Catholic nationalists had advocated the establishment of a large German state under the Catholic Hapsburgs of Austria vis-à-vis the small German state under the Protestant Hohenzollerns of Prussia. The Catholics of Alsace-Lorraine, provinces absorbed into Germany as the prize of victory over France, were viewed as potential sympathizers in any French reprisals against Germany. After the *Syllabus of Errors* and the infallibility decree, Bismarck concluded that by faith Catholics were compelled to be more loyal to Rome than to Berlin. By pursuing an anti-Catholic line, the Conservative German chancellor would gain support among German Liberals who held strong anticlerical and anti-Catholic biases. He needed such support against the Center party, which was originally a broad social-justice party but in 1870 had reconstituted itself as the proponent of Catholic views on social and political issues. Lastly, he was confronted not with a unified German Catholic Church but one suffering the trauma of the controversy over infallibility. Relying upon support from the Conservative and Liberal parties and the "Old Catholics," Bismarck launched a full-scale attack upon the Catholic Church. He aimed to curtail the self-determination of the church, to weaken the Catholic Center party, and to prevent the formation of any Papal-French-German Catholic coalition.[1] The *Kulturkampf* expressed itself in a series of laws beginning in 1871 with the dissolution of the Catholic Department within the Ministry of Public Worship and Education, and the Pulpit Law, which was aimed at preventing the Catholics from antistate preaching.[2]

In 1872 all Catholic schools were placed under state supervision and the Jesuit and Redemptorist orders were dissolved and forced into exile. The following year the first May Laws were passed by which the state imposed rules on seminary training, hiring of clergymen, and the internal governance of the

154

church. Obligatory civil marriage was made the law for Prussia in 1874 and for all of Germany in 1875. The most severe May Laws were those of 1875 whereby all houses and institutions maintained by religious orders, except those engaged in nursing the sick, were dissolved. Though thousands of religious were forced into exile, though an estimated 1,000 parishes were without priests because of either expulsion or harassment, and though many Catholics were threatened with and/or suffered fines and imprisonment, the church responded with a united front, the Catholic Center party gained strength in the Reichstag and Catholic loyalty to Rome remained strong.[3] Faced with such opposition and confident that a Catholic anti-German conspiracy was not a real threat, Bismarck, with the aid of Pope Leo XIII's policy of reconciliation, began gradually to diminish the enforcement of the *Kulturkampf* legislation in 1880.[4]

The Aachen Alexian Brothers who, under the direction of Brother Clement, had achieved papal congregation status in 1870, were obviously not attracted to the "Old Catholic Church." On the contrary, they were extremely proud of their renewed ties with the papacy and were grateful to Pius IX. Because their traditional notions of the austerity of the religious life appear to have been derived from a reaction against the secularism infecting their house during the late eighteenth and early nineteenth centuries, they were probably in accord with the spirit of the *Syllabus of Errors*. Though they had engaged in struggles with the Prussian state in their attempt to win independence from secular authorities, the Brothers seem to have considered themselves loyal Prussian subjects. Indeed, they were proud to serve as battlefield nurses in the Danish War and even in the war with Catholic Austria. As an indication that they viewed such service appropriate to their vocation, the Alexians incorporated battlefield nursing into the constitutional provision setting forth their religious works of charity. In the Franco-Prussian War (1870–1871) eight Brothers were stationed at the München-Gladbach military hospital, eleven at Krefeld hospital, twenty-one at a reserve hospital in Aachen, while fifteen nursed soldiers in field hospitals in France and for nearly four weeks seventeen Alexians transported wounded soldiers from the Rhine Railway to military hosptials.[5]

As a nursing order the Alexians were unaffected by the anti-Catholic legislation. However, shortly before the *Kulturkampf* the Aachen Brothers had accepted responsibility for running two convalescent/retirement homes for priests. On December 24, 1869, the vicar general of the Cologne diocese wrote to Brother Clement requesting the Alexians to manage the diocesan home for retired priests at Kaiserwerth near Düsseldorf; the Holy Ghost Fathers wished to discontinue their ministry there due to a lack of vocations.[6] After a brief period of negotations, on February 26, 1870, three Brothers assumed control of the house. Archbishop Melchers of Cologne also asked the Brothers to manage another retirement home for priests at Mariental near Siegburg and to care for the chapel there which housed a picture of the Sorrowful Mother, popularly considered miraculous by a continuous stream of pilgrims. Though Brother Clement was hesitant he submitted to the archbishop's request and in October 1873 sent several Brothers to Mariental. Because the German state did not consider caring for convalescent and retired priests as nursing, the houses were suppressed under the May Laws of 1875.[8]

After such strenuous nursing service during the wars which culminated in the establishment of the German Empire, the Alexians were deeply distressed by the anti-Catholic persecution. Even though their nursing apostolate protected them from wholesale suppression there was a period (1872–1875) when they dreaded the possibility that the entire church would be controlled by the state, that exile would become the lesser of the evils, or a time when the existence of a religious order would be proscribed.

In 1874 Professor Paul Hinschius, a distinguished Protestant professor of secular and church law, published a book on the Catholic orders and congregations in Prussia. He worked closely with Adalbert Falk, the *Kultusminister*, in drafting of the *Kulturkampf* legislation. Hinschius authored an 1874 work, which was a Liberal's apologia for such legislation. By this time religious had been excluded from teaching in public schools and the Jesuits, Redemptorists, Vincentians, Holy Ghost Fathers, and the Religious of the Sacred Heart had been expelled from the German Empire. Hinschius's book set the stage for the 1875 law expelling all non-nursing orders.[9]

He first mentioned the Alexians in a chapter outlining the constitutions of the various orders. He clearly intended to illustrate how the Alexian authority structure suppresses individualism, and how the Brothers' loyalty to the state is secondary to their superior, their bishop, and ultimately to the Pope.[10] Hinschius quoted from the Alexian rule to further indict the congregation's raison d'être as contrary to nature: "In order that they may advance in virtue, it is expedient, nay, it is altogether necessary, that all give themselves to perfect obedience, so that they acknowledge their Superior, whoever he may be, as the representative of our Lord Jesus Christ, and yield him all reverence and love." Later he quoted the daily schedule of the Alexians, noting the many hours at prayer, to show that their purpose was primarily religious.[11] And Hinschius culminated his exposé of the Alexians' religious rather than nursing purpose when he included those passages from the statutes that direct the Brothers to minister to the spiritual needs of their patients.

As a quasi-public institution under the authority of the City Poverty Administration, the Alexian asylum in Aachen, implied Hinschius, violated its public trust by directing the Brothers to spread church propaganda ("kirchliche . . . Propaganda").[12] However, the last quoted rule (no. 13) was lifted from the Brothers' religious duties in home nursing, i.e., private vis-à-vis public nursing. Hinschius then quoted from this last rule, regarding hospital or asylum nursing, which states that the "preceding chapter," i.e., in home care, should apply also to hospitals but only "so far as it is possible to apply them."[13] The latter qualifications could only have been intended to place an obvious restraint upon the Brothers' religious duties within the pluralistic hospital setting. By placing it at the end of a list of religious duties, Hinschius seems to have consciously deemphasized that qualification, as if to say that the above religious responsibilities are to be followed without regard to the conscience or religious affiliation of the hospital patients. That this was not the Brothers' intention was clearly evident, not only in the "whenever it is possible" qualification but also in the then four-hundred-year tradition of nursing the sick and burying the dead without regard to class or religious affiliation and their recent adoption of the battlefield-nursing practice.

The early Cellites were *Seelenbrüder* (Soul Brothers) and the modern Alexians were self-consciously *Seelensorger* (pastoral ministers). The later role was expressed implicitly in their vocation and tradition but explicitly only when it was prudent. In short, the Brothers were realists who, because they had been nursing in a pluralistic world for four centuries, were conscious of the need to restrain their *Seelensorger* role as they developed modern hospitals suitable for the general public. Erwin Gatz points out that Hinschius was convinced that nursing congregations gained great prestige among the masses and that even the "intelligent classes" approved of religious nurses. In spite of the fact that Hinschius believed their ultimate purpose was religious rather than humanitarian, the state could not afford to close their institutions.[14]

From the open letter to Brother Paul in which an anonymous Brother accused Paul of being a follower of Hinschius, whose work was placed on the Catholic Index of forbidden books, we can infer that the contents of his 1874 books were well known throughout the Alexian community. Brother Clement, implicitly portrayed as a religious tyrant, wrote, "Distress and fear filled our hearts for in keeping with the proposals according to which the laws were to obtain force, we all had to be ready to be suppressed."[15] No doubt the Alexians recalled the period of French occupation when the state regulated religious orders. Indeed they must have identified state control with that period during which they reached their nadir. Brother Dominic Brock's reforms were aimed at liberating the Brothers from the secularism that had permeated the monastery as a result of the Brothers' becoming city nurses entirely under the control of the civil authorities. The profession of the vow of poverty marked a liberation from the role of salaried nurses to a full participation in religious life, but the Alexian institutions were still under state supervision. Brother Clement Wallrath vigorously struggled to gain institutional autonomy not in matters of state supervision over the quality of health care but over the direction of their property. From 1864 to 1873 he petitioned several Prussian agencies to recognize the Alexian Brothers' asylums and hospitals as members of an independent corporation free from the controls of the Poverty Administration. Brother Ignatius Wiegers reports that Pater Clement had made a personal visit to Berlin: "Once he had even nearly approached King William I in the

Kurpack of Ems in the summer of 1867 in order to obtain liberation from the French laws of 1803 [the legal basis for the authority of the Poverty Administration—but in vain! Seven times the contract over admitting and nursing the sick in Mariabrunn had to be changed."[16] When the *Kulturkampf* legislation threatened to impose further controls—particularly upon institutions like Mariabrunn, which was under contract with the city—Brother Clement decided to explore the possibility of selling the asylum to the Aachen city government. Sometime before the *Kulturkampf* crisis the mayor of Aachen had proposed the purchase to Brother Clement; after some brief price negotiations the sale was consummated on May 8, 1875, for 85,000 marks.[17]

While Brother Clement and his council were involved in the negotiations to sell Mariabrunn they were also searching for a site for a new asylum free from the dangers of the *Kulturkampf*. Through a friend they were led to Chateau Baelen, or de Ruyff, near Henri Chapelle, Belgium.[18] Two chateaus prominently presided over the surrounding countryside; one had been bought by an order of teaching brothers from Burtscheid near Aachen, the other, Nouveau de Ruyff, was for sale. Brother Clement was so impressed with the site that he decided to purchase the property regardless of the outcome of the *Kulturkampf*. Brother Ignatius traced the earliest historical evidence of the property to an 1172 document testifying to its fiefdom in the old Duchy of Limburg.[19] The chateau was and still is a fine representation of classic eighteenth-century architecture. The final purchase agreement was made on May 3, 1875; for the sum of 126,000 marks the General Council of the Alexian Brothers received the large chateau, farm buildings, and 136 acres of farm land, primarily meadow.[20] Though the price was high (the seller was a land speculator), shortly after the Brothers bought the property a group of Ursuline Sisters, refugees from the *Kulturkampf*, offered 180,000 marks for the property. Brother Clement, sympathetic to their plight, was willing to sell it at the 126,000-mark price, but the Sisters ultimately decided to search elsewhere for a new convent site.[21] Holland and Belgium were inundated by German religious-order emigrants and the Alexians, unsure of their future, were grateful that they had a Belgian house located just a few miles from Aachen.

Five days after the purchase of Chateau Baelen, the Alexians sold their large Mariabrunn Asylum on the outskirts of Aachen. With characteristic business acumen, Brother Clement immediately took the cash from the sale along with surplus money, roughly 225,000 marks, over the border to Belgium where it was safe from the German state.[22] Six weeks later the Aachen police chief was sent to investigate the whereabouts of the money from the sale of Mariabrunn. Pater Clement reportedly laughed and bluntly stated, "You can well imagine that we immediately put this money into safety, and you will not be able to put your hands on it." When the police chief asked Brother Clement what he should place in his report, he answered, "Just write that the owners had received their share and that all was in safe keeping."[23] Apparently that satisfied the authorites as the issue never surfaced again. After much renovation, at a cost of 12,000 marks, the Alexian asylum at Henri Chapelle was approved by the Belgian government in 1876. Unlike the Aachen asylum on Alexianergraben, which housed patients from all classes, Chateau de Baelen was most suitable for private and semiprivate rooms, which made it an institution for first- and second-class patients.[24]

The *Kulturkampf* had a profound impact upon the Aachen Alexians. Not only did the anti-Catholic legislation prompt Brother Clement to purchase property in Belgium and sell Mariabrunn, but it seems to have added cement to the cloister walls separating the German Alexians from the modern world. Brother Clement's correspondence during this period to the American Provincial, Brother Leonard Jansen, contained many references to the tensions created by the *Kulturkampf*. We have explored the German influence upon the New World Province as characterized by the imposition of the Old World religious traditions of formalism, hierarchical structure, and a studied aloofness of the secular world. This emphasis upon monastic discipline, derived from the reform period of Brother Dominic Brock, was strongly confirmed by the German state-church conflict of the 1870s. One may infer, therefore, that Brother Clement's extremely stringent stress upon traditional religious decorum was not limited to his view of traditional Alexian monastic discipline, nor to his Old World notions, but also resulted from his bitter experiences with the *Kulturkampf*. He must have viewed the advance of the modern world in terms of the German state's anti-Catholic policies buttressed by anticlerical Liberals.

Professor Hinschius could have been easily portrayed as the embodiment of the Antichrist character of the modern age. A siege mentality, though perhaps seldom conscious, was implicit in the evolution of the character of the two German provinces. The dangerously threatening world beyond the cloister walls was one of the traditional concepts held by the person who sought to fulfill a religious vocation. When religious symbol and ritual were eclipsed by the advance of the modern world, religious orders tended to identify tradition almost as an end in itself. When confronted with persecution from the modern state, that tendency gains momentum. Because the German Alexians were primarily asylum nurses who worked extremely long hours, their contacts with the secular world were largely limited to their mental patents, rejects of the modern world. Hence they nurtured their formal traditions into a strong defensive posture. Today's American or English-Irish Alexian Brothers who visit a German house are struck by the persistence of tradition. However, to conclude that the Aachen Alexians are formalist, tradition-bound Germans is a half-truth bordering on a stereotype. Instead one must attempt to penetrate their traditional perspective as it was formed in a culture-battle with Bismarck, the harsh reality of World War I, the depression and the catastrophic culture battle with Nazism and World War II. Though other German religious orders have reconciled themselves to the modern world, it will take some time for these asylum Brothers to reach an accommodation with a culture from which they are separated by monastery and asylum enclosures.

The *Kulturkampf* laws remained on the statue book until the early twentieth century, but by 1880 Bismarck had shifted from an anti-Catholic to an anti-Socialist position, which meant that he was compelled to seek support from the increasingly strong Catholic Center Party, necessitating a relaxation in the implementation of the anti-Catholic laws. Though the state-church battles threatened the Alexians as a religious order, the practical considerations of maintaining their health-care institutions were pressing realities demanding their continuous attention.

Briefly, in spite of the dangers to their religious life they could not be distracted from the daily needs of their patients.

The establishment of the Chateau de Baelen Asylum somewhat compensated for the loss of Mariabrunn. The generalate and the novitiate, which were housed at Mariabrunn, returned to the Aachen house on Alexianergraben. During the 1860s the Aachen institution developed from a hospice with twenty patients to a modern asylum with over one hundred patients. During the '70s the Brothers expanded their rental property by constructing flats above and below the asylum along Alexianergraben. With this income they were able to continue the modernization of their mental hospital. By 1881 the Aachen Alexians, numbering twenty-one professed, seven novies, and six postulants, were caring for an average of 178 patients per day. Still maintaining their ancient burial apostolate they were funeral witnesses, pallbearers, for 1,058 adults and 1,416 children in 1881. Another ancient tradition, home nursing, occupied six Brothers during that year.[25]

The general trend toward the continuous updating of the Alexian institutions in Germany was clearly illustrated in München-Gladbach and Krefeld. When the former community was founded (1857) the Brothers were primarily engaged in home nursing. In 1860 Brother Rector Aloys Speck sought approval from the General Council for his plans to construct an Alexian asylum at München-Gladbach. After receiving permission from the Prussian authorities in Berlin and after Brother Bonaventure Thelen, later of American fame, had received permission from the president of Rhine Province for a public fund-raising effort, construction of the new asylum began; the first wing was completed in 1863. Over the next twenty years the asylum and the Brothers' cloister were enlarged to accommodate the high demands for care of the mentally ill. From its humble origins in 1857, when there were merely three Brothers begging from door to door and caring for the sick in their homes, the München-Gladbach's community expanded to fifteen professed Brothers in 1885 who cared for 150 mental patients and provided in-home nursing for 650 patients. They had expanded their property to include a farm of nineteen acres. Characteristic of the Alexian houses in all the provinces, this community became self-sufficient with a farm, bakery, tailor shop, shoe shop, and engineering department.[26]

After the rather bizarre origins of the Krefeld house (see chap. 5), the Brothers flourished as nurses in the Workers' Hospital and established a small hospice for all types of incurable patients at the site of a former amusement park. Because Krefeld was a rapidly expanding industrial city there was a growing need for mental-health-care facilities. In 1871 the Alexians received permission from the German authorities in Berlin to conduct an insane asylum.[27] Brother Bonaventure was not only a master-builder of the American Province but before and after his pioneering in the United States he was associated with the expansion of the German institutions. Instrumental in the development of the München-Gladbach Asylum in the mid-sixties, he also made his mark on the expansion of the Krefeld Asylum in 1875. By 1885 there were nineteen professed Brothers attending to 150 patients in the Krefeld Asylum, some of whom still nursed in homes and at the Workers' Hospital.[28]

The Brothers at München-Gladbach and particularly Krefeld developed close relationships with the townspeople, like the Elizabeth Brothers in the American Province and the Manchester Brothers in the English Province. Unlike the Brothers in Aachen, who had been serving the city since the fourteenth century, the Alexians in these four cities were like missionary Brothers responding to the needs of burgeoning industrial towns. Mainly drawn from poorer classes themselves, they easily identified with the needs of the workers in these urban areas. Visitng Krefeld, Manchester, and Elizabeth and chatting with Brothers who have served in these hospitals and in München-Gladbach, one understands that they have a common character derived from their shared experiences. In each of these cities the Brothers were witnesses in the church's urban nursing apostolate. Though their religious life was highly regulated and monastic in character, the Alexians in these four cities lived close to and were warmly appreciated by the townspeople; both the town and the Alexian cloister were able to express their mutual needs in simple but visible, concrete terms, in contrast to the relationship in ancient cosmopolitan Aachen where the Brothers had, after centuries of service, developed rather formalized relations with the townspeople.

Pater Clement presided over the phenomenal expansion of the Brothers' works in each of the provinces. His favorite project seems to have been Mariabrunn, but the Kulturkampf pressured him to sell that extremely modern asylum. Though the acquisition of Chateau de Baelen provided some compensation for its loss, after the threats of the anti-Catholic legislation subsided Pater Clement once again became interested in developing the Alexian presence in the vicinity of Aachen. However, when he did found a new asylum it was more by accident than design. The expansion of the asylum on Alexianergraben necessitated a search for farm land from which they could supply foodstuffs for the additional patients and Brothers. In 1878 the Alexians bought ten acres of property near the Berg estate outside Aachen, which they called Mariaberg. Almost immediately Pater Clement, urged on by other Brothers, decided to negotiate for the purchase of the entire Berg estate. After a two-year entanglement in legal and financial issues the Alexians purchased the forty acres, a large residence, and farm buildings for 120,000 marks. No sooner had Pater Clement submitted plans for the construction of a five-hundred to six-hundred-bed asylum than the city authorities demanded that the congregation pay for the construction of new streets. Four years later, in 1884, the matter was settled in favor of the Alexians and construction began in March of that year under the direction of a contractor who had built many of the additions to the München-Gladbach and Krefeld hospitals. By June of the following year the first wing was completed to accommodate one hundred patients. By 1889, after a massive fund-raising effort, two other wings had been completed. Mariaberg now housed 350 patients nursed by twenty Brothers and twelve lay assistants. The first rector of Mariaberg was the indefatigable Brother Bonaventure, who had recently returned from the English Province. Under his and his successor's direction the asylum continued to expand until in 1893 it was accommodating 650 patients.[29]

The fertility of the Aachen Motherhouse was extraordinary; from the mid-fifties to the mid-eighties she generated ten houses in four provinces. The Cologne and Belgian Alexians experienced gradual growth during the second half of the nineteenth century but the Aachen community was by far the most dynamic. Until 1870, when the Motherhouse received papal approval for her statutes, she was, like all other Alexian houses, a diocesan congregation under the authority of her ordinary. By gaining papal approval the Aachen Alexians became a canonically "exempt Institute." All religious orders are by definition exempt from the ordinary's authority; one of the marks of the membership in a religious order is the profession of solemn vows. Because the Brothers professed simple rather than solemn vows, they were not members of a religious order but a religious congregation. In contrast to the Cologne and Belgian houses, Aachen was the Motherhouse of a "Papal Congregation." In the late fifteenth and early sixteenth centuries when Popes Sixtus IV and Julius II approved the Cellites, canon law did not distinguish between solemn and simple vows. However, there were religious institutes under the ordinary and others papally exempt. Because the Cellites did receive exemptions, they were from their origins in that line of canon-law development which would have eventually led to the profession of solemn vows. But the Reformation resulted in the breakdown of the Cellite authority structures, and the Council of Trent granted so much supervisory authority to the bishops that without a central authority structure and learned canon lawyers within the community the Cellites devolved to de facto diocesan congregations. Though there were provincial structures intact in Brabant and the Rhineland up to the period of the French Revolution (1789–1815), the authority of provincial chapters and brothers provincial appears to have been limited by the bishops. The French occupation led to the condition of de jure diocesan-congregation status for all the Cellite houses.

The mid-nineteenth century revival of the Aachen Alexians was symbolized by the profession of perpetual vows. Before that time the Brothers seem to have been comfortable with temporary vows while the French and later the Prussian authorities imposed salaried-nurse status upon the Brothers, which precluded the profession of the final vow of poverty. As a result of the Prussian Constitution of January 31, 1850, the Brothers were granted autonomy in their internal affairs. Under the leadership of Brother Dominic Brock, the Aachen Brothers seized the opportunity to seek permission from their ordinary, the archbishop of Cologne, for the profession of perpetual vows. When the Aachen house founded the American mission their diocesan-congregation status became impractical; the archbishop of Cologne could not be responsible for the Chicago Brothers and if the latter were placed under the authority of an American bishop the Aachen house would have lost affiliation with their German Brothers in the United States. Hence Pater Clement placed the issue before the papacy and in the process achieved papal exemptions for the Aachen Alexians.

The Cologne and Belgian Alexians, who did not expand and were not led by such vigorous persons as Dominic Brock and Clement Wallrath, remained tied to their bishops. However, documents reveal that in 1869 Belgian Brothers in the diocese of Mechlin sought an investigation into their proper status. The issue hinged on the question as to whether the Brothers were to profess solemn or simple vows. If they were allowed to take solemn vows then they were de jure a religious congregation with full exemption from their bishops. Ultimately the Congregation for Religious within the Papal Curia decided on September 28, 1883, that the Alexians were to profess simple vows.[30]

Brother Ignatius Wiegers reports that the superior of the Belgian Alexian community at Lierre, Brother William Boovers, who was under the authority of the bishop of Mechlin, visited Aachen in early 1884.[31] He reported to Pater Clement that he had been responsible for initiating the investigation which led to the 1883 decrees because of a conflict over the interpretation of vows within his community. Brother William, armed with the decree urging Alexian unification, sought Pater Clement's approval for the Aachen Congregation's annexation of the Lierre house.[32]

Pater Clement was reluctant to respond to Brother William's request without first receiving a clarification of the 1883 decree from Rome. He therefore wrote to his agent at the Vatican, who gave the following reply, dated February 2, 1884.

> Although the wording of the enclosed decree of the Holy Congregation admits of no other explanation, save that all the Houses

of the Cellites, consequently also those of Cologne and Neuss, are to accept the Constitutions of the Motherhouse in Aachen, still I have made inquiry of the Auditor of the Sacred Congregation about the meaning of the decree. He told me expressly that the intention of the Sacred Congregation had precisely been to induce the Houses still separated from the Motherhouse of the Alexians in Aachen to join it by accepting its Constitutions.

They were to make a uniform whole, under the supreme direction of the Rector General unto the joy and glory of the Church and unto the welfare of the entire Alexian Institute, which the Holy See recognizes as a Community well deserving of the Church and of Religion.

Hence, if the Alexian Houses in the diocese of Mechlin still entertained doubts about the meaning and the intention of the decree of the Sacred Congregation, it is for them to apply to the Sacred Congregation with a petition for written explanation. There can be no doubt but that the Congregation will answer as explained above.

But you are acting very correctly, my dear Clement, by remaining neutral for the present. However, in case the Houses of Mechlin and later the House of Cologne apply to you in join up with the Motherhouse at Aachen, it is undoubtedly your duty to be kindly disposed to them and to receive them lovingly in Christ, presuming that they accept and follow the Constitutions of 1870.[33]

The controversy stirred up by Lierre's appeal for annexation did indeed require a posture of diplomatic neutrality on the part of Pater Clement. The archbishop of Mechlin, who was responsible for the Lierre Brothers as well as other Belgian Alexians, was bitterly opposed to the annexation. Rumors that Pater Clement represented German imperialism were spread in a climate of nationalism. The superior of the Cellites at Antwerp wrote to the Pope indicating their firm desire to remain "under the immediate jurisdiction of the Cardinal Archbishop of Malines [Mechlin]."[34] Brother Ignatius Wiegers stated that because most of the Belgian Brothers were unwilling to assume the religious discipline demanded by the Aachen Congregation, with its perpetual simple vows, they did not wish to be annexed. The Antwerp superior's rationale contradicts that interpretation. He wrote the Pope that he had heard of Lierre's petition for annexation, but that he considered such a move contrary to the spirit of religious discipline. He explained that when the Belgian Brothers were tied to the provincial structure before the French Revolution many abuses crept into the community and that discipline had greatly improved under the leadership of the cardinal archbishop of Mechlin. "It is our opinion that being governed by direct authority of the diocese is best and most regular."[35]

Brother William Boovers appealed to Rome for annexation but the Curia was reluctant to place pressure upon the archbishop of Mechlin. The official visitator of the Alexians in the Mechlin diocese apparently urged Rome to reject Lierre's appeal on the basis that national German-Belgian tensions would lead to the Belgian house's absorption into a German Congregation. Pater Clement replied to Brother William concerning such accusations.

If the Visitator, the Canon of Mechlin, speaks of a German union, and above all characterizes our Community as a German Community, as I glean from your letters and from the remarks of the Brothers there,—that is not correct. After our Institute received the Apostolic approval, as is really the case, it has received the character of an International Community, i.e., the Community is thereby placed directly under the Holy See and has been approved for the whole Church. Accordingly, it is neither a German nor a French Community, nor that of any other country, but a Roman Catholic Community, destined for the whole Church. That the Motherhouse is at present in Aachen does not affect the matter. If there were no revolutionary conditions in Rome, it would probably be located there. Hence, the Rector-General is not of necessity a German. The General Chapter has the right to choose the General Superior from any other country, just as long as he is a Cellite.

If the Belgium Cellite convents deem it proper to join us, they join an ecclesiastical Community approved by the Holy See which is destined to spread in the world and this is certainly the purpose of all regulated Congregations. If it is this that the Cellite convents of Belgium fear, they may keep their national Belgium character but they cannot then lay claim to being an ecclesiastical Order, especially if the single Houses so anxiously try to preserve their individual character.

We have no special interest in desiring a union with these convents; our Community will go its way whither God directs it and will spread still more with God's help.

It would certainly be to the greatest interest of the Belgium convents to join the well organized body of our Community which is already spread over several countries. Whither would the Brothers flee if the same happened in Belgium that happened here in the seventies? That Rome desires a union of the Belgium Alexians with our Community is a fact known to all. And as to your noble endeavor, my respected Superior, to carry out the decree of the Sacred Congregation, you may rest assured that God will bless your intention. Let us now leave the matter entirely in His hands and do continue to work with courage and confidence. Meanwhile I have the honor to be your well disposed. . . .[36]

Brother William of Lierre, sensitive to the general concern that the Belgian Brothers maintain their identity, proposed the formation of a Belgian Province with the seat of provincial authority at Henri Chapelle, federally incorporated into the Papal Congregation of Aachen.

Among the Belgian houses only Brother William's community at Lierre was willing to seek annexation, and on May 18, 1885, he and eleven other Brothers signed the document of unification which shifted their allegiance from the archbishop of Mechlin to the rector-general of the Alexian Congregation at Aachen. In accord with the 1883 decree urging unification, the papacy confirmed the union on July 5 and directed the hierarchy involved in the matter not to interfere with the annexation. On October 2, 1885, the twelve Lierre Brothers assembled in their chapel and professed perpetual vows according to the constitution of 1870.[37]

In contrast to the modern Alexian asylums in Germany, the Lierre Alexians represent the traditional-world Cellite ministries. In their relatively small hospice they cared for twenty to twenty-five elderly men, nursed the sick in their homes, and buried the dead. Though the Aachen Brothers maintained the city cemetery the Lierre Brothers were called upon to perform the traditional rites from preparing the body for the wake and funeral to participating in the burial ceremony at the cemetery. As late as the 1930s whenever a man of the town died the family would call upon the Alexians.

The pre-annexation statutes of the Lierre Brothers followed the general pattern of the 1711 statutes for the Brabant Province. Though they were detailed regulations for the eighteenth-century cloisters, they appear to be general principles in contrast to the 1870 statutes for Aachen.[38] Besides the obvious difference in their authority structures (i.e., local superior in Lierre, rector-general over four provinces in Aachen) the Brothers' traditional ministries in Lierre did not entail nursing in large asylums. While the Aachen statutes included a long list of offenses and punishments, those for Lierre were relatively brief.

They appear to have shared traditional Cellite spirituality with its focus on the office of the Holy Cross. Unlike the Aachen rule, the Lierre statutes explicitly hark back to the *Devotio Moderna* spirituality infused into the Cellite origins as the Brothers were instructed to read Thomas à Kempis. The Lierre and Aachen Brothers also shared a common daily schedule with the exception that the Lierre community began prayers at 4:00 A.M., half an hour earlier than in Aachen.[39]

The international character of the Aachen Alexians expanded with the annexation of Lierre. By 1888 the Aachen Motherhouse contributed large sums of money to enlarge her newly acquired Belgian house which gradually developed into a moderate-sized hospital for the aged. But the Lierre house preserved its identity and many Brothers were occupied in the traditional Cellite ministry to the dead. Lierre was the last Aachen house with which Pater Clement Wallrath was directly associated as rector-general. In 1886, having been pater of the Aachen House for twelve and rector-general for fifteen years, he retired.

The strong role of the state in the control and supervision of the Alexian institutions haunted Brother Clement throughout his tenure. Ever since the days of the French occupation, the Alexians had been under a welfare commission. Though for centuries they had dwelt in a contractual relationship with city councils, their religious status protected them from the civil authority's abusing its power. When the Brothers were declared public servants, i.e., nurses, under the authority of the French and then the Prussians, who had strong tendencies toward centralization and anticlerical and anti-Catholic biases, the Brothers' property as well as their communal life was subjected to the will of the state. Even before the Kulturkampf Pater Clement had earnestly, at times passionately, appealed for persmission to incorporate the Alexian Brothers as a legal person with full right under the law. Frustrated at every turn and deeply afraid that ultimately the Kulturkampf would be revived, Pater Clement designed a scheme by which members of the General Council, using their baptismal vis-à-vis their religious names, incorporated themselves as the Aachen Joint-Stock Company for the Support of Needy Men.[40] With a capital base valued at 304,000 marks, the company incorporated in 1885 and issued three hunrded shares at 1,000 marks per share. Presumably the officers of the corporation, i.e., the General Council, held all three hundred shares. In the event of state suppression or persecution those assets would be protected by the law. After his retirement Pater Clement continued his management of the joint-stock company. Though age and the stress of office encouraged him to announce his retirement at the 1886 General Chapter, his thirty years in authority were rewarded when he was elected assistant rector-general to the new pater, Brother Quirinus Bank. Apparently he felt the need to play a greater role in the governance of the congregation, for in 1887 he "humbly" asked Pope Leo XIII to appoint him visitator to facilitate a "smooth transition of power" within the context of good discipline. We have no evidence of Pope Leo's immediate reply but at a meeting of the General Council (June 8, 1887), Clement's appeal was rejected and in February 1889 that decision was approved by the papacy.[41]

During his long tenure in office Pater Clement laid the basis for the evolution of the modern Alexians. He demanded rational efficiency in the administration and nursing at the many asylums and hospitals constructed under his leadership. When he entered the novitiate, the Aachen community numbered less than twenty Brothers located in one house. When he retired there were over two hundred Brothers in the Aachen Congregation, located in Germany, Belgium, England, and the United States. Author of the 1870 statutes, Pater Clement provided extremely well-defined authority structures for every aspect of Alexian life. These statutes, which granted the rector-general almost absolute authority, reflect Pater Clement's personality and world-view. He was as efficient in his leadership, indeed almost compulsive in his concern for the minutiae of administrative work, as the statutes efficiently regulated every detail of the Brothers' life. His world-view was colored by the realization that without highly disciplined and austere cloisters and deep traditional devotion to the religious life, the Alexians would be vulnerable to the snares of the secular world such as had entangled the Aachen house prior to Brother Dominic Brock's reforms. Pater Clement viewed the ideal Alexian Brother as one who cherished the ancient Alexian tradition setting him apart from the world, who willingly suppressed his own will in deference to his superiors and his senior Brothers, who fastened himself to a rigorous prayer and work schedule, and who took pride in the contemporary character of the Alexian institutions.

11

Dawn of the Twentieth Century and World Conflict

Brother Clement Wallrath made such an impact upon the evolution of the authority structures, the tone of leadership, and the general direction of the congregation that he may be considered, along with Brother Dominic Brock, as a co-founder of the modern Alexians. His successor, Brother Quirinus Bank, was well suited to maintain the high character of the office of rector-general. During his twenty years in office (1886–1906), Pater Quirinus presided over the continuous expansion of the congregation in each of its four provinces with a clear vision of his role as pater. Considering the extraordinary achievements under Pater Clement's leadership, there was no apparent reason for Pater Quirinus to deviate from his predecessor's stress upon a strong enforcement of the monastic character of the Brothers as the means by which their vocation as religious in a modern nursing apostolate were to be safely moored to the church.

Before tracing the expansion of the Alexians in Westphalia and the Rhineland, which Pater Quirinus with his General Council orchestrated, it seems appropriate to capture the personal style with which the second rector-general led the congregation. In examining the reports of his visitations to the American Province, one may discover his self-image as a spiritual father of the Alexians.

Though these reports also instruct us in the distinctions between the German and American provinces, their significance is derived from the rector-general's point of view of the Alexian way of life, one which was expressed in terms of the ideal. Because his remarks flow from his role as interpreter of the ideal his reports, intended as public statements, should be viewed as commentaries on raising the real to the ideal rather than as objective statements on the actual conditions of the real.

After his 1888 visitation to the American Province—the first by a rector-general—Pater Quirinus reported to the American Brothers on August 25, 1888. In general he was impressed with the American houses and particularly gratified by the fine reputation the congregation had established in the various communities.[1] The greater part of the letter was concerned, however, with problems which endangered a monasterylike atmosphere. He noted that some Brothers were absent during the hours of prayer and meditation, that there were frequent visitors in the monastic enclosure, and that the Brothers' reading material was abundant and secular. He urged immediate rectification of these problems and ordered a limitation on the Brothers' reading to one Catholic Sunday newspaper. Pater Quirinus persisted in exhorting the Brothers to improve the communal prayer life.[2] In 1903, fifteen years after his first visitation, he remarked on the necessity of common prayer: "prayer comes before work."[3] His notion of the ideal Alexian included minimum personal contact between Brothers and laity.[4] Thus he urged that Brother-doctor relationships be limited to professional contact,[5] and that women visitors not be allowed to remain overnight in the patient rooms because such a practice "disrupts monastic life."[6] With a deep sense of traditional Alexian decorum, Pater Quirinus was shocked by American Brothers visiting saloons and reminded them that such practices were strictly for-

174

bidden: "Brothers must remember that they are religious people and conduct themselves accordingly."[7]

Pater Quirinus was strongly concerned about the relationships between Brothers and their superiors. Though he stressed the "goodness and necessity of obedience,"[7] he directed superiors to be sensitive to the feelings of the Brothers by couching their orders in kind terms. In order that Brothers Rector may "better know the problems, intentions etc. of the Brothers," Pater Quirinus reminded them of their duty to make daily rounds of the hospitals.[9] He said little about the Brothers' nursing apostolate other than to order the novice master to provde weekly "detailed instructions . . . in the company of the head Doctor"[10] to the novices on the care of the sick and to extol Brothers for maintaining their home-nursing component of the general apostolate.[11]

Pater Quirinus consistently prefaced his critical remarks with general approbation of the Brothers' religious life and ministry. Like his predecessor he was an avowed traditionalist but he appears to have embodied his ideals in a greater sense of compassion than did Brother Clement. His personal style of leadership included a keen sensitivity to the spiritual character of his office, which he equated with directions for communal prayer, religious decorum, and the general monastic quality of life. Pater Clement had laid the foundations for law and order, and in the process he strongly enforced his statutes on traditional monastic duties. Pater Quirinus followed suit but seems to have been more personal in the ways in which he expressed his authority. For example, during his third visitation in 1897 he was interviewed by a reporter for the *St. Louis Republican*. The article, subtitled, "A Benevolent Character," contained numerous quotes that reveal Pater Quirinus's rather cosmopolitan, easeful character.[12] Questioned on his reaction to the general conditions of the United States since his last visit (1895), the Alexian pater said, via an interpreter, that he had been in America for only one week but had been informed of the "unusual business stagnation," which, he said, was "also true in Germany. I cannot but observe the tendency of people to congregate in cities. They drift into the large cities and . . . suffer, instead of remaining on farms."[13] In spite of economic distress he was pleased with

175

the continuous progress of the Alexian hospitals. He proudly pointed out that the Alexians maintained thirteen hospitals and asylums—four in the United States, two in England, two in Belgium, and five in Germany. "Most of them are quite modern and in good condition."[14] Without distinguishing between Brothers in temporary or perpetual vows, Pater Quirinus placed the total number of Brothers at 350.[15]

The reporter's impression of the Alexian pater substantiates the view of him as a cosmopolitan, charming personality. "He is a man of broad culture and experience in charitable relief work. . . . In appearance the director general [sic] is the personification of benevolence. His face is open and beams with kindliness under a closely cut crop of iron-grey hair. He wears the regulation dress of the order, which consists of a black gown reaching down to the floor, white collar and plain leather belt."[16] Pater Clement also appears to have been very knowledgeable of the world, but he was never known as a person who "beamed with kindliness."

Of the thirteen Alexian houses in existence in 1897, the Elizabeth hospital in America, the Middlesbrough home in England, and two asylums in Germany were founded during Pater Quirinus's long tenure of office. Because of the continuous increase in vocations, particularly in Germany, the congregation had the manpower necessary for expansion. It is almost axiomatic that the vibrancy of a religious community has been traditionally evaluated on the norms of vocations and expansion. Paters Clement and Quirinus were both fortunate in that they presided over an expanding congregation matching their hopes to make the Alexian presence known. On September 16, 1886, before the end of his first year in office, Pater Quirinus wrote to the bishop of Münster seeking permission to establish an insane asylum in that ancient Catholic city of Westphalia.[17] Though the bishop welcomed the Brothers he stipulated that the Brothers should not plan the project for the city but should instead build in the countryside.[18] A Münster merchant must have been informed of the Brothers' intention, for in the spring of 1887 he offered to sell them a 175-acre estate entitled Haus Kannen.[19] The property had a rich history as a baronial estate dating from the thirteenth century.[20] The Jesuits had leased the land since

1859, maintained the farm, used the house as a recreation center for the Münster scholastics, and added a wing with a chapel. *Kulturkampf* legislation expelled the Jesuits but they were still allowed to remain as renters. However, Haus Kannen was no longer useful for the few Jesuits remaining in the area. On June 27, 1887, the Brothers purchased the land and buildings for 60,000 marks; later they paid the Jesuit Provincial, then residing in Stockholm, 18,000 marks for the furnishings. On the following September 1 Pater Quirinus and five other Brothers took possession of the property; five months later the first patient entered the new Alexian Asylum, a transfer patient from the mental-illness section of Clement Hospital, Münster.[21]

From the outset Haus Kannen was conceived as a large, modern institution. The asylum's chief physician, Dr. Dereken, was a major force in promoting the institution among the political authorities, particularly the provincial administration in Münster. With the devolution of *Kulturkampf*, the civil authority even assumed part of the interest payments on Haus Kannen's indebtedness, which reached 246,000 marks in 1906. In a beautiful pastoral setting within a few miles of Münster, Haus Kannen experienced a rapid growth. It developed along the lines of other Alexian institutions with its own blacksmith, carpentry shop, and bakery. But because of its large farm it appears to have been the most self-sufficient of all the Alexian asylums. By its twenty-fifth year—1912—it housed 370 patients cared for by forty-five Brothers. The following newspaper account, taken from the September 29, 1912, edition of *Westphalen Merkur*, highlights significant events that characterized the asylum's rich history.[22]

Twenty-five years have elapsed since the Alexian Community took over the former little Jesuit convent at Amelsbueren in order to exercise also here, in addition to their numerous foundations at home and abroad, the care and nursing of the mentally ill of the male sex without respect to their class or religion. Already after two years the original convent proved to be too small owing to the admission of so many insane. This was a proof that the Religious Brothers enjoyed universal confidence, not only of the State and Communal authorities, but also of those families who had been placed in the sad position of consigning their mentally ill loved ones to their provident care, who recognize as their first and principal vocation the difficult task of caring for the mentally ill, a task which not rarely endangered their own life.

From a small foundation consisting of three sick and five Brothers, a building complex with a water tower that has just been completed and can be seen all over the territory has been developed in the course of these 25 years. The building has all the modern equipment of our day, is arranged in every respect to suit its purpose and accommodates at present 370 patients and 45 Brothers. The asylum is directed medically by the medical adviser Dr. Dereken, who is assisted by the medical adviser, Dr. Weddige. The first named Psychiatrist can also look back upon an activity of 25 years, which he has spent in the service of the Community since the foundation of the Brothers at Haus Kannen, in most faithful fulfillment of his duties and with the greatest conscientiousness and devotion.

Last Sunday the celebration commemorating the founding was begun with a High Mass in the very beautiful convent-chapel which is built in Roman style. After the general congratulations, of which Dr. Dereken as Jubilarian formed the center, and while the Provincial and the House Rector expressed their heartfelt thanks for the congratulations extended to the Community, all remained as guests of the Brothers. But also the sick had been remembered in a very special way since the Alexian Brothers endeavor above all to oppose the opinion still very prevalent, that in insane asylums the days pass slowly, unhappily and without sympathy, until death puts out the spark of life. . . .

On the Jubilee day the patients received very special food as also beer, wine, and cigars; and in several wards even a little dance to music was arranged. After the close of the Day's celebration the Brothers assembled, as they are wont to do every evening in the refectory, to end the feast day in informal recreation. Thereafter came the night prayers in the chapel and the convent was again hushed in deep peace. May the many good wishes which were extended to the House from friends be realized in richest measure unto the best of suffering humanity and for the welfare of men![23]

On the eve of World War I Haus Kannen was on the territorial periphery of the Second German Province but, almost from its origin, its superb location, its stately dignity and its medieval-manor character placed it as the treasured jewel of the Alexian Congregation in Germany.

Paters Clement and Quirinus had been urged by the archbishop of Cologne, Philipp Krementz, to establish a house in Cologne or Düsseldorf. Though there had been an Alexian house in Cologne since the early fourteenth century it had, like the Aachen house in the eighteenth century, devolved into a diocesan congregation. The Cologne Brothers refused to follow the lead of Brother Dominic's reforms as they rejected the Cologne vicar general's proposal that they profess perpetual vows.[24] The Cologne Alexians appear to have been more rigidly regulated by the civil authorities than their Aachen cousins. By 1886 reforms comparable to those of Brother Dominic's in 1854 gained support among the Cologne Brothers. Indeed, their affiliate house in Neuss had professed in 1886. Complex negotiations between the diocesan and civil authorities in Berlin delayed profession of vows until 1893.[25] By that time the Aachen Alexians had been established for five years in Cologne-Lindenthal, a suburb of the ancient Rhenish city. Archbishop Krementz's request for such an institution should not be construed as a preference for the Aachen Congregation over the local Cologne Alexians. Rather, one should view it in the context of Cologne's population growth, which required expanded health care. Also the Cologne Alexians were a relatively small community, numbering around twenty-five Brothers who cared for fifty to sixty patients in the home in St. Mauritius' Parish.[26]

The Aachen Alexians, at first discouraged in their attempt to locate in the Cologne vicinity, were drawn to the city when on January 15, 1888, a Dr. Massen placed his private asylum and its surrounding nine-acre plot on sale. On February 20, 1888, the congregation purchased the property for 79,500 marks on the condition that the diocesan and civil authorities would approve the Alexian proposal to maintain an asylum there. On March 3 Archbishop Krementz gave his consent and hoped that the Brothers would also provide home nursing for the parishioners in Cologne-Lindenthal. The civil authorities also gave their approval and six Brothers under the Rector Brother Leo Domalsky moved into the small asylum which housed twenty-five patients formerly under Dr. Massen's care.[27] By 1889 a large building program was underway, one which culminated in the fall of 1890 with enough asylum space to house (by 1892) 136 patients, sixteen Brothers, and a chapel. Over the next seven years further improvements were made, but plans for expansion were obstructed by the city's development scheme, which called for streets to be paved out to the asylum.[28] In 1905 the street-development plan had been implemented to the point where the asylum's privacy was placed in jeopardy. The General Council was compelled therefore to search for a new location. In February 1904 they found a most suitable site in Ensen, a small town located above Cologne on the right bank of the Rhine. The site included nearly 120 acres but no buildings suitable for patients. The construction project began on April 1, 1905, and the asylum was finally ready for occupancy on October 21, 1908, when the patients and Brothers from Cologne-Lindenthal were transferred to Ensen. Ultimately the city of Cologne-Lindenthal bought the Brothers' property for 395,000 marks.[29] The Ensen asylum was designed on the chateau model with the impressive onion-shaped towers very similar to Chateau de Baelen at Henri Chapelle. Since the new asylum was an extremely modern facility with a 260-bed capacity (Cologne-Lindenthal could accommodate only one hundred patients) Ensen was a vast improvement. It also housed the provincialate for the Second German Province; Brother Herman Peutz, an outstanding provincial during the early twentieth century, lived there within an hour's train ride from the Aachen Motherhouse. On the eve of World War I Ensen housed thirty-four Brothers who cared for 254 patients, most of whom were mentally ill but there were many alcoholics and several drug addicts treated in the Alexian asylum.[30]

Coincidentally, the Cologne Alexians moved to Cologne-Lindenthal shortly before the Aachen Alexians transferred their asylum to Ensen. In 1894 after years of struggle both within the community and with the ecclesiastical and civil authorities, the Cologne Alexians professed the three principal vows. The Cologne counterpart to Brother Dominic Brock, Brother Mathias Gilles, was the superior most instrumental in preparing the way for the profession of vows. Though he died three years before the profession ceremony, the latter was celebrated as a triumph for him.[31] On May 10, 1894, thirteen Cologne Brothers professed the vow of poverty, which had been proscribed during the French occupation and the 1826 statutes. Because perpetual vows had to be preceded by five-year vows, it was not until September 30, 1900, that fifteen Cologne Brothers professed perpetual vows. By this time the Cologne civil authorities had notified the community that they must move from their hospice in St. Mauritius Parish. The city's decision was ostensibly the compromise product of long-standing negotiations in which the Cologne Alexians attempted to free themselves from the controls of the civil authorities. The latter contended that the Brothers held the property and the service to the city as a privilege granted by the city and that they should be accountable to the secular authority. The Brothers cited their historic ties to the ecclesiastical authority dating back to the late Middle Ages.[32] It seems as if both sides had valid points due to the nature of the medieval city-welfare establishment, which was infused with both a secular and a religious sense of duty. In examining which authority had provided more sustenance to the Cologne Alexians, the secular was by far the more prominent. However, because the modern nineteenth-century welfare establishment was not infused with a strong sense of religious duty, in the then-current negotiations the ecclesiastical authority was a more prominent source of sustenance.[33]

The compromise whereby the city was willing to give up its power of control clearly illustrates its purely secular motivation. It would allow the Brothers to be placed entirely under ecclesiastical authority on condition that the Brothers turn over their property to the city along with an additional 350,000 marks as compensation for its support over the centuries. The compromise reached its legal culmination in 1899.[34] Anticipating their eventual withdrawal from the property, the Cologne Alexians acquired a six-and-one-half acre site for a new institution in Cologne-Lindenthal.[35] Unlike the asylum character of their hospice, the new institution, which was ready for occupancy in January 1901, was a large general hospital.[36] Because the Cologne Brothers had been engaged in general nursing in homes of the sick, this was not a drastic break from tradition. However, in 1851 their hospice had been listed as one of the "Public Institutions for the Insane in Prussia" with nine incurable patients.[37] Their "affiliate" house in Neuss, which became a large asylum in the latter half of the nineteenth century, was also listed as caring for twenty-five incurable patients.[38] When the Cologne Alexians established a general hospital in Cologne-Lindenthal they were, therefore, not in competition with the

Aachen Brothers who maintained an asylum there until 1905.

As indicated in the preceding chapter, the Aachen Alexians under Pater Clement had attempted to liberate their institutions from controls by the Poverty Administration. Perhaps the Cologne Brothers' achievement of this goal in 1893 encouraged the Aachen Brothers to once again pursue their independence from civil authorities. However, it was not until 1897 that Pater Quirinus successfully negotiated a settlement. On September 18, 1897, three days after he had personally presented his case to Mayor Weltmann of Aachen, Pater Quirinus wrote to him:

> Referring to the negotiation hitherto carried on between the city and the Alexian Community concerning the rights over the local Alexian convent, I now take the liberty to make the following proposal, namely, that the city of Aachen renounced rights to the Alexian Convent and also to all other property belonging to it, so that in future the community alone will have the right of its free disposal, whilst the Alexian Community will pay the city 40,000 marks indemnity.[39]

On March 10, 1898, the city, after convincing Pater Quirinus that the indemnity sum should be 50,000 marks, officially renounced all rights of control over the administration and properties of the Aachen Alexians.[40] After ninety-five years of subservience to the French and then the Prussian authorities, the Aachen Brothers gained their autonomy at a relatively small cost compared with the 350,000-mark indemnity paid by the Cologne Brothers.

The major disappointment during Pater Quirinus's tenure of office was the 1896 sale of Mariaberg, which was considered the model asylum of the province. Mariaberg was founded in 1878 and became the largest Alexian institution, reaching in 1893 an occupancy of 650 patients. Pater Quirinus had supported the expansion of Mariaberg in spite of the fact that the city's development scheme, introduced in 1889, threatened to intersect the property with streets.[41] Though the implementation of the street scheme was ostensibly responsible for the sale of the institution, Pater Quirinus and his General Council might have struggled to maintain control had it not been for a vastly publicized scandal that cast a shadow of suspicion upon the Alexians in general and Mariaberg in particular.

The scandal erupted with the 1895 publication of a pamphlet authored by a Freemason, a Mr. Mellage of Iserkoln, Westphalia, and a renegade priest (Father X) who had lived for six weeks as an alcoholic patient in the Mariaberg asylum. Brother Ignatius Wiegers described the pamphlet as "containing the most disgraceful caricatures" of the Alexian Brothers.[42] The authors wrote a spurious "exposé" of Mariaberg as a house of utter cruelty. The pamphlet's notoriety, locally charged by Freemason lodges in the Aachen area and other places of anticlericalism, resulted in an investigation of Mariaberg. Subsequently Aachen's prosecuting attorney filed charges of libelous slander against Mellage and those associated with the pamphlet's publication. Brother Pius Welter, provincial rector of the First Province, lodged a civil charge against them.[43] Perhaps the jury was deeply influenced by the climate of anti-Catholic opinion, for in June 1895 the court declared Mellage et al. innocent and accused two Brothers of perjury. However, since the presiding judge had been a grand master of the Aachen Freemason Lodge, as had one of the chief witnesses for the defense, and since the judge allowed testimony from mentally ill patients who were later proven to be hallucinating, the court was clearly biased against the Alexians.[44] The tables were turned in a subsequent trial (October 1895) in which the two Brothers accused of perjury were declared innocent of all charges. After the first trial the German government initiated a meticulous investigation of all asylums in the Rhineland and Westphalia, the results of which completely cleared the Alexians of all suspicion. Indeed, it held that the Alexian asylum in Krefeld was a model institution.[45] The mayor of Aachen, who had never been a close friend of the Alexians, wrote in May 1875

> that the investigations ordered by the courts have no other positive results, save the complete lack of support of the accusations of unlawful incarceration and mistreatment of the sick, and that in the asylum of Mariaberg only minor irregularities had been found, as would certainly be found in all other institutions of a like nature.[46]

The Aachen Alexians had suffered grave injustices and public ridicule during this encounter with the forces of anticlericalism. Father X and Mellage, once considered popular heroes, soon fell from grace; the former's alcoholism became acute and he died in a convent, the latter was shot to death during the heat of an argument with his lawyer.[47]

This story of the Mariaberg scandal is derived from Brother Ignatius Wiegers's book on the Aachen Alexians. Because he does not delve deeply into the cause of the Brothers' sale of the asylum the story becomes equivocal at that point. Apparently the Poverty Administration, which was still playing a supervisory role during the scandal, advised the General Council to lease the asylum. Ostensibly the immediate cause for the sale was the implementation of the 1889 street-development scheme but, since the Brothers sold the asylum to the city of Aachen for 850,000 marks on July 1, 1896, the city did not view the street scheme as a hindrance to maintaining the asylum.[48] It appears, therefore, that either the scandal so affected the reputation of Mariaberg that the Brothers unloaded a heavy burden, or the city took advantage of its authority over the asylum and pressured the Brothers to sell. Nevertheless, the Brothers must have departed from Mariaberg with ambivalent feelings; Mariaberg, the model Alexian institution, had lost its public glamour, but the Brothers could hardly forget their strong attachment to their most modern asylum. Indeed the 850,000-mark price for Mariaberg indicates the asylum's vast size and its modern facilities. Less than a year later (April 1897) the Brothers purchased twenty-five acres of farming land just outside Aachen as compensation for the loss of their farm attached to Mariaberg. Eventually they added to the acreage and built a small residence and chapel for patients and Brothers who together farmed and managed the land.[49] It was not an asylum but, rather, a "family" farm whose produce today still supplies the dining tables of the patients and Brothers at the asylum on Alexianergraben.

During Pater Quirinus's term of office a few constitutional changes occurred which illustrate the gradual modernization of the Alexians. In 1891, upon the order of the Congregation of Bishops and Religious, temporary professed Brothers could attend and vote at chapter meetings.[50] Though one may logically infer that this rule could have eventuated in an injection of youthful idealism into the chapter meetings, there is no evidence to support such an inference. The decisions of the four

General Chapters held between 1891 and 1906 also reveal certain modern features. To provide for greater accountability in 1891 the chapter resolved that a Brother could not be both provincial and house rector, that a Brother could not be both a house consultor and a provincial consultor and that when the rector-general appoints Brothers to a house he must first seek his assistant's advice.[51] A practice which has recently been revived was also made a part of the statutes in 1891: an aspirant should spend time working in one or more of the houses for four months before entering the novitiate. Recognizing the need for professionalism the chapter of 1891 allowed superiors to hire lay secretaries but they were not to be concerned with monastery matters. Education was a consistent concern of the chapters. In 1891 educational lectures were encouraged at evening recreation, and in 1896 novice masters were directed to provide for regular catechetical instructions by a priest.[52]

Pater Quirinus not only negotiated the congregation's independence from civil authorities but was influential in promoting the congregation's release from its dependence on its ordinary in Cologne. Though by receiving the status of a papally exempt institute in 1870 the Alexians were free from their ordinary's jurisdiction, German-papal relations and the *Kulturkampf* influenced the Congregation of Bishops and Religious to appoint the archbishop of Cologne as visitator in 1873.[53] After the Mariaberg incident had terminated in the Brothers' favor, Pater Quirinus successfully appealed to Rome for a new cardinal protector who, besides having visitation rights, would act as the Brothers' liaison with the papacy. In 1899 the papal secretary of state appointed Andreas Cardinal Stienhuber, a German Jesuit, as the protector of the Alexians, symbolizing the final culmination of the Aachen Alexians as a papal congregation.[54]

Except for the unfortunate Mariaberg incident, Pater Quirinus presided over the continuously smooth expansion and modern development of the Alexian Brothers. Haus Kannen and Ensen in Germany, Twyford Abbey in England, and Elizabeth in the United States were founded during his long and prosperous term of office. So popular was this pater among the chapter delegates that in 1901 he was voted into office for a fourth term, an action requiring the prior approval of Rome.[55]

In 1906 Brother Paul Overbeck was elected rector-general and Brother Quirinus his first assistant; once again by referring to the reports of the pater's visitation in the American Province, one may perceive his attitudes toward the Alexian way of life. After touring the province Pater Paul wrote a circular letter to all the Brothers during his final stop at Elizabeth before his return to Aachen. Dated July 14, 1910, the letter opened with an exhortation to those Brothers who "have maintained a proper and fruitful life to pray for those weaker Brothers who find life in the order difficult."[56] Pater Paul was particularly concerned with the proprieties relating to the Brothers when they leave the house. They were ordered to wear religious garb, not to be taking pleasure trips or "going to places of amusement of any kind, to notify Superiors when going on and returning from an outside visit and to have an escort on all such visitations."[57] Pater Paul then listed nine more directives, including such general remarks as demanding obedience to the rules of the order and attendance at prayer and meditation. The remaining seven included specific orders: weekly house cleaning, supervision and control of the kitchen to guarantee proper diets according to patients' needs, prohibition of all games involving winning money, allowing occasional visits of outsiders during evening recreation, forbidding "light jokes lest the authority of the superior be evaded," prohibition of all discussion of house or order matters between Brothers and the laity, and a reminder to all superiors that they are accountable to God.[58] Pater Paul seems to have been more in the tradition of Brother Clement than his predecessor, Brother Quirinus. All three shared the same values but Paul and Clement placed a heavier stress upon a thorough rationalization of the monastic life than did Brother Quirinus.

Pater Paul was reelected rector-general at the 1911 chapter. The most significant item of new business for the delegates to that chapter was the rewriting of the constitution in order to place the statutes within the new Vatican directives on canon law for religious. In the constituion *Conditae a Christo* (December 8, 1900) Pope Leo XIII clarified the relationships between religious congregations, both diocesan and papal, and their ordinaries.[59] Because of the vast proliferation of religious institutes, each of which sought papal approval, the Sacred

Congregation of Bishops and Regulars introduced a guide for drawing up a constitution for the intended use of the founders and their ordinaries. Published on June 28, 1901, this guide listed the "Norms [rules] usually followed by the Sacred Congregation of Bishops and Regulars in the approval of new institutes with simple vows."[60] It did not bind religious by law, as it was merely advisory. The second part was a model constitution for religious congregations in accord with the then current attitudes of the papacy.[61]

The process of updating the constitution entailed engaging a specialist in canon law, consulting with those congregations whose constitutions had recently been approved by Rome, establishing a commission to formulate the revised statutes, and finally submitting them to the Holy See for its approbation.[62] After consulting with the Brothers of Mercy and the Franciscan Brothers, and after the canon-law specialist, Father Corbinian Wirtz, o.s.b., of Merkelbeck Abbey had drawn up a rough draft, a commission was convened on February 13, 1913. This commission was composed of representatives from each of the four provinces: Pater Paul Overbeck, former Pater Quirinus Bank, American Provincial Alexius Jansen, and the first American-born Brother, Novice-Master Cyprian Goesser; English Provincial Remigius Kochaneck, and an English-born Brother, Gilbert Holmes; Brother Leopole Elfrath of Haus Kannen and Brother Felix Jamers from Lierre, Belgium. After twelve sessions the new constitution was ready for papal consideration. As the result of a March 19, 1913, decision by the General Council, Pater Paul and his assistant, Brother Ludolf Niessen, traveled to Rome to present the new statutes to the Holy See personally. After the statutes had been translated into Italian, a task Pater Paul had not foreseen, they were approved on June 13, 1913. Before leaving Rome the Pater and his assistant received an audience with the Pope in which Pius X extended his pontifical blessing upon the Alexian Congregation.[63] The Alexians were abundantly grateful that the arduous constitution-revision process had achieved a successful culmination and that for the second time in their over six-hundred-year history an Alexian Brother had met with the Pope.

The 1913 constitution was not an extensive revision of the

1870 document. The new statutes were placed in a more logically developed scheme and their syntax was noticeably improved. Indeed, in comparing the 1870 "The End of the Congregation" with the 1913 "Object of the Congregation," one will note the impact of modernization upon the Brothers' self-image.[64] Instead of "care of sick persons" the 1913 document reads "nursing the sick"; in place of "directing institutions for the insane, the feeble, or other destitute persons of the male sex," one finds "Management of mental hospitals."[65] Because 8the Brothers in England did not manage hospitals but, rather, hospices for elderly men, the 1913 constitution included as one of the congregation's objects the management "of homes for the aged."[66] The regulations on Alexian deportment and the principal religious guidelines for nursing the sick in homes and in hospitals and asylums, the care of cemeteries, etc., did not undergo any substantial changes from the 1870 statutes other than an improvement in syntax. The daily schedule also remained the same with the exception that the 1913 rule gave the Brothers an additional half hour of sleep in the morning, until 5:00 A.M. [67]

According to Pater Paul Overbeck's circular letter to all the Alexian houses, which was intended to highlight the changes, two new statutes were most significant: when a professed Brother leaves the community he does so *quam singulare* (i.e., on his own), and after a Brother has professed temporary or perpetual vows he can have no say over his wealth or his beneficiary.[68] Pater Paul also clarified those statutes forbidding a Brother to occupy two important offices, i.e., rector and novice master, simultaneously, and he informed the Brothers of the appointment of Brother Ludolf Niessen and Brother Antonius Murelle as secretary general and procurator general respectively.[69] These were new offices, which symbolized the updating of the Alexian Congregation. Since the 1870 constitution, which was a refinement of the 1859 document, the General Council's responsibility had greatly expanded; it had to pass on complex measures involving many asylums in Germany, hospitals in the United States and nursing homes in England.

The secretary general's responsibility included establishing files for all deeds and documents relating "to the affairs and management of the Congregation," taking the council minutes, and writing all business letters for the congregation.[70] The procurator general was directed to administer "all personal and real estate belonging to the whole congregation."[71] According to the administrative chart, the office of procurator general was a staff rather than a line position, i.e., administrative duties without policy-making authority, which was lodged in the council. He was ordered to present the books to the General Council for approval every six months. All valuable papers and cash were to be stored in a safe which, to guarantee security, was to be opened with three keys belonging to the rector general, one of his assistants, and the procurator general. On the provincial level procurators were to be appointed, while rectors fulfilled that responsibility on the local level.[72] The heavily centralized character of the authority structures was expanded by the 1913 constitution; each house rector was directed to hand over one-third of his balance in cash to the rector-general and one-third to the provincial rector. In turn the provincial was to hand over all surplus cash to the rector-general, whose treasury would subsidize all major renovation and building projects on the local level.[73]

The 1913 rules governing the spiritual formation of the Brothers, which were contained in the chapter "Compulsory Prayers and Other Devotional Exercises"[74] included only one innovation. According to the then recent directive from the papacy, the Brothers were encouraged to receive Holy Communion frequently.[75] The general tone of all those regulations, which together portray the ideal Alexian Brother, was merely a further elaboration of the basic principles embodied in Pater Clement Wallrath's earlier constitution.

The modernization of the Brothers' institutions was not solely the product of the Alexian drive for rationalization and efficiency. From the last quarter of the nineteenth century to the present the state had assumed an increasingly expansive role as the author and monitor of hospital standards. In 1907 the Berlin government issued regulations on the training and examination of nurses.[76] In 1910 Pater Paul, pressed by this ordinance and realizing that the former methods of training, in which the young Brothers were instructed at bedside by older Brothers and the medical staff, were outdated, purchased land near the Krefeld Asylum for the establishment of a small hospital specifically intended as a training center for the Brothers.[77] After encountering delays in receiving permission from church and civil authorities, the seventy-bed hospital was completed in the summer of 1914. The Minister of the Interior approved the training school on the condition that it provide a one-year course according to the law, and he also granted permission to hold state examinations there. Shortly after the opening of the Krefeld hospital, Maria-Hilf (Mary's Help), plans to begin nursing classes were postponed as the hospital was almost completely immersed in the care of wounded soldiers from the then most cataclysmic of all wars, World War I.[78]

The shock of World War I reverberated throughout the Alexian Congregation. Thirty-seven German Brothers were drafted as combatants; fifteen Brothers volunteered as military nurses, attached to the Knights of Malta, a papal confraternity. The direct lines of communication from the Motherhouse to the British Province were immediately broken.[79] Pater Paul wrote that in spite of "the gloomy shadows cast over our congregation by the war . . . our distressed hearts lift up to God in cheerful thanks" for the strong character of those Brothers who were combatants on the front.[80] He proudly informed the American Alexians that three Brothers received the Iron Cross, five were promoted to lance corporal, and many had received "praise for their works from the highest quarters."[81] In turn these Brothers praised the soldiers for their respectful behavior. One Brother wrote from the front that Catholic and Protestant soldiers pray the rosary each day, which led Pater Paul to conclude: "In general the religious awakening of the army, like our own *volk*, [is] an unappreciated and pleasant fact in these pressing times."[82]

By 1916, 128 of the 250 German Brothers were absorbed in the war effort: fifty were on the front, twenty-four were in military hospitals and the remainder were nursing soldiers in Alexian institutions.[83] Pater Paul's New Year's circular letter of 1916 bears the imprint of eighteen months of wartime suffering. With the Motherhouse located at one of the major crossroads to and from the Western Front, Pater Paul had a clear view of the horrors. As a deeply religious person immersed in the gross indignities of the conflict, Pater Paul urged the Brothers to model themselves after Job: "Man born of woman, living for a short time, is filled with many miseries."[84] Recognizing that men "easily recoil from suffering" he exhorted the Brothers to accept willingly "the difficulties of daily life. The present time makes man depressed and ill humored. We can find consolation only in our divine model and in our holy Religion."[85] He directed all Alexians to offer to God all "corporal sufferings and difficulties . . . the annoyances caused by the sick, all the little crosses of Religious life, all the privations brought on by the war, . . . in order that He curtail the present affliction."[86]

In 1916 the American Brothers, who numbered approximately one hundred professed Brothers, temporarily remote from the European conflagration, celebrated the Golden Jubilee of the province's first hospital in Chicago. The English Province, however, was completely severed from direct contact with the Motherhouse. In 1914 the British Province numbered twenty-seven professed Brothers, six novices, and six postulants. According to Pater Paul's 1920 report on the activity of the congregation during the war years, three German Brothers at Twyford Abbey were conscripted into the German army, and three German Brothers, at Twyford Abbey and one at St. Mary's Home, Manchester, were placed in an internment camp on the Isle of Man.[87]

Brother Remigius Kochanek, the English provincial who had been rector at Oshkosh and other American houses, wrote to the American provincial, Brother Alexius Jansen, about his experiences during the war:

> As a result of the war, some Brothers have left the Order and there are now no postulants. Hence you can imagine in what a predicament we are, and all the more so, since one cannot get reliable workers even at a maximum salary . . . all hands (secular help) are gone either to Ireland or to the Army. . . . Moreover, our houses are filled to capacity with the sick. Everything is very expensive. . . . The Brothers are exempt from military service.[88]

Since many Brothers were from Ireland, the Easter Rebellion of 1916 compounded the troubles of the Brothers in England.

The Belgian houses of the German Province, Henri Chapelle and Lierre, were in the path of the German army's first attack in August 1914. Henri Chapelle's location, a few miles from the German border, allowed her to dwell in relative peace as the German army rapidly seized the area. Besides billeting soldiers and suffering some slight damage, the house experienced little wartime suffering.[89]

According to the German army's vantage point, Lierre was strategically situated along the line of attack leading to the great commercial center of Antwerp. Twelve Brothers and thirty mentally ill pensioners resided at the Alexian hospice. With the outbreak of hostilities the German Brothers had fled to the Motherhouse. The siege of Lierre, which began in late September 1914, eventually drove the remaining Belgian Alexians and their patients to seek shelter in Antwerp, but because of a lack of accommodations they gradually made their way to Oudenbosch, North Brabant, where they were cordially welcomed at the Elizabeth Institute. By mid-November when Pater Paul and Brother Ludolf visisted Lierre, the Alexians and fifteen patients had returned to find their house badly damaged by the war and many of their belongings looted by the German soldiers.[90] Fortunately one part of the building remained to house the Brothers and patients. Their terrifying experiences precluded calm living until peace was declared. In January of 1915, total damages to the Lierre hospice were valued at 57,276.80 Belgian francs.[91]

Wartime scarcity affected the German Brothers most severely. Rationing imposed great hardships upon the Brothers and patients at those hospitals without large farms, such as München-Gladbach. To illustrate the intense inflation spiral during the war, Pater Paul included a price chart comparing 1914 and 1916 in his report, which contained such items as coffee, which rose from 95 marks per hundred pounds to 315 marks and bacon from 65 to 300 marks.[92]

When the Allied advance gained momentum in 1918 as a result of the large influx of American soldiers, the German army retreated through the vicinity of Aachen. Fearing that their valuables would be tempting booty for the Allied soldiers, the General Council decided (October 8, 1918) to transfer all the Brothers' precious church articles and their treasured documents to Haus Kannen for safekeeping.[93] By this time the German government, confronted with the imminent collapse of its army in retreat, and with antiwar ferment at home, had pursued an armistice through a Berlin-Washington communiqué. President Wilson replied that an armistice could be realized only if German autocracy gave way to a more democratic government. On October 9, 1918, Wilson issued his famous Fourteen Points program for peace. Though the German government initiated moderate reforms as a peace gesture, the advancing Allied forces and revolutions within so fractured Germany that the government fell and was replaced by a coalition of parties representing the forces of democracy and peace. On November 11 the German delegates signed the armistice terms submitted by the French Allied Commander, General Foch. After four years of history's most disastrous war, in which approximately 10 million died and 20 million were wounded, came to a close.

An extensive report on the impact of the war upon the Alexian Congregations, written by Pater Paul Overbeck, contains the following statistics, which reveal the enormous nursing role of the Brothers during the conflagration:

1) 86 Brothers fought on the front, 13 of whom "met a hero's death," 11 were wounded, 15 suffered illness on the front and 11 were captured by the Allies.
2) 6 Brothers were military nurses for the reserves behind the lines and 5 served in the military hospital in Germany.
3) 24 Brothers nursed in four field hospitals which, from 1914–1919, housed 11,832 wounded and mentally ill soldiers.
4) By the end of the war 36 Brothers nursed mentally ill soldiers in the Alexian asylums at Aachen, Ensen, München-Gladbach, Krefeld (Maria-Hilf) and Haus Kannen. Throughout the war 12,276 soldiers were cared for by the Brothers in the asylums with total nursing days totaling 559,760.[94]

Also the brothers distributed tens of thousands of pounds of bread and thousands of noon meals to the wartime poor, "a holy responsibility," wrote Pater Paul.[95]

Of the several testimonials on the Brothers' wartime nursing efforts, that of Father Raymond Dreiling, O.F.M., the commandant of one of the military hospitals, is typical:

Everybody here knows and acknowledges that the local Alexian Brothers have cared for the psychiatric divisions of the military hospital VII, the most difficult branch of all therapeutics, and by their faithful, unselfish activity have achieved most glorious results.[96]

The Antwerp Alexians, who settled in Boechout in 1876, remained a small family of Brothers and patients. Between 1876 and 1914 the number of professed Brothers never exceeded seventeen.[97] Though the number of patients more than doubled during this period, reaching a high of ninety-one in 1910, the Boechout Hospital never experienced the rationalization so characteristic of those asylums attached to the Aachen Motherhouse. Brother Damien Stayaert, an expert on Alexian history, reports that until far into the twentieth century each patient was assigned to a Brother rather than to a ward. This very personal Brother-patient relationship remained intact even when a patient was transferred from one ward to another. In most of the Belgian houses the Brothers dined with the patients. A strong family spirit prevailed but the Brothers were directed to maintain a respectful formality toward their patients, illustrated by addressing each patient as "Mister" rather than with the familiar first name. The Boechout Brothers expanded their ministry when, in 1907, they founded a tubercular-care hospital in Son. Located in the south of the Netherlands, this foundation marked the first reestablishment of the Alexians in the Dutch Protestant state since the Reformation. Like their original ministry to plague victims, the Alexian response to the tubercular exiles represented a ministry to the outsider. Though the Boechout and Son hospitals were well respected for their quality of care, in contrast to the large asylums attached to the Aachen Congregation they appear to have been a remnant of the medieval Cellite family.

The Boechout community was not seriously threatened during the war. Because many of the Brothers were citizens of the Netherlands, the flag of that neutral nation was flown over the Boechout Hospital. Forty-six patients, with a collective passport and a handful of Dutch Brothers, traveled to the Alexian Tubercular Hospital in Son where they remained until the end of the war. Only five Brothers and eighteen patients stayed at Boechout. Though the latter suffered many wartime discomforts, in contrast to the Lierre community they were quite fortunate.

The postwar Alexians did not evidence great disillusionment with their traditions in the General Chapter of 1920. On the contrary, because their religious observances had suffered dur-

194

ing the war, the General Chapter strongly urged all superiors and Brothers to regenerate their lives according to the traditional statutes and customs of the congregation. From Pater Paul's second circular letter (Autumn 1919) in preparation for the first postwar General Chapter, it is evident that he was, at best, moderately apprehensive about convening delegates from the former enemy nations, England, United States, Belgium, and Germany. By this time the victorious states at the Versailles Peace Conference had declared Germany totally responsible for the outbreak of war. Pater Paul must have been deeply worried that nationalistic attitudes of the Brothers might engender severe ruptures at the General Chapter of 1920. He wrote: "All Superiors and Brothers must mutually work together, that the wounds of this terrible war which has struck our Congregation, and at the General Chapter, the elected Deputies may work together with fraternal love, for the good of our Congregation and that these wounds may be healed."[98]

When the delegates met on April 21, 1920, the chapter elected Brother Alexius Jansen rector-general; Brother Paul Overbeck was elected as first assistant, a practice which originated with Clement Wallrath's election as first assistant after his terms of office had expired.[99] Two other members of the new council had served as provincial or on the previous council. Indeed, since the 1870s the circulation of Brothers through the entire authority structure occurred along the chain of command: superior, provincial, or novice master, general council, rector-general. Though this guaranteed continuity and the preservation of tradition, it did not encourage innovation. As the first American-based Brother to be elected rector-general and the first not to have had prior leadership experience in Germany, Brother Alexius represented a slight departure from traditional practices. One measure passed by the General Chapter, which directly involved the new rector-general, was a strong break with tradition; "it is herewith permitted to admit coloured candidates and to admit them into the Brotherhood of the American Province."[100]

Immediately prior to the General Chapter, a black youth from Trinidad wrote to the American novice master seeking permission to enter the Alexians. He was advised to meet with Brother Alexius, who was at the Elizabeth house on his way to the General Chapter. Without hesitation the soon-to-be-elected pater consented to the youth's appeal. Brother Hilarion Pencheon, the first black Alexian Brother, professed temporary vows in 1922 and after serving in many posts—X-ray technician, novice master, secretary general—is currently the superior general's secretary at the American Motherhouse, Signal Mountain, Tennessee.[101]

One chapter resolution was implicitly intended to heal the wounds of war: "The interchanging of American and German Brothers is hereby recommended."[102] The decline in vocations as a result of the outbreak of war prompted the delegates to resolve that all the Brothers should promote vocations "with all their means."[103] To achieve the expansion of the congregation, the chapter recommended "the nursing of the poor in private houses."[104] With modern vocation-recruitment procedures yet to be designed, the Brothers fell back upon their traditional home-nursing apostolate as the most feasible way of reaching out to the youth. Such contact came only in the American Province with its general hospitals; the English and German Brothers's hospice and asylum work prevented them from frequent contact with the public. Hence home nursing was considered a valuable asset for recruiting vocations. However, nursing the poor in their homes was not the general trend of the day, as most in-home hursing patients tended to be relatively affluent laymen and clergymen. The chapter's concern for the poor may have resulted from the discernment that by following the congregation's most traditional ministry, that to the poor, the Brothers would naturally attract vocations.

Other than the resolution to accept black candidates, the only modern feature of the chapter's resolutions was the strong endorsement to ground all novices in a solid education in both the religious life and nursing. The remainder of the resolutions by the chapter underscored the importance of the constitution and the traditional customs in the formation of the ideal Alexian Brother.

At the end of one of mankind's most disastrous wars, the general mood was to seek confidence and security in the old prewar precepts. There were several intellectuals, artists, and statesmen who realized the impossibility of satisfying the recreation of the past; they were of course correct. The Alexian Brothers reflected the dominant mood by stressing the need for a strong retrieval of the fundamental traditions of the congregation, those ideals so explicitly enunciated by Paters Clement Wallrath and Dominic Brock: austere monastic discipline and continuous modernization of the Alexian institutions.

These ideals were mediated differently in each of the cultures. The German Alexians' asylum apostolate, their Old World authoritarianism, their bitter encounters with stringent anticlericalism, and the *Kulturkampf* urged them to draw clear lines of demarcation between their religious life and the dangerous character of the secular world. During its formative years, the American Province experienced a conflict between Old World traditions and frontier innovations. Though the German customs dominated the American scene, providing a strong sense of discipline, order, and hard work, the German-American character of the Province developed along distinctive lines. Their general-hospital ministry was enthusiastically supported by Catholic immigrants and, in contrast to the German *Kulturkampf*, the American climate, though containing the winds of anticlericalism, did not appear threatening to the religious life. If the Aachen Motherhouse projected a remote, stately image, the Chicago provincialate projected a youthful, self-confident, and socially engaged image. The German and the German-American Brothers outlined their day according to the same statutes, but American culture with its informality, its buoyant optimism, and its rapidly accelerating pace of social change was imposing a distinctive imprint upon Alexians of the New World.

In contrast to the strongly institution-bound character of the other provinces, the British perpetuated the ancient Cellite traditions, the burial and hospice ministries. The German-Anglo-Irish character of the province, which dwelt in a society permeated with anti-Catholic and anti-Irish attitudes, compelled the Brothers to form a sort of enclave existence. Barred from the state-regulated nursing profession and from establishing an asylum, the Brothers in England eked out a meager existence in their cemeteries and hospices. With only twenty-nine Brothers in 1918, they appeared as missionary Alexians. Though circumstance compelled them to dwell very close to the ancient

Cellite burial and hospice ministries, they were no doubt self-conscious of their modest institutional growth and their quiet Alexian witness. Twyford Abbey was a stately residence but it bore neither the German marks of modernization nor the American spirit of buoyant self-confidence. The German imprint was visible in each of the provinces, but gradually the distinctive characters developed. This was not a continuously smooth process: depression, Nazism, and war profoundly affected the general Alexian life and tradition as well as the distinctive characters of each of the provinces.

PART THREE

✚

STRUGGLE
WITH MODERNITY,
1920-1970

The Alexian Motherhouse in Aachen, 1885

Henri-Chapelle, ca. 1950

Krefeld, 1883

München Gladbach, 1928

Haus Kannen, near Münster, ca. 1950

Ensen, near Cologne, ca. 1950

Pater Dominic Brock, Reformer
and Founder of the modern
Alexian Congregation

Brother Bonaventure Thelen,
Founder of the American Province

Pater Clement Wallrath, First
Rector General, 1860-1886

The First Chicago Hospital, 1866

The Belden Avenue Hospital in Chicago, ca. 1910

St. Louis Hospital, 1905

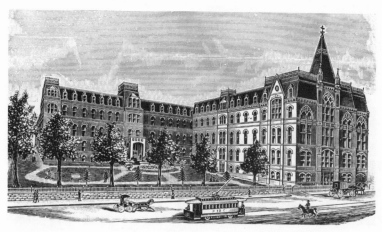

Oshkosh, Wisconsin,
ca. 1912

Elizabeth, New Jersey,
1892

Elizabeth, New Jersey,
ca. 1895

St. Joseph's Cemetery, ca. 1955

St. Mary's Home, Manchester, ca. 1955

Sacred Heart Home, Middlesbrough, ca. 1895

Pater Quirinus Bank, Second
Rector General, 1886-1906

Pater Paulus Overbeck, Third
Rector General, 1906-1920

Schänis, Switzerland, ca. 1930

Schloss Malseneck

Mt. St. Columb's, Warrenpoint, Northern Ireland, 1955

Stillington Hall, York, England, ca. 1935

Signal Mountain, Tenn.

Pater Frumentius Horn, Fifth
Rector General, 1932-1938

Pater Alexius Jansen, Fourth
Rector General, 1920-1932

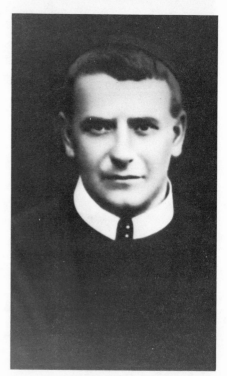

Pater Gilbert Holmes, Sixth
Rector General, 1938-1946

The Novitiate, Cobh, Ireland, 1977

The Novitiate, Gresham, Wisconsin, ca. 1955

The School of Nursing, Chicago, ca. 1965

San Jose, California,
1977

Elk Grove Village,
Illinois, 1977

Elizabeth, New Jersey, 1977

St. Louis, Missouri, 1977

St. Mary's Home, Manchester, England, 1977

Mount St. Columb's, Warrenpoint, Northern Ireland, 1977

Twyford Abbey, London, 1977

The Hostel for the Poor and Destitute, Limerick, Ireland, 1977

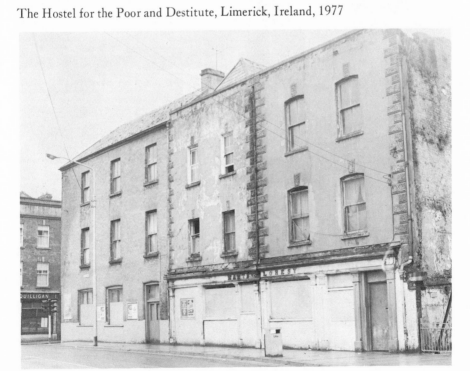

Pater Ludolf Sattler, Eighth
Rector General, 1952-1958

Pater Anthony Wessel, Seventh
Rector General, 1946-1952

Pater Melchoir Wimmer, Ninth
Rector General, 1958-1962

The delegates to the General Chapter, Aachen, 1969

The delegates to the General Chapter, Signal Mountain, 1974

The Bush Clinic

Brothers Mark, Dominic and Vianney, the pioneer Alexians in Nigeria, locate the area near Minnia, where their Bush Clinic was established.

Pater Ludolf Sattler and Brother Florian Eberle (left to right from Pope Pius XII) at the Vatican

Brother Felix Bettendorf, Superior General, and his Assistant, Brother Edmund Kelly (in the background), chat with Pope Paul VI

Alexian Brothers and their patients enjoy a *sommerfest* in the gardens of the hospital, Aachen, 1975.

Brother Felix Bettendorf, Eleventh
Superior General, 1968-1974

Brother Herman Joseph Berkes,
Tenth Superior General, 1962-1968

Brother Augustine Lohman, Twelfth
Superior General, 1974-

Boechout

Grimbergen

Henri-Chapelle

12

Postwar Adaptation

I

Postwar Germany was economically depressed, socially dislocated, psychologically disillusioned, and politically disjointed. The Allies occupied the Rhineland, managed the coal mines in the Saar, limited the German army and navy to a token force, blamed the entire war on Germany, and subsequently burdened her with heavy reparations. The Weimar Republic arose from the ashes of the defeat of the German Empire. Though constitutionally it was governed democratically, strong remnants of Imperial Germany persisted to form an authoritarian shadow enshrouding the republic. In 1923 gradual economic recovery was halted by galloping inflation due to Germany's anti-French policy by which it printed money to subsidize the anti-French workers in the Saar valley.[1] By the autumn of 1923 one American dollar was valued at 4.2 trillion marks. Because the Alexian houses in Henri Chapelle and Lierre were German-owned, they were subjected to the threat of confiscation in early 1919. Though these houses were temporarily accountable to the Belgian authorities, the Aachen Motherhouse, through the intervention of the apostolic nuncio in Munich, Eugenio Cardinal Pacelli (later Pope Pius XII), succeeded in gaining autonomous status for them by 1922. A previously promulgated decree aimed at deporting all Germans from Belgium was rescinded. Henri Chapelle and Lierre were safely tied to the Motherhouse. However, because the German mark had been devalued by nearly 50 percent, in Belgium the Brothers suffered economic losses, particularly in patients' fees.[2]

Catholicism experienced a rich renaissance in Weimar Germany. Though the Catholic Workers movement had failed to attract large numbers among the urban proletariat, a religious consciousness expanded as a result of the war. Romano Guardini, the spokesman for the new liturgical movement, optimistically proclaimed that "a religious development of unforeseen impact has begun: The Church is awakening in the souls of men."[3] The stress upon liturgy, ecumenism, and the image of the church as the *corpus Christi mysticum* formed the new religious consciousness of the era. The Alexian Brothers appear to have been relatively untouched by the new trends in spirituality, but the large number of men attracted to their way of life illustrates the general religious awakening in Germany. The increase in vocations was so great that by 1929 there were sixty-eight novices and eighteen postulants in the two German provinces.[4] Since at the turn of the century there were roughly two hundred Brothers in the entire congregation, these figures represent the phenomenal growth of the German Alexians. If one uses the traditional criteria for evaluating the prosperity of a religious order, i.e., vocations and new foundations, then it may be stated that the German Alexians flourished in the twenties.

The pater of the congregation, Brother Alexius Jansen, who presided over the expansion, had been provincial in America and had served in each of the Alexian provinces. In June 1920, a few months after he was elected rector-general, Pater Alexius traveled to Rome where he personally reported to Pope Benedict XV on the general condition of the Alexians and sought the appointment of a cardinal protector for the congregation. The Pope was pleased with his report and appointed William Cardinal van Rossum as protector. Pater Alexius also succeeded in his appeal to the Sacred Congregation of Rites for elevating to first-class status (limited to Alexian houses) the three feasts of the congregation: St. Alexius, St. John of God, and St. Augustine.[5]

A return visit to Rome the following year seems to have been motivated by Pater Alexius's intention to establish an Alexian foundation in Rome. As the congregation expanded and modernized, the relationship with the papacy became more complex. Rather than hire an agent to negotiate Alexian business in Rome, Pater Alexius considered it more efficient to appoint Brothers to conduct Alexian affairs directly. The prestige of a Roman foundation, in line with so many ancient religious orders, must have also been a motivating factor.

The congregation's cardinal protector was not very encouraging. "If you wish to erect only a 'boarding house' then it is my duty to dissuade you from it. According to your statutes your activity consists in nursing, the burial of the dead, and in the care and supervising of cemeteries. For as soon as Religious begin to apply themselves to extraneous affairs, there is either a decline in spiritual life or the undertaking fails financially. I have made these experiences as a Visitator of convents for many years before I was made Cardinal."[6] Pope Benedict echoed these sentiments but he did urge the Alexians to "come directly to me" in the event that they found a suitable location for an asylum.[7] It seems as if Pater Alexius considered the Alexians unprepared to embark on such an adventure.

The first postwar Alexian foundation was in Bavaria, a state with a wealthy Catholic heritage. Pater Clement Wallrath had seriously pursued the civil authorities for permission to establish a house there but had been frustrated at every turn. In 1921 Pater Alexius received word, via Monsignor Baumgarten, that a castle on a one-hundred-acre estate near the town of Kraiburg on the Inn River was for sale.[8] On July 21, 1921, after the General Council had sent a delegation to explore the suitability of the site and after the church and civil authorities approved the project, the congregation purchased the property for one and a half million marks. Castle Malseneck, named by Count Malsen who built it shortly before the war, was initially intended as a home for retired and sick priests but later became a small asylum. Under the leadership of Brother Rector Wolfgang Wollender, the Brothers moved into their new Bavarian home in the autumn of 1921.[9] The following description contained in one of its early brochures highlights the pastoral character of the asylum.

Castle Malseneck has an excellent, idyllic location. It is situated on a wooded height of the upper Bavarian Plateau 450 meters above sea level. Surrounded by a large, beautifully laid out park of about 11 acres, the southwest side offers an enchanting view both at close range and in the distance, directly into the Inn valley and at a distance the Alpine chain with the high mountains in the background.

According to the judgment of medical experts, Malseneck is most suitable for the treatment of ailments of the nervous system and of general debility of every kind, as also of mild psychic illness. The air is pure and perfectly free from dust.

All clinically tested, physical and medicinal treatments are taken into consideration as curative remedies. Dr. Waldvogel is the physician in charge. The careful and conscientious nursing is in the hands of the Alexian Brothers.[10]

Schloss Malseneck was then a relatively small asylum, which in 1929 had but six Brothers, two novices and four postulants to care for their patients. The Alexian presence in Bavaria was significant not only as an extension of their apostolate but also because Bavaria became a major source of vocations.[11]

Pater Alexius, thwarted in his plans to establish a house in Rome, presided over the erection of a generalate building adjacent to the asylum on Alexianergraben. The initial plans for a separate facility for the administration of the congregation originated in 1912, but the war precluded its development beyond the concept phase. In 1921, after the postwar situation stabilized, the General Council made plans which reached the cornerstone stage on October 15, 1922. Because construction was severely delayed during the inflation of 1923, the building was not completed until the end of 1924. Designed in the style of a spacious country house, the generalate building symbolized the maturity of the congregation. The first of two floors included two parlors, the offices of the rector-general, secretary, and bursar. The second floor was highlighted by a beautifully appointed chapter room with the congregation's coat of arms carved into the wood as well as the national symbols of the American, English and two German provinces. The American Province, under the leadership of Brother Frumentius Horn, provided strong financial support not only for construction of the generalate headquarters, but during the inflation period it sent $600 a month so the Motherhouse could feed the hundreds of hungry Aacheners who were dependent upon the asylum's kitchen.[12] Within the American Province stories have been circulating for decades that the American provincial surreptitiously subsidized the new generalate construction at the expense of funding necessary improvements and much desired expansion within his own province. Though Brother Ignatius Wiegers denies such stories, the fact that they still linger today indicates the strength of dissent against the flow of money from America for what many considered to be a nonapostolic endeavor.

On September 22, 1922, a few weeks before construction began on the new generalate, the Alexian Brothers in Aachen ministered at their last funeral service at the Adalbertsteinweg Cemetery.[13] The people of Aachen were particularly insistent that the Alexians remain burial Brothers, but by 1922 Aachen had grown by more than 115,000 people in less than a century, requiring a large number of Brothers to service the many funerals.[14] Because of this, and the strong trend toward developing the Brothers as first-rate nurses, the Alexians discontinued their nearly six-hundred-year-old burial ministry in Aachen. The last vestige of the ancient ministry persisted in Manchester, England, where four Brothers lived and worked at St. Joseph's Cemetery.

Nearly every year of his first term of office, Pater Alexius was deeply involved in wide-ranging decisions. In the summer of 1924, just as the new generalate was reaching completion, Pater Alexius was confronted with an offer to purchase a medieval convent in the town of Schänis in the canton of St. Gall, Switzerland. Within a short time the General Council, upon the advice of a delegation sent to examine the property, signed a ten-year lease for the convent. The buildings of "Tenthof," a name derived from its ninth-century origin, were believed to have been built over a relic of the Holy Cross. The General Council considered the fifty-room convent and its beautiful garden and park to be most suitable for a home for aged men. In 1927, three years after Pater Alexius signed the lease, the congregation purchased the property from its owner, Dr. Stiener, for approximately 125,000 Swiss francs. Generally eight Brothers were stationed at Schänis where they cared for fifteen to twenty men and for the novitiate, which was designed particularly for Swiss vocations.[15] Though Tenthof was an impressive home possessing a rich religious heritage and located in a strikingly beautiful setting, it never really flourished as either an institution or a source of many vocations. Apparently its remote location in a sparsely populated district of Switzerland prevented its growth and expansion into a financially stable institution.

The Maria-Hilf Hospital in Krefeld had been envisioned as providing nurses' training courses for the Brothers, but the war obstructed its development and the postwar Belgian occupation of the hospital further delayed its use until January 1926, when it was turned over to the Alexians once again. Because of previous expansion into Bavaria and Switzerland, the building of a new generalate, and the recently initiated construction of a new chapel and other sections of the Motherhouse, Maria-Hilf became a heavy financial burden. Yet modern trends in nursing required this expense of maintaining a general hospital suitable for training the Brothers. In September 1928 four Alexians passed the state nursing exam, having received a two-year training course at Maria-Hilf.[16] This event is historically significant not only because it marks a new phase in the modernization of the Alexians, but also because, with professionalization of nursing, a new type of Brother emerged, one who developed a different perspective on the world from his unschooled confrere in the cloister.

Immediately following the completion of the generalate, construction began on a new section of the Motherhouse where the Brothers' rooms, refectory, and novitiate were to be located. Upon its completion in 1927, construction of a new chapel began. Forming a bridge between the generalate and the asylum, the chapel was of neo-Renaissance motif with the back of the rococo high altar of the old chapel marking a point of continuity with the 1683 chapel. Two Brothers built the pews, with the elaborately carved communion railing, a gift from Emperor Francis I commemorating his visit at the Motherhouse, playing a prominent role in the decor. The new chapel was solemnly dedicated on February 2, 1929. Bishop Herman Joseph Sträter, auxiliary of the Cologne archdiocese, presided at the ceremony during which the Brothers processed from the old to the new chapel carrying lighted candles and chanting a choral Mass. A few weeks later demolition of the 1683 chapel commenced to make room for a new section of the hospital.[17]

When Pater Alexius's first term of office expired in the spring of 1926 he was in the middle of many projects. However, according to precedent each rector-general had served at least two terms. It came as no surprise, therefore, that Pater Alexius was reelected at the General Chapter of April 21-23 held at Haus Kannen. The resolutions passed by the chapter did not break any new ground, except one which recommended that the American Province erect a "separate House for the novitiate . . . in order that the novices may have sufficient occupation and also may have an appropriate field for training as nurses. . . . this House ought to be accommodation for about 40 to 50 patients."[18] Apparently the chapter delegates had in mind Maria-Hilf as the model for a nurses' training facility in the United States. Though a separate American novitiate did become a reality in the late thirties, by that time the Chicago nursing school had evolved into a first-rate institution.

One regressive resolution originated in the American Province. At the Provincial Chapter, the United States delegates resolved: "It was decided to ask the General Chapter again to clarify the policy on accepting colored people in the order. Most of the brothers were against it [the nondiscriminatory policy] but Brother Hilarion Pencheon, the only colored man in the order, was considered to be a Holy Man."[19] The General Chapter did not rescind the policy initiated in 1920 but decided that "it was very advisable not to take any colored candidates into the order."[20] As if the Brothers were afraid of the very unlikely event of being inundated with black aspirants, they left the matter to the discretion of each province. Since the 1920 policy was extremely progressive for the time, it is not surprising that there would be some backlash, not directed at Brother Hilarion, but at the precedent. It was not until the post-World War II period that blacks were encouraged to enter the congregation.

After World War I the two German provinces were merged into one because of a lack of novices during the war and for the sake of efficiency. With the establishment of Malseneck, Schänis, and the reestablishment of Maria-Hilf, the General

207

Chapter of 1926 directed Pater Alexius to appeal to the Sacred Congregation for Religious to approve the reformation of two German provinces and to drop the minimum age for postulants from eighteen to fifteen years. On July 19, 1926, Rome acceded to these requests: Brother Siegfried Hermanns was appointed provincial of the First Province and Brother Winand Schmitt of the Second Province.[21] The new minimum age for postulants was in accord with the trends of the time and could have been prompted by the English Province, which by 1926 had expanded into Ireland where young vocations for many religious orders were quite common.

II

For decades the English Province had hoped to establish a house in Ireland. One may recall that in the 1890s a physician from Waterford had offered the Alexians a home, which he considered suitable for the care of alcoholics. At the 1919 Provincial Chapter the delegates associated an Ireland house with vocations: "It was suggested that in order to get a good increase of Postulants, it was found advisable to start on a small scale in Ireland at the first most favorable opportunity."[22] The General Chapter of the same year confirmed the resolution. The reference to a "small-scale" endeavor derived from the manpower shortage in the Province. Unlike the other provinces, the English Province had always been plagued by the vocation problem.

It also appears as if the province sensed that the Motherhouse never fully understood its situation. In the 1919 Provincial Chapter the delegates resolved to explore the possibility of amending the constitution to require that assistant rectors-general be representatives of the provinces, and in another resolution appealed to the rector-general to appoint English-speaking Brothers as interpreters during visitations to the province.[23] These illustrations of English self-assertiveness probably stemmed from the 1918 appointment of Brother Gilbert Holmes as provincial. For the first time in its history the English Province was led by a native Brother. Because Brother Gilbert was a quiet, conservative man who had been a tailor before entering the religious life, he represented the traditional character of the province rather than a point of departure from past trends. Though he was no innovator he appears to have been sympathetic to the moderate self-assertiveness of the postwar development in the province.

The English Province was never affluent. In his 1921 semiannual financial statement Brother Gilbert noted gifts to the province totalling a mere £15. St. Joseph's Cemetery was by far the largest institutional contributor to the provincial treasury, £315; St. Mary's Home contributed only £28. Since the interest on bank deposits came to only a little over £14, the principal must have amounted to less than £300.[24] Without the rectorgeneral's £516 loan the province would have operated in the red, but because the provincialate and novitiate were located at Twyford Abbey, the province paid out roughly £170 to that house for food and lodging. Traveling expenses, including the cost of sending three Brothers to America, came to nearly £210. An interesting expense item indicates the charity of the English Brothers within their slim budget. "Alms and presents of Tobacco to Germany and Belgium £26.2.5." Of the superior general's £516 loan the province returned £378 to the Motherhouse. The entire operating budget came to £245.18.2 income; £937.3.3 expenses, with £305.3.2 as cash on hand.[25] Without comparative figures one may guess that these amounts would be the equivalent to one month's budget for the other Alexian provinces, which underlines the English Province's plan to develop a house in Ireland on a "small scale." Perhaps the financial conditions prompted Pater Alexius to suggest to Provincial Rector Brother Gilbert that his council consider merging the province with the two Belgian houses to form a new Anglo-Belgian Province. On February 15, 1922, the council unanimously voted against the proposal, which would certainly have drastically affected the autonomy and character of the English Province.[26]

The political situation in Ireland blocked the Alexians' plan for a new house. Irish nationalism had achieved Parliamentary strength in the late nineteenth century. On the eve of World War I Parliament passed an Irish home rule bill but the war prevented its implementation. However, because the "six counties" of the north with a Protestant majority would never have accepted the bill, its implementation could not have been pursued peacefully. The Easter Rebellion of 1916 was a failure but it did further polarize the situation in which neither the north nor the south would accept home rule; the former demanded British rule while the latter was veering toward full sovereignty. The 1918 elections to Parliament returned more than seventy members of the Sinn Fein ("We ourselves") party, who formed a Dublin Parliament and proclaimed Ireland a sovereign state. In the fall of 1919 the war-weary Lloyd George government sent a volunteer force, "the Black and Tan" (generally composed of prisoners whose sentences were reduced upon volunteering) to support the Irish police in suppressing the insurrection. An ill-disciplined terrorist-type civil war ensued until a tenuous peace treaty was achieved in December 1921, through which the six northern counties remained British with a modicum of home rule and the southern counties achieved dominion status comparable to Canada. However, the Sinn Fein was not satisfied until, after World War II, the south gained sovereignty while its extremist wing still will not be satisfied until all of Ireland is ruled from Dublin.[27]

The so-called Irish troubles directly obstructed the Alexians' plans. On July 12, 1920, Michael Cardinal Logue, archbishop of Armagh, Ireland, wrote to Brother Gilbert informing him that the mansion the Brothers had hoped to purchase "was unfortunately burned in the present disturbance . . . one of the many miseries to which we have been unhappily subjected." Even in peacetime the Alexians would have encountered many problems because so many Irish dioceses had already been deluged by requests for settlements from numerous religious congregations, most of which had many Irish institutions and friends to support their requests.[28]

In 1923 Brother Gilbert found a suitable location in county Down located in the Protestant Northern Ireland. The Bishop of Dromore refused to grant permission and apparently Brother Gilbert's reticient personality prevented him from pressuring the bishop.[29] When in the following year Brother Camillus McGill was appointed provincial, the negotiations with the reluctant bishop took a different turn. Brother Camillus was known for his single-minded perseverence in the pursuit of his goals and was a shrewd businessman with a broad vision on the modernization of the province. His Irish heritage gave him more than a slight edge over Brother Gilbert Holmes in negotiating with an Irish bishop. Within a year Brother Camillus had received the latter's permission to buy an eighteenth-century twenty-room home located on a large estate between the villages of Warrenpoint and Rostrevor.[30] Only an Irishman could aptly describe the new Alexian home's idyllic location "where the mountains of Mourne roll down to the sea. Divine Providence has been more than bountiful here, as elsewhere in Ulster. We might say lavish. He has not been content to endow Rostrevor and Warrenpoint with a lovely lough [an arm of the Irish sea] and fine mountain views, but he has added to them the magnificence of the Mournes. . . . It would be too much to assert that the road across the Mournes is the most beautiful in the world. But it is in all truth stated that it is nearly unmatched for its beauty."[31] Though the Alexian home was in predominantly Protestant Northern Ireland, it was within a Catholic district and close to the Catholic county of Armagh.

Brother Columcille McGuinness was an ideal choice as the home's first rector. He named the home in honor of his own religious namesake and the patron saint of Derry, Brother Columcille's home town; St. Columcille is known as the "apostle of the North" (Ulster); Columcille, "Dove of the Church." The Irish say they can detect a Derryman by his charming frankness and salesmanlike verbosity. From the stories which have reached the proportions of legends, Brother Columcille was a thoroughbred Derryman. Brother Dunstan O'Neill recalled that Brother Columcille was a man "who would fit into our times, as he mixed with and gathered together many non-Catholics who were always impressed with him."[32] Within four years he expanded the residence from twenty to forty-three rooms and had placed Mount St. Columb's on the Irish religious map.

In 1926 he introduced into Ulster the first Corpus Christi procession since the Reformation. The bishop of Dromore carried the monstrance in a procession of thousands of Catholics from all of Ireland. The youth of Warrenpoint constructed triumphal arches for the procession but, because of the fear of anti-Catholic disturbance, guarded their work throughout the night.[33] Brother Columcille was not at all hesitant to display Ireland's Catholic heritage. Under his direction Stations of the Cross were built along the landscape.

Mount St. Columb's was a convalescent home along the lines of St. Mary's, Manchester. E. P. Carey remarked that the Brothers were "skilled in the care of nervous, neurasthenic, senile, paralytic, chronic, and other ailments."[34] However, patients with mental, alcoholic, or infectious diseases were not accepted, as the Brothers in Ulster were under British law, which required nurses' training. The home was also a holiday retreat for men who wished to be relaxed "from business worries" or who suffered from "over-anxiety in other causes."[35] Carey painted an appealing picture of the Brothers' holiday home:

> All the warmth of traditional monastic hospitality awaits the comer, who thus receives, during the first hour, an encouraging sense of having escaped that something in the environment and role of the average hotel and boardinghouse which renders the holiday feeling uncomfortably like that of a prisoner of war on parole . . . a word for the pleasant, gentlemanly company at the pensionnaire during my own stay there. To have met there a society of the kind has not been surprising in the after-light of my own experiences, for Mount St. Columb's is the ideal vacation retreat for the clergy, the professional and literary classes, as well as for the mind-jaded man of business and the toil weary artisan.[36]

The holiday character of St. Columb's was derived not only from its idyllic location but also because there were few Irishmen who would convalesce in an institution. Ireland was still a traditional society where nursing in the home was the rule.

The English Province had intended its new Irish establishment to become a strong source of vocations. But before it could appeal to the youth of Ireland it had to break down their traditional bias against male nursing. Hence in Mount St. Columb's Almanacs of the mid-thirties there were articles on the tradition of Christian nursing extolling the virtues of St. John of God, St. Camillus de Lellis and St. Vincent de Paul, and "the nursing Brothers of St. Alexius [who] offer mankind the greatest possible assurance of perfection and hope."[37] A juniorate was established at St. Columb's where Irish aspirants could be introduced to the Alexian life before traveling to London for their novitiate at Twyford Abbey.

During the first ten years after the war the English Province had expanded from eighteen Brothers and two novices in 1918 to forty-three Brothers, thirteen novices, and five postulants by 1928. Since ten of the thirteen novices were Irish it appears as if Mount St. Columb's had succeeded as a source of vocations.[38] It had also succeeded as a convalescent home as well. One of the four houses in the English-Irish Province in 1929, Mount St. Columb's housed the greatest number of Brothers. However, as Brother Camillus remarked in a 1925 council meeting (July 10, 1925), "Financially and spiritually St. Joseph's Cemetery leads the way by far."[39] St. Mary's Home continued to be a financial burden during the twenties. On September 12, 1926, the Provincial Council agreed "to sell St. Mary's Home . . . if we could find a suitable place elsewhere which might be used for the treatment of the temporary insane, feeble minded, or border line cases."[40] Because the Brothers never found a suitable location, St. Mary's remained an Alexian institution. Financial problems harassed Brother Camillus as they did Brother Gilbert. To help defray expenses the Provincial Council "suggested to get as much of the work done by ourselves instead of employing helpers or servants."[40]

In 1930 the bishop of the Salford diocese (Manchester), Dr. Hearnshaw, purchased a stately Tudor home, Wardley Hall. In the autumn of that year he negotiated an agreement with the Alexians whereby the Brothers would give the bishop thirteen pieces of antique furniture from St. Mary's Home's for his new residence; in exchange the bishop purchased "good modern furniture" for the home.[42] Though the Brothers were aware that the bishop gained from the agreement, they appear to have been somewhat pressured as the bishop had been negotiating with them for two months. When Bishop Hearnshaw initiated plans for a second cemetery in the diocese, to be located adjacent to Wardley Hall, he naturally turned to the Alexians for its care and maintenance. The Brothers notified him that they would accept a "formal invitation to take charge of the new cemetery . . . and form a small community there."[43] The diocese built a new house for the Brothers and in August 1932 agreed to the following points of the contract:

> The Brother Registrar received an annual salary of £150 and £150 annual bonus; "the emoluments from the people for out-of-time funerals, keeping the graves clean, etc. to be perquisite of the Brothers as at Moston"; Church collection and candle money went to the Cemetery Board for the upkeep of the Chapel; the Board paid the Brothers' household utilities and taxes.[44]

Brother Gilbert, who had been appointed provincial in 1930, negotiated the contract for Wardley Cemetery, which was solemnly consecrated by Bishop Hearnshaw on June 17, 1933. Unlike Bishop Vaughan's Victorian elegy on the ties between the living and the dead, published on the occasion of the consecration of Moston Cemetery, Bishop Hearnshaw merely stressed the rules of the church and the practical need for a second cemetery in Manchester.[45]

Brother Gilbert assigned three German Brothers to Wardley Cemetery: Brothers Alban Viehs, Serenus Engel, and Ephrem Vogel.[46] Financially the province greatly benefited from the salaries and donations collected at Moston and Wardley cemeteries, and the expansion in vocations and financial stability allowed the Anglo-Irish Province to seek a site for new foundation. After two years of searching, the Provincial Council decided to purchase an eighteenth-century mansion in Yorkshire, not far from Ampleforth Abbey where the Brothers had frequently nursed sick Benedictine monks. Stillington Hall, located in the village of Stillington on the moors of Yorkshire, possessed a rich history; before the Reformation the property belonged to the archbishop of York, and the Croft family had held the land until the late nineteenth century. One anecdote relates how Stephen Croft salvaged the manuscript of *Tristram Shandy* after its author, Laurence Sterne, had bitterly tossed it into the fireplace.[47]

On May 12, 1935, Brothers Anselm Hopkins and Vincent Brewer, rector and assistant rector, moved into the old mansion. Brother Joseph Newell, one of the pioneers at Stillington, recalled the early days:

> When the Brothers went to Stillington there was a lot of opposition. The people who were standing at their doors would look the other

way when the Brothers passed; and this went on for the first year. When the people knew the Brothers were [moving into] the house they thought that they [would] find work for the tradesmen and were disappointed when no one was employed. . . . In 1937 there was an open house at Stillington Hall for the people of the village and many people came to see the work of the Brothers.[48]

However, the Anglican vicar, Reverend J. Smith, advised against mixing with the Catholic Brothers, so an attitude of cool coexistence prevailed until the war. (Later Reverend Smith became a close friend of the Brothers and was nursed by the Alexians at York in his last illness.) Because of its remote location in a region sparsely populated by Catholics, Stillington Hall never became a success. However, with a thirteen-acre farm and garden the Brothers were relatively self-sufficient. In 1939, on the eve of the war, nine Brothers cared for approximately twenty-five aged men. The entire province numbered six houses, fifty-seven Brothers, ten novices, and eight postulants.

Between the wars the Alexian presence in England evolved from a German mission into an Anglo-Irish Province. Though the congregation's customs were either of German origin or derived from the general traditional canons for the religious life, the spirit expressed through these forms was primarily Anglo-Irish with a heavy accent on the Irish.

Brothers Gilbert Holmes and Camillus McGill provided the leadership for the province between the wars. With contrary personalities and temperaments, they no doubt had their arguments but they tended to balance each other: the reflective Gilbert and the impetuous Camillus; the conservative tailor and the progressive businessman; the restrained Englishman and the uninhibited Irishman. If there were bitter struggles on the Provincial Council they were not registered in the minutes. Indeed, the council seems to have acted from unanimity.

Only one modern trend, professional nurses' training for the Brothers, surfaced during this period. Though it was in 1926, when Brother Camillus was provincial, that the council agreed to allow "reliable Brothers" to volunteer for such training in America, it was not until the mid-thirties that the first Brothers from the Anglo-Irish Province made the journey.[49] For cultural and other reasons few finished the course, yet the American style of modernization gradually had an impact upon the Anglo-

Irish Province. For decades the province had persisted in its commitment to hospice and cemetery ministries which, except for its Irish expression, compelled the Brothers to dwell in Irish-Catholic enclaves within British Protestant society.

III

The American experience in World War I acted as a catalyst in the modernization process; the United States was rapidly becoming more industrialized, urbanized, technological, and standardized. For German immigrants the war acted as a catalyst in the Americanization process. Wartime propaganda caricaturing the German "Huns" spilled into impassioned public ridicule of German-American citizens. At times driven to excessive self-consciousness, many German-Americans discarded public symbols of loyalty to the old country. By the 1920s German Catholics were breaking through their protective cultural shells and assimilating with American society. Colman Barry, O.S.B., who has extensively researched the conflicts between German Catholic particularists and the American Catholic generalists, concludes that by the 1920s a synthesis had been achieved:

> . . . German Catholics eventually came to accept the position of the Americanizer. The mother tongue was dying out, American national habits were being assimilated, the United States was becoming recognized by them as a nation. No more protesting memorials were forwarded to Rome, since German parishes gradually became mixed parishes, national parishes slowly gave way to territorial parishes, and the German parishes were distinguished only by a spirit of German Catholicism as practiced by American citizens of German origin. Interest in the appointment of Bishops of German ancestry and tongue became an academic question as American Germans took their place in American life as one of the many elements that went to make up one people. . . . In all of this it was apparent and worthy of note that the German Catholics acted freely and in circumstances where they felt that their faith would not be endangered by the assimilation process.[50]

The postwar Alexians in America reflected general trends in church and culture. In the 1920s the Brothers' community prayers, other than the office of the Holy Cross which was recited in Latin, were in English for the first time. Before this time even the rosary had been said in German. Official minutes of the House and Provincial Council meetings were recorded in English. Though there was a preponderance of Alexians of German extraction, of the Brothers who professed temporary vows during the 1922–1928 period many were of non-German ancestry: Sebastian Brogan, Andrew McManus, Honoratius Doherty, Victor Scanlon, Innocent Doonan, Ruffinius Garrity, Romanus Higgins, Hilarion Pencheon, Eustachius Walsh, Vulgan Cunning, George Burke, Leo Longan, Raymond O'Connor.[51] Virtual provincial authority during the war had engendered American self-assertion. Alexians were gradually assimilated into American society but the customs of the congregation were German and because of the predominance of German and German-American Brothers, it was rare for a non-German to hold a position of responsibility. Since the cloister was still very remote from Main Street, the assimilation was very gradual.

The modernization of the Alexian Brothers' hospitals occurred at a much more rapid pace. The Belden Avenue Hospital in Chicago was ahead of its time at the turn of the century. During the postwar period new equipment was continuously introduced, including elevators and laundry machines. In their 1926 Annual Report the Brothers proudly cited new X-ray equipment, an addition to the clinical laboratory, new physical rehabilitation apparatus, and a new kitchen managed by professional dietitians as examples of the "progressive tendencies the Brothers have always shown."[52] The Chicago hospital cared for 3,758 patients during 1926, 1,285 of whom were full or partial charity patients. In accord with the traditional nondenominational character of their hospitals, the Brothers in Chicago treated over 1,500 non-Catholics during 1926.[53] One feature of their report illustrates the advance of the assimilation process, i.e., the patients were not listed according to national origin, as was traditional in the reports.

Mr. James Horton, who began his more than fifty years of service as an employee at the Belden Avenue Hospital, has left us a number of anecdotes about this period. As Brother Ambrose

Nussbaum's assistant during the early 1920s, he fondly recalled how Brothers would visit each patient in the morning before settling down at the Admittance Office. Mr. Horton testified to the transition from the hospital's personalist to its standardized character in recalling how many Brothers played jokes on each other in the old days, in contrast to the increasingly organized pace so characteristic of the contemporary hospital's tone.[54]

The St. Louis hospital had once been located on the periphery of the metropolitan area, but by 1920 the advance of the city meant that it was absorbed into the fullness of urban life. It was quite evident, therefore, that the hospital and its free dispensary must expand if it were to keep pace with the growing demand for hospital treatment. This increased demand was not merely the result of population growth but of the expanding awareness or medical sophistication among various groups in society. The 1920 report of the St. Louis Alexians eloquently addressed these issues:

> It is becoming more and more apparent that the sick and injured require hospitalization, and the public realizes this better as time goes on. The reaction to this realization is the tendency for the sick to come to hospitals more than ever before. On this account, all the hospitals have found their facilities inadequate to properly care for the numerous applicants for admission. Our hospital is no exception. We believe that every hospital should have a surplus of twenty per cent of its capacity available for emergency. This condition has not been obtained here. We have at times had all available space occupied and found it necessary to refuse admission to worthy and desirable patients owing to lack of room. Our hospital needs twice its present capacity and we hope some time in the near future to be able to bring about this desideratum.[55]

Economic distress in the postwar period prevented the Brothers from raising the funds necessary for expansion. The 1921 report included the words *sanitarium, hospital,* and *dispensary* in the institution's title as if to emphasize the psychiatric convalescent portion of its general character. The author of the report was extraordinarily candid in narrating the hospital's weak points along with its strengths. In 1921 the hospital cared for 227 fewer patients than in 1920, while the dispensary treated 1,484 more patients than the previous year. "This we believe reflects the economical conditions affecting the entire country. That the character of our work has improved cannot be questioned, but there is room for vast improvement still and the attainment of the highest possible degree of excellence is our goal."[56] Admitting that "our hospital is somewhat antiquated" and that need for improvement "is a self-evident fact" the author of the report questioned whether the general economic instability "didn't preclude that improvements will have to be delayed."[57] The dispensary was particularly in need of expansion, as its operation had increased 60 percent over the previous year. The improvement of the hospital was an intensely thorny question.

> The hospital problem is many more sided. We have a valuable property here which is inadequate and somewhat unsuited for the best accomplishment of our purposes. We have given a great deal of thought to the question of an additional wing with alterations in our old building and we do not consider this practical or feasible in view of the immense outlay of money it will require, and leave us a patch-work affair. The question of an entirely new plant is also out of the question at the present time on account of the great amount of money involved. The solution of the problem as it presents itself to us is the separation of our Sanitarium from our hospital proper by the erection of suitable buildings with agricultural environments so that our nervous patients may receive that kind of care, attention and treatment which is recognized as best suited to their needs. This plan also permits the use of our present nervous department with some alterations for general hospital purposes and will cause us to bend our efforts to enlarging our usefulness in this direction.
>
> We are ambitious and our ambitions are only limited by the size of our problems. We have improved and added to our facilities during the past year. We have expended fairly large sums for added equipment to our Laboratory and X-ray departments. We have tried to be economical but not at the expense of efficiency. For the co-operation we have received, we are truly grateful.[58]

The nation's improved economic situation after 1922 gradually filtered down to affect the Brothers' ability to make necessary improvements. In 1925 a new dispensary was completed at a cost of $75,000.[59] In 1930 a south wing was added to the hospital, one which provided much-needed living quarters for the Brothers as well as additional space for a closed roof garden for the mentally ill, for expansion of the hydrotherapy facilities and the creation of a Department of Occupational Therapy.[60]

The new south wing was intended as the first phase of a major building program aimed at replacing the entire hospital complex with modern buildings, but the depression and World War II halted the plan at phase one.

Though the 1920 Annual Report included *Sanitarium* in the title, by the late 1920s the Brothers were struggling against the misinformed public image of the hospital as almost exclusively dedicated to the care of the mentally ill and alcoholic patient. The 1928 Annual Report attempted to correct this mistaken image.

> For a great many years our Hospital has been known far and wide among other things for its Neuro-psychiatric Department and also for the fact that we have cared for a large number of patients suffering with acute and chronic alcoholism. These facts have been stressed in the consciousness of the people so that the work done in our Medical and Surgical Departments has been somewhat obscured.[61]

The Alexian Brothers' institution in Oshkosh, Wisconsin, evolved along lines similar to the German tradition, a hospital for the mentally ill, the convalescent, and the aged. In the twenties the hospital appears to have flourished; in 1928 eight rooms and solaria were added to each of its four floors and in 1930 the fourth floor was completely replaced. On September 1, 1930, the Oshkosh hospital celebrated its Golden Jubilee. In a brochure published during the depression, the Brothers listed the hospital's five major features:

1. A rest cure for men; conducted by men.
2. A hospital where precision and accuracy is always exercised in executing physicians' orders.
3. An atmosphere of cheerfulness and encouragement pervades the establishment and is always shown by the Brothers in their dealings with patients.
4. A haven for men of moderate means who wish to enjoy the evening of life in quiet, peaceful and understanding surroundings for a remuneration.
5. An opportunity to obtain the finest service, methods, measures and means to secure a complete restoration to mental and physical health.[62]

The brochure projected the image not of a confinement institution (though it contained a photo of the barred-window hospital) but of a guest house. It listed under the title "Prospective Guests" "Business and professional men, who, especially in these times of economic reversals, suffer from worry and anxiety with its concomitant physical and mental exhaustion" as well as persons who have suffered "nervous breakdowns."[63]

The Oshkosh hospital became well known among the bishops in the United States because of the Alexians' fine reputation in caring for priests suffering from alcoholism and mental illnesses. The above brochure may have been an accurate description of the Brothers' treatments and of the Brothers' hope for their Oshkosh hospital, but it was not a clear reflection of their views on the life at the institution. Care for the mentally ill was hard work, with little or no gratitude from patients and their families. It was particularly difficult for Brothers to give orders to priests. Not only were the patients confined, but the Brothers were also. Indeed upon receiving word that he was to be transferred to Oshkosh the typical Brother would immediately ask himself what he had done to deserve such punishment. Care for "problem priests" so isolated the institution that the Brothers nicknamed it the "Sacred Penitentiary." In spite of its poor image among the Brothers, the Oshkosh hospital was not treated as a stepbrother institution but, on the contrary, was strongly supported by the American Provincials.

If Oshkosh was the most socially isolated of the Alexian institutions, then Elizabeth was the most socially involved. For example, when Prohibition was imposed on the nation in 1919, the Elizabeth Alexians received permission to brew beer for their own consumption. Mr. Herman Kitzler, who as a young boy was a neighbor of the Brothers, recalled how policemen, firemen, and mailmen "found out how they could get beer" and made frequent visits to the hospital.[64] Kitzler said that when Brother Herman Joseph Berkes was appointed superior in 1932 he put an end to the practice because he considered it to have become an excessive violation of monastic discipline. The fact that Kitzler, a German Lutheran, entitled his memoirs "Our Alexian Brothers" clearly illustrates the warm relationship between the Brothers and the people of Elizabeth.[65]

The hospital in Elizabeth was also the smallest of the Alexian institutions, with a capacity of less than one hundred beds. In

1926 the Brothers cared for 1,733 patients, 880 of whom were charity cases. Unlike the introductions to annual reports of the Chicago and St. Louis hospitals, which were lengthy and elaborate analyses of the year's events and projections of future developments, the Elizabeth Brothers introduced their reports with merely a gloss on the statistics, as if they were in no need of strong public relations efforts. In 1928 a new annex was built, bringing the total capacity to 168 beds.[66] Because there was no city hospital in Elizabeth the Alexians were subsidized by the city and, of course, grew in accord with population growth. Like its Chicago and St. Louis counterparts, the Elizabeth hospital developed a busy outpatient clinic; 2,989 patients were treated there in 1929.[67] Further modernization occurred in 1931 with the addition of a new laundry building and in 1939 when new kitchen and auxiliary departments were constructed. In July 1940 the Brothers' residence building across the street from the hospital was ready for occupancy (the Brothers had previously lived on the top floor of the hospital). In the Golden Jubilee issue of its Annual Report, 1892–1942, the Brothers dedicated forty-four pages to commemorate their history in Elizabeth, their contribution to the community, and their gratitude to the people and city of Elizabeth for their strong support over the years.[68]

Brother Cajetan Theisen served four terms as rector of the Elizabeth community during the period from 1901 to 1927. He was a capable administrator who presided over the era's growth and modernization, as the major additions to the hospital in 1906 and 1928 occurred under his leadership. Brother Dominic Piotrowski, R.T., represented the trends toward professionalization among the American Alexians; an expert X-ray technician, he read a paper at the 1938 annual meeting of the American Society of X-Ray Technicians held in Madison, Wisconsin.[69] Though many Brothers had gained expertise in the various fields of nursing, the professionalization trend so clearly embodied in Brother Dominic was just budding in the 1930s. However, the seeds were sown in the 1920s when Chicago (and later St. Louis) developed a nursing school for the professional training of the Brothers.

The Chicago School of Nursing originated in a February 21,

1894, meeting of the hospital's medical staff. "A motion was passed to inaugurate a course of lectures (twenty-four), two lectures a week. The Medical lecture on Tuesday. The Surgical lecture on Friday."[70] On November 28, 1898, the staff resolved to appoint "Dr. Schmidt as a committee of one to confer with the Brothers in regard to the establishment of a male lay training school in the hospital."[71] Brother Aloysius Schyns, who was provincial at the time and had presided over the hospital's move to Belden Avenue, possessed a keen appreciation of the trends in health care. After responding positively to the doctor's request he assumed full responsibility for laying the groundwork. He wrote to the director of the D. O. Mills School of Nursing, founded in 1888 as a unit of Bellevue Hospital in New York City, asking him to recommend a qualified person to administer the Alexian Brothers school. On December 4, 1899, a Mr. Hearst, who graduated from the D. O. Mills School, was appointed superintendent.[72]

Before the school could get under way Brother Aloysius died (January 9, 1900) and his replacement, Brother Bernard Kleppel, was not a strong advocate of modernization. On May 30, 1900, Pater Quirinus Bank attended a meeting of the medical staff during which the latter's chairman, Dr. J. B. Murphy, urged the Brothers to maintain the school in order that the hospital might be provided with well-trained nurses, both Alexians and laymen, in accord with its high standards. Though a few laymen had been allowed to enroll in the school, Dr. Murphy noted the need for a greater number of lay students to meet the nursing demands of the hospital. According to Brother Ignatius Wiegers the school was a threat to Alexian tradition. "The School, however, had developed in such a manner that the Superiors lost control, the Brothers were brushed aside in nursing, and the Institution was on the way of becoming completely secularized. Pater Quirinus Bank, who had come to America in 1900 on the occasion of the Visitation, had to use all his official and personal influence against the opposition of the twenty-six doctors at the hospital, in order to remedy the matter. He dissolved the school, whose members were mostly Protestant, and also dismissed the superintendent who had interfered."[73]

Shortly after World War I the School of Nursing was revived

but without laymen. In September 1919 Brother Ferdinand Schmidt was appointed superintendent of nursing but it was Brother Ludolf Sattler, appointed superintendent in September 1920, who seems to have effected professional progress.[74] The 1920 student body included thirteen novice Brothers and twelve postulants. The curriculum included ten subjects ranging from Nursing Ethics to Bacteriology, which were taught by medical doctors or Alexians. Brother Ludolf had included in his personal file his recollection of the first Alexian Brothers to receive the title "R.N."[75] In the early twenties the Missouri legislature passed the Modern Nursing Act which, among other things, stipulated that persons who had been nursing for three or more years might apply for the "R.N." provided they had attended a nursing school with an approved curriculum. Brother Ludolf stated that five Brothers, Frumentius Horn, Ignatius Schneider, Louis Roy, Norbert Kreidler, and Sergius Nowicki, received the R.N. after the Missouri Board of Education accepted the curriculum submitted.[76] In April 1925 the school was accredited and the next month Brother Sebastian Brogan and Brother Camillus Snyder passed their state exams; the former was superintendent in Chicago, while the latter became the first superintendent of the St. Louis Brothers School of Nursing in 1928. During the next two years twenty-one Brothers became R.N.s.[77] From the outset the newly accredited school was a controversial issue in the province. At its April 1, 1925, meeting Brother Sebastian reported that "the opposition to the school is very pronounced in certain Brothers."[78]

Traditionally the novitiate was a period for training one's will for discipline in the rigors of the religious life, not for school. No doubt the opposition was critical of educating postulants and novices who might leave the community. Perhaps more than a few Brothers were apprehensive of the divisive implications of an R.N. versus non-R.N. community. In October 1926 Brother Sebastian noted that a school "down state" had sought affiliation but he had "to refuse as there is no way of getting all the Superiors to see the necessity of having things up-to-date. The Provincial and Rector did not object."[79] According to Brother Rigobert Meyer's recollection of the school's early days, Brother Sebastian faced "an uphill fight" in his struggle to modernize the school. The novice master, Brother Cyprian, considered it too secularistic, and the rector did not object.[80] The superiors must have feared mixing young Alexians with seculars. By 1928 the school was accepting a few laymen but in January 1929 Brother Sebastian told the various superiors, "We will not develop a school for the seculars. Our experience with secular nurses cannot be called a failure. We simply do not need them sufficiently to make the extensive preparations and alterations such a work demands."[81]

One of the persistent problems associated with the professionalization of the Brothers' nurses' training was integrating school with work duties in the hospital. The conservative view, which did not admit the necessity of education, distrusted any changes in the work schedule as invasions of secularism. Though flaming liberals never surfaced in opposition, moderates urged some flexibility to suit the demands of a more modernized hospital and a professionalized training of novices. Immediately prior to the 1925 Provincial Chapter meeting Brother Simplicius Eberle, on behalf "of many Brothers,"[82] wrote a letter to the delegates to the chapter urging moderate changes in the schedule. He opened his letter with a summary of the general trends in health care.

> Nursing has reached the point today where it is regarded as a profession which demands precise and thorough study and education. People and habits and circumstances have changed. Patients in hospitals demand polite and capable nurses who had graduated. Not only the rich, but also the workers make these demands, and rightly so, for attentive care speeds up their betterment and brings about good health more quickly.[83]

Brother Simplicius noted how these trends have made necessary the providing of a good professional training for Alexian novices but because they also must conform to a severe work schedule many novices "fall apart under the burden of work and leave the order."[84] The recent ruling requiring completion of high school or passing an equivalence exam before entering nurses' training intensified the novices' work load. Because he did emphasize the heavy burdens placed upon the novices, Brother Simplicius's proposals appear quite moderate.

> Taking into consideration the well being of our young brothers, we ask that the time for wakening be changed from 4:20 . . . to 4:45. . . . In our opinion it would be of great benefit if a good substantial

breakfast be served, and the 9:00 [A.M.] snack be omitted. . . . There is hardly a religious society in our country whose members have to get up at 4:20 A.M. Everyone who knows our climatic conditions and the strains of nursing must add that longer rest is of benefit to both nurses and the sick.[85]

Brother Simplicius had been nearly twenty-five years in vows when he wrote this letter. The fact that it was written in German indicates that he was loyal to tradition. Yet the moderation of his proposals illustrates the degree to which most Alexians viewed the monastic schedule as sacred. To tamper with the monastic time was akin to tampering with the soul of the religious cloister.

The problem of reconciling professional training with the novices' traditional work load prompted the delegates to the 1926 General Chapter to recommend that the American Province erect a separate novitiate to be attached to a small forty- or fifty-bed hospital.[86] However, the 1926 recommendation to establish a novitiate attached to a small hospital does not appear to have been received by the American provincial with a sense of urgency. The catastrophic economic situation seriously affected the congregation.

At the 1932 General Chapter, when Brother Frumentius Horn was elected pater, the retiring pater, Brother Alexius Jansen, requested "that all the houses of the Congregation should exercise the greatest economy and abstain from all not absolutely necessary expenses in order to enable the Congregation to meet the considerable [financial] obligations accumulated the last few years."[87] In spite of this plea, the chapter once again resolved to erect a separate novitiate in the American Province. "The Provincial Council should take immediate steps to acquire a proper location and report the progress to the General Council."[88] Brother Gerard Kuhn, who had been rector of the Chicago house, was appointed provincial in 1932, with the mandate to follow the above resolution. However, it was not until 1936 that a suitable location was found. Brother Gerard purchased land in Waukegan, Illinois, for developing a novitiate-nursing home, but after examining a piece of property in the Chattanooga, Tennessee, area, which struck him as more economical than the Illinois site, the provincial purchased a 140-room resort hotel located on a thirty-five-acre lot at the top of Signal Mountain, Tennessee. Once one of the luxury hotels of the south, the Signal Mountain Hotel was unable to weather the storm of economic depression. Because its mortgage was tied to bonds in default, a court had to pass on the sale contract. On September 27, 1936, the Alexians were permitted to buy the property and all its buildings for $125,000 and its furniture for $7,500. Even in the depression years this sale price was quite low. However, the cost of constructing a monastery to house fifty Brothers and a chapel, refectory, laundry, kitchen addition, and boiler-maintenance building amounted to $226,572.[89]

Signal Mountain had been entirely developed by Charles James. An imaginative entrepreneur, James constructed the hotel on Walden's Ridge with a panoramic view of the mountain range and the Tennessee River valley. The hotel grounds included fifteen summer cottages and a large dance pavillion. James also developed housing, roads, and tram transportation up to the mountain to encourage settlement. Motivated by a blend of anti-Catholic bias and economic self-interest, an impassioned group of Signal Mountain residents strongly opposed the Brothers' purchase of the property.[90]

On September 17, two days after the negotiations had been made public, three hundred residents of Signal Mountain attended a protest meeting to consider ways of obstructing the sale of the hotel. Brother Gerard had publicly stated in the press that the Alexians intended to establish a health resort for convalescent and retired men and not a mental hospital. He also informed the public of the Alexians' traditional practice to care for men of all religions.[91] Wild rumors circulated. A Mrs. Estill questioned the propriety of a Catholic institution in a predominantly Presbyterian area, as if the Brothers' chapel represented a center of proselytization. She asked the gathering if they "wanted this to be a Catholic community. We're Presbyterians now, but they would have to erect a chapel."[92] Her husband, Judge Estill, referred to the Alexians as a Mexican order: "If these Mexican gentlemen will run it as a hotel we'll be glad of it . . . a hotel open to everybody to come and enjoy a stay. But we don't want an eyesore under our noses . . . we don't want this hotel used for a lot of broken down old stiffs. I know of nothing more uninteresting than a sick old man."[93] Estill's sarcasm encompassed Brother Gerard and Brother Aloys: those "Mexican gentlemen . . . Mutt and Jeff."[94] At a September 22 meeting of the Laymen's Dinner Club of Sts. Peter and Paul Catholic Parish in Chattanooga the club endorsed the resolution in which it "protested against the unfairness of these newspaper articles and against the unfairness of certain residents of Signal Mountain. . . ."[95] Though the Brothers' opponents attempted to obstruct them by a zoning act and other legal maneuvers, the Alexians successfully consummated the purchase on September 27, 1936.[96] After incorporating themselves as a nonprofit institution, the Brothers initiated an extensive redevelopment plan, which took nearly two years to complete.[97] On the feast of St. Alexius, July 17, 1938, Brother Vincent Geist, a registered nurse, was appointed first rector of the Alexian Brothers Rest Home. His vice rector, Brother Alphonse Honnewinkle, who had extensive engineering experience, had been responsible for overseeing the construction of the monastery chapel and other buildings. With a buoyant personality and a strong diplomatic sensitivity, Brother Vincent was an excellent choice as administrator responsible for breaking the ice with the once hostile portion of the Signal Mountain residents. As a sign of the Alexians' good citizenship, Brother Vincent sent a check for $1,000 to the town of Signal Mountain on August 22, 1938.[98]

Because there was a growing population of Catholics on the mountain, Bishop Adrian of Nashville made the Alexian Chapel, dedicated to St. Augustine, their parish church. On November 22 he consecrated the chapel and blessed every room in the rest home and monastery.[99] As another goodwill geature to the entire Chattanooga community, the Alexians hosted an open house on November 23 and 24. Over 1,300 people passed through the home, a sign that the ice had indeed been broken.[100] By this time the first resident, Joseph Miller, had moved into the rest home (November 8) and the first novice to persevere, Brother Jerome Revak, had entered the sixty-five-room novitiate (August 31). (In 1974 Brother Jerome became director (superior) of the Alexian community at Signal Mountain. In 1977 Brother Vincent Geist, the home's first superior, was cheerfully greeting guests at the home's reception desk.) By November 1938 sixteen novices, under the direction of Brother Anthony Wessel, were in formation there.

The Signal Mountain novitiate was extremely remote from the other Alexian institutions. The rest home was not a hospital. The novices' work there was more custodial than professional. The home was never filled to capacity. Hence in June 1940 clergy retreats were initiated to compensate for the relatively low occupancy rate. However, as long as it remained a novitiate the Brothers did not expect the home to break even financially. Though placing novices in a remote unprofessional setting was not in accord with the modernization trend it was in harmony with church trends, which encouraged an isolated novitiate characterized by prayer, study and work, and free from the distractions of active apostolates. The issue of a separate novitiate has elicited controversy from its inception. Some Brothers still feel that isolation prevented practical preparation for Alexian life, while others stressed the necessity of isolation for strong religious formation.

13

The Third Reich
and World War II

I

The rise of the Nazi party in Germany was directly linked with the great depression, which originated in the United States in late 1929 and spread throughout the industrial world within a matter of months.

The rector-general during the first years of the Third Reich was the former American provincial, Brother Frumentius Horn. Because of frequent harassment by the Gestapo and other government officials, Pater Frumentius emigrated to Henri Chapelle in 1935. A new generalate was constructed on the grounds, one which was considered the Alexian Motherhouse in exile. The Brothers in Germany, like members of all religious orders, were subjected to slanderous attacks upon their morality as if the religious cloisters were houses of ill repute.

The Nazi propaganda attacks upon clergy and religious elicited a firm response from the Bishops' Conference at Fulda. In an August 25, 1935, document the bishops stated that they lodged a protest with Hitler against "the concerted action which is going on against the clergy" and alluded to the press propaganda in which priestly celibacy, the confessional, and veneration of saints were dragged "in the mud."[1] Anti-Catholicism was occasionally united with anti-Semitism: "When will man's heavy bonds be cut? When will earth's gloom be banished? When, strangled with the last priest's gut, the last of the Jews has vanished."[2] Gestapo investigations leading to the so-called "morality trials," in which religious and clergy were to be convicted of sexual deviations of the most absurd stripe, touched the Alexians of Krefeld and Aachen. Though the Alexians were subjected to such Gestapo harassment they were never brought to trial. Besides these indignities many of the younger Alexians were conscripted into the domestic public-works programs and, after 1936, were conscripted into the army. In 1933 there were forty-two Brothers at the Motherhouse, while by 1938 there were only thirty. Each house experienced a proportionate fall in Brothers, but new vocations fell disastrously. In 1932 there were seventy-three novices and twenty-one postulants, while in 1938 the numbers were ten and two, respectively.[3]

The sterilization and euthanasia issues deeply touched the Alexians as hospital and asylum Brothers. The Nazi sterilization law, requiring every bearer of specific hereditary diseases to be sterilized, contained an escape clause for Catholic doctors and nurses. Maria-Hilf at Krefeld, the only general hospital among the Alexian institutions in Germany, was for the most part exempt from the law. The bishops had protested all sterilizations, voluntary or involuntary, but according to Brother Camillus Snyder, an American Brother who was the pharmacist at Krefeld during the early thirties, the ruling of their bishops was at first equivocal, so that a few sterilization procedures occurred at Maria-Hilf in 1933. This practice may have been initiated by the hospital non-Catholic physicians and lasted only a short time. However, the law required hospitals to report to the government all those cases of hereditary illness, and through an exaggerated twist of logic the church allowed Catholics to report such incidents as if such reporting were morally indifferent "material cooperation" rather than "formal cooperation."[4] There is no extant evidence related to the Brothers' reporting such cases, but, since the Nazi anti-Catholic campaign was intensified during the mid-thirties, one may infer that there was little or no cooperation with the letter of the law.

Hitler's euthanasia policy was initiated on September 1, 1939, the opening day of World War II. The practical motivation behind this "Aryan" extermination policy was that by murdering all the incurably ill, the "useless eaters" would be removed from the scene, thereby providing more hospital space. Between December 1939 and August 1941, 30,000 patients in Germany were murdered, most of whom were mentally retarded or terminally insane.[5] In 1941 the Alexian Brothers' asylums in Ensen and near Münster (Haus Kannen) were notified to turn over to the state-asylum authorities all those patients whose bills were paid by the government.[6] Hence in the guise of a war-economy measure the Nazi government pursued what by this time was an "open secret" policy of mass murder. Since the Brothers at Ensen and Haus Kannen had certainly heard euthanasia horror stories, they undoubtedly sensed the fate of their patients (one hundred at Haus Kannen were turned over). However, all the young Brothers were fighting in the war and the older (approximately twenty Brothers between ages sixty and eighty years) felt helpless before the Nazi officials. Perhaps the few who may have been able to muster the courage to protest against the policy (which was in official disguise) may have deferred to the church leaders. In 1940 Cardinals Betram and Faulhaber had lodged formal protests against the policy and on August 3, 1941, Bishop Graf von Galen of Münster, perhaps responding to the plea of the Alexians and the plight of their patients, eloquently defended the sanctity of human life: " 'Woe unto the German people,' Galen declared, 'when innocents not only could be killed, but their slayers remain unpunished.' "[7] Bishop von Galen's speech was well publicized and nearly resulted in his arrest and execution for treason. Rather than make him a martyr, Hitler restrained his rage and, because of the impact of the sermon, officially terminated the euthanasia program. The Catholic Church, prompted by public opinion, assumed strong moral leadership, which in part compelled Hitler to halt the program. Unfortunately neither public opinion nor moral leadership responded to the plight of the Jews. Gunter Lewy points out that "wild euthanasia" persisted but the mass-murder program was never revived.[8] On July 11, 1943, 135 patients of the Krefeld asylum were forcibly loaded on buses and, according to Brother Ignatius Wiegers, "the majority of them were never seen again."[9] Once again the Alexians felt helpless.

The war's impact upon the Alexians is best detailed by the

Brothers themselves. Brother Evergistus Sonneck wrote about Haus Kannen:

> During the war years approximately twenty Brothers between the ages of 60 and 80 years remained here to care for our 500 patients; and it is wonderful how Almighty God has sustained them and blessed their efforts. Many of us younger men had already gone away to fulfill the military service required of us and had returned by 1939 to our very happy community, only to be compelled to make the double sacrifice of once more leaving our dear conventual home to face a cruelly uncertain future. Five Brothers from this largest house of our province have lost their lives, two we have not heard from in the last few years, and one of us is still a prisoner of war in Russia.[10]

On July 9, 1941, Münster was heavily bombed. St. Clement Hospital was destroyed. Since the Alexians had just added a wing to their asylum, it was made available to the refugee patients and nuns. Eventually St. Clement's patients occupied 350 of the 500 beds at Haus Kannen. Other than some broken windows and roof damage as a result of one bomb exploding near the asylum Haus Kannen escaped the physical ravages of the war.[11]

In 1941 Schloss Malseneck was seized by the government and transformed into a political school for the Nazi party. Brother Corbinian Benzkofer described the situation there:

> We younger Brothers were ordered to leave our convent for the military. The house was confiscated in March, 1941 and used as a *political-school* for some 80-100 children from bomb-damaged towns and cities. The barns were left to Brothers Boniface, Rector, and Brother Burkhard. The chapel was desecrated and used as a dining room with the usual party symbols and images prominently displayed. Since the Nazi regime and the departure of the American military, who used it as a small hospital for soldiers, the house has been renovated and the chapel restored. The Holy Sacrifice of the Mass is once more offered daily in atonement and reparation for the dishonor done to God and the injustice and disgrace brought upon this home in the recent years. We received our first refugees here on September 4, 1946, the house was solemnly reopened by dignitaries of both Church and State on the 16th, and we celebrated the twenty-fifth anniversary of the House's foundation on September 21st, 1946. This latter occasion was made doubly joyous by the return of Brother Wilhelm from prison camp. . . .[12]

The asylum at München-Gladbach suffered the most extensive damage. As a result of 1944 "obliteration bombing" the chapel was "a gutted shell open to the heavens,"[13] and two wings were terribly burned by incendiary bombs. The Krefeld asylum was not directly hit but did experience grave damage by an explosion nearby. Due to a shortage in Alexian manpower Maria-Hilf in Krefeld had been turned over to the Augustinian Sisters (Cellitenen) and had withstood some serious damage when the convent floor was entirely demolished.[14] The Ensen asylum was transformed into a military hospital, but because of its location near a railway switching station it was extremely hard hit during the air attacks of the winter of 1944–1945. On February 6, 1945, when American forces took Cologne, the bombing finally stopped, leaving the Ensen hospital in shell-like condition.[15] Henri Chapelle's location within a few miles of the German border meant that she "led a dizzy existence under the duress of occupation and counter-occupation, but suffered no damage."[16] At the end of the war Henri Chapelle housed the war homeless, a contingent of American troops, and refugees from Lierre.[17] With only four elderly and overworked Brothers at Lierre and with little hope of enough vocations, the Alexians closed the house in 1945, only to sell it in 1946 to a community of Black Sisters, Flemish Cellite Sisters.[18] Lierre was the last Alexian house still embedded in the ancient Cellite tradition of preparing the body for burial. Of all the houses, Schänis, nestled in its remote Alpine enclave, was the least affected by the war.

The Aachen Motherhouse stood directly in the path of destruction. However, the largest Allied air offensive of hundreds of planes ravaged the Rhineland area from Aachen to Cologne. From the first days of the war the Motherhouse had been occupied, first by police, then by reserves and security police and other government agencies. The chapel and the generalate had been almost destroyed in April 1944.[19] With the advance of the American army toward Aachen in September, all civilians were ordered to leave the city. Brothers Columbanus, Candidus, and Eugen, five patients and Father Faust, from the Jesuit parish nearby, remained in the Motherhouse, which became a bomb shelter and refuge for many of the townspeople.

II

The governance of the congregation during the war years devolved to the provincial level. At the 1938 General Chapter, the only Brother from the Anglo-Irish Province to lead the Alexians, Brother Gilbert Holmes, was elected rector-general. It was a wise choice for with the outbreak of war the British pater could at least maintain links between England and the United States. Indeed, when the war started, Pater Gilbert was touring the American Province. In mid-September he returned to England where blackouts characterized the wartime fear and anxiety. Unable to dwell in the Belgian generalate, which was in Nazi hands, Pater Gilbert resided in England throughout the war. Brother Andrew McKenzie, a member of the Anglo-Irish Province who had been stationed in Lierre and Henri Chapelle before the war, wrote that "Twyford Abbey had many narrow escapes during the blitz [of 1940]. One night a land-mine dropped in the meadow a few yards from the house, and another landed at the gate obliterating the water main. Our water from thence on was carted from elsewhere. . . . During these raids the Abbey suffered considerable damage from the blast. Many of the windows were blown in and schrapnel pitted the walls of the building."[20] Because of the danger and because the British army was occupying part of the abbey, the Brothers looked for a wartime residence. In October 1940 Twyford Abbey was taken over by the management of the Guinness Brewing Company, which was located adjacent to the Brothers' property. The novitiate was moved to Warrenpoint, Northern Ireland, which was physically undisturbed by the war while the provincialate, community and residents moved to Wales. Brother Andrew McKenzie recalled the journey:

At 9:00 A.M., October 3rd, 1940 we left London for Llysdulas, Angelsey, North Wales, in two large motor coaches and several ambulances, the Abbey to be occupied immediately by the office staff of the Guinness Brewing Company. Our caravan lunched at Stratford-on-Avon, the birthplace of William Shakespeare. . . . We arrived at Llysdulas somewhere around midnite, where Brother John

Lynch, the Provincial, had a smashing tea waiting for us. . . . Exhausted from our long journey we settled down for the night in makeshift beds. Morning revealed Llysdulas in all its sylvan loveliness. It was an ancient Gothic manor . . . situated atop a wooded hill overlooking sweet Dulas Bay at a point where a mile-long yellow strand stood out in contrast to the blue sea and the green banks. . . . In comparison to London, Llysdulas was a solitude, but a very lovely and delightful one. At times life was hard and strenuous there, but we settled down nicely to a quiet country life, thanking God for His goodness when so many others had to face the raging storm of war and its horrible consequences. God was good to us indeed. . . .[21]

III

The Belgian Brothers also suffered many casualties during the war. On Friday, May 10, 1940, the German blitzkrieg shot through Belgium.[22] Because they had turned off the radio early that morning the Boechout Brothers had no news of the advancing attack. Upon hearing of the destruction of the Brothers' of Charity House, eight Brothers, under the leadership of Brother Vincentius, left for Antwerp where they worked in the infirmary. Unlike the German Brothers, the Belgian Alexians were not drafted as combatants but as medical corpsmen, whereas the Dutch Brothers were not drafted at all.

German occupation imposed severe hardships among the Belgian people. The psychological terror entailed in living within earshot of the firing squads and in the threat of deportation if one were caught violating the rationing and other laws was most severe. For example, Brother Clemens Aarts and Brother Cornelius were arrested for attempting to smuggle a piece of bacon to the confreres in Brussels. Fortunately the arresting soldier was lenient with them as he set them free after he seized the bacon. Yet he warned them that if caught again they would be deported to Dachau or Buchenwald. Four Louvain Alexians were imprisoned in those infamous institutions of death, terror, and torture because they had been found hiding a wanted man in their house. Two Brothers were sent from Boechout to take their place at the asylum in Louvain.

The Dutch Brothers, barred from traveling to the Netherlands, were very anxious for their families. Aided by a sister of one of the patients at Boechout who lived in a border town, Brothers Paulus and Clemens risked a clandestine crossing into the Netherlands. After successfully evading the border guards they were caught and interrogated by SS troops. Once again Brother Clemens avoided imprisonment; the German troops merely fined the group 100 francs.

Shortly before the end of the war, tragedy struck the Alexians; on November 17, 1944, Pater Alphons was mortally wounded by a V-2 rocket. He had been superior of the Boechout community for forty-one years. He founded the TB sanitarium at Son and was deeply dedicated to the cause of Cellite unity in Belgium. Because the Belgian Brothers professed vows to both their superior and their ordinary as official visitator, and because bishops defended their right, Pater Alphons made only gradual headway in pursuit of unity and the reestablishment of province status in Belgium. He did succeed in leading the Elsene Alexian community to join Boechout, while in 1937 Joseph Cardinal Von Roey encouraged unity when he designated Boechout as the novitiate for all Belgian Alexians. In 1941 Grimbergen and in 1950 Tienen joined the Boechout family. After the war Brother Christopher Lynch encouraged Belgian-German unity but formal talks did not pursue such a merger until 1949.

Brother John Lynch was the Anglo-Irish Provincial during the war. According to Brother Anselm, Brother John "was the right Brother needed to guide the Province during the war."[23] He appears to have been an inveterate optimist; he "was a man full of charity and heart full of other people, he was one for the down and out. . . . If you were in trouble or needed to be uplifted he would be the first to help you. . . . He was a very spiritual man but had no hard and fast rules about him, but in this way he got much more from others than if he had laid down the law, because you wanted to do the right thing for him."[24]

St. Mary's Home in Manchester was not damaged during the blitz. Indeed it "offered good protection for neighboring families who used its cellars as air raid shelters."[25] Stillington Hall in remote Yorkshire was undisturbed by German air raids. The Brothers there assumed a most unusual task when they agreed to house young boys and their schoolmasters who had been evacuated from the bomb-devastated town of Hull. The Brothers improved the farmhouses on their property for some fifty new boarders. Brother Anselm Hopkins, who was the superior at Stillington during this time, recalled the many discipline problems these Alexian foster-fathers experienced. From the boys' point of view life in the large country estate must have been one continuous adventure.[26]

The war hastened the modernization of the Anglo-Irish Province. Due to a wartime shortage of nurses, to the flexibility and openness of Brother John Lynch, and to the progressive foresight of Brother Anselm Hopkins, the Brothers were able to train as nurses at York City Hospital in 1943. First residing at Stillington Hall, the student nurses moved to the city where they lived in a home rented from the Poor Clares. Brother Joseph Newell was one of the first British-trained R.N.s and a pioneer at the new home called St. Michael's House.[27] Had some of the Brothers not become R.N.s their hospices would not have qualified as nursing homes under the British Public Health system when it was introduced a few years after the war. On October 3, 1945, exactly five years after the Brothers had left Twyford Abbey, the Alexians returned to their London residence. Many of the Brothers and sixty patients left their Welsh home by the sea reluctantly, but there was general joy upon arriving back at Twyford Abbey.

IV

In April 1941, while the conflagration continued in Europe, the American Alexians, free from the impact of war until the end of that year, celebrated the seventy-fifth anniversary of the Chicago foundation, the first Alexian house in the United States. To honor the occasion Archbishop Samuel A. Stritch celebrated a solemn pontifical Mass at the Brothers' chapel, and at the Lake Shore Country Club the Brothers were honored by a gala fete attended by Chicago's mayor and other civic dignitaries.[28]

The following September Archbishop Thomas Walsh of the

Newark archdiocese blessed the Brothers' new residence in Elizabeth, one which is located across the street from the hospital and is still occupied by the Brothers. The war dampened the civic celebrations of Elizabeth's Golden Jubilee in 1942 and St. Louis's Diamond Jubilee in 1944, but each was commemorated with a solemn pontifical Mass. The capacity of each of these hospitals had grown to 175 beds.[29] Unlike their German and Anglo-Irish confreres, the American Brothers were not directly involved in the war. However, vocations were drastically reduced and their hospitals suffered an acute shortage of personnel.

When the Selective Service began conscription in the spring of 1941 the Brothers, who feared that the shortage of student nurses would severely affect Alexian health care at the hospital, were able to obtain only six-month deferrals for their students. After some lobbying efforts in Washington, D.C., Brother Hugh Miller, rector at Chicago, traveled to Springfield, Illinois, for discussions about draft deferrals. The officials could not offer much encouragement but did inform Brother Hugh of the possibility of recruiting conscientious objectors to work at the hospital.[30]

In the fall of 1941 Brothers Hugh and Basil met with those authorities responsible for conscientious objector (CO) camps. After a Colonel Kosch toured the Belden Avenue Hospital he promised to urge General L. B. Hershey to speed up the process of transferring CO's from a reforestation camp to the Alexian Brothers hospital. "On March 5, 1942, a few months after the bombing of Pearl Harbor, the first hospital unit [of CO's] was opened at the Alexian Brothers Hospital of Chicago, and was designated as CPS Unit #26."[31] Of the first eighteen men assigned to the hospital, twelve were sponsored by the Association of Catholic Conscientious Objectors. Throughout the war a total of 101 men entered the unit, with the highest unit strength at seventy-six. Eleven of the original eighteen entered the School of Nursing in June 1942, receiving their R.N. three years later, while most of the others became either practical nurses or worked in plant maintenance, etc.[32] At first some of the Brothers opposed locating a CO camp at the hospital, as if they were harboring unpatriotic cowards. In contrast Brother John of God wrote: "In justice to the men, it can be said, that they were found to be of good character, efficient in their work, cooperative with patients, superiors and everyone with whom they came in contact."[32] "While they considered their motives, in being conscientious objectors, never did they advertise or argue their course to others during their time at the hospital."[33] So valuable were the new lay personnel that the Brothers "would have been compelled to limit the number of patients . . . had it not been for the assistance we received from the CO's."[34] The additional nursing staff also allowed Brothers to be transferred from Chicago to other houses "where they [were] badly needed."[35]

The St. Louis hospital temporarily closed its nursing school and relied upon voluntary help to fill the manpower gap. Many students from Christian Brothers College donated their time, and a contract was successfully negotiated with the St. Louis State Training School whereby some delinquent boys were placed under the direction of the Brothers on a trial basis. So successful was the program that it developed into a regular feature of the school's rehabilitation system. Mr. E. V. McMahon, then director of the hospital's Social Services Department and monitor of the program, reported that many of the boys remained on as permanent employees.[36] Other volunteers came from city and church organizations, eight of whom "became the first nurses' aides in the city."[37]

Brother Basil Wilwerding, provincial from 1938 to 1944, seems to have been comparable to his counterpart in the Anglo-Irish Province. Like Brother John Lynch, he was a warm, flexible leader but, unlike Brother John, he was a shrewd businessman with keen political insight. His circle of friends included bishops and stockbrokers, the latter advising him on the management of the Alexian Brothers' corporations. He seems to have considered Signal Mountain an albatross, as he pursued a new location for a novitiate in New Jersey. In the spring of 1944 the Brothers purchased property in Summit, New Jersey, located near Elizabeth in the Newark diocese. The American provincial purchased the property only after receiving the permission from Archbishop Thomas J. Walsh, who successfully appealed for further permission from the apostolic delegate, Archbishop Cicognani.[38] However, after Brother Basil had purchased the property, Pater Gilbert wrote to him refusing permission to move the novitiate to the New Jersey site.[39] After visiting the property with his vicar general and Brother Conrad Christie, rector at Elizabeth, Archbishop Walsh advised Brother Basil to "hold title to this Summit property and consider the proposition to establish thereon a home for convalescents or other similar institution."[40] It is unclear whether Pater Gilbert vetoed this proposal or Brother Basil rejected it because of a lack of Brothers, but the property was sold, apparently for a small profit.[41]

Brother Basil's flexibility and openness seem to have included a less stringent enforcement of the rules regarding smoking and recreation time in general. During the war when Brother Hugh and Brother Jude Thaddeus Eckrich were rector and vice-rector, the Belden Avenue Hospital had been compelled to use many secular employees, some of whom were women. With the inclusion of the lay nursing students and the COs there was naturally a breakdown in the traditional monastic remoteness from the laity. Many of the Brothers who had been well-trained nurses and felt the need for a more professional atmosphere were grateful for the more relaxed atmosphere. A traditionalist wing under the leadership of Brother Gerard Kuhn appealed to Pater Gilbert; without consultation with other American Brothers, Pater Gilbert appointed Brother Gerard as provincial rather than reappoint Brother Basil for a third term, which most Brothers had anticipated as the most likely decision during wartime. The new provincial and his council replaced Brothers Hugh and Jude and established a stringently traditional rule for the province. Though Brother Gerard was deeply motivated to revive the monastic ideals of the province, his methods, such as placing on bulletin boards accusatory notes about a particular Brother's lax ways, alienated many of the Brothers. Indeed shortly after Brother Gerard was appointed provincial a group of anti-Gerard Brothers visited with Cardinal Stritch to seek his intervention in what had developed into an extremely polarized situation.[42] Father James J. Mertz, s.j., of Loyola University recalled a most significant conflict during this period:

> On September 11, 1944 I was called to the Chancery Office by His Eminence, Samuel Cardinal Stritch, Archbishop of Chicago, Illinois. A letter, dated September 2, 1944 by His Excellency Archbishop A. G. Cicognani, Apostolic Delegate, was presented to me

by the Cardinal, together with a letter, dated Rome, August 28, from the Sacred Congregation of Religious, signed by the secretary Fr. L. Pasetto. In these letters I was appointed Apostolic Visitor to the Alexian Brothers of the United States, "with all necessary and opportune faculties" ad inquirendum et referendum (to make inquiry and report).[43]

As apostolic visitor, Father Mertz was to conduct an unbiased investigation. Hence Brother Gerard, confident of his interpretation of the spirit of the community, warmly welcomed Father Mertz. According to the Father Mertz–Brother Gerard correspondence, the education of the young Brothers both in nursing and in the university was a thorny issue between the progressives and the traditionalists. Apparently Brother Gerard refused to allow young Brothers in St. Louis to attend the nursing school there. The school's director, Brother Athanasius, had notified Father Mertz of the problem; he, in turn, as the final authority in the province, wrote to Brother Gerard urging him to send Brothers to the school if only for continuity. Brother Gerard considered the origin of the dissenter's criticism: "The men are unhappy because they realize their unfortunate condition. As long as they were permitted to have their easy going life they had some consolation from the frequent intercourse with the outside world; now, since the Superiors are trying to correct the irregularities, they are deprived of this consolation and their consciences give them no satisfaction of assurance that they are doing the right thing."[44] He also told Father Mertz how the dissenters complained about the rule and constitution and superiors, "since it is these which deprive them of their unrestrained liberties."[45] This December 31, 1944, letter to Father Mertz ended with Brother Gerard's plea for his help in stemming the tide of monastic abuse.[46] Recognizing the danger in delving into personalities during this critical time, it appears appropriate to place this authority crisis in light of modernization. The opponents to Brother Gerard appeared to be striving toward a recognition of their maturity as modern professional men within the religious life, a condition which demands greater freedom of conscience and association with lay colleagues. Regardless of how he mediated his traditionalism, Brother Gerard appears to have viewed this tendency as indicative of a gross violation of the religious vocations as Alexian Brothers. Because of the polarized condition, the dissenters who lashed out at the legitimate authority probably appeared radical but their goals were actually quite moderate.

On May 20, the feast of Pentecost, Father Mertz wrote a circular letter to the Brothers of the province, providing them with "a digest of the recommendations made by the Sacred Congregation of Religious subsequent to my report after the Visitation of the Province of America."[47] By this time Brother Gerard had been notified that he, his council, and all the superiors of the houses were to be replaced. The Sacred Congregation's recommendations, paraphrased by Father Mertz, stressed the need for separate facilities for novices and candidates or postulants, for sophisticated spiritual formation in the novitiate, and in each house some monthly instructions including "the explanation of Christian Doctrines" to be given to the entire community.[48] He pointed to the necessity of a suitably furnished recreation room where Brothers can relax and read material which will "help to keep the Brothers posted on current events of the day" as well as religious and devotional materials. Explicitly endorsing secular reading supported the moderates. His stress upon the "importance of education" places Father Mertz squarely behind the modernism of the moderates.[49] He recommended the R.N. and advanced degrees for all those qualified "so that to the nursing of the sick all those proper technical methods can be applied that are so imperative at present in all hospital work."[50]

The Sacred Congregation also stressed the sanctity of the individual religious's conscience, the need for superiors to respect that sanctity by permitting Brothers to send letters free from all inspection to the Holy See, its legate in the country, to their cardinal protector, to their own major superior, etc., and to receive untampered letters from these authorities.[51] Though the latter clarification seems to imply that there had been many violations of conscience, it confirmed the superior's privilege of opening general outgoing and incoming mail "with prudence and charity and under the seal of secrecy."[52] The final recommendation was a directive to Father Mertz to draw up a new Provincial Custom Book aimed to help "regulate the individual house, as far as that is possible, and give greater community of interests to all the members of the Province."[53] Though working in consultation with the Brothers, Father Mertz did not introduce many substantial changes into the customs of the province. In general the changes reflect the gradual movement away from the traditional monastic life toward a fuller appreciation for the Brothers as active professional nurses and hospital personnel with time to cultivate outside interests and pursue healthy entertainment, recreation, and relaxation.

Prayers after breakfast were dropped and a Brother could leave the table when he was finished.[54] The Seven Penitential Psalms were dropped from the 2:00 P.M. visitation to the Blessed Sacrament, while Stations of the Cross were to be said privately.[55] Father Mertz's Jesuit background was evidenced in the Ignatian-like schedule for the Brothers' retreat program.[56] Rectors were bound to follow specific guidelines for meals, such as meat twice a day, beer and wine available at dinner, and beer at supper.[57] Smoking was permitted in the Brothers' rooms as well as in the traditional place, the recreation room.[58] The 7:00 to 8:45 P.M. recreation period was divided into two parts, the first to be devoted to personal work or needs and the second to community recreation. The Brothers were to be allowed one day each week at the country cottage with evening return-hour at 8:00 or 8:15 except in July and August when it was to be 9:00 or 9:30 P.M. A few times a year they could spend a weekend at the cottage. Movies of appropriate character were to be shown in the house once or twice a month at the rector's discretion. Brothers might attend concerts and entertainments of a high order. Though this Custom Book appears stringent by today's standards it was, in contrast to tradition and those customs guiding the European provinces, quite liberal.[59] On July 6, 1946, the book received Cardinal Stritch's *imprimatur* and was immediately put into effect.

On June 8, 1945, Brother Vulgan replaced Brother Gerard as provincial. A new council was appointed, which in turn appointed new house rectors. At the suggestion of Father Mertz the office of Brother Rector was separated from the administration of the hospital because of the burden of dual leadership embodied in one Brother and because the spiritual life and temporal ministry required two separate abilities, which some felt were not frequently found in one man. Though others would contend that leadership is leadership regardless of the spiritual or temporal sphere, the division has been maintained in the American Province and was later introduced as an option in the Anglo-Irish and German provinces. Divided authority works smoothly as long as the persons involved respect each other's autonomy and sense that often fuzzy dividing line. Father Mertz's recommendation to separate the postulancy from the novitiate was fulfilled in the spring of 1946 when the novices, under Brother Anthony Wessel's direction, moved into their new novitiate on the Schoenberg Estate located in what was then referred to as Clayton, Missouri. Entitled Our Lady of St. Alexius, the new novitiate was situated in a lovely rural setting approximately seven miles west of that is today downtown Clayton. Because of the Brothers' warm affection for the then recently deceased archbishop of St. Louis, John Cardinal Glennon, they named the new foundation Glennondale. The postulancy under Brother Kevin Gruss remained at Signal Mountain.

V

As the American Province was experiencing the renewal of unity after the 1944 rupture and as the Anglo-Irish Province was eking out a meager living during the severe postwar scarcity amid the bitterly cold winter of 1945–1946, the German Province, war-shattered in a struggle for survival, mourned the many maimed, lost, killed, and alienated Brothers. Of the eighty-five Brothers who had experienced battle, twenty-six were killed; three noncombatant Brothers lost their lives as a result of the Allied bombing raids. Between 1933 and 1945 the German Province lost 150 Brothers, some by the hand of death, others by leaving the religious life.[60] Brother Ignatius Wiegers had witnessed the horrors of Nazi terror and war:

> Finally after 6 years the cannons are silent and useless dying has ceased. But what a terrible inheritance the National-socialistic System has bequeathed! Millions of dead are in their graves; millions

of cripples stagger along in distress. The army of a million of an entire nation has been captured. Families are disrupted; none knows the whereabouts of the other; women are looking for their husbands, parents for their children, everything is thrown into confusion and uprooted in flight. The most beautiful cities are lying in ashes; countless quiet towns and extensive stretches of fertile land are devastated. Hunger is knocking at the door. The conqueror is in the country; Germany's fate lies in his power. For all this we are indebted to the Fuehrer.[61]

For over a year the German Province limped along on its own. Haus Kannen, the least damaged asylum, sent building materials, clothing, and general nonfood supplies to the desperate Alexian institutions to the south, many of which were feeding and clothing the refugees of war. The General Chapter, originally scheduled for 1944, had been postponed until after the war; permission to travel to Henri Chapelle was granted in October 1946. When the chapter convened on October 22, the German Provincial, Brother Leontius, and the two delegates, Brother Aloysius Prehm and Brother Gereon Wittkamp, were unable to obtain visas for travel to Belgium. Three Brothers from Henri Chapelle were chosen as substitutes. A commission composed of Brother Anthony Wessel of the American Province, Brother John Lynch of the Anglo-Irish Province, and Brother Baldomer Dole of the German Province was mandated by the chapter to examine the rector-general's report and to classify the proposals for the chapter's consideration.[62]

Three days later the delegates elected Brother Anthony Wessel, the American novice master, as rector-general. His council was almost evenly representative of the three provinces: first, second, and fourth assistants from Germany, Brothers Wolfgang Wollender, Crespian Mouthe, and Baldomer Dole; third assistant, Edmund Kelly of England; secretary general and bursar general, Brothers Christopher Lynch and Basil Wilwerding of the American Province. Pater Anthony was highly regarded for his quiet piety; the choice of two Americans to handle clerical and business matters appears more than coincidental.

The American proposals and resolutions stressed the need for democratic reform, for greater province autonomy, for historical consciousness, and for spiritual renewal.

The proposals for democratic reform included requests that the life professed Brothers of the American Province elect their own provincial and that the life professed Brothers nominate three Brothers for provincial, one of which would be chosen by the General Council[63]. The autonomy resolutions stated:

1. That the American Province be given autonomy in all matters concerning finances, new foundations and abolishing old ones, constructions or alterations of buildings, establishing of policies regarding education of members, public relations and charitable activities.
2. That this Province be associated with the General Motherhouse by identity of Rule, traditional customs, requirements for membership, in religious and canonical matters.[64]

Both sets of recommendations were voted down by an identical 12 to 3 vote. Considering that provincials and ex-provincials were ex-officio delegates to the chapter and that the Anglo-Irish Province was deeply tied to tradition, the three affirmative votes were undoubtedly registered from the American delegates at large.[65] This was a young Turk trio within the chapter, but it had the support of twenty-one of the twenty-two delegates at the American Provincial Chapter.[66] Again, with nearly unanimous support from the American Chapter, the reformers had also proposed changing the election rules governing General Chapters. They recommended that for each provincial attending the chapter an at-large delegate be added to the total representing the province.[67]

Brother Baldomer Dole, as a member of the Commission of Examiners, authored a report on the democratic reform proposals. Defending the hierarchical principle as being in conformity with the structure of the church, Brother Baldomer concluded, "our Divine Lord . . . *nominated* the Apostles as Bishops or as it were Cardinals and amongst them St. Peter as the Supreme Head. Therefore if we are disciples of Christ then all must retain the hierarchical form."[68]

Brother Baldomer recommended that, to ensure unity and impartiality on the General Council, each of the provinces be represented and that the generalate be moved to Rome, both of which were approved at the chapter.[69] The American proposals that "more stress be put upon the historical aspect of our

Congregation and a reliable history of the Congregation, giving a more detailed picture of the various Brothers in establishing new foundations etc., be compiled as soon as possible" was unanimously accepted and the General Council was "charged with its execution."[70] The specific reference to new foundations within the historical perspective appears to have been related to another American proposal endorsing and encouraging new ministries such as "Public Health Work in Schools and Colleges, and the establishment and maintaining of residences and recreation agencies for the young."[71] The chapter referred this to the provincial authorities.

In contrast to the American Province the Anglo-Irish Province did not propose any major changes. Indeed all of its proposals were referred back to the provincial level for decisions. The Anglo-Irish delegation sought confirmation of the need to extend their houses in Ireland, to establish a juniorate, to establish a novitiate in Ireland and to divide it into a spiritual year and nurse's training year.[72]

The German delegation proposed to extend the financial autonomy of the province, to establish a generalate in Rome, and due to postwar communication problems, to place Henri Chapelle and Schänis under the authority of the General Council rather than the German Provincial Council. The first two proposals barely passed, while the latter was postponed until canon-law issues were resolved.[73]

The reform movement within the American Province, buoyant from its experience with Father Mertz and his progressive Custom Book, received a severe setback at the General Chapter. The German and Anglo-Irish provinces were not ready to break with the hierarchical centralized authority structure. There is no doubt that the two European provinces admired the American Alexian style of modernization within the general hospital context, but after experiencing the tragedy of war, cut off from the traditional structures, they cherished those principles which the American reformers criticized. Ultimately these reforms were codified into the constitution, but not until after John XXIII convened Vatican Council II.

14

The Ascendancy of
the American Province

The theme of modernization reaches a climax in this and the
final chapters dealing with the Alexian Brother as a professional
nurse-minister in an increasingly complex technological hospital
setting and as a post-Vatican II religious groping for renewed
ways of mediating the gospel within the context of the unique
charism of the Alexians, or Cellites. The period from 1946 to
1965 is characterized by such rapid social change that the usual
generation span of twenty years contains many generations. For
example, we speak of youth's cultural sensibilities in terms of
decades, '40s, '50s, '60s, but actually one could subdivide them
into early and late '50s, etc. Because Vatican Council II sym-
bolizes a profound shift in Catholic perspectives one speaks of
pre- and post-Vatican II generations in the church. Religious
communities composed of many postwar generations and both
pre- and post-Vatican II religious were hard hit by generational
conflict and attitudinal tensions. The 1944 authority crisis in the
American Province was in a sense a conflict engendered by social
changes within the province; i.e., the demand for more professional and educational opportunities versus the traditional dichotomy between the cloister and the secular world. This
chapter explores the evolution of the professional Alexian
Brother within the varying cultural and church contexts in
America, England-Ireland and Germany.

With the ruptures of war still not fully mended and with the American Province strongly asserting itself in demands for democratic reform and provincial self-determination, the first postwar congregational publication, the 1948 *Alexiana,* opened with a plea for unity. The secretary-general, Brother Christopher Lynch, editor of *Alexiana,* stated, "In a little international family such as ours dissensions, the party spirit, or excessive national pride wound us with their lethal toxins much more than they would a larger group."[1] After quoting Pater Clement Wallrath on how the Alexian congregation was "destined to extend itself throughout the entire universe," Brother Christopher asked, "Are we worthy sons of such a father? Or are we too preoccupied with the difficulties of the present moment or circumstance to be concerned with family solidarity and apostolic vision?"[2]

In March 1948 Pater Anthony and Brother Christopher journyed to Rome. Just as Pater Alexius Jansen pursued an Alexian residence in Rome after World War I, Pater Anthony, under a mandate from the 1946 General Chapter, pursued a residence after World War II. Though a Rome-based generalate would have simplified Alexian-Vatican relations and given the congregation a sense of status equal to other international papal congregations, the postwar trend to break down nationalism and engender unity among the provinces seems to have been a significant motivating factor. Pater Anthony and Brother Christopher Lynch enjoyed a "special audience" with Pope Pius XII, the former cardinal protector of the Alexians; after inquiring about the affairs of the congregation His Holiness blessed "the Pater, the Congregation, its works, and the Brothers individually."[3] The Alexians left Rome with the hope of negotiating a residence sometime in the future. Though Pater Anthony received positive responses from Cardinal Protector Micara and the vicar of Rome, Cardinal Marchetti, the Alexians never settled in the Eternal City. Perhaps the advice rendered to Pater Alexius in the 1920s had an impact: do not establish a house in Rome unless it conforms to the general ministerial character of your order, i.e., hospital, asylum, hospice. Since the Alexians' goal was not ministerial but merely administrative it did not conform to this rule. The cold-war tensions in Eastern and Central Europe symbolized by the Berlin blockade of 1948 urged the Alexian General Council to decide (December 28, 1948) to move to the United States. In the spring of 1949 the Sacred Congregation of Religious approved the transfer of the generalate from Henri Chapelle to Lake Villa, Illinois, the Chicago Alexians' country cottage about an hour's drive from the city.[4]

Just as the Marshall Plan and the formation of NATO represent America's leadership role in European affairs, so the establishment of the generalate near Chicago represents the predominance of the American Province in the affairs of the congregation. Indeed, during the reconstruction phase in Germany, Brothers Christopher Lynch and Basil Wilwerding had been closely associated with postwar relief work in the Aachen area. From September 1947 to January 1948 they were attached to *Caritas Virband,* which collaborated with the Vatican Mission and the Quaker Relief Team of Aachen. They were primarily engaged in transporting apples from Belgium to Germany.[5] Brother Christopher recorded the experience in the 1949 *Alexiana:*

> These transports averaged two to four a week with as many as four trucks involved. It was not exactly an entertaining task and often proved exhausting in the extreme, but it did carry with it its little joys and considerable interior satisfaction. Brother Christopher handled the customs and frontier controls; Brother Basil frequently had to drive one of the military trucks. Fortunately we were able to include large quantities of personal goods in the transports, destined for our Brothers in Germany: sheeting, habit material, shirts, socks, oatmeal by the hundredweight, tinned meat, shoes, brushes, tinned milk and vegetables, soap, tooth paste, brooms and innumerable food and clothing parcels destined for convents and private families in need. We made the last transport in January, supplying the Motherhouse with 20 mattresses and pillows to replace those burned during the bombardment of Aachen, and bringing the total tonnage of apples up to 170. Our Brothers will owe an everlasting debt of gratitutde to Mr. Vernon Thomas and Miss Olive Goodykoontz of the Quaker Relief Team in Aachen for the time, hard work and good will they generously contributed during these months.[6]

Brother Christopher Lynch's experience eventually led to his being chosen as head of War Relief Services (NCWC) in the British Zone of Germany.[7] Because of his efforts during the 1948 Berlin crisis, Brother Christopher was awarded the *Pro Ecclesiae et Pontifici* medal.

The Anglo-Irish Province had been slightly influenced by the American Brothers through those young nursing students who returned from the Chicago School of Nursing bearing the marks of their American experiences. Shortly after the close of the 1946 General Chapter, Pater Anthony Wessel, Brother Provincial Vulgan, and Brother Athanasius Savary visited the Anglo-Irish houses. On April 1, 1947, after he had made his canonical visitation in the Anglo-Irish Province, Pater Anthony with the consent of the General Council appointed an American, Brother Camillus Snyder, to provincial of the Anglo-Irish Province.[8] Brother Camillus, one of the first Alexian R.N.s, had been well known for his keen professional leadership. In 1928 he became the first director of the School of Nursing in the St. Louis Alexian Hospital. From 1932 to 1935 Brother Camillus was laboratory technician and supervisor of the pharmacy at the Maria-Hilf General Hospital in Krefeld, Germany. In an undated document entitled "Pre-Visitation Remarks" Brother Camillus gives us a glimpse of his role as an American provincial of a foreign province. Written as a rough draft, the "Remarks" opened with a plea for advice from all the Brothers, as if he were appointed to upgrade and expand the province. He wrote, "It is difficult for me, a stranger, to know what should be done first. As I look over the houses I find things so entirely different from our American institutions. Our hospitals there are modern and scientifically on as high a plane as any in that country. I have been told that you wish modern nursing home establishments."[9] In contrast to the American Province the Anglo-Irish houses no doubt struck Brother Camillus as extremely primitive. The poverty of the province also shocked him. "They only had one wireless in the entire Province," he later recalled.[10] After visiting St. Mary's Home, Manchester, Brother Camillus remarked that he was "surprised and shocked to find the Holy days of the Church and our order have not been receiving the recognition and solemnity they deserve."[11] He suggested a feast-day schedule which included an 8:30 A.M. Missa Cantata with "something extra" added to the meals and wine at dinner and again at recreation along with cakes or sweets. "These days should be observed with joy and gladness as becomes the chosen souls of our Lord. God has been good to us, we certainly can afford these little extras in our ordinary life. We want to be happy and remember the day was a special one in the liturgical calendar."[12]

With wartime rationing still in effect in 1947 the financial situation of the province was uppermost in Brother Camillus's concerns. To relieve the financial burden the American provincial almost immediately decided to close Stillington Hall and to withdraw the Brothers from Wardley Cemetery, Manchester. At his first Provincial Council Meeting (May 20, 1947) Brother Camillus agreed that because few Brothers like cemetery work and because community life was irregular there, Wardley House should be closed.[13] They verbally agreed to sell Stillington Hall, a thoroughly unprofitable venture after twelve years. In a scratched-out portion of the rough draft of "Pre-Visitation Remarks," he wrote, "There are reasons why I would like to be relieved of Wardley Cemetery. . . . There is the matter of Stillington Hall. It never has been a profitable venture because it is too far from a large city and the house needs so much repair that it would seem advisable to acquire a more useful location in some other city."[14]

The superior at Wardley, Brother Alban Viehs, was in frequent correspondence with Brother Camillus regarding the decision. He had had many conflicts with Bishop Marshall, who lived at Wardley Hall adjacent to the cemetery. The tensions appear to have stemmed from minor issues, such as responsibility for maintaining the fence, but, according to Brother Alban, Bishop Marshall was given to severe bouts of temper, which made life quite uncomfortable for the Alexian superior.[15] Concurrent with the process of disengaging from Wardley Cemetery was the decision to sell Stillington Hall. Since Brother Anselm Hopkins, the founding rector of ?. ?all, was a provincial councillor to Brother Camillus, the decision was not that of an American but, rather, of all the Brothers on the Provincial Council. The Brothers left Wardley at the end of 1947 and Stillington toward the end of 1949.

Brother Camillus's most notable achievement as provincial was to expand the province into the Republic of Ireland. According to his own account of the "Search for Novitiate House in Irish Free State," Brother Camillus and Brother Gerard

Byrne (a Dubliner), a member of his council, set forth on a journey through Ireland seeking a bishop's permission.[16] The archbishop of Dublin replied with an emphatic "No" and the bishop of Limerick would not even provide for a visitation.[17] The bishops of Kerry and Kildare said that their dioceses were already overcrowded with religious congregations.[18] From the bishops' point of view a novitiate was only a drain on a diocese; it provided no service for the laity, while it consumed the time of a priest-confessor and could be a source of competition for candidates to the priesthood. After visiting the bishop of Cork the Brothers visited the adjacent diocese of Cloyne, centered in Cobh, where Bishop Roche informed them that he "felt sure his canons would not agree to it."[19] After another disappointing talk with the bishop of Carlow, Brothers Camillus and Gerard "dejected and tired drove into Warrenpoint feeling [they] had tried [their] best and failed. Upon arrival the Brothers poured out to meet us very happy with a telegram for Brother from Bishop James Roche of Cloyne, 'Have Brother Camillus come back to see me.' "[20]Upon their revisitation to the diocese of Cloyne, Bishop Roche informed them that after Friday Mass he had asked himself, "Why shouldn't I let those Alexian Brothers come into my diocese?"[21] Brother Camilus recorded his response. "I told him that was St. Joseph pushing you around."[22] A week after he had arrived in London to assume his duties as provincial, Brother Camillus had noted a real-estate advertisement on Bennett's Court, an eighteenth-century mansion located on one of the highest hills overlooking the Atlantic's majestic entrance through the Cobh (Queenstown), port of call to the busy harbor at Cork. Upon receiving word of Bishop Roche's permission to settle in Cobh—September 20, 1947—Brother Camillus set in motion the necessary real-estate and congregation negotiations for the purchase of Bennett's Court. However, before the new novitiate opened, Brother Camillus, after consulting with his council and Pater Anthony, resigned as provincial of the Sacred Heart Province in March 1948.[23]

In a circular letter to all the Brothers of the province, Brother Camillus stated that for reasons of health "and other worries" he considered it best to resign and "thus allow one of your own province to take over the office of Provincial."[24] The "other worries" appear to have been very deep feelings that his style of leadership and his ideas on the future of the province had not been warmly received by many of the Brothers. Though he stated that he had received kind support from the Brothers, he said, "You have your customs and way of life which is somewhat different than those I have known. It became increasingly evident to me that I did not 'fit in' and I doubt that I could ever adjust myself even with time. It is difficult to transplant an old tree."[25] Brother Camillus left with pride in his major impact on the history of the province, the purchase of Bennett's Court for the establishment of a novitiate in the Republic of Ireland, a goal of all the provincials since 1919.

One speculates that perhaps Brother Camillus attempted to do too much too soon, a change of pace which could have alienated many Brothers unaccustomed to such rapid-fire decisions. Not to "fit in" could also have meant that Brother Camillus was setting rather high standards regarding the professionalization and modernization of the province. Had a native provincial attempted to achieve the same goals, but in a low-keyed manner, then he might have not elicited strong opposition. The American style, which could have been viewed as impetuous and impatient, engendered at least enough opposition to provide Brother Camillus with his "other worries." One further source of anti-Camillus sentiment could have developed in opposition to the establishment of an independent novitiate. Though the trends in canon law encouraged separating the novices from the works of the institute and though General Chapters went on record favoring a separate novitiate, some Brothers opposed the idea on the grounds that by separating novices one encourages a shallow religious naiveté rather than the ethos of practical hard work gleaned from living within an established Alexian institution. This latter sentiment is still representative of legitimate opinion on formation and it was an even stronger factor thirty years ago.

Brother Edmund Kelly (familiar with both the German and American provinces) resigned as assistant rector-general to accept the appointment as provincial. During a visit to the United States, he was enrolled in a course on Canon Law at the Jesuits' St. Louis University. A traditionalist on cloister matters, he nevertheless was foresighted regarding the professionalization and updating of the province. Under his direction, St. Michael's House, the Alexian student-nurse residence in York, was enlarged and improved.[26]

According to the minutes of his first Provincial Council meeting (March 9, 1948), Brother Edmund asked the council to share the burden of decision-making and to submit to the will of the majority in the council. Though he had been superior and a member of the Provincial Council, Brother Edmund felt ill-prepared for assuming responsibility, according to recent comments of his. The papers of a provincial were traditionally considered his private possession and consultations between retiring and newly appointed provincials were rare.[27] After Brothers Gerard Byrne, Philip Walker, Ignatius Swan, Stanislaus Fitzgibbon and Stephen Russell had spent months preparing the house and property (eighty acres) Cobh was ready for occupancy in June 1948.[28] During the next six years as provincial, Brother Edmund presided over many major events: the opening of the Cobh novitiate under the chaplaincy of Father Ernest Mackey, s.j., the sale of Stillington Hall, the certification of the Brothers' institutions in London, Manchester, and Warrenpoint under the National Health and Insurance Act, and the subsequent modernization of the Alexian Brothers nursing homes.[29] Indeed in a brief period the aspirations of Brother Camillus Snyder were realized; the Brothers' homes were transformed from residences or hospices to genuine health-care institutions staffed by many Brothers who had pursued professional training.

The traditional character of the province was gradually breaking down during this period. Lay advisory committees were formed to provide liaison with the community and to be a fundraising arm of the Alexian institutions. Though the province was developing along American lines, the Anglo-Irish Brothers were professionals within a nursing-home context, in contrast to the American Brothers who worked in a highly technological general-hospital setting. Meanwhile the German Province developed along its traditional ministerial line—the care for the mentally ill.

Postwar relief and reconstruction placed a heavy burden on the German Brothers. From late 1947 through 1948 the Alexians in Aachen spent many hours a day on the reception and distribution of relief supplies.[30] In spite of the back-breaking work, the task provided them with great satisfaction. Indeed during all of 1948 the Brothers' soup kitchen fed an average of five hundred persons a day.[31] Brother Gereon Wittkamp, who became Provincial on June 8, 1948, provided strong leadership during these critical years. A large, stately figure radiating dignity and authority, Brother Gereon was well prepared for the appointment, having served as rector of Haus Kannen, the province's largest institution, during the war years. At the 1948 Provincial Chapter the delegates seem to have been most concerned with reviving spirituality and its vocation appeal.[32] Besides mandating an updating of the Customs Book the chapter made reforms of the community prayer life "in keeping with the very advanced Liturgical Movement in Germany, and the use of vernacular in all Prayers excluding the Office of the Holy Cross."[33] Though the Americans were the most modern Brothers scientifically, the German Alexians led the way in advanced liturgical practices.

The liturgical movement developed within the context of a revival of the scriptural foundation of Catholicism. The Office of the Holy Cross, a series of devotional prayers thematically integrated around the passion theme, was of late medieval origin and was adopted by the Alexians in the late sixteenth century. In light of the trends in liturgy and Scripture studies, the Alexians in Germany adopted the series of scriptural prayers, comparable to the Short Breviary in English compiled by the Aachen Alexians and their good friend, Professor Dr. Schnitzler, a priest of the Cologne diocese.[34] These communal prayers were said in the vernacular, while the Office of the Holy Cross was still said in Latin. On January 11, 1949, the new prayer book received the imprimatur of the bishop of Aachen.[35]

On August 23, 1951, the Provincial Council of the Anglo-Irish Province discussed an English translation of the Divine Office (abbreviated form) "now being said by our Brothers of the German Province."[36] The minutes did not contain the pros and cons of the discussion but only the remark: ". . . after some discussion on the matter it was turned down."[37] The new Prayer Book evolved into a congregationwide issue, which culminated at the

1952 General Chapter at Signal Mountain, Tennessee. Delegates from the Anglo-Irish Province sought consideration of the "whole question of the community prayers, with the reform of the community prayer book of the German Province, in 1948 as a precedence and norm."[38] The chapter supported "the principles for liturgical reform" as well as vernacular prayer "for true comprehension."[39] The delegates unanimously resolved to adopt the Short Breviary.[40]

The spirituality of the German Province was revived during a period when its institutional body was suffering the wounds of war. The Swiss House, Schänis, which had been a financial drain as early as 1932, became an unbearable burden for the postwar German Alexians. For both financial and manpower reasons Pater Anthony and his General Council decided to discontinue the institute.[41] After renting the house for nearly three years the Styl Mission Sisters bought it in 1952.[42] The American Province and the West German government provided the necessary funding for the reconstruction of those hospitals hit hard by the war. By 1954 the Krefeld, Ensen, and Aachen hospitals were back intact and, of course, greatly improved by postwar modernization. Haus Kannen and later the Krefeld general hospital, which had been placed in the hands of the Cellite Sisters of Cologne, were training centers for the Alexians.[43] With the professionalization of many German Brothers and with the medical progress in the treatment of the mentally ill, their nursing ministry tended away from custodial to a highly scientific and technological character.

The postwar modernization of the American general hospital occurred at such a rapid pace that it caused grave concern among some Brothers. Brother Julian Ford, the administrator of the Chicago hospital, authored "A Report on Administrative Problems in Our Hospital," which was circulated among members of the Provincial and General Councils.[44] Dated September 1951, the report contains valuable insights on the evolution of the general hospital as well as on modernization's traumatic impact upon the province. Noting how wars effect improvements in medicine, Brother Julian stated that "Following the Second World War, the improvements in therapeutic and prophylactic medicine have been most outstanding. The various agencies concerned with hospitals mushroomed after the war. . . . In 1950 thirty-three national, state and city groups inspected our Hospital for various reasons."[45] Since each of these groups imposed a set of minimum standards upon such areas as medical education, nursing education, physical facilities, professionally trained personnel on the nursing staff in ratio to the number of patients, Brother Julian urged the authorities to insist that the nursing school in Chicago be vastly improved to meet demands for professional standards.[46] Brother Julian issued a severe warning:

> We can no longer hide our head in the sand and say that we are different from other hospitals, and we do not have to worry about standards. We should have sufficient proof of this fact when in 1949, we lost our approval by the American Medical Association for the education of interns, just because we could not meet their minimum standards. *The day of using our specialization as an excuse is gone.* The Brothers must face the cold reality of a situation where we must meet other groups on a competitive level.[47]

The conflict between those Brothers who advocated advanced professional training and those who criticized its antitradition character was dramatically illustrated by Brother Julian:

> To some of our Brothers such a presentation [on the need for modernization] will seem strange and perhaps unorthodox. Any time the words "education" and "advancement" are presented by various individuals in the Community, they are classed as "radicals; proud intellectuals; or poor Religious." Yet, after viewing the complete situation in the hospital field, we should become aware of our responsibilities to continue the scientific and technical training of our Brothers, even though such training now requires greater sacrifice on the part of the Community and the individual Brothers.[48]

Brother Julian followed this strong exhortation with a set of statistics which substantiated his pro-education thesis. In 1950 90 percent of the lay graduate-nursing staff were pursuing a university degree, compared to only three Brothers who were so enrolled. It was evident to him that if the Brothers were to maintain a quality nursing school then they must become more deeply involved in nursing-education programs at the university level. "I can assure you it is neither my idea, nor my ideal of what nursing should be; nevertheless we must face certain facts of minimum standards, if Brothers are to conduct our School of Nursing."[49] Further education was not only required for the Brothers on the faculty and administrators of the school but, according to Brother Julian, by 1955 the director of nurses must have a master's degree while the education director, guidance director, clinical instructor, and floor supervisor must have bachelor's degrees, and the head nurse must be preparing for a B.S.[50] Hence Brother Julian strongly endorsed upgrading the standards of the School of Nursing, in order to continue the affiliation with DePaul University. To counter those who argued that a "formal education [was] completely foreign to our vocation,"[51] he reminded them of the Alexian pursuit of excellence; fifty years ago "the Brothers were setting standards in the Hospital and Medical field. The early pioneers of this Hospital were possessed with great foresight and courage. They were not only interested in the care of the sick, but in the most modern and scientific treatment they could give along with that care."[52] Instead of education being merely tolerated, either a strong program ought to be established and promoted or its incompatability with the religious life should be clearly stated.

The following points illustrate the Chicago hospital's modernization during the forties:

(1) Twelve years ago we gave care to less than 3,000 patients; in 1950 our services were offered to over 6,000 patients. This increase in patient service, as well as all hospital diagnostic activities, has caused a tremendous increase in operating expenses.

(2) In 1939, there was somewhat less than seventy-five paid employees on the staff; in 1950 we had two hundred and thirty-five paid employees. Salaries alone have taken fifty-two percent of our income. The cost of personnel has increased from $150,000.00 in 1940 to $580,000.00 in 1950.

(3) Twelve years ago we had only two women employed at the Hospital; in 1950 we had close to seventy-five. It has become more and more difficult to obtain professionally trained men for such Departments as X-ray, laboratory, etc. As an example, today there are four women technicians in our laboratory, one Brother technician, and one student Brother.

(4) When working with such a large group of personnel there are many additional problems presented. We must consider the factors of adequate wages, social security benefits, hospital plans,

and working conditions. The hours of labor have changed from
sixty to seventy-two hours per week in 1939, to forty or forty-
four hours in 1951.

(5) With all of these outstanding changes and constant demands on
the Brothers, we have not made any great effort to properly
prepare Brothers in the business administration of our
Hospitals.[53]

By way of summary, Brother Julian stated that amid the growing complexity of hospital activities, the Brothers' "service to
charity patients has increased." Yet that very complexity had
transformed the nursing profession and had subjected the Brothers, particularly the young professed so unaccustomed to the
demands of nursing, to "great pressure and nervous tensions."[54]
Finally, he warned of the possibility of the unionization of hospital personnel. In order to prevent the formation of a "third
party from interfering with our care of the sick," he advocated
the establishment of "industrial councils" composed of employ-
ers and employees as outlined in the social encyclicals of Popes
Leo XIII and Pius XI and the engendering of a spirit of
"harmonious family life" within the hospital.[55]

After the Provincial Council, chaired by Provincial Rector
Brother Ludolf Sattler, had responded favorably to Brother Julian's report, Pater Anthony Wessel, on behalf of the General
Council, issued a Memorandum on Education for the Province
of the Immaculate Conception. Concurring with the Provincial
Council, Pater Anthony stated that "The General Council . . .
recognizes the necessity of both the nursing school and higher
education for the Brothers in order to maintain standards, the
efficient service of the patients and the professional status of
the Brothers of the United States."[56] To substantiate the pro-
education position, Pater Anthony quoted Pope Pius XI who
urged nursing religious to be "leaders in hospital work" and
particularly addressed the issue to St. John of God Brothers by
stating, "Charity must not appear to be separated from progress."[57] Pater Anthony directly responded to those Brothers who
opposed education on religious grounds: ". . . it is an error to
believe that in education we are confronted with an enemy of
our salvation or sanctification, a point of view rejected by Holy
Mother Church."[58] Responding to those who criticize education

261

as the source of Brothers' leaving the order, he stated, "Defections are not caused by the educative process, but rather by qualities inherent in the individual."[59]

Pater Anthony encouraged the American Brothers not to allow themselves to be preoccupied with the "problems of the modern hospital and those associated with the professional training of the Brothers"[60] to the point where they were blind to new apostolates in the United States and the needs of the entire congregation. Recalling the Alexians' origins, when the Brothers responded to a neglected need in society, he urged the Brothers to be sensitive to those fields currently neglected in America. He reminded the Brothers of the essential need to be concerned with the future of the entire congregation and directed the Brothers "to look beyond today and its burdens toward new ground to be gained and new goals for the community as a whole."[61]

At the 1952 Provincial Chapter, the delegates settled the education issue by establishing a provincial education committee to be comprised of house rectors and three other Brothers of the province "for the coordination, supervision and promotion of the education of our Brothers."[62] Though the newly appointed provincial, Brother Florian Eberle, was a moderately strong advocate of education, it was not until the late 1950s and early '60s that young Brothers were strongly encouraged to pursue advanced degrees. Until then a rector would not directly oppose the pursuit of a university degree, he just would not allow time off for such study. During the early fifties Brother Felix Bettendorf attended evening classes at DePaul on a part-time basis in tandem with a full week's nursing at the Chicago hospital and full attendance at religious exercises, whereas the present superior general, Brother Augustine Lohman, was the first American Brother allowed to attend a university (St. Louis University) on a full-time basis. Since this was also in the early fifties, Brother Augustine's privilege represents the exception that proved the rule. Hence the education committee did not have much impact until the general attitude changed.

The evolution of the general hospital obviously required a continuously progressive nursing education scheme, but nevertheless many Brothers refused to adapt to the demands. The conflict became severe because professionalization engendered a new type of Brother, one more attached to professional values and a modern perspective on self-fulfillment, who obviously clashed with traditional Alexian stress on the asceticism of the cloister. Though the German and Anglo-Irish provinces upgraded their educational program, the education issue was not as intense in Europe as in the United States. Nursing in Alexian mental institutions left room for a certain amount of custodial nursing of mentally deficient and senile patients and the small size of the Anglo-Irish nursing homes allowed the nonprofessional Brothers to play a visible role in the institutions. Nevertheless, the advance of education has engendered a class consciousness throughout the congregation, but fraternal charity frequently assuages the human conflict within the context of the religious life. Other religious congregations experienced conflicts of generation, class, and modern versus traditional world. Like the Alexian Brothers these other congregations did not fully grapple with their significance until Vatican Council II encouraged total reevaluation of the nature of the religious life. During the transition period between the increasing modernization of the hospital and the modernization of the religious authority structures, the Alexians advanced in vocations and, particularly in the United States, in new foundations.

The Alexians shared the general rise in vocations during the postwar period. The growth rate of the twenties, which culminated in 1928 with 357 professed Alexians in nineteen houses, was surpassed in the postwar years: in 1947 there were 399 professed Brothers, ninety of whom were under thirty years of age.[63] German postwar dislocation severely affected vocations; whereas there were sixty American Brothers and thirty Anglo-Irish Brothers under thirty years of age, there were only three German Brothers in that category. [64] Indeed over 50 percent of the German Province was over fifty, while the figures were 25 percent and 22 percent for the American and Anglo-Irish provinces, respectively.[65] Total Brothers per province came to: German, 123; American, 185; Anglo-Irish, 91.[66] The ascendancy of the American Province is quite evident, but in terms of Alexian-patient ratio, the small nursing homes in England and Ireland provided that province with the leadership in that category. The

German Province showed a gain in vocations during the next decade, but it never reached its former status. Hence in 1954 the München-Gladbach Asylum was closed and in 1975 Krefeld was turned over to Caritasverband, a national Catholic Charities association. However, state medical insurance programs and wise investments over the years guaranteed the German Province a modicum of financial security during the era of declining vocations. Brother Camillus Snyder, provincial of the Anglo-Irish Province (1948–1949), had laid the foundation for a separate novitiate at Cobh, which until the late sixties was able to accommodate the upsurge in vocations. Under the direction of Brother Maurus O'Sullivan, Cobh had sixteen novices in 1950.[67] After the war the German Province reopened its novitiate at the Aachen Motherhouse. To establish a separate facility would have been a travesty of tradition. Recalling the reopening of the novitiate, one German Brother wrote:

> Who would deny that it is a great and powerful inspiration for a prospective member to know that he is standing on the same spot on which high-minded men, 600 years ago, dedicated themselves to the service of God and suffering mankind, those men whose spirit of love for God and fellow men is a challenge to present novices to acquire and transmit to further generations.[68]

Brother Thomas Poier, who was the first postwar novice master, oversaw the reconstruction of the novitiate. At first the novices were "lodged directly under the roof of the hospital, in small attic rooms, which received air and light through small trap doors."[69] By 1950 the novitiate had moved four times, the last move being into their permanent quarters located in the hospital's main administration building. In 1950, when Brother Evergislus Sonneck was novice master, there were six novices and three postulants in the novitiate.[70] Though small in comparison to the pre-1935 period, these figures represented a rather healthy vocation scene for the times.

The American novitiate, Glennondale, founded in 1946, was well filled in 1949 with twenty-nine novices.[71] With twenty postulants housed at Signal Mountain in 1949, the American Province was experiencing a veritable vocation explosion. Pater Anthony Wessel, a former American novice master, must have been extremely gratified by the postwar vocation scene. Indeed when Mrs. F. M. Peters gave the Brothers a 210-acre estate and a striking stone mansion, Pater Anthony urged the American Provincial Council to move the novitiate from Clayton, Missouri, to Gresham, Wisconsin, located in the diocese of Green Bay. On June 29, 1950, Brother Nicholas Bartelme arrived at Gresham as the first rector, but it was not until March 29, 1951, after the mansion had been renovated to accommodate twenty-six novices and eight professed Brothers, that the first novice class, numbering fourteen, arrived at the new novitiate. The Brothers sold the Glennondale property to the Passionists at a profit comparable to renovation costs.[72]

Because the Gresham novitiate was located in the remote Wisconsin wilderness far from an Alexian institution the move engendered some controversy. The opponents cited Glennondale's proximity to the St. Louis hospital and criticized Gresham's wilderness location as symbolic of its isolation from the Alexian way of life. The proponents of the new novitiate stressed the setting's retreat character as essential to the novices' entrance into Alexian spirituality. Much of the anti-Gresham/pro-Glennondale criticism developed after the decline in vocations. In the early seventies new directions in religious formation engendered the novitiate's move from Gresham to Chicago. Yet an entire generation of American Brothers are products of the Gresham formation experience, including such Brothers as the recently elected provincial, Brother Robert Wilde; the current novice master and recruiter, Brothers Warren Longo and Eugene Gizzi; and many others in leadership roles.

With the general postwar rise in numbers of Brothers and a revival of internationalism, the Brothers became very mission-conscious. The first exploration for a suitable Alexian mission occurred in 1935 when Pater Frumentius Horn, accompanied by Provincial Rector Brother Gilbert Holmes, visited Cape Town, South Africa. In the fall of 1935 the bishop of Cape Town wrote to Pater Frumentius seeking the Brothers' ministry for his diocese.[73] In a letter to his vicar, Brother Wolfgang Wollender, Pater Frumentius listed the disadvantages of locating in Cape Town: "Catholic sisters' institutions are abundant; there appear to be plenty of state and private asylums; cost of construction would require a large investment; [and] all the dead are buried in the so-called public cemetery."[74] Unable to detect any potentially viable ministerial expression in accord with Alexian tradition, Pater Frumentius and Brother Gilbert returned to Europe.

During Brother Anthony Wessel's time as rector-general (1946–1952), the mission ideal was revived. In mid-1951 the ideal achieved concrete form. On July 19, 1951, Pater Anthony informed the Brothers of the General Council's decision to establish a mission in Brazil. He introduced the decision with some general remarks:

> For some time there has been a lively discussion in all the Provinces of the Congregation of the possibility of new foundations and missions. In the course of the past five years we have considered opportunities for the Brothers to labor for Christ in Japan, the Belgian Congo and South America. Not since the Congregation was invited to England by the late Cardinal Vaughan . . . has the congregation been introduced into a new country.[75]

Brother Regis Apel was selected to explore both São Paulc and Rio de Janeiro to find out which was the more "desirable location for a community such as ours."[76] On October 21, 1951, Brother Regis informed Pater Anthony that the Alexians were sorely needed in Brazil, particularly because of the lack of trained nurses and because "it is only now that the Church is waking up to the fact that 'Catholic Hospitals should be Catholic,' that is they must maintain the proper standards and practice 'Catholic action' at the bed-side of the sick."[77] Brother Regis recommended establishing the mission in São Paulo "for many reasons: climate, size of the city, American-minded Cardinal Archbishop, and ease of adjustment from the English German manner of living to the Latin."[78] São Paulo was also attractive because the Franciscan Sisters of Mary had offered to provide the Alexians with temporary positions in their hospital until such time as the Brothers had learned Portuguese and acclimated themselves to the medical customs of the country, when they would be ready to establish their own institution.[79] Impressed with Brother Regis's enthusiastic reports from São Paulo, Pater Anthony formally announced on February 20, 1952, the formation of an interprovincial missionary community to be established in São Paulo and to be associated with the Franciscan Sisters of Mary.[80] Brother Goar Nalewaja represented the German Province, Brothers Camillus McGarry and Placidus Dalton of the Anglo-Irish Province, and Brothers Regis Apel, Aloysius Troyan, and Francis X. Joerger the American Province.[81]

In December 1952 Brother Ludolf Sattler, elected rector-general the previous May, sent an eight-item questionnaire to Brother Francis X. Joerger, rector of the São Paulo Alexians.[82] (Brother Regis Apel had left the congregation.) Brother Francis's item-by-item response formed a clear picture of the spiritual, ministerial, and community life of the Alexian missionaries. While Brother Francis said that the "religious spirit is good," and that the association with the hospital sisters and relations with the local church authorities were encouraging, he also reported that community life was tense, that the Brothers' missionary zeal had greatly deteriorated, and that the prospects for an independent Alexian institution and for native vocations were bleak.[83]

Community life was characterized by personality conflicts, homesickness, and ill health. Contrary to Brother Regis's optimistic account of the great need for the Brothers, Brother Francis discovered that an independent Alexian hospital was not the way to meet the health needs, as most hospitals were state-owned and staffed by state-salaried sisters. He considered the Alexian nursing ministry to be too unappealing to Brazilian youth to anticipate a healthy vocation situation. Brother Francis was most disturbed with the low level of community spirit which, when combined with the other problems, led him to respond to the question on maintaining the mission with an emphatic "*No.* . . . This may sound like a lack of courage and faith on my part, but it still remains my honest opinion as I see it."[84]

After Brother Ludolf gained firsthand experience during a visitation to São Paulo, he announced on February 12, 1954, that the General Council had decided to discontinue their mission in Brazil.[85] Citing many of the internal and external problems reported by Brother Francis, Brother Ludolf pointed to a lack of preparedness and the "inability" of the Brothers there to form a vital community as major reasons for the failure of the mission. "Other than attendance at morning prayers and Mass in a body in the Hospital Chapel, there are no other spiritual exercises or recreation held in common. The outstanding variety of characters and the difference in nationalities has tended to keep the Brothers from molding into a unity."[86]

Distressing as the São Paulo situation may have been, Pater Ludolf said that "the mission life must not be abandoned, but we must continue our efforts toward its realization."[87] He reported that the bishop of Malacca in British Malaya had invited the Alexians to work in his diocese. As if to imply that an interprovincial mission has too many built-in problems, Pater Ludolf indicated that a medical mission in Malaya "may well be the answer to the pressing need of an outlet for [the Anglo-Irish Brothers'] specialized training."[87] Though these Brothers did venture into the mission field some fifteen years later, they went to Nigeria, not Malaya.

The postwar surge of vocations in the American Province was an impetus to expansion. Brother Florian Eberle, provincial from 1952 to 1958, was a cautious expansionist with keen insight into administrative problems. In the spring of 1955, he received a letter, dated March 31, from Monsignor Nicholas Wenger, director of Father Flanagan's Boys' Home, requesting the Alexians to take over the administration and operation of the new forty-bed hospital at Boys' Town. Founded in December 1917, Boys' Town had achieved a national reputation. In 1955 it housed nearly 1,000 homeless, hard to handle, and delinquent boys on a large 1,500-acre estate located ten miles west of Omaha, Nebraska. According to the views of the administration, the new Boys' Town hospital then under the direction of lay-women nurses, would be more in accord with the character of the institution if it were staffed by male religious nurses.[88]

After visiting Boys' Town, Brother Florian remarked that the invitation had "great possibilities."[89] He referred to the harmony between the Boys' Town project and the sentiments expressed at recent Provincial Chapters that the Brothers expand into new apostolates. Brother Florian noted that the project would require true sacrifice from Brothers so accustomed to large community life but saw great compensation in serving the needs of homeless and rejected. He presented to his Provincial Council an eight-point proposal accepting the invitation and putting forth the need to formulate all the necessary policies related to the administration of the small hospital.[90]

On August 20, 1955, Brother Gregory Isenhart, the first rector-administrator, arrived at Boys' Town. Two days later he was joined by Brothers Boniface Wood, Angelus Patin, and Elmo Gizzi. Each of them was an R.N., and Brother Boniface specialized in radiology.[91] Brother Florian's stress on sacrifice proved to be accurate; the small team of four Brothers frequently worked more than a twelve-hour day. Because the postwar growth of the Anglo-Irish Province exceeded the nursing needs of their three hospices, in 1958 the superior general requested that the American provincial turn over Boys' Town to the Anglo-Irish Brothers. At the October 9 meeting of the American Provincial Council the suggestion was rejected, but the council did propose that Anglo-Irish Brothers be transferred to the United States for work in the Alexian general hospitals.[92]

Brother Gregory, valedictorian of his high-school class, had served in the business offices of the Chicago, St. Louis, and Elizabeth hospitals, had been director of postulants and, previous to his appointment to Boys' Town, was assistant administrator of the Chicago hospital. During his three years at Boys' Town he successfully laid the foundation for a professional hospital and he formulated equally professional policies relating to the relations between the Alexian community and the Boys' Town administration. In short, under his direction the Brothers at Boys' Town evolved from a pioneer to an ongoing community. In 1958, when Brother Gregory was transferred to Chicago, Brother Arthur Sanford was provincial and Brother Melchior Wimmer was rector-general; both brought valuable experience to their offices.

Pater Melchior, the only German-Province Brother to be elected rector-general since 1932, had been drafted into the German army and had been captured and imprisoned by the Allies in Manchester, England and in Canada. After the war he returned to Germany where he served in various offices, including that of provincial in 1951–1952. Pater Melchior is fondly remembered for his warm, gentle spirit and his genuine happy piety as well as his deep pride in Alexian spirit and tradition.

Brother Arthur Sanford entered the Alexians at the age of fifty-five. A successful businessman and widower with one son, he made his final vows when he was sixty-one and became provincial seven years later, in 1958. Like Pater Melchior, Brother Arthur became known for his warmth and good humor. His indefatigable energy allowed him to keep pace with a Brother half his age. During his two terms as provincial, he worked closely with those young superiors appointed by his predecessor. For example, in 1961 Brother Fidelis Kennedy, age thirty-three, was rector of the Chicago community and Brother Reginald Gleasure, age thirty-four, was rector at Elizabeth. The rectors of St. Louis and Gresham, Brothers Ronald Ruberg and Cajetan Garvonovich, were in their early forties. By 1961 Brother Felix Bettendorf, then thirty-eight years old, had begun laying the groundwork for a new Alexian hospital (the first since 1893) in San Jose, California.

In the late 1940s Mr. Francis Crocker was a lay nurse under Brother Felix's authority at the Brothers' hospital in Chicago. After working there for nearly a year, Mr. Crocker moved west, ultimately receiving a position as a private nurse to Mr. E. J. Overfelt of San Jose, California. Though Mr. Overfelt died in 1956, Mr. Crocker continued to live at the Overfelt Ranch as a friend and companion to Miss Mildred Overfelt, who was in her late seventies when her brother died. When Miss Overfelt decided to dispose of portions of her ranch, Mr. Crocker suggested the Alexian Brothers as the recipient of part of the land for the site of a hospital. In the summer of 1959 she offered the Brothers seventeen acres in East San Jose for the express purpose of establishing a hospital for men. After a November visit to San Jose by Brother Arthur, accompanied by one of his councillors, Brother Augustine Lohman and Pater Melchior's first assistant, Brother Herman Joseph Berkes, the Alexians were impressed with the property, the need for a general hospital, and the strong general support promised by church, public, and medical groups.[93]

On December 29 Brother Felix Bettendorf was appointed special representative to San Jose.[94] When he and Brother Arthur visited Miss Overfelt and Mr. Crocker the following March, they confronted the first of many obstacles in the path to realizing the new hospital. A gross misunderstanding arose on the issue of when the Brothers were to receive the land. During his fall visit Brother Arthur received the impression that the Alexians were to take over the property in 1962 when the then current lease ran out.[95] Because the Brothers had been encouraged by the community support for the immediate need for the hospital they had hoped that they could receive the land in 1960 rather than wait until 1962.[96] Now they were faced with an indefinite delay. The intensity of the conflict was compounded by the issue of federal financing of the hospital, which would have necessitated allowing female patients, a drastic departure from Alexian tradition and contrary to Miss Overfelt's stipulation that the land be used for a men's hospital.[97] Though the Alexians had been considering setting aside their exclusively male-patient tradition because of pressure from physicians concerned with placing both female and male patients in the same hospital, Mr. Crocker and Miss Overfelt refused to consider altering the deed.

After Brother Arthur had returned to Chicago, Brother Felix spent weeks informing key church, legal, health-care, and community persons of the recent turn of events. Confident of the city's need for a general hospital, yet discouraged by the land issue, Brother Felix returned to Chicago in early April.[98] When the Provincial Council considered the entire matter it decided that in the event that Miss Overfelt's position did not change, the Brothers would pursue an alternative San Jose site for their new hospital. Then on April 11, 1960, Mr. Crocker phoned Brother Arthur informing him that since he had discovered that the Brothers were not being pressured by local people but by the federal government to press for an immediate proposal to establish a general hospital for patients of both sexes, Miss Overfelt had agreed to alter the deed in conformity with the Brothers' wishes.[99]

Brother Felix returned to San Jose with a proposal for Hill-Burton aid in hand. After many months of frustration, he was confident of federal, state, and local financial support. Meanwhile, on June 14, 1960, the deed for the property was signed, and on January 1, 1962, the property came into the possession of the Alexian Brothers. During the intervening period, Brother Felix was thoroughly engaged in seeking state, federal, and local-community funds. Just as the foundation of the Belden Avenue Hospital (Chicago) was almost entirely the work of Brother Aloysius Schyns, so the San Jose hospital was virtually founded by Brother Felix. However, Provincial Rector Arthur and Pater Melchior were continuously supportive of his pioneering efforts by expressing their implicit confidence in his judgment. On the other hand, Brother Felix was scrupulously accountable to his superiors regarding the entire project. Brother Felix cemented strong community ties which ultimately led to his formation of a lay advisory board attached to the administration of the hospital.[100]

The entire San Jose complex—hospital, chapel, monastery—cost over $6 million. Government funds covered nearly two-thirds the cost, while fund-raising and a $1.6 million mortgage made up the difference.[101] When it admitted its first patients on July 19, 1965, the 180-bed hospital, located on twenty-five acres (the Brothers had purchased an additional eight acres) of beautifully landscaped property, was immediately recognized as one of the most striking buildings in the area. The San Jose hospital not only marked the Alexians' westward expansion but represented the most modern trends in medical care and, by adopting a policy of admitting patients of both sexes, it edged the Brothers closer to the modern world.

With the precedent established in the policy for the San Jose hospital, the Elizabeth hospital became the first Alexian hospital actually to admit a woman patient January 15, 1962.[102] The previous November Brother Reginald Gleasure, rector-administrator at Elizabeth, had written to Brother Arthur requesting permission to employ female nurses and accept female patients.[103] To support his request he pointed to the unavailability of male nurses and physicians' pressure for bringing all the patients to one hospital. Because some physicians were driven away by the regulation, the occupancy rate for the first nine months of 1961 had fallen 10 percent below the 1960 figure.[104] (Before the Alexians could admit women patients, the congregation had to alter its constitution, which required papal approval.)

A young man of thirty-four, Brother Reginald developed his policy for both practical and social-justice reasons. As he stated to one newspaper reporter, "It's been talked about for the last ten years. . . . And there were a number of reasons—the needs of the community, that is overcrowding in the hospitals and of course the question of discrimination."[105]

At first the Alexians placed a limited number of beds located on separate floors or wings for women patients. The Brothers attempted to maintain as much tradition as possible; they did not nurse women and women were permitted on their floors under only special conditions.

In late 1961, as the newest Alexian hospital was assuming shape on the architect's designing board, the Planning Committee of the oldest American hospital, on Belden Avenue, was designing a bold future for the Chicago Alexians. Encouraged by nearly a century of strong community support, and bolstered by a steady flow of vocations, the Planning Committee decided to develop a second Alexian hospital in the metropolitan area in accord with the city's expansion. On November 14, 1961, the Provincial Council unanimously approved a proposal by the committee in which it requested permission to purchase twenty-five acres of ground in Elk Grove Village, a western suburb of Chicago, at a cost of $4,000 per acre and to receive a gift of five acres for the purpose of building a new Alexian Brothers hospital.[106]

Brother Gregory Isenhart was the project's first director and the hospital's first rector-administrator. He was confronted with myriad questions related to every aspect of developing a general hospital from scratch. Like Brother Felix, the pioneer of the San Jose hospital, Brother Gregory was a keen administrator; but whereas Brother Felix was an extreme activist, Brother Gregory was more reflective. Until the hospital was well under way, Brother Gregory lived at the Belden Avenue Hospital and commuted to Elk Grove Village nearly every day. As director of the project he had the implicit trust of his superiors and he had them at hand for both support and direction.

The Planning Committee had specifically stated the intention to maintain both the old and the new hospitals.[107] Nevertheless rumors persisted to the point that the Provincial Council held a special meeting on January 1, 1963, to develop a policy statement on the issue. The result was the following:

. . . the Chicago Hospital will continue operating as a general hospital as long as there is a clearly demonstrated need for such a hospital and it can be operated on a sound financial basis, and can

273

be adequately staffed by the Medical Profession. The Board of Directors and the local management have no plans for the sale of any of the present property, or a change in its method of operation.[108]

Brother Gregory envisioned a moderate-sized hospital with three hundred beds. The Elk Grove area had been growing, but it did not appear that a larger hospital was needed. In June 1966 the Elk Grove hospital admitted its first patient and within a year the size of the hospital became an issue. Brother Gregory was determined to keep the hospital from expanding too quickly. He feared that rapid growth would alter the Brothers' influence on the institution. In contrast, the opposing opinion favored a full response to what appeared to be a strong community need for a larger hospital. With Provincial Rector Brother Flavian Renaud's support, the expansionist view prevailed. The Brothers' residence floor was turned over to patients and the Brothers moved into three houses located in a subdivision close to the hospital property. In June 1967, a year after Brother Gregory assumed the office of rector-administrator, Brother Ferdinand Leyva was appointed administrator. Brother Gregory was transferred to Boys' Town and was soon a major spokesman for tradition at the General Chapter meetings during 1968–1969.[109] By 1969 the Elk Grove hospital had 289 beds; in 1975 it could accommodate 400 patients. A thoroughly modern health-care facility, the hospital is so designed that each floor's nursing center is the hub from which the rooms off the spokelike corridors may be easily observed and attended. To distinguish it from Belden Avenue hospital, the Elk Grove institution was named St. Alexius Hospital. In 1971 it became the Alexian Brothers Medical Center, since by that time the Alexian Brothers hospital on Belden Avenue had been closed.

The 1968 decision to close what had once been considered the prize Alexian institution was preceded by a twenty-month feasibility study. Three major factors prompted the decision: the high cost of renovation to meet state and local standards, the fact that area hospitals could easily compensate for the loss, the manpower shortage within the province.[110] According to remarks of Mr. Hiram Sibley, then executive director of the Hospital Planning Council of Metropolitan Chicago, the five other hospitals in the area served by the Brothers' hospital could expand and easily compensate for the loss.[111] Lutheran Deaconess Hospital, located in the same area, announced its closing in tandem with the Brothers' announcement. Mr. Sibley pointed out that there was a "tremendous obsolescence problem" with most of the older Chicago hospitals and that both the Deaconess and Alexian Brothers hospitals failed to meet state standards.[112] Provincial Rector Brother Flavian Renaud reflected the province's strong emotional ties to Belden Avenue Hospital when he stated that "This decision is one of the most difficult and painful tasks I have ever undertaken. But it is in the best interest of our patients and the community at large."[113] The San Jose and Elk Grove hospitals were developed during a high-vocation phase, but by 1968 the rate of vocations had fallen seriously. To thoroughly renovate Belden Avenue Hospital, which was experiencing a declining patient census simultaneous with expansion of the Elk Grove hospital, would have placed an extremely heavy financial burden upon the province.

The decision to close the old Chicago hospital was preceded by the decision to close the nursing school. In deference to its nursing students, the school did not close its doors until the summer of 1969. Except for the war years, the school had been graduating nurses since 1927. Dr. Peter Latz had been instrumental in arranging cooperative ventures with other hospitals leading toward the school's accreditation and registration for its graduates.[114] However, it was Brother Sebastian Brogan who infused a spirit of academic excellence into the school.[115] During the thirties and forties Brother John of God Blackledge was the guiding spirit. In 1938 he negotiated the affiliation with DePaul and during the war years he supported housing and training of conscientious objectors, a controversial position within the community.[116] In 1951 the St. Louis School of Nursing pioneered by Brother Camillus Snyder and affiliated with St. Louis University School of Nursing merged with the Chicago school. From 1953 to its termination Brother Maurice Wilson was director of the school. His career reflects the trend toward continuous professional upgrading of the Brothers. He received a B.S. and an M.S. in Nursing from DePaul University and served in administrative posts in many professional nursing organizations. Under Brother Innocent Doonan's direction a new school and residence building were constructed (1952–1953). Brother Maurice succeeded him in October 1953 and the students moved into the new building in September 1954. Accreditation by the National League of Nursing was soon achieved.[117] Because of Brother Maurice's energetic leadership the school gained a national reputation for excellence. Since the closing of the nursing school young Brothers pursued the B.S. in nursing at St. Xavier College and other colleges and universities.

The second oldest hospital in the American Province in St. Louis persevered on its original site on South Broadway. In the late forties a fund-raising effort for a new hospital fell far short of its goal, owing to the brisk competition for charity funds among many of the area's hospitals.[118] When the hospital once again pursued expansion the administrator, Brother Jude Eckrich, gathered support from the Civic Advisory Board formed in 1954. Under the direction of J. Harry Vatterot, a prominent St. Louis Catholic layman, and energetically aided by Monsignor Lloyd A. Sullivan of Epiphany Parish, the board was able to raise enough money to fund a large addition to the hospital. However, construction was delayed because the provincial, Brother Florian Eberle, considered two other construction efforts of higher priority than the St. Louis project. The lay board, which had raised one and a half million dollars, was quite bitter, particularly when Brother Jude was transferred. Eventually the funds were used to construct a new wing.

Since its formation in 1951, the Ladies' Auxiliary, primarily initiated by physicians' wives, has been an extremely strong volunteer arm of the hospital. On July 1, 1962, the first woman patient was admitted, but the psychiatric department persisted as entirely male. In 1963 a new wing, containing a pharmacy, X-ray department, and chapel was added and in 1966 an intensive-care unit was introduced.[119] Though it celebrated its centennial (1969) with nearly all its original buildings still functional, the St. Louis hospital had kept abreast of the advances in medical technology, particularly in the field of industrial medicine. The Alexian Brothers of St. Louis have been most widely respected for their care of the mentally ill and alcoholics. The Catholic archdiocese has been particularly grateful to the Brothers for the hospitality shown to alcoholic and other sick priests.

Their discretion in dealing with highly sensitive cases was severely tested when a Jesuit sought them out to admit a young boy to whom he had administered the rites of exorcism. Brother Rector Thomas Knosalla and Brother Silverius Case, administrator, immediately consented to the request. When William Blatty's book *The Exorcist* achieved national fame, the news media correctly reported that the research had been largely based upon the report of the exorcism of this boy nursed by the St. Louis Alexian Brothers. To their credit the leaks to the news media never emanated from the Brothers. It seems more than a coincidence that the Alexians were asked to care for the boy. Indeed, the situation reveals the persistence of the Alexian charism to the outsider.[120]

Brother Athanasius Savary has served as either rector or administrator of the St. Louis hospital for seventeen years. Since his first years as rector (1939–1945) he has been involved in most of the hospital's major developments. He was rector-administrator during the tedious negotiations with St. Anthony's Hospital. In the early 1970s the two institutions decided on a cooperative endeavor, the product of which was to be a new hospital. The venture was abandoned in 1972 after the two parties reached an impasse over joint-administration issues.[121] Since 1975 Brother Athanasius has been presiding over the planning and construction of a new hospital and Brothers' residence on the original site purchased by Brother Bonaventure Thelen in 1869.[122]

The Oshkosh mental hospital was the Alexian institution least affected by modernization until early 1953 when Brother Eugene Ratley was appointed rector-administrator. Though the 1884 building had been renovated in the 1930s, the hospital's primary care for alcoholics, the mentally ill, and the aged, particularly priests of the first two categories, isolated the Brothers from the Oshkosh community. Its nickname, "The Sacred Penitentiary," illustrates its unfavorable character among both Alexians and priests.[123] Brother Eugene succeeded in breaking down the town-sanitarium barriers. He personally pursued a vigorous public-relations effort and strongly supported a shift in the general direction toward a nursing-home character symbolized by removing the bars from many of the windows. Hence, when the Oshkosh hospital celebrated its Diamond Jubilee in 1955, a newspaper headline aptly described the occasion: "Air of Festivity Pervades Alexian Brothers Sanitarium."[124] In spite of the efforts of Brother Eugene's two successors, Brother Benedict Roll (1956–1962) and Brother Bede Guyon (1962–1965), the eighty-six-bed sanitarium fell on hard financial times. In October 1963 Provincial Rector Brother Arthur sought the General Council's permission to close the institution.[125] He pointed out that its accommodations deterred broad appeal to prospective nursing-home patients. Because a new two-hundred-bed nursing home was due to open in Oshkosh on January 1, 1964, the need for the Alexian institution was greatly diminished.[126] To modernize the old building would have been a very risky expense, particularly since most of the Brothers found the work unappealing. However, Brother Arthur and the Provincial Council, confident that nursing the elderly was an important component in the Alexian apostolate, proposed searching for a new site for an Alexian Brothers nursing home.[127] Upon the sanitarium's closing in March 1965, Brother Arthur's successor, Brother Flavian, was quoted by one Oshkosh reporter as stating that "it is our hope that eventually after present construction of general hospitals is completed in Elk Grove, Ill. and San Jose, Calif., we can consider a suitable location for a new home for the aged."[128] Though that hope never perished, the vocation-crisis of the late sixties precluded serious consideration of reviving that aspect of the Alexian heritage.

Of the four nineteenth-century American foundations, the Elizabeth hospital has been the most flourishing. Amid the complex evolution of the general hospital it persisted in its traditionally warm human character; in 1977 the townspeople still fondly refer to it as "the Brothers' hospital." Brothers Herman Joseph Berkes, Conrad Christie, Theophane Lawrence and Innocent Doonan embodied the spirit of the Elizabeth Alexians. A thoroughly professional nurse with R.N., B.S. and M.A. degrees, Brother Innocent had been superintendent of nurses at the Alexians' St. Louis School of Nursing, and had fifteen years' experience as a surgical nurse before assuming the position of rector.[129]

The townspeople's deep affection for the Brothers was clearly demonstrated in the formation of the Alexian Brothers Hospital Foundation in 1948. Encouraged by Brother Innocent's successor, Brother Urban Wiegand, a group of laymen bound themselves together in concern for serving the needs of the institution.[130] Under the strong leadership of Mr. Harry A. Grassman, president of the Alexian Brothers Foundation from 1951–1959, this lay group absorbed men from every ethnic group in the area: German, Irish, Italian, Polish, Bohemian, some of whom were non-Catholic such as Mr. Cohn, a Jewish lawyer who was still associated with the hospital on a professional and personal basis in 1977. Mr. Grassman's contributions were greatly appreciated by the Brothers as he became an associate member of the congregation. The political significance of both the foundation and the Brothers' hospital was highlighted when in 1949 three mayors of municipalities serviced by the hospital were members of the foundation's board.[131] The first year's recruitment efforts netted 672 members, while the fund drive resulted in the purchase of a new ambulance, construction of a new ambulance entrance, and plans to build a new $80,000 operating room.[132] Brother Reginald Gleasure, rector from 1958–1964, presided over the opening of a new addition to the hospital in 1960, which included a suite of operating rooms, a pharmacy, a blood bank, and fourteen semiprivate rooms. The following year, the Elizabeth hospital was the first Alexian institution to depart from tradition when it admitted its first woman patient. Since Brother Reginald is gifted with a cool diplomatlike personality, he was superbly suited to breaking down traditional barriers with minimum damage to the sanctity of custom and maximum impact upon public relations between the hospital and the community. Brother Ronald Ruberg, who succeeded him in 1964, blends the diplomatic style of Brother Reginald with his own keen administrative skills. Still chief executive officer in 1977, Brother Ronald's leadership resulted in a major expansion which entailed replacing the pre-1960 structures with modern wings, one completed in 1966, the others in 1974 and 1977. Such a large investment represents the Alexian commitment to an inner city characterized by all the problems associated with neglect and poverty. In the short span of fifteen years the Elizabeth hospital expanded from 180 to 375 beds.

Breaking through the impersonal barriers of hospital technology is that Alexian warmth and the close personal ties between the Brothers and the townspeople. Passing through the halls with Brother Ronald one is struck by the naturally friendly way in which he greets patients and staff, frequently on a first-name basis.[133]

At the southernmost extremity of the American Province lies the Alexian Brothers' Rest Home atop Signal Mountain, Tennessee. When the novitiate relocated to the St. Louis area in 1949, the home passed through an identity crisis. It served as home for elderly men, formation residence for postulants, and in 1950 it housed the generalate of the congregation. Though the latter arrangement was intended as temporary, the generalate was still located there in 1977. Its occupancy rate as a rest home never provided the income necessary to match expenses until the late 1960s. [134] An attempt to attract retreats and days of recollection was moderately successful but the home continued to place a great financial strain upon the province.[135] In 1955 the Provincial Council unanimously favored selling the property, but the necessary permission from the General Council was never achieved. Without full documentation on why permission was withheld one may only speculate that the council had hopes for the home's future. In 1964, when Brother Peter Mannion, a member of the General Council from the Anglo-Irish Province, was rector, the home was extensively renovated to accommodate women guests. Since women form such a large portion of the clientele for such homes, the innovation generated a rising occupancy rate. Brother Emmet Roach administered the home from 1966 to 1976, a period characterized by modernization of the guest facilities and developing those floors dedicated to nursing. Brother Emmet had a phenomenal impact upon the home's character. A gracious host, a meticulous master of good housekeeping, and an able administrator, he will forever be associated with the home's crucial entrance into a modern residence hotel and nursing home. Since mid-1976, Mr. Roger Ochse has been administrator. He brought professional experience and a rich background in gerontology and nursing-home management to the position. Though major capital improvements were required to meet various standards and maintain broad appeal to prospective patients, the proposal to sell the property was in 1977 a minority position.[36]

Though contemporary American Alexian Brothers are more than simply the products of the evolution of the general hospitals, developments in their profession have had a profound impact upon their perspective. Before modernization occurred at its accelerated postwar phase, Alexian Brothers were found in every occupation throughout the hospital. By 1977 the Brothers formed a tiny minority within the hospitals' administration and staff. It may appear that the decline in vocations is responsible for this trend, but in 1951, when Brother Julian Ford wrote his commentary on the need for professionally trained Brothers, vocations were high, and yet the need for lay help had been increasing. It is evident, therefore, that the proliferation of specialties and subspecialties within the general hospital eventuated a rate of increase in hospital personnel far beyond the rate of decline in vocations; had vocations remained steady the Brothers would still be in a minority. Though that minority presence would be stronger than in 1977, the professionalism of the contemporary American Brothers represents a significant shift from the perspectives of the old days. First the contemporary American Brother is by profession middle class. His education and training have introduced him to the need for continuous upgrading of his skills. Attendance at committee meetings and professional meetings at the local, regional, and national levels, authoring and reading complex reports on intricate medical, technological, and business topics, and the general strain of dwelling in the hospital subculture mark the contemporary American Alexian Brother as an extreme activist. Even before Vatican Council II broke down the dichotomy between the cloister and Main Street, the latter had so invaded the hospital that many Alexians were questioning the viability of the traditionally monasticlike character of the congregation.

Generational tensions were not limited to the American Province. The state medical-care schemes in Germany and England were catalysts for the professionalization and modernization processes. From the fifties on the Aachen Motherhouse, Maria-Hilf, Haus Kannen, and Malseneck have evolved into thoroughly modern mental hospitals. The vocation crisis, compounded by financial strain, led the province to decide against rebuilding München-Gladbach after the war. It was sold in 1956. The German Brothers received excellent training at Maria-Hilf and later at Haus Kannen. Under the strong leadership of Provincial Rectors Gereon and Melchior in the forties and fifties the professionalization progressed with a heavy accent upon tradition. Provincial Rector Ludger, a highly trained nurse and a skilled administrator and businessman, presided over the province's institutional modernization from the mid-sixties to the mid-seventies. He too placed a premium upon the traditional monastic character of the congregation. However, the sanctity of custom among the German Alexians has been strongly buttressed by the Catholic milieu in Germany and the Alexian ministry to the mentally ill. Though the German church has produced many of the world's most famous theologians, social critics, and liturgists, there lingers in the cloisters a strong legacy formed by Bismarck's *Kulturkampf* and Hitler's *Mein Kampf*. Though other German religious orders who possess the same legacy appear less conservative than the Alexians, the Alexian ministry to the mentally ill, those exiles from "normal society," strengthened their separation from the world. Tensions between the younger professional nursing Brothers and those who were trained as more custodial nurses has been minimized by the nature of their mental hospitals. Many of the Brothers' patients are mental deficients who require only custodial supervison. Hence the Brothers trained in the old school play a significant role within the institution and do not feel estranged from the highly skilled psychiatric nurse. The ancient roots of Alexian experience in Germany further strengthen a traditionalist spirit. For example, in April 1951 the local diocesan paper dedicated a cover story to the Brothers, entitled "600 Years of Alexian Brothers' Activity in Aachen."[137] A deep sense of pride in their centuries of service on Alexianergraben permeates the life of the German Alexian Brothers. Gradual changes in their style of life have developed along with the respect for tradition. Prayer in the vernacular and the shift from devotional to scriptural prayer was initiated in the German Province. Vacation periods have been liberalized and the contacts between Brothers and laity have become more frequent and more open. However, to

282

the American visitor, the German adaptations appear to be moving at a glacial pace. When younger Brothers assume positions of leadership, the rigidly standardized prayer and work schedules may be reformed but the traditional character of the province will no doubt be preserved.

During the 1950s and 1960s the ministry of the Anglo-Irish Province evolved from hospice custodial service to modern nursing-home and psychiatric care. Because many young Brothers had been studying nursing at York General Hospital since 1944, the province had a steady flow of professional nurses, allowing Twyford Abbey, St. Mary's Home (Manchester) and Mount St. Columb's (Warrenpoint, Northern Ireland) gradually to be absorbed into the National Health scheme. Though not all the Brothers qualified or desired to attend nursing schools, conflicts between nursing and non-nursing Brothers never achieved critical dimensions because the province's relatively small institutions allowed each Brother to have a sense of his individual impact regardless of his role. To illustrate the low-keyed nature of the conflict, Brothers Edmund Kelly and Pascal Boland were not trained nurses, but nevertheless as provincials (1948–1954 and 1954–1957 respectively) they promoted, in varying degrees, education throughout the province. Once absorbed into the National Health scheme, the Alexian nursing homes expanded and modernized to meet the patient demand. With a high patient census the homes could afford the expenses entailed in upgrading their institutions. Though their lay personnel expanded, Brothers were engaged in every type of work, thereby holding down the need for lay staff. Nursing homes in England and Ireland are not refuges for the elderly who can no longer fully care for themselves but extended-care facilities; after the general hospital has reached its limit of care, patients are transferred to nursing homes for further treatment. In 1952 Twyford Abbey received official recognition as a Registered Nursing Home. Continuous modernization of the abbey ensued. In 1960 five new wards were constructed and in 1962 a new wing was added which provided for "twenty-three additional beds, a new administration section and guest rooms."[138] On December 6, 1962, the new wing was formally opened by Lord Boyd of Merton amid a festive gathering of friends and benefactors.[139] This social gathering represents a new postwar trend within the province. Traditionally the Alexians at Twyford Abbey had been remote from the community, forming a sort of Catholic enclave. Their new nursing apostolate broke down traditional barriers, and committees of lay supporters were formed in each of the nursing homes. A 1960 articles in *What's On in London*, informing its readers of the life and work of the Alexian Brothers, illustrates Twyford Abbey's shift from relative obscurity to prominence in the public eye.[140] St. Mary's Home, Manchester, was in the vanguard of this move toward close Alexian ties with the community. A 1961 report from the province states, "St. Mary's Home holds the honor for having established the most active lay committee yet known in any of our houses. One of its latest schemes is for the erection and equipment of a new hospital for the Brothers."[141] Brother Gerard Byrne was working closely with influential Catholic and non-Catholic laymen for nearly two decades.

The rationalization and modernization of the Anglo-Irish institutions was almost entirely due to the leadership of Brother Cormac O'Reilly, the first professionally trained Brother to serve as provincial (1960–1966). He not only expanded and updated the nursing facilities but also appointed young professionally trained Brothers as administrators in each of the nursing homes, where they were responsible for admission, discharge, and medical care of the patients, duties that had belonged to the superior of the community. During Brother Cormac's tenure as provincial, the province's corporate status was drastically altered. Incorporated as "The Manchester Joint-Share Company Limited," registered as a nonprofit company, the province had incurred a heavy tax debt by the early sixties. After complex legal negotiations, Brother Cormac succeeded in incorporating the province as a charitable foundation listed under the Registered Charities Act, i.e., it received tax-free status. Brother Cormac's enthusiastic support for the Alexian missionary efforts in Nigeria was characteristic of his dynamic leadership in every aspect of Alexian life in England and Ireland. The province experienced a severe blow when cancer ended Brother Cormac's life in 1968.

Over the years the Provincial Council has been confronted with a variety of requests to expand into new health areas. In

1954 when Brother Pascal was provincial, a Dr. Malone proposed establishing an Alexian Brothers psychiatric hospital in Dublin, to which the council replied that the Brothers "were not interested in mental nursing as their qualifications covered general and T.B. nursing."[142] However, in 1962, when Brother Cormac O'Reilly was provincial, he enthusiastically noted in the Provincial Council Minute Book that since Warrenpoint has been successfully negotiating for permission to nurse psychiatric patients under the National Health scheme, "A new era could be opened for psychiatric nursing in the Province."[143]

Tragedy struck Mount St. Columb's in early March 1964 when a fire broke out, threatening the lives of eighty patients and twenty-three Brothers. Though there were no major injuries, damages exceeded £50,000. After many months of fundraising efforts, including television appeals, cash became available to help subsidize the reconstruction, which had begun almost immediately after the fire. The American and German provinces also helped finance the new building program. In early 1965 Mount St. Columb's was once again fully operational as a nursing home with a psychiatric ward and facilities for the aged. As it looks out upon the point leading to the Irish Sea, Mount St. Columb's radiates with dignity and pride as the only Alexian Brothers nursing home in Ireland.[144]

In 1955 Brother Provincial Paschal Boland received a letter from Pater Ludolf Sattler requesting that the Brothers be removed from Moston Cemetery "as soon as conveniently possible."[145] Apparently Pater Ludolf and his General Council considered such work an anachronism. After over a year's deliberation the Provincial Council resolved that Brother Paschal should appeal to Pater Ludolf "to rescind his previous order to withdraw the Brothers."[146] In 1962 the Provincial Council minutes report on problems at Moston; though these appear to have been of a financial nature, a consensus in favor of withdrawing developed over the next four years. On August 7, 1966, shortly after Brother Peter Mannion became provincial, the council unanimously decided to leave Moston Cemetery.[147] Though many lamented the final dissolution of the ancient Alexian burial ministry, on the same day that the Anglo-Irish Provincial Council decided to leave Moston, Brother Peter informed the council that Monsignor Fitzgibbon (the brother of Brother Stanislaus

Fitzgibbon) had offered the Brothers a residence and chaplain in the bush section of his diocese in Minna, Nigeria. Ten days later Brother Peter exclaimed that a "golden opportunity had been offered us . . . We should accept the invitations."[148]

The invitation to do missionary work originated in 1964 when a Canon Murphy, who was a frequent visitor to the Brothers' home in Manchester and had contacts in Nigeria, made the first overture that the Brothers consider a mission in Nigeria. Brother Dominic Walsh passed on the invitation to his provincial, Brother Cormac O'Reilly, who with Brother Peter Mannion visited Bishop McGetterick in Biafra, Nigeria in 1965. After Monsignor Fitzgibbon's 1966 offer, Brother Peter, who had been appointed provincial in March 1966, and Rector-General Brother Herman Joseph Berkes visited Minna, whereupon the decision to embark on the missionary endeavor was made. (In hindsight, the decision to settle in the northwest was most advantageous as civil war in Biafra would have precluded an Alexian mission in Nigeria.)

Brothers Vianney Kerr and Dominic Walsh entered special training in tropical medicine in January 1967, while Brother Mark Brennan, a builder, studied automobile and electrical engineering in preparation for building the Rural Health Center and maintaining the physical plant in Kafin-Koro near Minna, Nigeria. The political situation in Nigeria delayed embarking on the mission until September 1967. When they reached Kafin-Koro, the three Irish pioneer Alexians had to build a health center and adjust to the severe demands of bush culture. After a long period of frustration with the culture gap, with poor communications systems, and Nigerian bureaucracy, the Brothers managed to achieve their goal of bringing modern medicine to the poor.[149] Brother Dominic Walsh was particularly suited to the work, one which was certainly in accord with the Alexian ministry to the outsider.

15

Aggiornamento

Alexian aggiornamento, renewal or new beginning, may be viewed within the context of Pope John's XXIII's call for general Catholic renewal. Just as the mainstreams of discussion at the Vatican Council were fed by the theological tributaries of the previous decades, so the renewal discussions among the Alexian Brothers had antecedents in previous Provincial and General chapters. The council's general theme, the church in the modern world, stood in sharp contrast to the implicit theme of Vatican I, the church against the modern world. The latter theme characterized many religious orders and congregations, including the Alexian Brothers, who developed a dichotomous perspective toward the sacred cloister and the profane world.

By the time of the council's first session in 1962, the Alexian Brothers had been influenced by the new liturgical awakening, had introduced scriptural prayer to integrate their communal chapel-life, and had become professional nurses working alongside and dependent upon highly trained lay people. The accelerated pace of change within its general-hospital ministry placed the American Province in the vanguard of the renewal movement within the congregation.

The postwar rectors-general had not been great reformers, but each of them indirectly contributed to the development of the reform atmosphere. Pater Anthony Wessel, a quiet, peaceful past novice master, revived the missionary zeal upon which the non-German provinces were established. Pater Ludolf Sattler brought a sound professionalism to the congregation's leadership. Pater Melchoir Wimmer, endowed with a warm, confident personality, encouraged expansion, particularly the westward movement to San Jose, California. In early 1962, conscious that he was dying of cancer, Pater Melchior wrote a touching letter to the entire congregation extending a confident farewell and urging all the Brothers to joyfully dwell within the Alexian spirit.[1] Special travel accommodations were arranged for his flight to Germany soon followed by his death, funeral and burial at the Krefeld House.

Pater Melchior's first assistant, Brother Herman Joseph Berkes, became temporary rector-general. According to the statutes he invoked a General Chapter for November 1962, at which Brother Herman Joseph was elected superior general.[2] In terms of reform the chapter was uneventful. There were no significant proposals similar to those presented to the 1946 chapter calling for election of provincials, enlargement of provincial authority, and expansion into new ministries. The education of the Brothers in the American Province was once again an issue at the chapter. The General Council was authorized to set up an education fund, which eventually allowed more American Brothers to pursue undergraduate and graduate degrees.[3] In 1965 there were forty-nine American Brothers attending sixteen educational institutions, including forty full-time students.[4] A three-week vacation was granted to the German Brothers because they did not have a weekly outing, but the American Province was refused an extension beyond two weeks, while the Anglo-Irish Province decided not to propose such an extension.[5] Other than allowing radios and phonographs to be played during Lent, excluding Holy Week, the chapter did not reduce the traditional regulations for the monastic character of the Alexians' communal life.[6] Indeed, the delegates admonished those who were reading "improper magazines and books," maintained standardized street wear but granted alternatives of either white shirt and black tie or a collar with a rabat.[7] The American Province requested that the limitation of one alcoholic drink on days when "extraordinary refreshment" was permitted be abolished as it "implied an untrustful attitude toward the Brothers who should be considered mature."[8] The matter was referred to the General Council for consideration. Because this latter proposal invoked the principle of respect for individual freedom and responsibility for the Brothers it heralded the new conflict on the nature of the religious life—law versus freedom. The most far-reaching decision of the chapter was to establish constitution-revision committees within each of the provinces three years before the 1968 chapter.[9] Since this proposal, along with sixteen others of the twenty-nine submitted to the General Chapter, originated in the American Province the interests of the American Brothers dominated the chapter.

In April 1965 Pater Herman Joseph, and his General Council followed the wishes of the chapter by appointing constitution-revision committees in each of the provinces. However, these committees were almost immediately dissolved in deference to the Alexian procurator in Rome, who advised postponing constitution revision until after the revision of canon law for religious.[10] By this time the American Province, stimulated by the discussions of the Vatican Council (formally convened on October 11, 1962) became very renewal-conscious. Reflecting this burgeoning consciousness, Brother Flavian Renaud submitted to the General Council renewal proposals, which would lead to major revisions of the constitution. On December 4, 1965, Brother Flavian sent a circular letter to all the Brothers of the province announcing the General Council's decision to reactivate the constitution-revision committee, composed of himself as chairman, and Brothers Florian Eberle and Gregory Isenhart. The committee's immediate task was to direct discussions of the constitution at each of the local houses in order to receive a sense of the province's views as well as to encourage every Brother to contribute "toward adaptation and renewal of the religious life."[11] This was the first time in the history of the Alexian Brothers that all Brothers regardless of office and seniority were asked to discuss serious issues, including their very raison d'être as religious.

The Constitutional-Revision Committee entitled itself The Central Self-Study Committee for Adaptation and Renewal after the Vatican Council's "Decree on Adaptation and Renewal of Religious Life." By the end of March 1966 it presented a comprehensive report to the entire province.[12] After noting the origins of the committee, the report described the house-chapter discussion process, directing house group leaders to submit the results of discussions to the Central Committee.[13] Reflecting the advanced thought of the Vatican Council, the committee stated that the ultimate goal "of our Congregation is to help the individual member grow in the love of God by carrying on as a work of love, our apostolate of service to mankind."[14] The following "specifics" were listed as directly related to the aim of the congregations.

1. We must undertake deep spiritual renewal
2. We must acquire greater vision and flexibility
3. We must take a truly catholic outlook on our apostolate
4. We must become more involved in contemporary problems
5. We must nurture in ourselves the spirit of love, kindness and concern which gives deeper meaning to our professional endeavors
6. We must fully develop every member as a person in community[15]

The objectives established by the committee were, in abbreviated form, "to imbue every member with the spirit and thought of the Ecumenical Council," to revitalize Alexian prayer life in accord with contemporary liturgical development, "to adapt our religious life to the adequate fulfillment of our apostolate," to develop to the utmost the "apostolic professional excellence of each Brother," to foster and develop vocations, to give priority to those works "most closely associated with our apostolate," to participate in the ecumenical movement, to encourage the laity and other religious "to fulfill their apostolate" and "to participate in ours" and to develop a well-organized and integrated formation program.[16] Just as these aims and objectives reveal the committee's total immersion in the streams of Vatican II, so the committee directed the entire province to immerse itself totally in discussing every facet of the Alexian way of life. Each house was directed to discuss seven major topics over a seven-month period: (1) The Spirit of the Congregation, (2) Prayer of the Congregation and Acts of Piety, (3) The Vows, (4) The Apostolate of the Congregation—A Witness to Christ, (5) Community Living, (6) Philosophy of Formation for Members of the Congregation, (7) Organization and Government of the Congregations.[17]

The local chapter discussions on the fundamental aspects of the Alexian way of life frequently reached a consensus. Most of the Brothers agreed on the need for a new, more positive approach to the vows, for a liturgically and scripturally based prayer life, for reducing communal prayer and enlarging the individual Brother's responsibility for his own devotional and mental prayer, for considering new apostolates, for expanding contacts with the clergy, laity, and interfaith groups, for revising the governance system, for a more open and flexible recreation period, and for a revival of the usable past.[18] There were many divisions along traditionalist-reformer lines within each of these groups and, of course, the normal dosage of personality and semantic conflicts. Though both traditionalists and reformers were imbued with the spirit of Vatican II, the reformers promoted immediate experimentation, while traditionalists stressed caution and moderation. The traditionalists, not entirely anti-reform, stressed Alexian service to the honor and glory of God and viewed the apostolate as a means to this end. They criticized the committee's discussion questions as too vague, as too imponderable, and as encouraging disloyal dissent and individualism. Many Brothers questioned the emphasis upon new apostolates as impractical in light of maintaining the general-hospital apostolate. Though traditionalists agreed with many of the renewal aims, they disagreed with the reformers on the means to achieve those ends. For example, both groups agreed on the need to retrieve the original spirit of the Alexians but were divided on just what was that spirit and how should it be incorporated into new apostolates. The reformers stressed the non-institutional apostolate and small family communal character of the fourteenth-century Beghard Alexians and proposed training more Brothers in pastoral ministry and social work, establishing small clinics for the poor, and in general reaching out as Christian witnesses to those in need. The traditionalists were unsure of the original spirit and doubted the feasibility of developing these new apostolates while maintaining large health-care institutions. These divisions often polarized the discussion and precluded a consensus.[19]

Throughout this period, April to December 1966, the Central Committee was advised by experts in renewal and canon law, Father Edward Stokes, s.j.. of St. Mary of the Lake Seminary, Mundelein, Illinois, and Father Paul Boyle, c.p., professor of canon law at St. Meinrad Seminary in Indiana. In May 1966 the

Provincial Council, under Brother Flavian's leadership, proposed a period of experimentation concurrent with the renewal discussions. On May 22 Brother Flavian sought permission from Brother Herman Joseph and his General Council to adopt three changes in the communal life as experiments in "accordance with the thinking of Vatican II."[20] Common recreation was to be reduced to forty-five minutes (6:45–7:30) followed by night prayers and free time until 10:00 P.M. The midday meal was to be buffet-style with meal-prayer private, no reading or talking permitted. During morning and afternoon collation (coffee break), talking was to be allowed.[21] Two days later Brother Herman Joseph wrote to Brother Flavian a formal letter in which he directed the Provincial to "conduct adequate and prudent experimentations" in accord with the "Decree on the Adaptation and Renewal of the Religious Life."[22] Besides the previously mentioned experiments the provincial Council introduced (October 1966) such changes as discontinuing the censorship of mail, liberalizing television regulations, injecting flexibility into devotional customs (such as the frequency of Benediction on retreat, May and October devotions), dropping the usage of the title "Brother Superior," and other like changes.[23]

In the January 1967 issue of *Review for Religious*, Father Joseph Gallen, S.J., categorically stated that the General Council of a religious order or congregation may not engage in experimentation because that authority resides in the General Chapter.[24] Brother Flavian consulted with Father Edward Stokes, S.J. on this issue; in a March 9, 1967, letter, Father Stokes, stated that contrary to Father Gallen's interpretation on experimentation, the decree *Perfectae Caritatis* states that experimentation "is the responsibility of competent authorities, *especially* (and therefore not exclusively) of the General Chapter to allow for a right amount of prudent experimentation."[25]

Confident of the authority to experiment, the Provincial Council sought Brother Herman Joseph's permission to alter the province's formation program and to change the principles upon which delegates were elected to the General Chapter. On March 12 Brother Herman Joseph sought advice from Father Edward L. Heston, C.S.C., procurator general of the Congregation of the Holy Cross and an expert in canon law residing in Rome, and the Alexians' representative to the Sacred Congregation of Religious within the Papal Curia.[26] Seven days later Father Heston responded to the questions in the same vein as Father Gallen's article, i.e., only the General Chapter is authorized to engage in such experimentation.[27] After Brother Flavian received a copy of Father Heston's letter he wrote to Fathers Stokes and Boyle, both of whom expressed views contrary to those of Father Heston.[28] However, Brother Herman Joseph followed the advice of Father Heston and informed Brother Flavian (April 11, 1967) that "we should not start any new experimentation until after the 1968 General Chapter is convened."[29] Brother Herman Joseph considered it prudent to allow the previous experimentations to "remain in force," since they were implemented "in good faith" and since stopping them would have caused "a reaction among the Brothers that [would have been] harmful to the religious life and spirit of the Province."[30] Though experimentation was brought to an abrupt halt, proposals for renewal and adaption were evolving in preparation for the Provincial Chapter to be held eight months later.

In the summer of 1967 the Provincial Council formed seven committees composed largely of volunteer members. Each committee was directed "to study the Community's relationship to a given area of the Brothers' activity, and to make to the Provincial Chapter whatever recommendations seemed suitable in light of the Vatican Council's desire that religious undertake appropriate measures to renew themselves."[31] Brother Fidelis Kennedy, a member of the Provincial Council, had been transferred from San Jose to the provincialate in order to coordinate the pre-chapter committee work. The following committees replaced the Central Committee, which had directed and supported the adaptation and renewal process and had prepared for the writing of a new constitution by collating the reports of the local-chapter discussions: Spirit and Purposes, Government of the Congregation, Community Living, Basic Formation, Community Worship and Personal Prayer, Apostolic Formation and Continuing Education, Habit.[32] Never had any province been so thoroughly prepared for a chapter meeting in the history of the congregation. Indeed before the January 6, 1968, opening session, the delegates attended a pre-chapter workshop on renewal during which Father Paul M. Boyle, c.p., spoke on spiritual renewal, Father Bernard Cooke, s.j., spoke on apostolic spirituality, and Monsignor John R. Gorman spoke on the psychology of renewal.[33] Another precedent was established at this chapter; the delegates were elected proportionately according to age. Five Brothers were elected from the over fifty-five and the under thirty age-groups, while the Brothers between thirty-five and fifty-five years of age elected fourteen delegates. A majority of the Brothers were of the postwar generation who leaned toward moderate reform. Brothers Fidelis Kennedy, Cletus Howard, and Warren Longo were strong advocates of reform; Brothers Gregory Isenhart, Ronald Ruberg, and Athanasius Savary were spokesmen for tradition.[34] Because reform was implicit in the renewal and adaptation themes for the chapter, the reformer-traditionalist breakdown was relative and many delegates voted with both groups, depending on the issue.

Among the resolutions passed by the Provincial Chapter and approved by the General Council, the most liberal was "authorization to experiment with any proposition of the custom book which does not involve any of the articles of the constitutions."[35] Other resolutions concerned the establishment of a medico-missionary foundation in Chulacanas, Peru; the possibility of a geriatric center in Florida; a moratorium on the establishment of new general hospitals until the 1974 General Chapter; the consideration of broadening apostolic works; permission to wear informal dress, to use the recreation room at any time during the day, and to serve liquor on all major celebrations and at any time "at the discretion of the Superior." Resolutions related to spirituality authorized continuous experimentation for Benediction, encouraging Bible Vigils and visits to the cemetery.[36]

Many of the province's resolutions were presented to the first session of the General Chapter. Because of the many complexities involved in writing a new constitution, the General Chapter decided to divide the chapter into two sessions, May 1968 and May 1969. The first order of business was the election of a superior general. When Brother Felix Bettendorf was elected to the office, the chapter seemed to have sensed the congregation's need for moderate, progressive yet practical leadership. Forty-four years of age and a silver jubiliarian in 1968, Brother Felix became the youngest superior general among the eleven paters elected since Clement Wallrath's success in gaining papal congregation status in 1870. Brother Felix was neither a traditionalist nor a reformer in the ideological sense of the terms; yet his instincts and his thoroughly modern sensibilities led him to side more often with the progressive wing of the province. Though impatient with theoretical discourse, he possesses a strong facility to broker compromise and the boundless energy and rugged persistence to direct nearly any problem or conflict to a viable resolution. As the chairman of the chapter mandated to write a new constitution, Brother Felix was the ideal person to preside over the tedious parliamentary struggle entailed in the process of forming a consensus on a new constitution. Brother Edmund Kelly, who had gained large stature as Provincial of the Anglo-Irish Province, was elected assistant superior general.

Prior to the first session of the General Chapter, the American delegates, Brothers Fidelis Kennedy, Gregory Isenhart, Felix Bettendorf, and Flavian Renaud, toured the German and Anglo-Irish provinces as well as visited the unaffiliated Alexians in Germany as part of their preparation for designing new statutes for the entire congregation. Anglo-Irish delegates also toured the American Province before the chapter. Brother Fridolin Wimmer, assistant superior general, insisted that the German delegation abide by tradition and tour the province after the first session. Such visits were very beneficial not only because they provided mutual insights into the cultural diversity among the provinces but also because they allowed the various delegates to get to know one another prior to exchanging ideas and opinions within the "constitutional convention." Though the new constitution was not to be finally approved until the second session of the chapter, scheduled for May 1969, at the May-June 1968 session the chapter did approve major constitutional changes of which the most significant was the change in the congregation's entire authority structure.

The heavily centralized structure, designed by Pater Clement Wallrath and modeled on the Jesuit system, was first officially criticized by the American delegates to the 1946 chapter when they proposed the election of Provincials and greater provincial autonomy. The principles of individual responsibility, accountability, and collegiality derived from the thought of Vatican II strengthened the legitimacy of the reformers. The German and Anglo-Irish provinces, which since 1948 had been governed by a General Council residing in the United States and by American rectors-general (except for Pater Melchior), gradually shifted their position to the side of reform. The chapter easily reached a consensus on altering the governance system; Brother Cletus Howard enthusiastically reported on the changes in *The Alexian*:

> . . . the Alexians have now re-structured all internal government. The highest superior (Superior General) is now counseled by one assistant plus the regional superiors (Provincials), who make up the General Senate. Then, the regional superior is Executive Chairman of the Provincial Senate which is made up of the best minds in the region. At the local setting, the superior will now turn to the whole body of Brothers living under his direction and will take counsel with them. You might ask, "so what?" Well, our former government structure placed broad and sweeping power in the hands of the General, some independent power in the hands of the Provincial, and limited independent governing power in the hands of the local superior. Now our philosophy is . . . the individual Brother must accept the responsibility of making a "go" of the local house, and this frees the Provincial for high level planning and implementation. The Superior General is now guiding the creativity and uniqueness of each separate Province, stimulating growth and success, and thus serving as the torch which permits the travelers to move ahead. Remember, the torch is held high . . . but held by persons who must move ahead . . . the torch is a light and aid (yes, even a source of security) as the persons move on. Without this personal, grass-roots movement, there is no one to hold the torch and it just sits there burning brightly . . . but, sitting there all the same![37]

The first session of the chapter also approved many American proposals for adaptations to the modern world. Brothers could adopt baptismal rather than religious names; could live in small communities within neighborhoods (a decision provoked by the need of the Elk Grove Brothers to vacate their living quarters to make room for patients); were permitted to wear professional uniforms and were encouraged to participate in cultural and rec-reational activities. The chapter changed the vow of chastity to celibacy, which reflected the new theological notion that all Christians are called to be chaste but the religious goes beyond chastity to celibacy, a condition suitable only to those willing to become a special witness.[38] The ramifications of the vow of poverty were seriously discussed from many points of view rang-ing from the traditional to the most radical notion of living as poor people.[39] The period of temporary vows was changed from five years to a suitable time between three and seven years.

The chapter directed the superior general to establish an international commission composed of one Brother from each province. Under the supervision of the superior general, the commission was charged with responsibility to work on the constitution in preparation for the second session of the chapter to be held at Aachen in May 1969.

After a one-week visit to Rome where they had an audience with Pope Paul VI, the delegates convened in Aachen for the opening of the second session on May 9, 1969. In accord with a resolution of the first session, each province elected an additional delegate. The ex-officio delegates included Brother Felix Bettendorf, superior general, Brother Edmund Kelly, assistant superior general, Brother Ludger Göller, the German provincial, Brother Charles (formerly Flavian), the American provincial, Brother Peter Mannion, the Anglo-Irish provincial, Brother Fridolin Wimmer, the assistant superior general, and Hilarion Pencheon, general secretary. All were members of the previous General Council. Former superiors general, Brothers Ludolf Sattler and Herman Joseph Berkes, excused themselves for reasons of health. Representing the German Province were Brothers Ludolf van der Coelen, Thomas Poier, Christopher Schrudde, and Joseph Welsch. Brothers Philip Kennedy, Gregory Isenhart, and Warren Longo represented the American Province. The Anglo-Irish delegates included Brothers Anthony Ferri, Walter Sharkey, Montfort Eames, and Aquinas Anderson. In March the delegates had received working papers drafted by the International Commission. Each province had held its own chapter in January, the resolutions from which clearly illustrate the direction of the province.

The German Provincial Chapter remained traditionalist. For example, it voted to observe recreation as in the past, to maintain seniority seating at meal time, not to engage in any new apostolates, and not to permit a Brother to change from his religious to his baptismal name.[40] The American Province stood at the other end of the spectrum. Nearly four years of renewal and the establishment of various provincial commissions to encourage adaptation had resulted in a plethora of reform proposals. At its two sessions the American Provincial Chapter produced well over two hundred resolutions, far more than the other two provinces combined. Democracy, individual responsibility, accountability by those in authority, popular trends in scriptural prayer, and continuous experimentation mark the character of its resolutions.[41] For example, superiors were to be nominated by the Brothers of each house; the title of "local superior" was changed to "director," and individual Brothers who wished to go out for whatever reason had only to notify their Brother director.[42]

The Anglo-English Province assumed a moderate position. Local superiors were to be nominated by the local community, with the Provincial Council empowered to choose a Brother from a list of nominees. Reading at meals was discontinued; baptismal names were permitted; Brothers were allowed to eat out as circumstances warranted; broad experimentation in modes of dress was encouraged. The incorporation of Bible Vigils during the Advent and Lent prayer schedule was voted down by two votes.[43]

The conservative-to-liberal breakdown did not fully reflect the general characteristics of the Catholic Church in Germany, America, and England-Ireland. Some German religious communities were far to the left of the Alexians but there were few American Alexian communities that had not moved to the left. There were broad differences among the religious in England and Ireland; the Alexians were noticeably to the right of many of the Sisters' communities. To discover the causes of the divergent characteristics within the Alexian Congregation one should review the postwar developments within each province. With few vocations the German Province was not pushed by young Brothers to engage in reforms. Brothers were professionally trained within Alexian institutions providing little contact with the secular world. Though their hospitals were extremely modern, their mental-health character precluded broad contacts with the secular city. As provincial during the post-Vatican II period, Brother Ludger Göller, a young professionally trained nurse who had to deal with complex business matters, was imbued with the German-Alexian tradition and deferred to the sensibilities of the older Brothers who formed a majority of the province. Bitter experiences with Bismarck's *Kulturkampf* and Hitler's *Mein Kampf* had led the German Province to preserve its tradition and its nineteenth-century notion of the rigid separation between the cloister and the modern world.

The American Province experienced a vocation boom from the late forties to the early sixties. The evolution of the general hospital demanded highly trained Brothers. In the sixties many young Brothers studied at universities where they were introduced to new theological perspectives, including a radical reexamination of every aspect of the religious life. Brother Flavian Renaud, deeply influenced by Vatican II, provided the crucial leadership for renewal, adaptation, and experimentation. A more traditional provincial could have obstructed the movement to the left, but the education trends within the province would have engendered a liberal character. No doubt the political climate infused with the idealism of John F. Kennedy's New Frontier and Lyndon B. Johnson's Great Society and the general ferment of the civil-rights and antiwar movements had a strong impact upon many American Brothers.

The Anglo-Irish Province had shifted from custodial to professional nursing homes and had experienced a vocation boom. However, its nursing homes were quiet enclaves in contrast to the American general hospitals. Many Brothers had received professional training but none were allowed free time to pursue university degrees. Brother Cormac O'Reilly, provincial during Vatican II, was more concerned with upgrading the professional character of the province than with the reform thought of the day. Appointed provincial at the age of thirty-six, Brother Cormac was a very dynamic leader who appointed many young Brothers to positions of responsibility. Anglo-Irish distrust of reform theorizing also expressed itself in Brother Peter Mannion, appointed provincial in March 1966. Though open-minded toward reform, Brother Peter proceeded cautiously, patiently awaiting the General Chapter of 1968.

The delegates to the General Chapter reflected the majority position of their provinces. The American Province delegation formed an exceptional mix. As superior general, Brother Felix expressed the neutrality of chairman but was determined not to allow conflicts to rupture the congregation. Brother Flavian, a provincial dedicated to implementing the principles of collegiality, did not impose his reform views upon the American delegation. Brother Fidelis Kennedy was the most articulate proponent of change. Well known for his brilliant mind and his keen rhetorical style, Brother Fidelis pursued the liberal cause with the acumen of a seasoned constitutional lawyer. The recently elected delegate Brother Warren Longo had been invited to present a paper on "Formation" to the first session at Signal Mountain. Reflecting the newest trends in formation, Brother Warren's paper, which juxtaposed Alexian traditional *monastic* training with futurisitc *apostolic* formation, marked him as a radical among the European delegations. Brother Gregory Isenhart had long been a proponent of simplifying the monastic regulations that implied the Brothers were lacking in maturity and individual responsibility. Though he was also influenced by Vatican II, Brother Gregory gradually became disenchanted with what he thought was reform faddism, thoroughly lacking any sensitivity to the older Brothers' views and feelings. He was shocked at the excessive individualism contained in the American Province and feared a total breakdown in community life. He did not oppose liturgical innovation but viewed the small community movement within the province as deeply divisive. With his strong analytical mind and his keen command of the language he was an equal match to Brother Fidelis. Indeed, during periods of the debate at the second session of the chapter, the German and Anglo-Irish Brothers were astounded to hear Brother Gregory articulate their position against the American liberals better than they could have done themselves.

The traditionalist-reformist conflict surfaced on the first day of the second session when the delegates debated a proposal from the American Province that called for allowing priests within the congregation. It had been discussed at the first session but final consideration had been postponed for further study. The reformers agreed that Alexian priests could serve liturgical needs of the Brothers, the pastoral-ministry character of the congregation, and the spiritual needs of the patients.[44] The traditionalists argued that the entire lay-Brother character of the congregation must be preserved to prevent the establishment of first- and second-class Brothers within the congregation. The traditional anticlericalism of the Alexians also influenced the opposition. The chapter accepted the reform position with six qualifying stipulations:

1) The Congregation maintain its lay character; 2) primary purpose for introducing the priesthood is to serve the needs of local communities, though spiritual care of patients is a secondary function which may also be filled; 3) the clerics are always to be considered brothers who are ordained; 4) they wear the Alexian habit and are called Brother within the Congregation and their own community . . . ; 5) priests desirous of joining the Congregation may do so under certain conditions; 6) none of the above becomes effective in any province until the provincial Chapter recognizes the need for the priestly services these men can offer.

The procedures for approving a Brother candidate for the priesthood were later amended. The stipulation granting provincial authority full sovereignty on the issues of the priesthood became a guiding principle for resolving other interprovincial conflicts. Theoretically referred to as "subsidiarity," the principle was implemented when the chapter decided on introduction of a diaconate, provincial election procedures, the order of precedence (e.g., seniority seating at meals), and other decisions that granted the provincial authority full sovereignty on specific matters.[45] Subsidiarity was not a theory that descended upon the chapter but, rather, it surfaced during the debates when it became necessary to devise an acceptable formula whereby the American reform and experimentation, German traditionalism, and Anglo-Irish gradualism could coexist within the congregation. Prior to the 1968–1969 chapter, congregational standardization and centralization characterized governance. Subsidiarity reversed tradition but it was the only practical means to guarantee cultural diversity among the provinces and to prevent one province from dominating the entire congregation.

The traditionalists did achieve a modest victory when they led the chapter to limit the broad authority of the Commission on Experimentation established in the American Province. The commission, composed of the Provincial Senate and one representative from each house, had been empowered to decide on experimentation in all areas except formation, education, government, and the apostolate.[46] Hence it possessed great authority for experiments in communal and prayer life. The traditionalists pointed out that the extra-regular commission violated sound principles of governance embedded in canon law because it possessed legislative authority equal to the regularly constituted authority, i.e., the Provincial Senate. The chapter decided to alter its authority from legislative to consultative.[47]

One recently established American Province regulation, which stipulated that Brothers were required but not bound by the rule to attend daily Mass, was deeply opposed by many delegates to the chapter as well as the many Brothers who wrote letters to the chapter. The chapter refused to alter the American regulation.[48] One may infer that some of the German and Anglo-Irish delegates joined with the liberal American delegates on this issue, not because they were sympathetic to the regulation but because they were reluctant to tamper with subsidiarity, which prevented American interference in their affairs.

After some revisions in language the new constitution was published under the title *Way of Life for the Congregation of Cellites or Alexian Brothers*. Prefaced by "The Essence of the Rule of St. Augustine," *Way of Life* is steeped in Scripture, Vatican II thought on the nature of the church, and the principles of the religious life. The following illustrates the extremely divergent ideals between *Way of Life* and the pre-Vatican II constitution published in 1949. One will note that the ideal Alexian Brother is no longer in monastic remoteness from the world but, rather, is called to be a witness within the world.

1949

THE TITLE AND THE SCOPE
OF THE CONGREGATION

1. The Congregation is recognized by Holy Mother, the Church, under the title; CONGREGATION OF CELLITES OR ALEXIAN BROTHERS.

1969
I. SPIRIT

THE SPIRIT OF THE BEGHARDS—
SPIRIT OF THE CONGREGATION

1. Where people join to live and work together, a particular atmosphere is generated which is more felt and experienced than definitively known. This is the spirit of the group—its energy-force. Spirit is not a simple concept: it embraces the sum of all forces involved in the heritage and the present-day situation of a group. Spirit cannot exist in abstract form, but only in the people whose energy-force it is.

302

2. The Congregation rigidly maintains its original scope which, through the years, has been repeatedly approved and confirmed by significant and benevolent Papal Bulls.

2. Our lives are oriented toward a communal witness to Christ Who loves the sick; to Christ the Healer; to Christ the Concerned One. By our caring for others we live our Christian lives as a loving response to Man's needs. Therefore, our specific spirit is basically an intensification of the universal Christian spirit.

3. This scope is two-fold, namely:

First, the general scope of the Congregation is the individual perfection and sanctification of its Brothers through the observance of the three simple vows of Religion following the Rule of Saint Augustine and these present Constitutions. Its members shall strive to honor God in a special way by generously fulfilling His holy will and conforming their own lives to the life and doctrine of Jesus Christ.

Second, its specific aim is the practice of charity towards our fellow-men. This comprises, in particular:

a. Caring for male patients regardless of their religious affiliation, and for the poor and outcast as well as for people of means, either in their own homes or in the Establishments and Hospitals that are under the supervision of the Congregation.

b. Supervising mental institutions and hospices for either aged-infirm males or other men in need of custodial care.

c. Burying the dead, especially during epidemics. Failing other provision, the Congregation undertakes the establishment and full administration of cemeteries. [pp. 25-26]

3. This orientation of spirit has always been our motivating force since the first grouping of the Beghards, the concerned ones of the Middle Ages. Men of their times, they responded in a community way to the pressing health needs of their society. Theirs was a totally selfless dedication and an uncomplicated love of God and Mankind. These men who were a source of inspiration to their contemporaries, were the seed from which we have grown. In their spirit we modern Alexian Brothers must continually replant the seed of our legacy, nurturing and bringing it to maturity in a manner consistent with the times in which we live. . . .[49]

303

The 1968–1969 General Chapter occurred during a critical period in the congregation's history. There was a severe drop in vocations and many professed Brothers were seeking dispensations from their vows. The traditionalists viewed these developments as proof that because change was occurring at such a rapid pace confusion reigned. Accordingly, young men found such confusion unappealing, while both traditionalists and reformers left the congregation because either change was occurring too rapidly or not rapidly enough. Though the latter development was most characteristic of the American Province, each province experienced a serious vocation crisis, one which is still severe in the German Province and has only recently begun to diminish in the Anglo-Irish and American provinces.

It is fruitless to engage in an "if only" interpretation of the crisis by attempting to guess what might have occurred had the Alexians gradually changed or had Vatican II occurred thirty years earlier. One fact is clear: just as the majority of Roman Catholics would not like to return to the days when the priest "said Mass" with his back to the congregation, so would few Alexian Brothers like to return to the days when they were directed to turn their back to the modern world. Pater Clement Wallrath's constitution reflected the antimodern spirit of Vatican Council I, while the *Way of Life* reflects the principle—the sanctification of the modern world—so characteristic of the thought of Vatican Council II. During the time-span between the two councils, Western culture passed through the profound phases of industrialism, urbanization, and secularism and experienced history's two worst wars. The church gradually opened itself to the modern world through the social encyclicals and through the encouragement of the lay apostolate.

Though unconscious of its revolutionary impact, the church encouraged the revival of its scriptural foundations and the development of a theology of the laity—trends which eventuated modern philosophical and theological explorations on the nature of the early church. These explorations gathered great strength from Vatican II, engendering strong criticism of traditional devotionalism and the ghetto and fortress mentality derived from Vatican I.

By the mid-sixties the Alexians had become highly professional nurses and hospital administrators with the Americans setting the pace. Hence, with the American Province most in touch with the trends within the church and within the congregation, many American Alexians began to criticize the traditional cloister mentality and to search for new ways to incorporate their original charism as folk mendicants. Just as an agonizing polarization struck many religious orders in the post-Vatican II period, so the Alexians were divided within and among their provinces. At their 1968–1969 chapter the traditionalist-reformist conflicts were resolved by the principle of subsidiarity. Now each province has great autonomy in dealing with the ways in which its ministerial, communal, and prayer lives shall implement the Vatican II principles imbedded in the *Way of Life*. Just as Dominic Brock and Clement Wallrath responded to the nineteenth-century needs of the congregation and to those to whom it ministered according to what they considered to be Alexian tradition and according to the spirit of Vatican I, so will the modern Brothers be influenced by their notions of Alexian tradition, Vatican II, and the diverse cultures of each of the provinces. The congregation's rise under Pater Clement occurred during a profound vocation boom throughout Catholic Europe. A spirit of defense against the anti-Catholic and anticlerical attacks of the modern liberal free-thinkers led him and others to cultivate an antimodern-world cloister. Contemporary Alexian Brothers have been called by Vatican II to sanctify the world and to discern how their charism may best be incorporated into their ministry. As Brothers of each province work their way through the crisis and to the spirit of the anonymous founder-Beghards and -Lollards, they may gather some nourishment for the agonizing journey by recalling the words by the fourteenth-century German mystic, Meister Eckhart:

> God's foundation is my foundation and my foundation is God's foundation. Here I am on my ground, just as God is on his ground. Actions spring up from this ground without asking *why?*

Epilogue

1970-1977

I

Pluralism is one of the most predominant characteristics of modern culture. At the General Chapter of 1968–1969 the Alexian Brothers, following the lead of the Vatican Council fathers, opened themselves to the modern world. Since renewal and adaptation are not mechanical devices but, rather, organic processes of development the Alexians of the seventies have only begun to discern how their way of life is to be adapted to the needs of the times and how the Alexian message is best expressed within a pluralistic society replete with diverse messages.

The new governance principles of subsidiarity and collegiality may be viewed as symbols of the congregation's recognition of its own pluralism; each province is to develop according to how it perceives its role within the Alexian family. Though the modernization of their institutions and the professionalization of the Brothers persist as the most common characteristics of all the provinces, the events of the seventies fall into patterns in accord with the diverse culture and movements within each province.

Under the leadership of Brother Provincial Ludger Göller (1964–1976), the mental hospitals of the German Province flourished. However, the severe vocation crisis compelled the Provincial Council to withdraw the Brothers from the Krefeld house in 1975. The Cellitinen Sisters, who had assumed management of the Maria-Hilf General Hospital adjacent to the Brothers' mental hospital there, had withdrawn the previous year.[1] With so few young Brothers, the province struggles to maintain hope in its future. Brother Ludger and his successor, Brother Thomas Poier (elected in 1976), keenly aware of the nearly seven-century presence of the Brothers on Alexianergraben, represent strong leadership during these critical times. The traditional Alexian cloister life with its formal recreation period, its standardized daily schedule, and its general remoteness from secular life still characterize the province but there are signs of changing attitudes. The Brothers are not required to wear their habits during certain portions of the day, including recreation; women patients are admitted to the hospital; a new Brothers' residence has been constructed on the site of the old generalate, and each Brother has his own private bath; a new recruitment drive has encouraged many Brothers that the vocation crisis will diminish.

Hospitality is a hallmark of the German Province. Visitors from the United States are overwhelmed with the natural ease with which the Brothers concern themselves with the guests' every need. Hospitality also characterizes the Brothers' attitude toward their patients. As administrator of the Aachen hospital, Brother Joachim Wetzke greets nearly every patient by name. Brother Adelbert Hau, a gifted, enthusiastic musician, has developed his own style of music therapy. Nearly all the Brothers, regardless of training, experience patient-care situations. Though in numbers secular personnel dominate the German hospitals, Alexian hospitality permeates the atmosphere. Whether one is visiting the Aachen Motherhouse, Haus Kannen, near Münster, Ensen near Cologne, or the Bavarian house, Malseneck, one will easily detect the genuine spirit of hospitality together with a healthy pride in the ancient Alexian tradition and the modern Alexian health care.

II

As the American Province entered the seventies it too experienced a serious vocation crisis. For a variety of reasons, over forty American Brothers had left the congregation between 1966 and 1970. Brother Charles (Flavian) Renaud, who had presided over the high peaks of post-Vatican II renewal and the low valleys of the vocation crisis resigned as provincial in June 1971. He felt he could not satisfy either the traditionalist alienated by change or the reformer eager to continue experimentation.[2] Brother Charles is currently serving as the first Alexian priest. A chaplain at the Elk Grove hospital and for the Brothers located there, Brother Charles represents the pluralism of the American Province. While many Brothers supported his pursuit of ordination there is still a strong anticlerical feeling within the provinces, which is derived from the traditional hierarchical ladder from which priests frequently looked down upon communities of Brothers.

During Brother Charles's terms as provincial, two mission endeavors stemming from the Provincial Chapters were initiated. On June 26, 1968, almost immediately after the first session of the General Chapter, Brothers Christopher Schmitz, Pius Baker, and Robert Fleming left for Lima, Peru, where they were to be enrolled in a language school prior to establishing a clinic in Chulucanas, Peru. Before leaving for their mission they had received training in obstetrical nursing and public health.[3] They had originally intended to establish a mobile clinic to serve the people in the rural areas, but upon the advice of their bishop, John McNabb, they dedicated themselves to training Peruvians in health care. Under the direction of Sister Thomas More, M.D., the government health officer in the area, they developed a public health program. However, because of an insufficient number of Brothers the Peru mission was "temporarily" discontinued in 1971.[4]

In the summer of 1969 the American Province established a mobile health clinic for the rural area around Waterboro, South Carolina. Among the nine volunteers, Brothers Maurice Wilson, John Greider, Kenneth Mulholland, and Raymond Levesque were chosen to run the clinic. The idealism of Vatican II blended with the War on Poverty as the Office of Economic Opportunity funded much of the Alexian support. Besides providing health care, the Alexian mobile clinic was dedicated to instruct families on the principles of good health, to work with other social agencies for referrals, and to participate in community health planning. On June 22, 1970, Robert M. Strickland, a director of the Economic Development Corporation in the area, wrote the following letter to the Provincial; it clearly indicates the Alexian impact in the Waterboro area.

Dear Brother Charles:

I am writing this letter as a means of expressing my personal appreciation for the services rendered by four Alexian Brothers with whom I have had the pleasure of being associated.

I met my first "Brother" in June of 1969 when I was introduced to Brother Maurice Wilson, c.f.a. My first thought, being a Baptist and a resident of this area for 22 years was that of suspicion. I wondered why a man would give up so many worldly pleasures to dedicate his life to helping others. Shortly after, Brother Maurice was joined by Brother Kenneth Mulholland, Brother Raymond Levesque and Brother John Greider who completed his staff. From this time forth these four volunteer nurses have given me an insight into human relations and feelings that could never be from experience.

These men work hard and diligently toward their goal of bringing professional health services to their less fortunate brothers. I am held in complete awe and respect for their dedication and character. Men such as these who would put in that extra hour or go another twenty miles if it meant being of service to anyone, regardless of race, color or religion are hard to find. Their work in our Mobile Health Unit Project has been unsurpassed.

After being in their home on several occasions and discussing private and public matters, I must say that many of the rest of us have fallen down on the job. These men do not know what it means to say, "I can't do this," or "That is impossible." . . .

Their efforts this past year have probably meant survival as many families struggle in their primitive environment. Beyond their professional services, the Brothers have served as a communication media between the people of our area and the Alexian order and even the Catholic faith. These men carry their banner high and they carry it proudly for their beliefs and convictions. I feel their services can be expanded in the future.

In closing, may I say that my personal respect for these four Alexians exceeds all else. I pray that one day all men may have the faith and trust exemplified by Brother Maurice, Brother Kenneth, Brother Raymond and Brother John.[5]

The project experienced many of the bureaucratic problems so characteristic of government-sponsored programs. Just as great a problem was the fact that as the idealism of the sixties waned, new volunteers among the Brothers did not come forth to replace those on duty. When federal funds were cut off by the Nixon administration in early 1973, the Provincial Senate decided to terminate the project.[6] However, in 1977 Brother John Greider was still living in Waterboro as the sole Alexian witness to the health needs of the rural poor.

Brother Florian Eberle was elected provincial to replace Brother Charles. Since Brother Philip (Fidelis) Kennedy, a strong proponent of change, was also on the ballot, Brother Florian's election represented the general will to moderate the pace of change and consolidate the reforms of the post-Vatican II period. Brother Florian's term as provincial was marked by low-keyed renewal workshops and a movement toward a strongly centralized corporate management of the five American Alexian institutions.

Brother Florian and his Provincial Senate sponsored a variety of community workshops ranging from community-living to discernment-of-the-Spirit themes. Though such renewal efforts have been extremely well planned and led by experts in various fields, it was difficult to satisfy the many diverse views of the Brothers. One workshop may have been well received by younger, more change-oriented communities at Elk Grove and San Jose and the same one poorly received at the more traditionalist communities at St. Louis and Signal Mountain.[7]

The pluralism of the American Province is aptly illustrated by the evolution of formation thought during Brother Florian's tenure of office. In 1969 the novitiate moved from Gresham to the Chicago scholasticate adjacent to the old Belden Avenue Hospital and Nursing School. With the closing of the latter two institutions, the novitiate was temporarily established at the provincialate at Elk Grove. In 1971 Brother Warren Longo was appointed novice master. Holding an M.A. in theology and being very innovative in his formation ideas, Brother Warren received permission to purchase a house on Glenlake Avenue as the site for a new novitiate. Stressing small communal living as opposed to institution-bound communal life, poverty, hospitality, and apostolic witness to the poor, Brother Warren represented a continuity with the experimentation days of the sixties. During the next few years the novitiate alienated a majority of the Brothers. Some Brothers blamed the vocation crisis on the radical Glenlake experiment. After an intense controversy and deep personal conflict, the novitiate was moved to the provincialate, which in 1972 had been established on North Kenmore Avenue near Loyola University. When the provincialate returned to Elk Grove in the summer of 1977 the novitiate remained as a small community closely resembling the Glenlake experiment, with less emphasis on direct apostolic witness and more on apostolic spirituality. Brother Warren still presides over the novitiate but now with full support from almost the entire province.[8]

When Brother Florian was first provincial, 1952–1958, he participated in the establishment of the Alexian Brothers clinic at Boys' Town. Though for many years the clinic thrived, during the early seventies changes in administrative policy resulted in a drop in enrollment from 925 to 350 boys. Whereas in the sixties the Brothers treated an average of 150 boys daily, by 1976 the number had dropped to 30. The low census of the clinic and the manpower shortage of the province caused Brother Florian to initiate a thorough reevaluation of the Brothers' presence there. In January 1976 the Provincial Senate, in consultation with the local Alexian community and the administration of Boys' Town, closed the Brothers' house.[9]

Brother Florian possesses a keen business sense, which is expressed through a rigorous work day. At his desk as early as 4:00 A.M., Brother Florian has vigorously pursued a restructuring of the institutional management of the province. The process began under Brother Charles when he appointed Mr. Al Bushman, a professor of economics at Washington University, St. Louis, Missouri, as the province's chief financial adviser. Mr. Bushman's top priority was to centralize the province's financial processes. With the introduction of medicare and the growing need to direct and support the many complex facets of the general hospital, Brother Florian decided to further centralize the management of the province. He was assisted in the process by Mr. Neil Bennett, a former hospital administrator and a C.P.A. The product of their efforts was the establishment of the Alexian Brothers of America, Inc. (ABA, Inc.), composed of a parent Board of Trustees and local boards of trustees. The provincial

311

is president and chairman of the parent board, which is composed of the Provincial Senate. He is also an ex-officio member of each local Board of Trustees. Though Brother Florian is no longer provincial, Mr. Bennett provides continuity in the corporate management as he is the chief staff officer of the Shared Services wing of ABA, Inc. Supported by an expert staff, Brother Robert Wilde (elected provincial in April 1977), Brother Florian, and Mr. Bennett can proudly point to the success of ABA, Inc., measured by a nearly 50 percent increase in the equitable assets of the province.[10]

Brother Robert Wilde was elected provincial after ill health had forced Brother Florian to resign. With ABA, Inc., thriving, Brother Robert has placed community life and recruitment at the top of his priority list. Reflecting the consensus of the 1976 Provincial Chapter, he has established task forces to study small-community life, the retirement issue, and many other topics. Brother Robert, thirty-eight years of age, is a former head of recruitment and assistant provincial and, like some Brothers, is deeply involved in the charismatic movement. Setting an extremely optimistic tone, Brother Robert's style of leadership harks back to the theme of the Provincial Chapter of 1968–1969, "To Build and to Plant."[11]

On January 1, 1975, when Brother Florian was recovering from open-heart surgery, the province was confronted with a challenge unique in its history. On New Year's day word reached the provincialiate that several armed Menominee Indians had seized the Alexian Brothers' property in Gresham, Wisconsin, and were holding six hostages, two men, two women, and two children.[12] The property, which had been for sale for years, was seized by representatives of a radical splinter faction of the tribe who viewed it as rightfully belonging to native Americans of the area. Brother Robert Wilde, acting provincial, quickly dispatched Brother Maurice Wilson, a member of the Provincial Senate, and Mr. Neil Bennett to the scene. After assuring the Indians that he would stay in Gresham and negotiate with them in good faith, Brother Maurice convinced them to release their hostages.

Town-tribe relations, which had never achieved a spirit of

312

congeniality, reached a peak of intensity threatening an outbreak of violence. By January 6 the National Guard had been
called in to maintain law and order. The radical Menominees,
i.e., the Menominee Warrior Society, the moderates, and the
American Indian movement entered into the negotiations. The
lines of authority among the sheriff, the district attorney, and
the commanding officer of the National Guard often became
blurred. Negotiating within a potentially explosive atmosphere,
Brother Maurice established as his first priority the pursuit of a
nonviolent, just resolution of the conflict. During the next four
weeks Brother Maurice and Neil Bennett, assisted by many
consultants among the Brothers, the Green Bay diocese, other
religious orders, and Protestant organizations concerned with
peace and justice, negotiated with moderate and radical Menominees. Finally, on February 2 a peaceful settlement was
reached that brought an end to the occupation of the property.
The Alexian Brothers promised to convey title to the novitiate
property to the Menominee tribe as soon as it regained legal
tribal status. The property was to be used for humanitarian purposes in the areas of health, education, or social services.

The decision was greeted with relief by many Brothers and
national observers. Because it appeared to some as a capitulation
to radicalism it was bitterly criticized. For example, Father Andrew Greeley rebuked the Alexians for not standing their ground
against the Warrior lawbreakers. Columnist Tom Wicker took
a diametrically opposite view. Having witnessed the violence at
Attica, New York, he praised the Brothers for their wise human
accommodation to the Warriors' demands and lamented the fact
that such concern was absent in the Attica negotiations.

During the following seven months, tribal officials would neither accept nor reject the title. Because the Menominee tribe
was ruled by moderates, acceptance of the title would have been
tacit recognition of the radical element, while rejection would
have left the door open for another radical maneuver. On July
9, with no resolution in sight, the Brothers announced that they
had fulfilled the February agreement as best as possible and
promised to consider all proposals, including those from the
Menominee tribe, for a final disposition of the property.

313

In mid-August the Brothers announced a September 15th deadline for submission of proposals. Of the eight proposals submitted, the Brothers decided on that presented by the Crossroads Academy. On November 13, 1975, Brother Maurice Wilson issued the following concluding statement on the disposition of the Gresham property:

> The Alexian Brothers' former novitiate in Gresham, Wisconsin, has been the subject of much discussion since January 1st of this year. It was at that time that a group calling itself the Menominee Warrior Society began its 34 day occupation of the facility. Through a series of difficult negotiating sessions with the occupants of the novitiate, an agreement calling for their peaceful withdrawal was reached on February 2nd. Under the terms of that agreement, the Alexian Brothers agreed to offer title of the novitiate to the Menominee Indian Tribe.
>
> For six months following that agreement, no tribal official would agree to accept or reject title to the novitiate. Because of the standstill that had been reached, the Alexian Brothers announced on July 9th that the terms of the February agreement had been fulfilled as best possible. At that same time, the Brothers announced that they would consider any and all proposals, including those from the Menominee Indian Tribe, for final disposition of the novitiate if they:
>
> - Are meaningful, humanitarian and truly serve the needs of the Gresham area as reflected by input from community leaders, both Indian and non-Indian.
> - Are submitted by responsible parties that are able to demonstrate program self-sufficiency in terms of perpetuation, management and financing.
> - Are of such nature and scope that implementation, including conveyance by deed, could be accomplished within a reasonable period of time following final approval.
>
> In mid-August, a September 15th deadline for submission of proposals was announced by the Alexian Brothers. On the date of the deadline, eight proposals had been received. All proposals were then submitted to an Ad Hoc Advisory Committee of the Alexian Brothers for review and consideration. The Advisory Committee included Alexian Brothers, attorneys, Gresham area residents as well as individuals familiar with Indian affairs. After careful screening, the proposals that best met the established criteria were submitted to the Board of Directors for final action.
>
> Brother Florian Eberle, Alexian Brothers Provincial, has asked me to advise you of the decision reached today by the Board.
>
> As of this date, the former Alexian Brothers novitiate in Gresham, Wisconsin, along with approximately 186 acres of land has been deeded to Crossroads Academy, Incorporated, of Milwaukee, Wis-

consin. Crossroads Academy is a non-profit organization providing therapeutic, educational and recreational services in Milwaukee, Cudahy, Waukesha, Green Bay and Sturgeon Bay, Wisconsin. The services of Crossroads Academy are offered to all people, regardless of race, color or creed.

In addition, title to the remaining Alexian Brothers property in Gresham, approximately 56 acres of Red River frontage, has been deeded to the town of Richmond, in Shawano County, for use as a recreational park by all people.

It is the opinion of the Alexian Brothers that the proposal submitted by Crossroads Academy best met the established criteria, especially in relation to serving the needs of the Gresham area.

During discussions with Gresham area residents, it became apparent that there existed a genuine desire to preserve a portion of the Red River land in its natural state for use as a recreational area. It was for that reason as well as the desire of the Alexian Brothers to preserve the ecological integrity of a portion of their land for community use that the decision deeding title to the town of Richmond was reached.

Although the Alexian Brothers recognize that there is no "perfect" solution to the problem of the Gresham novitiate, the Brothers sincerely feel the decisions announced today are truly in accord with their desire to reach a peaceful and humanitarian resolution of this matter.[13]

When the ten-month ordeal was finally terminated Brother Maurice Wilson was greatly relieved of a heavy burden. As former administrator of the Chicago Nursing School and of the Waterboro mobile clinic he had had many contacts with persons of diverse backgrounds. Tolerant and peaceful by temperament, Brother Maurice was placed in an extremely tense situation. During many chats with this historian, Brother Maurice discussed his point of view as a negotiator. He represented the Alexian Brothers not as property owners but as the conscience of the Catholic Church in America sensitive to the need for reconciliation with native Americans. Though the confrontation at Gresham sparked this conscience, Brother Maurice and other Brothers were singular witnesses to reconciliation with one of America's most alienated outside groups. No representative of the American Catholic hierarchy became publicly involved in the negotiations. Once they were confronted with the situation, the Alexian Brothers responded according to their traditional charism as ministers to the outsider.

315

III

Since 1972 the Anglo-Irish Province has been under the direction of Brother Dominic Walsh. His predecessor, Brother Peter Mannion, witnessed the first phase of the general vocation crisis. To upgrade the intellectual and spiritual character of the novitiate at Cobh, the Provincial Council appointed Brother Fidelis O'Sullivan novice master in August 1969.[14] The following spring Brother Fidelis presided over the construction of a new building adjacent to the eighteenth-century mansion. Still novice master in 1977, Brother Fidelis is a meticulous administrator, well versed in current theological trends and projecting a warm father-figure at the novitiate.

Brother Dominic Walsh was a pioneer at the Alexian mission near Minna in northwestern Nigeria. The Irish missionary tradition is strongly expressed in Brother Dominic's concern to maintain the Alexian presence in Nigeria. However, political instability there and the government's 1975 announcement that it would soon control all health-care centers compelled the Brothers to reevaluate their mission. Because of the abundance of government forms, one Brother was compelled to spend nearly all of his time on bureaucratic work. Almost simultaneous with the Nigerian government's announcement, Brother Dominic received a request that the Brothers participate in the Irish Missionary Union Team's "Faith and Hope Project" in Cairo, Egypt. Brother Dominic responded favorably and Brothers John Anderson and Robert Fleming, two of the Alexian volunteers for the project, were sent for special training in preparation for paramedical work in the poverty areas of Cairo.[15] However, by the time Brothers John and Robert were ready to embark for Egypt, Brother Dominic received discouraging news from those missionaries who had initiated the project in 1975. Indeed, administrative and personnel problems had become so heavy that the project was terminated in the spring of 1977.[16]

Brother Dominic has received many other requests for missionaries. The most appealing came from the bishop of the Navrongo diocese in Ghana. After his annual visitation to the Nigerian mission in the spring of 1977, Brother Dominic traveled to Navrongo, where he enjoyed a promising visit with the bishop.[17] It appears that the Alexian presence in Africa may be extended to Ghana.

Each of the Brothers' nursing homes in Manchester, London, and Warrenpoint was modernized during the seventies. On June 7, 1975, the province celebrated its centennial with a solemn High Mass at St. Patrick's Church, Manchester, followed by a gala luncheon for over four hundred friends and benefactors. After concelebrating Mass and attending the luncheon, Bishop Holland made an informal tour of the Brothers' new residence at St. Mary's Home. Superior General Brother Augustine Lohman, Brother Ludger Göller, and other German Brothers joined their English-Irish confreres in the festivities.[18]

The modernization of Twyford Abbey has been a problem for years. Because it comes under the regulations of the National Trust, intended to preserve historic homes and places throughout England, Twyford Abbey has many limitations for renovation placed upon it. If the Brothers could find a buyer they would be very tempted to sell the property. In 1977 the situation was compounded when the government announced that financial exigencies compelled it to reduce the number of patients sent to private nursing homes. Even before the government announced its austerity program, the Provincial Council decided to renovate Twyford Abbey to make it suitable for the admission of female patients.[19] Since the Brothers' nurses' training included contact with women patients and since the missionary Alexians engaged in midwifery procedures, the decision to admit women into their nursing homes was not a drastic departure from their tradition.

The spirit of the Anglo-Irish Province has been shaped by its relatively small nursing-home m... ..ry. Though lay staff greatly outnumber Alexians at each of their institutions, the Brother-patient ratio is much lower than in the other two provinces. The nursing-home ministry allows for the growth of a strong personalist spirit, one which is unobstructed by the medical technology so characteristic of the general hospitals. Because the nursing homes are relatively remote from the secular city, the Anglo-Irish Alexians minister within quiet enclaves. The spirit is also partially shaped by the province's missionary thrust in Africa and, since 1972, its home mission to down-and-out alcoholics in Limerick, Ireland.

The latter missionary activity originated in Manchester in 1969. Brothers Stephen Russell, Joseph Newel, and others volunteered to work at the Morning Star Hostel. A prominent Manchester Catholic layman, Mr. Joseph Cox, had purchased a large mansion, which became the Morning Star. Because Brother Stephen, who had been on the road recruiting vocations, had such a natural rapport with the down-and-out, he was Brother Dominic's obvious choice when the Brothers were invited by the Limerick Social Service Council to engage in that type of work. On November 4, 1972, Brother Stephen and Brother Anthony Ferri were assigned to establish the Limerick Mission for alcoholics.[20]

IV

Brother Felix Bettendorf was an activist superior general. Though the 1968–1969 General Chapter had greatly decentralized authority within the congregation, Brother Felix fully exploited the superior general's moral authority. In order to strengthen his familiarity with the German Province he attended the Goethe Institute where he immersed himself in the German language. Under his direction, General Council meetings, which were formerly held in America, convened in each province at least once a year. He was determined to break through the centuries-old barrier that separated the Belgian and Neuss (descendants of the ancient Cologne house on the Lungengasse) Alexian families from the congregation. The reunion process with the Belgian Alexians originated after World War II. Brother Christopher Lynch, assistant superior general, had visited Belgian houses, and Pater Anthony Wessel and the Belgian provincial had corresponded on reunion issues with enthusiastic optimism. However, it was not until 1965, when Herman Joseph was superior general, that he and the provincial of the Belgian Alexians, Brother Clemens Aarts, located at Boechout near Antwerp, achieved a general understanding on the principle of reunion. Though Leon Cardinal Suenens, archbishop of Malines-Brussels, appears to have held favorable views, he deferred to the ordinary of the Antwerp diocese, Bishop J. V. Daem.[21] Unwilling to relinquish his authority over the Alexians, Bishop Daem was reluctant to grant the province permission to call a provincial-like chapter, which was a necessary step in the reunion process. Some Brothers speculated that Bishop Daem was just waiting for the small province (in 1969, thirty Brothers in four houses) to dissolve, allowing him to seize their property. Nevertheless the congregation and the Belgian Brothers continued to pursue the matter in Rome.[22]

On the evening of May 8, 1969, prior to the opening of the second session of the General Chapter in Aachen, the General Council of the congregation met with representatives of the Alexians of Boechout with filial houses in Brussels, Grimbergen, and Tienen. After discussing the characteristics of the Belgian Province, the bishop of Antwerp's unwillingness to permit a Provincial Chapter, and pursuit of reunion in Rome, the General Council unanimously resolved "That the Alexian Brothers of Belgium become a part of our congregation, as a separate Province, and that we begin the necessary operation to effect this, subject to the approval of the General Chapter.[23] At the meeting of the General Chapter on the following day, the delegates unanimously approved the principle contained in the above resolution, with an amendment (proposed by Brother Philip Kennedy) that the General Council be authorized also to pursue the incorporation of all other Alexian institutes into the congregations.[24]

After six years of correspondence with the Sacred Congregations for Religious, after visits to its Rome offices by Brothers Felix and Clemens, and after many meetings between representatives of the Belgian Province and the congregation, Rome finally approved reunion in March 1975. At the General Council meeting at Cobh, Ireland, the following September, with Brother Clemens Aarts and other representatives in attendance, norms for a five-year trial period for the Belgian houses as a vice-province were proposed.[25] On November 11, 1975, Brother Clemens reported to Superior General Brother Augustine Lohman that his council had unanimously approved the norms that incorporated the Belgian Province into the authority structure of the congregation; but until full union is established its property is retained by the vice-province.[26] The Belgian provincial is a member of the General Council with voting rights limited to those matters which affect the vice-province, while delegates to the General Chapter would have a voice but no vote. In September 1976, at a Provincial Chapter, the Belgian Brothers approved new statutes with the General Council of the congregation in attendance.[27] After having met their last norm, the Belgian family became the vice-province with St. Augustine as its patron. On September 18, 1976, the General Council joined the Brothers of Boechout for the centennial celebration of the house, which was founded in 1876 after the Antwerp Alexians had decided to move from the burgeoning mercantile city where they had resided since 1345.

Over the years Brothers Felix and Augustine had established strong familial ties with the Neuss Alexians. Their superior Brother Erhard Flotzinger, has hosted his German, Anglo-Irish, and American confreres on a number of occasions, and in 1974 journeyed to Signal Mountain, Tennessee, to be an observer at the General Chapter. An auspicious occasion indeed; for the first time since the Reformation representatives from the various Alexian branches held a family reunion. Though the relationship between the Neuss Brothers and the congregation is still on a familial basis, no doubt it will reach juridical status sometime in the future.

Delegates to the 1974 chapter were surprised to find Brother Felix Bettendorf's name absent from the list of nominees for superior general. Because his term was marked with a strong popular leadership within each of the provinces, there was little doubt that had he not removed his name Brother Felix would have been reelected. Though he was somewhat torn he decided to respond to the American Province's call for an experienced administrator to fill a recent vacancy at Elk Grove hospital. A low patient census, financial and construction problems, and staff-administration conflicts compounded the need for an administrator with Brother Felix's background. The delegates proceeded to elect Brother Augustine Lohman, who was then superior of the St. Louis community, as the new superior general.

One of the first Brothers to be allowed to attend the university on a full-time basis, Brother Augustine received his B.S. in laboratory technology from St. Louis University in 1952. A former supervisor of the labs at Belden Avenue Hospital in Chicago and at Elk Grove hospital, he had also served on the Provincial Council during the early sixties and was a very popular superior in St. Louis. When Brother Augustine received word of the election results, while on an outing at the country cottage outside St. Louis, he was overwhelmed with surprise. He had not known that he was a candidate. Though there appears to have been no causal relationship, three months after the General Chapter adjourned, Brother Augustine suffered a stroke. Because the chapter had elected Brother Felix assistant superior general he provided the necessary continuity of leadership during Brother Augustine's three-month recovery period.

In contrast to Brother Felix's activist-personalist style of leadership, Brother Augustine's leadership is marked by his stress on collegiality. With his warm, unassuming manner he radiates enthusiastic optimism on the future of the congregation. His top priority has been to lead the congregation through the vocation crisis with calm confidence and to instill within all Brothers a healthy pride in the Alexian way of life.

Under the leadership of Brothers Felix and Augustine, the principles of subsidiarity and collegiality have been nurtured to full bloom. Provincial diversity has become fully respected and indeed cherished. Throughout the dramatic years of post-Vatican II introspection, renewal, and adaptation, and the quiescent years of the seventies, the Alexian Brothers have preserved their unique spirit of quiet inconspicuousness. They have sharpened their historical sense and have focused on their founderless origins, their charism to the outsider, and their collective heroism rather than a long list of individual heroes. Proud that they were once Tamers of Death, they pursue the ministry of healing in pluralistic ways, roles like those of modern nurses, administrators, and pastoral ministers quietly responding to the sick, to those who dwell in a hospital subculture exiled from our antiseptic modern world.

Notes

Each of the Alexian Brothers Archives is arranged differently; therefore, citations to each reflect the varying methods of listing data. Following is a list of abbreviations used in these citations.

ABA-SM   Alexian Brothers Archive, Signal Mountain, Tennessee. The archive for the American Province and microfilm archive of all documents in the German Provincial and Congregational Archive, Aachen, Germany.

ABA-EGV   Alexian Brothers Archive, Elk Grove Village, Illinois. Current files of the American Province.

ABA-LON   Alexian Brothers Archive, London, England. The archive for the Anglo-Irish Province.

Introduction

1. Christopher J. Kauffman, *Tamers of Death; The History of the Alexian Brothers 1300–1789*, vol. I (New York: Seabury Press, 1976), p. 4.

Chapter 1

1. Bernhard Giergen, *Das Alexianer Kloster in Köln-Lindenthal in seiner geschichtlichen Entwicklung* (from the manuscript of the then deceased Thomas Paas) (Köln-Lindenthal, 1834). Ignatius Wiegers, C.F.A., *Die Aachener Alexianerbrüder, ihre Geschichte und ihr Ordensgeist* (Aachen, 1956).

2. Christopher J. Kauffman, *Tamers of Death: The History of the Alexian Brothers*, vol. I, 1300–1789, (New York: Seabury Press, 1977), pp. 9–97.

3. *Devotio Moderna* spirituality was embodied in Thomas à Kempis, who stressed simple, clear directives for devotion to the passion and death of Jesus.

4. *Vita apostolica*, the apostolic life, was interpreted in radical poverty terms by lay mendicants of the late Middle Ages.

5. Kauffman, pp. 131–35.

6. Ibid., pp. 190–93.

7. Ibid.

8. Ibid., pp. 197–98.

9. Ibid.

10. Klaus Epstein, *The Genesis of German Conservatism* (Princeton, N.J.: Princeton University Press, 1966), p. 154.

11. George Rude, *Europe in the Eighteenth Century, Aristocracy and the Bourgeois Challenge* (New York: Praeger Publishers, 1973), p. 126.

12. Ludwig Pastor, *The History of the Popes*, vol. XXXVII (London: Kegan, Paul, Trench, Trubner & Co., 1937), p. 379.

13. Epstein, p. 156.

14. Quoted by Epstein, p. 155.

15. Quoted by Pastor, vol. XXXVIII, p. 408.

16. Ibid., p. 412.

17. Epstein, p. 158.

18. Adrien de Meeüs, *History of the Belgians* (New York: Frederick A. Praeger, 1962), p. 238.

19. *The 1763 Constitution*, ABA-SM.

20. Ibid.

21. Giergen, p. 92.

22. Ibid.

23. Kauffman, pp. 209–210.

24. *The 1686 Constitution*, ABA-SM.

Chapter 2

1. Kenneth Scott Latourette, *A History of Christianity* (New York: Harper & Row, 1953), p. 1009.

2. Ibid., p. 1010.

3. Ibid., p. 1011.

4. Adrien de Meeüs, *History of the Belgians* (New York: Frederick A. Praeger, 1962), pp. 239–243.

5. Ibid., p. 242–243.

6. Quoted by Sydney Seymour Biro, *The German Policy of Revolutionary France: A Study in French Diplomacy during the War of the First Coalition*, 1792–95, vol. I (Cambridge, Mass.: Harvard University Press, 1957), p. 142.

7. Ibid., p. 143.

8. Ibid., p. 297.

9. Ibid., pp. 299–300.

10. Floris Prims, *Geschiedenis van Antwerpen*, vol IX (Antwerp, 1940), p. 160.

11. Ibid.

12. Ibid.

13. Ibid.

14. Ibid.
15. Ibid.
16. Ibid.
17. Ignatius Wiegers, C.F.A., *Die Aachener Alexianerbrüder, ihre Geschichte und ihr Ordensgeist* (Aachen, 1956), p. 54.
18. Ibid.
19. Ibid., pp. 54–55.
20. Ibid., p. 55.
21. Ibid.
22. Ibid.
23. Ibid., p. 56.
24. Bernhard Giergen, *Das Alexianer Kloster in Köln-Lindenthal in seiner geschlichtlichen Entwicklung* (from the manuscript of the then deceased Thomas Paas) (Köln-Lindenthal, 1934), p. 98.
25. Wiegers, p. 57.
26. Ibid.
27. Giergen, p. 99.
28. Ibid., p. 100.
29. Ibid.
30. Ibid., p. 101.
31. Ibid., pp. 102–103.
32. Ibid., p. 102.
33. Ibid.
34. Ibid.

Chapter 3

1. Henry Haag, "The Political Ideas of Belgian Catholics (1789–1914)," *Church and Society, Catholic Social and Political Thought and Movements*, ed. Joseph N. Moody (New York: Arts, Inc., 1953), pp. 281–298.
2. Ibid., pp. 279–298, 407–434.
3. Floris Prims, *Geschiedenis van Antwerpen*, vol. IX (Antwerp, 1940), p. 160.
4. Ibid.
5. Ibid.
6. Ibid.
7. Haag, p. 288.
8. Prims, vol. IX, p. 160.
9. Ibid.
10. *Regel van den Heiligen Vader Augustinus, Tot Gebruk van de orde Cellebruders, Te samed met Hune Statutes* (Sint-Truiden, 1862).
11. Christopher J. Kauffman, *Tamers of Death: The History of the Alexian Brothers*, vol. I, 1300–1789, (New York: Seabury Press, 1977), pp. 190–193.
12. Bernhard Giergen, *Das Alexianer Klosster in Köln-Lindenthal in seiner geschichtlichen Entwicklung* (from the manuscript of the then deceased Thomas Paas) (Köln-Lindenthal, 1934), p. 100.
13. Ibid.
14. Ibid., p. 103.
15. Ibid., p. 105.
16. Ibid., pp. 107–108.
17. Ibid., p. 109.

18. Ibid., pp. 109–110.

19. Erwin Gatz, *Kirche und Krankenpflege im 19. Jahrhundert* (Paderborn: Verlag Ferdinand Schöningh, 1971), p. 39.

20. Giergen, pp. 109–110.

21. Ibid., p. 111.

22. Ibid., pp. 111–112.

23. Ibid., pp. 113–114.

24. Ibid., p. 114.

25. Giergen, pp. 117–118. The Alexians at Nuess, a medieval daughter-house of Cologne, accepted these statutes on June 1, 1829. Cf. Giergen, p. 119.

26. Ibid., pp. 120–121.

27. Ibid., p. 123.

28. Ibid.

29. Ibid., p. 124.

30. Ibid., pp. 129–131.

31. Wiegers, p. 59.

32. Ibid.

33. Ibid., pp. 60–61.

34. Ibid., p. 62.

35. Ibid.

36. Ibid.

37. Ibid.

38. Ibid.

39. Quoted by Gatz, p. 195.

40. Ibid.

41. Ibid.

42. Ibid., p. 196.

43. Wiegers, pp. 63–64.

44. Gatz, p. 196.

45. Ibid.

46. Ibid.

47. Ibid.

48. Wiegers, p. 167.

49. Gatz, p. 196.

50. Wiegers, p. 68.

51. Alexander Dru, *The Contribution of German Catholicism* (New York: Hawthorn Books, 1963), p. 71.

52. Ibid., pp. 77–78.

53. Wiegers, p. 69.

54. Dru, p. 42.

55. Ibid., p. 44.

56. Quoted by Edgard Alexander, "Social and Political Movements and Ideas on German and Austrian Catholicism, 1789–1950," *Church and Society, Catholic Social and Political Thought and Movements*, ed. Joseph N. Moody (New York: Arts, Inc., 1953), p. 403.

57. Ibid., p. 540.

58. Gatz, p. 197.

59. Wiegers, p. 70.

60. Peter N. Stearns, *1848, The Revolutionary Tide in Europe* (New York: W. W. Norton, 1974), pp. 188–191.

61. Wiegers, p. 74.

62. Ibid.
63. Quoted by Katz, p. 198.
64. Wiegers, p. 75.
65. Ibid.
66. Ibid., p. 79.

Chapter 4

1. Michel Foucault, *Madness and Civilization, a History of Insanity in the Age of Reason* (New York: Pantheon Books, 1965), pp. 8–9; and Christopher J. Kauffman, *Tamers of Death: The History of the Alexian Brothers*, vol. 1, 1300–1789 (New York: Seabury Press, 1977), p. 207.
2. Kauffman, pp. 206–207.
3. Kauffman, pp. 209–210.
4. Foucault, pp. 74–78.
5. Ibid.
6. Ignatius Wiegers, C.F.A., *Die Aachener Alexianerbrüder, ihre Geschichte und ihr Ordensgeist* (Aachen, 1956), p. 65.
7. Ibid.
8. Ibid., p. 66.
9. Ibid.
10. Ibid., p. 79.
11. Ibid., p. 77.
12. Ibid., pp. 77–78.
13. Ibid., pp. 78–79.
14. Ibid., pp. 80–81.
15. Ibid., pp. 80–81.
16. Ibid., p. 83.
17. Ibid., p. 84.
18. Ibid., p. 85.
19. Ibid.
20. Ibid.
21. Ibid., p. 86.
22. Ibid.
23. Ibid., p. 87.
24. Ibid., p. 88.
25. Ibid.
26. Ibid., p. 89.
27. Ibid.
28. Ibid., p. 90.
29. Ibid., pp. 110–113.
30. Ibid., p. 114.
31. Gregory Zillboorg, M.D., and George W. Henry, M.D., *A History of Medical Psychology* (New York: W. W. Norton & Company, 1941), p. 436.
32. Ibid., p. 441.
33. Ibid., p. 443.
34. Ibid., p. 446.
35. Henry C. Burdett, *Hospitals and Asylums of the World*, vol. I (London: J. & H. Churchill, 1891), pp. 402–403.
36. Ibid., p. 404.

37. *Constitution of the Alexian Brothers* (West Chester, N.Y., 1878), pp. 121–126.

38. Wiegers, p. 116.

39. Ibid.

40. *Constitution*, p. 1.

41. Ibid., pp. 1–2.

42. Wiegers, p. 114.

43. *Constitution*, pp. 4–8.

44. Ibid., pp. 27–43.

45. Ibid., p. 31.

46. Ibid., pp. 77–80.

47. Ibid., p. 80.

48. Ibid., pp. 81–83.

49. Ibid., pp. 86–87.

50. Ibid., p. 87.

51. Ibid., pp. 94–95.

52. Ibid., pp. 97–103.

53. Ibid., p. 109.

54. Ibid.

55. Ibid., p. 120.

56. Ibid., p. 121.

57. Ibid., pp. 126–130.

Chapter 5

1. Ignatius Wiegers, C.F.A., *Die Aachener Alexianerbrüder, ihre Geschichte und ihr Ordensgeist* (Aachen, 1956), p. 92.

2. "Action of the Council in Aachen, Appointment of Brother Bonaventure Thelen as 'Rector in America,' " Dec. 12, 1865, Document 4, PRO-1, Box 1, Folder 7, ABA-SM; also Wiegers, pp. 92–93.

3. Wiegers, p. 93.

4. Ibid., pp. 92–93.

5. Ibid., p. 96.

6. Ibid.

7. Ibid., pp. 93, 96.

8. Joseph James Thompson, *Diamond Jubilee of the Archdiocese of Chicago* (Des Plaines, Ill., 1920), p. 725.

9. Wiegers, p. 96.

10. Ibid., pp. 96–97.

11. "Permission of Bishop James Duggan, Chicago, for Foundation of House, March 31, 1866," Document 2, PRO-1, Box 4, Folder 3, ABA-SM; also Wiegers, p. 97.

12. Wiegers, p. 98.

13. Ibid.

14. Alfred Theodore Andreas, *History of Chicago*, vol. II (New York: Arno Press, reprint of the 1884–86 edition, 1975), p. 537.

15. Wiegers, p. 100.

16. Ibid. Because it is impossible to trace the last names of every Brother mentioned by Wiegers and those contained in primary material, I was compelled occasionally to refer to Brothers without attaching their surnames.

17. Andreas, vol. II, p. 551.

18. Wiegers, p. 100.

19. Ibid.

20. Andreas, vol. II, pp. 449, 513, 515, 521, 526, 557–558, 672, 684.

21. "Act of Incorporation," C-2, Box 1, Folder 1, ABA-SM.

22. Ibid.

23. Ibid.

24. Wiegers, p. 101.

25. John E. Rothensteiner, *History of the Archdiocese of St. Louis*, vol. II (St. Louis, 1928), p. 512.

26. Ibid., p. 222.

27. Wiegers, p. 101.

28. "Brief Diary of the Establishment of the St. Louis House," Sept. 14, 1869, Document 13, PRO-1, Box 3, Folder 1, ABA-SM.

29. Ibid.

30. Ibid.

31. Wiegers, p. 103.

32. Ibid.

33. "General Council Establishes U.S. Houses as a Province," Oct. 17, 1869, Document 24, PRO-1, Box 1, Folder 1, ABA-SM.

34. "Pater Clement to American Province," Nov. 14, 1869, PRO-1, Box 1, Folder 1, ABA-SM. Also Wiegers, p. 104.

35. Wiegers, p. 9.

36. "Pater Clement to the American Province," June 12, 1869, Document 9, PRO-1, Box 1, Folder 1, ABA-SM.

37. "Pater Clement's Appointment of Brother Albert Engeln as First Provincial," Oct. 17, 1869, Document 10, PRO-1, Box 1, Folder 1, ABA-SM.

38. Ibid.

Chapter 6

1. Ignatius Wiegers, C.F.A., *Die Aachener Alexianbrüder, ihre Geschichte und ihr Ordensgeist* (Aachen, 1956), p. 104.

2. Alfred Theodore Andreas, *History of Chicago*, vol. II (New York: Arno Press, reprint of the 1884–86 edition, 1975), p. 537.

3. Ibid., p. 725.

4. Wiegers, p. 105.

5. "Brother Paul to Pater Clement," Jan. 22, 1872, Document 25A, PRO-1, Box 1, Folder 2, ABA-SM.

6. "Pater Clement to Brother Paul," Document 25B, PRO-1, Box 1, Folder 2, ABA-SM.

7. Andreas, vol. II, p. 565.

8. Quoted by Wiegers, p. 106.

9. "Pater Clement to Brother Paul," Dec. 10, 1872, Document 27B, PRO-1, Box 1, Folder 1, ABA-SM.

10. "General Council to Brother Paul," May 28, 1873, Document 28, PRO-1, Box 1, Folder 2, ABA-SM.

11. John E. Rothensteiner, *History of the Archdiocese of St. Louis*, vol. II (St. Louis, 1928), p. 512.

12. "General Council to Brother Paul," May 25, 1873, Document 36A, PRO-1, Box 1, Folder 2, ABA-SM.

13. "Pater Clement to American Province," May 1, 1874, Document 39, PRO-1, Box 1, Folder 2, ABA-SM.

14. "Pater Clement Appoints Brother Leonard Jansen Provincial," July 25, 1874, Document 35, PRO-1, Box 1, Folder 2, ABA-SM.

15. Ibid. Cf. also *Constitutions of the Alexian Brothers* (West Chester, New York, 1878), pp. 14–15.

16. "Pater Clement to the American Province," July 29, 1874, Document 38, PRO-1, Box 1, Folder 2, ABA-SM.

17. "Pater Clement's Circular Letter Convoking First Provincial Chapter," Aug. 3, 1874, Document 36, PRO-1, Box 1, Folder 2, ABA-SM.

18. Ibid.

19. Ibid.

20. "Report of the Election of the General Council," May 24, 1871, Document 23, PRO-1, Box 1, Folder 2, ABA-SM.

21. "Archbishop of Cologne to Pastor de Roth," April 21, 1873, Document 29, PRO-1, Box 1, Folder 2, ABA-SM.

22. "General Council Writes about Visitation Procedures to Be Used in the U.S. by Brother Bonaventure Thelen . . .," April 3, 1877, Document 72, PRO-1, Box 1, Folder 4, ABA-SM.

23. *Constitutions*, p. 188.

24. Ibid., pp. 176–177.

25. Ibid., p. 177.

26. Ibid.

27. Ibid.

28. Ibid., p. 178.

29. Ibid., pp. 32–33.

30. Colman J. Barry, O.S.B., *The Catholic Church and German Americans* (Milwaukee: The Bruce Publishing Co., 1953), p. 25.

31. "Pater Clement to the American Province," Sept. 9, 1877, Document 73, PRO-1, Box 1, Folder 4, ABA-SM.

32. Ibid.

33. "Circular Letter from General Council to American Province," April 3, 1877, Document 72, PRO-1, Box 1, Folder 4, ABA-SM.

34. Ibid.

35. "Pater Clement to Brothers Bonaventure and Leonard," June 18, 1877, Document 71, PRO-1, Box 1, Folder 4, ABA-SM.

36. Ibid.

37. Ibid.

38. Ibid.

39. "Brother Bonaventure to Pater Clement," Aug. 14, 1877, Microfilm 17, section C, ABA-SM.

40. "Brother Bonaventure to Pater Clement," Oct. 6, 1877, Microfilm 17, section C, ABA-SM.

41. "Brother Leonard to Pater Clement," Oct. 1, 1877, Microfilm 17, section C.

42. "Brother Leonard to Pater Clement," Jan. 26, 1878, Document 109, PRO-1, Box 3, Folder 2, ABA-SM.

43. "Brother Leonard to Pater Clement," Dec. 15, 1877.

44. Ibid., Dec. 18, 1877.

45. Ibid.

46. "Pater Clement to the American Province," Jan. 29, 1874, Document 90, PRO-1, Box 3, Folder 2, ABA-SM.

47. Ibid.

48. "Brother Leonard to Pater Clement," Oct. 1, 1878, Microfilm 17, Section C, ABA-SM.

49. "A Pernicious Blunder," *New York Freeman's Journal and Catholic Register*, Oct. 19, 1878, vol. 39, no. 32, p. 4.

50. "The Alexian Brothers and The Freeman's Journal," *The Western Watchman*, Nov. 9, 1878, vol. X, no. 42, p. 8.

51. Ibid.

52. Ibid.

53. "Brother Leonard to Pater Clement," Nov. 22, 1878, Microfilm 17, section C, ABA-SM.

54. Ibid., April 9, 1878.

55. Ibid.

56. Ibid.

57. Newspaper cutting, Aug. 8, 1879, Microfilm 17 section C, ABA-SM.

58. "Brother Cunibert to Pater Clement," Aug. 16, 1879, Microfilm 17, section C, ABA-SM.

59. "Pater Clement to the American Province," Jan. 24, 1879, Document 148, PRO-1, Box 3, Folder 2, ABA-SM.

60. "Brother Leonard to Pater Clement," ca. December 1880, Microfilm 17, section C, ABA-SM.

61. "Brother Leonard to Pater Clement," Feb. 17, 1880, Microfilm 17, section C, ABA-SM.

62. Ibid.

63. Ibid.

64. Ibid.

65. "Brother Leonard to Pater Clement," March 26, 1880, Microfilm 17, section C, ABA-SM.

66. Wiegers, p. 158.

67. "Pater Clement to Vicar General Muhlsiepen," Feb. 7, 1882, Document 155, PRO-1, Box 3, Folder 3, ABA-SM.

68. Ibid.

69. Ibid.

70. Ibid.

71. Ibid.

Chapter 7

1. *Constitutions of the Alexian Brothers* (West Chester, N.Y., 1878), p. 164.

2. Ibid., pp. 165–166.

3. Ibid., p. 166.

4. Ibid.

5. Ibid.

6. Ibid., p. 167.

7. Ibid., p. 172.

8. Ibid.

9. Ibid., p. 169.

10. Ibid., pp. 170–171.

11. Ruth Meier, *The Alexian Brothers in Oshkosh* (Oshkosh, 1956); privately circulated manuscript, copy in ABA-SM, pp. 19–21.

12. Ibid., pp. 5–7.

13. Ibid., pp. 7–8.

14. Ibid., p. 9.

15. Ibid., p. 21.

16. "Pater Clement to Brother Stanislaus," Dec. 30, 1880, Document 120, PRO-1, Box 3, Folder 2, ABA-SM.

17. Ignatius Wiegers, C.F.A., *Die Aachener Alexianerbrüder, ihre Geschichte und ihr Ordensgeist* (Aachen, 1956), p. 158.

18. "Vicar General of Baltimore Diocese to Brother Stanislaus," Sept. 25, 1883, Document 36, PRO-1, Box 3, Folder 2, ABA-SM.

19. "Pater Clement to Brother Stanislaus," Oct. 1, 1884, Document 45, PRO-1, Box 3, Folder 1, ABA-SM.

20. "Pater Clement to Brother Stanislaus," Jan. 4, 1885, Document 62, PRO-1, Box 3, Folder 1, ABA-SM.

21. Meier, p. 50.

22. Wiegers, p. 158.

23. Alfred Theodore Andreas, *History of Chicago*, vol. II (New York: Arno Press, reprint of the 1884–86 edition, 1975), p. 537.

24. Ibid.

25. Ibid.

26. Ibid.

27. Andreas, vol, II, p. 527.

28. *Nineteenth Annual Report of the Alexian Brothers Hospital, Chicago, Ill.* (Chicago, 1886), p. 27.

29. Ibid., p. 12.

30. Ibid., p. 16.

31. Ibid., p. 11.

32. Newspaper cuttings, C-10, ABA-SM.

33. *Nineteenth Annual Report . . .*, pp. 113–115.

34. Newspaper cutting, C-10, ABA-SM.

35. Ibid.

36. *The Chicago Pilot*, newspaper cuttings, C 10, ABA-SM.

37. Newspaper cuttings, C-10, ABA-SM.

38. Ibid.

39. *Nineteenth Annual Report . . .*, p. 12.

40. *The Tribune*, Aug. 25, 1880, newspaper cuttings, C 10, ABA-SM.

41. Newspaper cuttings, C-10, ABA-SM.

42. Ibid.

43. "The Alexian Brothers," *The Catholic Record* (Chicago), Sept. 1886, vol. II, no. 6, p. 1.

44. "The General Council to Brother Aloysius," Oct. 25, 1894, Document 88, PRO-1, Box 3, Folder 2, ABA-SM.

45. "Brother Aloysius to Archbishop Feehan," Sept. 25, 1895, Document 227, PRO-1, Box 4, Folder 1, ABA-SM. *Brief History of the order of the Alexian Brothers and a Description of the New Alexian Brothers Hospital as a Souvenir of the Laying of the Cornerstone* (Chicago, 1896).

46. *Brief History . . .*, pp. 17–19, 21.

47. "Recollections of Dr. Alexander Horowitz," C 10, ABA-SM.

48. Ibid.

49. Ibid.

50. Ibid.

51. Ibid.

52. *Souvenir of the Golden Jubilee Year of the Alexian Brothers Hospital of Chicago* (Chicago, 1916), pp. 20–25.

53. "Contract between Bishop John J. Hogan and the Alexian Brothers of St. Louis," April 17, 1872, SL.-7, Box 1, Folder 2, ABA-SM.

54. "Pater Clement to Brother Leonard," Nov. 16, 1874, Document 33, PRO-1, Box 3, Folder 1, ABA-SM.

55. J. A. Ducas and J. W. Ball, *A Tour of St. Louis or Inside a Great City, St. Louis* (St. Louis: Western Publishing Co.,1878), p. 501.

56. "Provincial Council Minutes," Nov. 1, 1878, Document 114, PRO-1, Box 3, Folder 2, ABA-SM.

57. "Provincial Council Minutes," Jan. 21, 1879, Document 151, PRO-1, Box 3, Folder 2, ABA-SM.

58. Ibid.

59. Ibid.

60. "General Council Minutes," March 10, 1879, Document 83, PRO-1, Box 3, Folder 2, ABA-SM.

61. Ibid.

62. Ibid.

63. Ibid.

64. Ibid.

65. Newspaper cuttings, SL-9, Box 4, ABA-SM.

66. Ibid.

67. Ibid.

68. Ibid.

69. Ibid.

70 Christopher J. Kauffman, *Tamers of Death: The History of the Alexian Brothers, 1300–1789*, vol. I, (New York: Seabury Press, 1977), p. 205.

71. "Application for Admission into the Insane Department of the Alexian Brothers' Hospital," May 3, 1888, SL 3, Box 11, Folder 3, ABA-SM.

72. Ibid.

73. *Sixtieth Annual Report of the Alexian Brothers Hospital and Dispensary* (St. Louis, 1929), p. 7.

74. "House Council Proceedings," June 4, 1882, p. 32, SL-1, Box 1, Folder 1, ABA-SM.

75. "House Council Proceedings," Dec. 10, 1884, p. 46, SL-1, Box 1, Folder 1, ABA-SM.

76. *Golden Jubilee of the Alexian Brothers Hospital* (St. Louis, 1919), p. 2.

77. Ibid.

78. Newspaper cuttings, SL-9, Box 4, ABA-SM.

79. Ibid.

80. "House Council Proceedings," Feb. 11, 1902, pp. 113–114, SL-1, Box 1, Folder 1, ABA-SM.

81. *Golden Jubilee of the Alexian Brothers Hospital* (St. Louis, 1919), p. 4.

82. Ibid.

83. Ibid., p. 45.

84. "House Council Proceedings," Nov. 7, 1909, p. 146, SL-1, Box 1, Folder 1, ABA-SM.

85. "House Council Proceedings," Jan. 17, 1887, p. 60, SL-1, Box, 1, Folder 1, ABA-SM.

86. Rose Brigid Berry, "A History of the Alexian Brothers Hospital, St. Louis, Missouri, 1869–1949" (master's thesis, School of Social Work, St. Louis University, 1950), p. 45.

332

87. Wiegers, p. 175.

88. Ibid.

89. "Financial Report of the Alexian Brothers Hospital," Elizabeth, N.J., 1894, E-2, Box 2, Folder 3A, ABA-SM.

90. Ibid.

91. Ibid.

92. Ibid.

93. Ibid.

94. "Financial Report," 1896, E-2, Box 2, Folder 3, ABA-SM.

95. Ibid.

96. Ibid.

97. Wiegers, p. 178.

98. "Financial Report," 1907, E-2, Box 2, Folder 3A, ABA-SM.

99. Ibid.

100. Ibid.

101. "Elizabeth Institutions, The Alexian Hospital," *Elizabeth Evening News*, Saturday, July 22, 1905. E-9, ABA-SM.

102. *Twenty-fourth Annual Report of the Alexian Brothers Hospital of Elizabeth, N.J.* (Elizabeth, 1916), p. 16.

103. Ibid., p. 18.

104. Ibid., p. 21.

105. Ibid.

106. Ibid.

107. Ibid.

108. Ibid.

109. Newspaper cuttings found in the historical files of the Alexian Brothers Hospital, Elizabeth, New Jersey.

Chapter 8

1. Ignatius Wiegers, C.F.A., *Die Aachener Alexianerbrüder, ihre Geschichte und ihr Ordensgeist* (Aachen, 1956), p. 124.

2. Quoted by Rev. Gordon Wheeler, "The Archdiocese of Westminster," *The English Catholics, 1850–1950*, ed. George Andrew Beck (London: Burns, Oates, 1950), pp. 164–65.

3. Wiegers, p. 124.

4. J. G. Snead-Cox, *The Life of Cardinal Vaughan*, vol. I (London: Burns, Oates, 1910), p. 386.

5. Wiegers, p. 125.

6. Ibid.

7. Thomas Curley, *The Old Catholic History of Oldham* (East Yorkshire: St. Williams Press, 1911), p. 46.

8. Ibid.

9. Herbert Vaughan, Bishop of Salford Diocese, *Pastorals, etc.*, Salford Diocesan Archives, Wardley Hall, Manchester, England.

10. Ibid.

11. Ibid.

12. Ibid.

13. Ibid.

14. Wiegers, p. 127.
15. "Brother Leonard Jansen to Pater Clement Wallrath," Oct. 7, 1877, Microfilm 19, ABA-SM.
16. Ibid.
17. Quoted by Wiegers, p. 130.
18. Ibid., p. 132.
19. "Pater Clement Wallrath to Brother Leonard Jansen," March 28, 1879, PRO-1, Document 79, Box 3, Folder 2, ABA-SM.
20. William Llywelyn Parry-Jones, *The Trade in Lunacy* (London: Routledge & Kegan Paul, 1972), pp. 13–20.
21. Ibid., p. 20.
22. Ibid., p. 22.
23. Ibid., p. 26.
24. "House Council Minutes," Sept. 28, 1882, St. Mary's Home, ABA-LON.
25. Wiegers, p. 134.
26. "House Council Minutes," Feb. 15, 1884, St. Mary's Home, p. 4.
27. "Pater Clement Wallrath to Brother Andreas Harderer," Jan. 15, 1885, Document 60, PRO-1, Box 3, Folder 1, ABA-SM.
28. Ibid.
29. Ibid.
30. Ibid.
31. Ibid.
32. Ibid.
33. Ibid.
34. Ibid.
35. Ibid.
36. Ibid.
37. Ibid.
38. "House Council Minutes," March 1885, St. Mary's Home, ABA-SM.
39. Ibid., Dec. 2, 1885.
40. Ibid.
41. Ibid.
42. Ibid., Dec. 3, 1885.

Chapter 9

1. "House Council Minutes," May 1888, ABA-LON. Provincial Cyrillus's full ac- of this story is recorded as a retrospective account rather than as minutes.
2. Ibid.
3. Ibid.
4. Ibid.
5. Ibid.
6. Ibid.
7. Ibid.
8. Ibid., Dec. 1888.
9. Ibid., Dec. 2, 1885.
10. Ibid., Feb. 1889.
11. Ibid.
12. Ibid.
13. Ibid., Sept. 8, 1889.

14. Ibid.
15. Ibid.
16. Ibid.
17. Ibid., Oct. 28, 1889.
18. Ibid.
19. Ibid.
20. Ibid., Oct. 1, 1889.
21. Ignatius Wiegers, C.F.A., *Die Aachener Alexianerbrüder, ihre Geschichte und ihr Ordensgeist* (Aachen, 1956), pp. 134–135.
22. "House Council Minutes," Oct. 27, 1891, St. Mary's Home, ABA-LON.
23. Ibid., Feb. 1, 1892.
24. Ibid., March 11, 1894.
25. *Album of St. Joseph's Cemetery, Moston Lane* (Manchester, 1896), p. 22. ABA-LON.
26. Ibid.
27. Wiegers, p. 134.
28. *The Alexian Brothers, Sacred Heart Home, Oakleigh Villa, Lindthorpe, near Middlesbrough* (no pagination). ABA-LON.
29. Ibid.
30. "House Council Minutes," Jan. 1, 1849, St. Mary's Home, ABA-LON.
31. Ibid., Aug. 19, 1899.
32. Ibid., Oct. 11, 1899.
33. Cornelius Kearney, C.F.A., *The History of the District and Manor House of West Twyford* (an unpublished manuscript), pp. 5–7. ABA-LON.
34. Ibid., p. 26.
35. Cornelius Kearney, "History of the Sacred Heart Province" (an unpublished manuscript at ABA-LON), p. 9.
36. Ibid.
37. Ibid., p. 10.
38. In the spring of 1903 the Alexians sold the Middlesbrough home to the Marist Brothers, a teaching order.
39. Brother Brendan Weston's remembrances, ABA-LON.
40. John O'Keefe's remembrances, ABA-LON.
41. Ibid.
42. Oral tradition among the Alexian Brothers of the Sacred Heart Province, Summer 1975.
43. "House Council Minutes," Dec. 3, 1888, St. Mary's Home, ABA-LON.
44. "Brother Camillus McGill to Brother Remegius Kochaneck," June 1, 1909, ABA-LON.
45. Ibid., Aug. 5, 1909.
46. Ibid.
47. Ibid.
48. Ibid.
49. Ibid.
50. Ibid., Feb. 16, 1910.
51. Ibid.
52. Ibid, Feb, 19, 1910.
53. Ibid.
54. Ibid.
55. Ibid., Feb. 25, 1910.
56. Ibid.
57. Ibid.

58. Ibid.

59. "St. Mary's Home, Manchester: A Haven of Rest," *The Harvest* (Manchester, England), August 1913, vol. XXVI, no. 311, p. 205.

60. Ibid.

61. "The Alexian Brothers," *The Harvest*, December 1915, vol. XXVIII, no. 339, p. 321.

62. Ibid.

63. Ibid.

64. Ibid.

65. Ibid.

66. Ibid.

67. Ibid.

68. "Brother Camillus to Brother Remegius," Oct. 16, 1910, ABA-LON.

69. Ibid.

70. Cornelius Kearney, C.F.A., *The History of the District and Manor House of West Twyford*, (unpublished manuscript), p. 27. ABA-LON.

71. Quoted by Ibid., p. 27.

72. Vicar General (name illegible) to Brother Rector Columbcille McGuiness, June 24, 1912, ABA-LON.

73. Ibid.

74. Ibid.

Chapter 10

1. August Franzen and John P. Dolan, *A History of the Church* (New York: Herder and Herder, 1969), pp. 396–397.

2. Ibid., p. 397.

3. Ibid.

4. Ibid., p. 398.

5. Ignatius Wiegers, C.F.A., *Die Aachener Alexianerbrüder, ihre Geschichte und ihr Ordensgeist* (Aachen, 1956), p. 117.

6. Ibid., pp. 116–117.

7. Ibid., p. 117.

8. Ibid.

9. Paul Hinschius, *Die Katholische Kirche in Preussen*, (Berlin, 1874).

10. Ibid., pp. 35–36.

11. Ibid., p. 74.

12. Ibid., p. 86.

13. *Constitutions of the Alexian Brothers* (West Chester, N.Y. 1878), p. 86.

14. Erwin Gatz, *Kirche und Krankenpflege im 19. Jahrhundert* (Paderborn: Ferdinand Schöningh 1971), pp. 584–585.

15. Wiegers, p. 118.

16. Ibid.

17. Ibid., p. 119.

18. Ibid., p. 120.

19. Ibid., pp. 120–121.

20. Ibid., p. 122.

21. Ibid.

22. Ibid., p. 119.

23. Ibid., p. 120.

24. Ibid., pp. 123–124.
25. Ibid., pp. 143–144.
26. Ibid., pp. 146–148.
27. Ibid., pp. 148–150.
28. Ibid., pp. 150–152.
29. Ibid., pp. 153–155.
30. "Circular regarding Rome's Decision on the Vows Taken by Alexians," Document 157, PRO-1, Box 3, Folder 3, ABA-SM.
31. Wiegers, p. 136.
32. Ibid.
33. Ibid., p. 138.
34. Letter found in Alexian Brothers Archive, Boechout, Belgium.
35. Ibid.
36. Wiegers, p. 139.
37. Ibid., p. 140.
38. *Statuten der Cellebroeders Alexianen* (Lier, 1869).
39. Ibid., pp. 36–38.
40. Wiegers, p. 162.
41. "Circular regarding the General Council's Negative Decision on ex-Pater Clement's Appeal to Be Appointed Visitator," June 8, 1887, Document 169, PRO-1, Box 3, Folder 3, ABA-SM.

Chapter 11

1. "Pater Quirinus Bank's Report to the U.S. Province on His Visitation," Aug. 25, 1888, Document 221, PRO-1, Box 4, Folder 1, ABA-SM.
2. Ibid.
3. Ibid., Oct. 8, 1903, Document 208, PRO-1, Box 4, Folder 1, ABA-SM.
4. Ibid.
5. Ibid., Oct. 31, 1905, Document 211, PRO-1, Box 4, Folder 1, ABA-SM.
6. Ibid., July 17, 1900, Document 229, PRO-1, Box 4, Folder 1, ABA-SM.
7. Ibid., Oct. 31, 1905.
8. Ibid., July 17, 1900.
9. Ibid., Sept. 11, 1897, Document 195, PRO-1, Box 3, Folder 3, ABA-SM.
10. Ibid., Nov. 11, 1890, Document 171, PRO-1, Box 3, Folder 3, ABA-SM.
11. Ibid., Sept. 11, 1897.
12. *St. Louis Republican*, June 25, 1897, newspaper cuttings, SL-9, Box 4, ABA-SM.
13. Ibid.
14. Ibid.
15. Ibid.
16. Ibid.
17. Ignatius Wiegers, C.F.A., *Die Aachener Alexianerbrüder, ihre Geschichte und ihr Ordensgeist* (Aachen, 1956), p. 165.
18. Ibid.
19. Ibid.
20. Ibid., pp. 162–165.
21. Ibid., pp. 165–166.
22. Ibid., pp. 166–170.
23. Ibid., pp. 170–171.

24. Bernhard Giergen, *Das Alexianer Kloster in Köln-Lindenthal* (Köln-Lindenthal, 1934), p. 167.

25. Ibid., pp. 172–173.

26. Wiegers, pp. 130–131.

27. Ibid., pp. 172–173.

28. Ibid., pp. 173–174.

29. Ibid., p. 174.

30. Ibid., pp. 197–198.

31. Giergen, p. 174.

32. Ibid., p. 177.

33. Ibid., p. 178.

34. Ibid., pp. 178–179.

35. Ibid., p. 179.

36. Ibid., pp. 181–182.

37. "German Asylums," *Journal of Insanity,* October 1853, p. 142.

38. Ibid.

39. Wiegers, p. 191.

40. Ibid.

41. Ibid., pp. 154–155.

42. Ibid., p. 182.

43. Ibid., p. 183.

44. Ibid.

45. Ibid., p. 185.

46. Ibid., pp. 184–185.

47. Ibid., p. 186.

48. Ibid., p. 187.

49. Ibid., pp. 189–190.

50. "Pater Quirinus Bank Informs U.S. Province on New Rules Governing Delegates to the General Chapter," March 7, 1891, Document 174, PRO-1, Box 3, Folder 3, ABA-SM.

51. "Acts of the General Chapter, 1891," June 23, 1891, Document 177, PRO-1, Box 3, Folder 3, ABA-SM.

52. "Acts of the General Chapter, 1896," June 23, 1896, Document 189, PRO-1, Box 3, Folder 3, ABA-SM.

53. Wiegers, p. 187.

54. Ibid., pp. 188–189.

55. "Acts of the General Chapter, 1901," May 30, 1901, Document 230, PRO-1, Box 4, Folder 2, ABA-SM.

56. "Pater Paul to the U.S. Province, Report on Visitation," July 14, 1910, Document 253, PRO-1, Box 4, Folder 2, ABA-SM.

57. Ibid.

58. Ibid.

59. Joseph Creussen, S.J., *Religious Men and Women in Church Law* (Milwaukee: Bruce Publishing Co., 1958), p. 5.

60. Ibid.

61. Ibid.

62. Wiegers, p. 210.

63. Ibid., pp. 210–211.

64. *Rules and Statutes of the Alexian Brothers* (Chicago, 1913), p. 19; *Constitution of the Alexian Brothers* (West Chester, N.Y. 1878), pp. 1–2.

65. Ibid.

66. *Rules and Statutes,* p. 19.

Notes

67. Ibid., p. 95.

68. "Pater Paul Overbeck's Circular on the Changes in the Rule," Aug. 25, 1913, Document 278, PRO-1, Box 4, Folder 3, ABA-SM.

69. Ibid.

70. *Rules and Statutes*, p. 64.

71. Ibid., p. 65.

72. Ibid., pp. 65–66.

73. Ibid., p.67.

74. Ibid., pp. 32–34.

75. Ibid., p. 34.

76. Wiegers, p. 213.

77. Ibid.

78. Ibid., pp. 213–215.

79. Paulus Overbeck, C.F.A., *Rechenschaftsbericht des Generalrektor der Celliten oder Alexianerbrüder zu Aachen* . . . (Aachen, 1920), p. 18.

80. "Pater Paul to the U.S. Province," December 1914, Document 286, PRO-1, Box 4, Folder 4, ABA-SM.

81. Ibid.

82. Ibid.

83. Ibid.

84. Wiegers, p. 219.

85. Ibid., p. 220.

86. Ibid.

87. Overbeck, p. 18, and Cornelius Kearney, C.F.A., "History of the Sacred Heart Province" (unpublished manuscript), p. 12, ABA-LON.

88. Wiegers, pp. 226–227.

89. Wiegers, p. 218.

90. Overbeck, pp. 30–32.

91. Ibid., p. 32.

92. Ibid., p. 36.

93. Wiegers, p. 229.

94. Overbeck, pp. 23–26.

95. Ibid., p. 39.

96. Quoted by Wiegers, p. 230.

97. The following was gleaned from Brother Damien Stayaert's letters to the author.

98. "Pater Paul Overbeck to the U.S. Province," ca. Autumn 1919, Document 300, PRO-1, Box 4, Folder 3, ABA-SM.

99. "Acts of the General Chapter, 1920," April 28, 1920, Document 301, PRO-1, Box 4, Folder 3, ABA-SM.

100. Ibid.

101. C. J. Kauffman and Brother Hilarion Penchion, C.F.A., oral interview at Signal Mountain, Tenn., Jan. 23, 1977.

102. "Acts of the General Chapter, 1920."

103. Ibid.

104. Ibid.

Chapter 12

1. Felix Gilbert, *The End of the European Era 1890 to the Present* (New York: W. W. Norton, 1970), p. 179.

2. Ignatius Wiegers, C.F.A., *Die Aachener Alexianerbrüder, ihre Geschichte und ihr Ordensgeist* (Aachen, 1956), pp. 233–234.

3. August Franzen, *A History of the Church*, rev. and ed. John P. Dolan (New York: Herder and Herder, 1969), p. 406.

4. *St. Alexius Almanac* 1929 (Aachen: The Congregation of the Alexian Brothers, 1929), pp. 36, 42.

5. Wiegers, p. 236.

6. Ibid., pp. 237–238.

7. Ibid., p. 238.

8. Ibid.

9. Ibid., p. 239.

10. Ibid., p. 240.

11. *St. Alexius Almanac* 1929, p. 45.

12. Wiegers, pp. 240–244.

13. *St. Alexius Almanac* 1929, p. 29.

14. Wiegers, pp. 244–245.

15. Ibid., pp. 245–248.

16. Ibid., pp. 255–258.

17. Ibid., pp. 259–267.

18. "Minutes of the General Chapter of 1926," Document 324, PRO-1, Box 4, Folder 3, ABA-SM.

19. "Minutes of the Provincial Chapter of 1926," Document 321, PRO-1, Box 4, Folder 3, ABA-SM.

20. "Minutes of the General Chapter of 1926."

21. "Circular Letter, Sep. 4, 1926," Document 326, PRO-1, Box 4, Folder 3, ABA-SM.

22. "Minutes of the Provincial Chapter 1921, England," ABA-LON.

23. Ibid.

24. "Receipts and Expenses for 1921, Jan. 1922, English Province," ABA-LON.

25. Ibid.

26. "Minutes of the Provincial Council," Feb. 16, 1922, ABA-LON.

27. H. Stuart Hughes, *Contemporary Europe, a History* (Englewood Cliffs, N.J.: Prentice-Hall, 1967), p. 159.

28. Bishop Michael Cord to Brother Gilbert Holmes, July 12, 1920, ABA-LON.

29. Cornelius Kearney, C.F.A., *History of the Sacred Heart Province* (unpublished manuscript), p. 14, ABA-LON.

30. Ibid.

31. Soluis (pseudonym), "Where the Mountains of Mourne Roll Down to the Sea," reprinted in *Almanac and Yearbook* 1935–36 *Mount St. Columb's Warrenpoint*, ABA-LON.

32. Taped interview, Brother Cornelius Kearney and Brother Dunstan O'Neill, June 12, 1974, ABA-LON.

33. Wiegers, pp. 248–249.

34. F. P. Carey, "With the Brothers of St. Alexius of Carlingford Lough," a reprint from *The Irish Catholic*, Sept. 7, 1929, ABA-LON.

35. Ibid.

36. Ibid.

37. Benin (pseudonym), "The Catholic Church and Nursing," a reprint in *Almanac and Yearbook* 1935–36 *Mount St. Columb's Warrenpoint*, ABA-LON.

38. *St. Alexius Almanac* 1929, p. 50.

39. "Minutes of the Provincial Council," July 10, 1925, ABA-LON.

40. Ibid., Sept. 12, 1926.

41. Ibid.

42. Ibid., Nov. 7, 1930.

Notes

43. Ibid., July 15, 1931.

44. Ibid., Aug. 12, 1932.

45. "Wardley Cemetery Consecrated," *The Harvest* (Manchester), Aug. 5, 1933, vol. XLVI, no. 6. p. 249.

46. Wiegers, p. 281.

47. Kearney, p. 18.

48. Taped interview, Brother Cornelius Kearney and Brother Joseph Newell, Nov. 12, 1974, ABA-LON.

49. "Minutes of the Provincial Council," Nov. 12, 1926, ABA-LON.

50. Colman J. Barry, O.S.B., *The Catholic Church and German Americans* (Milwaukee: Bruce Publishing Co., 1953), p. 275.

51. *St. Alexius Almanac 1929*, pp. 25–35.

52. *Sixty-sixth Annual Report of the Alexian Brothers' Hospital* (Chicago, 1926), p. 9.

53. Ibid., p. 11.

54. Taped interview, Brother Gregory Isenhart, C.F.A. and Mr. Edward Horton, Feb. 22, 1974, Oral History File, ABA-SM.

55. Quoted by Rose Brigid Berry, "A History of the Alexian Brothers' Hospital, St. Louis, Missouri, 1869–1949" (master's thesis submitted to the School of Social Work, St. Louis University, St. Louis, 1950), p. 48.

56. *Fifty-second Annual Report of the Alexian Brothers' Hospital and Dispensary* (St. Louis, 1920), pp. 6–7, ABA-SM.

57. Ibid.

58. Ibid.

59. Berry, pp. 49–50.

60. *Sixty-second Annual Report of the Alexian Brothers' Hospital and Dispensary* (St. Louis, 1931), p. 7, ABA-SM.

61. Quoted by Berry, pp. 68–69.

62. *Alexian Brothers' Hospital, Oshkosh, Wisconsin* (no date, no pagination), ABA-SM.

63. Ibid.

64. Herman Kitzler, "Our Alexian Brothers" (unpublished manuscript on the Alexian Brothers in Elizabeth), ABA-SM.

65. Ibid.

66. *Thirty-fourth Annual Report Alexian Brothers' Hospital* (Elizabeth, 1928), no pagination, ABA-SM.

67. *Thirty-seventh Annual Report Alexian Brothers' Hospital* (Elizabeth, 1929), no pagination.

68. *Fiftieth Annual Report, Alexian Brothers' Hospital* (Elizabeth, 1952).

69. Brother Dominic Piotrowski, "Oblique View of the Ankle," *The X-Ray Technician*, vol. X, September 1938, p. 76.

70. Brothers Sebastian Brogan and John of God Blackledge, *Diary of the Alexian Brothers' School of Nursing*, (unpublished manuscript, no pagination), ABA-SM.

71. Ibid.

72. Ibid.

73. Wiegers, p. 208.

74. Brogan.

75. Brother Ludolf Sattler's personal file ABA-SM.

76. Ibid.

77. Brogan.

78. Ibid.

79. Ibid.

80. Taped interview, Brothers Gregory Isenhart and Regobert Meyer, March 16, 1975, Oral History File, ABA-SM.

81. Brogan.

82. "Brother Simplicius to the Conventual Chapter of the American Province," Oct. 6, 1925, Document 320, PRO-1, Box 4, Folder 3 ABA-SM.

83. Ibid.

84. Ibid.

85. Ibid.

86. "Minutes of the General Chapter 1926," Document 324, PRO-1, Box 4, Folder 3, ABA-SM.

87. "Minutes of the General Chapter 1932," ABA-LON.

88. Ibid.

89. Gregory Isenhart, C.F.A., "History," Inventory, p. 3, SM-1, ABA-SM.

90. "A History of the Alexian Brothers Novitiate and Resort at Signal Mountain, Tennessee," p. 2, SM-1, ABA-SM.

91. Newspaper cuttings, SM-9, ABA-SM.

92. Ibid.

93. Ibid.

94. Ibid.

95. Ibid.

96. Ibid.

97. "House Chronicle," SM-5, ABA-SM.

98. Ibid.

99. Ibid.

100. Ibid.

Chapter 13

1. *The Persecution of the Catholic Church in the Third Reich: Facts and Documents* (London: Burns and Oates, 1940), p. 246.

2. Ibid.

3. *St. Alexius Kalender* 1933 (Aachen, 1933), p. 48, and *St. Alexius Kalender* (Aachen, 1938), p. 11.

4. Oral interview, Christopher J. Kauffman and Brother Camillus Snyder, May 2, 1976. Also cf. Gunter Lewy, *The Catholic Church in Nazi Germany*, (New York: McGraw-Hill Book Company 1964): p. 258–263.

5. Lewy, pp. 263–264.

6. Ignatius Wiegers, C.F.A., *Die Aachener Alexianerbrüder, ihre Geschichte und ihr Ordensgeist* (Aachen, 1956), pp. 289–290.

7. Quoted by Lewy, p. 265.

8. Ibid., pp. 265–267.

9. Wiegers, p. 292.

10. Quoted in "Ecce quam bonum," *Alexiana*, 1948, p. 33.

11. Ibid.

12. Ibid.

13. Ibid., p. 34.

14. Ibid.

15. Ibid.

16. Ibid.

17. Ibid.

18. Wiegers, p. 306.

19. Ibid., p. 296.

20. Quoted in "Ecce quam bonum," *Alexiana*, 1948, p. 40.

Notes

21. Ibid., p. 41.
22. The following was gleaned from Brother Damien Stayaert's letters to this historian.
23. Taped interviews, Brother Cornelius Kearney and Brother Anselm Hopkins, Dec. 12, 1972, ABA-LON.
24. Ibid.
25. *The Alexian*, 1949, p. 44.
26. Taped interview, Dec. 12, 1972, ABA-LON.
27. Ibid.
28. *Souvenir Booklet Alexian Brothers Hospital, Chicago*, C-9, ABA-SM.
29. Wiegers, p. 288.
30. Sebastian Brogan and John of God Blackledge, *Diary of the Chicago School of Nursing*, (no pagination), NS, ABA-SM.
31. Ibid.
32. Ibid.
33. Ibid.
34. Ibid.
35. Ibid.
36. Rose Brigid Berry, "A History of the Alexian Brothers Hospital, St. Louis, Missouri, 1869–1949," (master's thesis, School of Social Work St. Louis University, 1950), pp. 59–60.
37. Ibid., p. 60.
38. "Brother Basil Wilwerding to the Most Reverend Thomas J. Walsh," Sept. 3, 1943, Alexian Brothers File, Archiocesan Archive, Newark, New Jersey.
39. Ibid., Feb. 21, 1944.
40. "The Most Reverend Thomas J. Walsh to Brother Basil Wilwerding," April 4, 1944, Alexian Brothers File, Archdiocesan Archive, Newark, New Jersey.
41. Ibid., May 17, 1944.
42. "Apostolic Visitation File," ABA-EGV.
43. Ibid.
44. "Brother Gerard Kuhn to Father James J. Mertz, S.J.," Dec. 31, 1944, ABA-EGV.
45. Ibid.
46. Ibid.
47. "Father James J. Mertz, S.J., to the American Province," ABA-EGV.
48. Ibid.
49. Ibid.
50. Ibid.
51. Ibid.
52. Ibid.
53. Ibid.
54. *Custom Book of the Cellites or Alexian Brothers of the United States*, 1946, p. 1, ABA-SM.
55. Ibid., p. 2.
56. Ibid., p. 10.
57. Ibid., p. 15.
58. Ibid., p. 6.
59. Ibid., pp. 7–10.
60. Wiegers, p. 303.
61. Ibid., pp. 299–300.
62. "Minutes of the General Chapter, 1946," ABA-LON.
63. Ibid.

64. Ibid.
65. Ibid.
66. "Minutes of the Provincial Chapter of the American Province, 1946."
67. "Minutes of the General Chapter 1946," ABA-LON.
68. Ibid.
69. Ibid.
70. Ibid.
71. Ibid.
72. Ibid.
73. Ibid.

Chapter 14

1. Christopher Lynch, C.F.A., "Caritas Christi Urget NOS!" *Alexiana*, 1948, p. 6.
2. Ibid., p. 7.
3. Christopher Lynch, C.F.A., "Ecce quam bonum," *Alexiana*, 1949, p. 44.
4. Ignatius Wiegers, C.F.A., *Die Aachener Alexianerbrüder ihre Geschichte und ihr Ordensgeist* (Aachen, 1956), p. 317.
5. Lynch, "Ecce quam bonum," p. 42.
6. Ibid.
7. Wiegers, p. 317.
8. Lynch, "Ecce quam bonum," p. 42.
9. Camillus Snyder, C.F.A., "Previsitation Remarks," ABA-LON.
10. Oral interview, Christopher J. Kauffman and Brother Camillus Snyder, May 3, 1976.
11. Camillus Snyder, C.F.A., "Manchester Visitation," July 6, 1947, ABA-LON.
12. Ibid.
13. "Provincial Council Minutes," May 20, 1947, ABA-LON.
14. Camillus Snyder, C.F.A., "Previsitation Remarks," ABA-LON.
15. "Brother Alban Viehs to Brother Camillus Snyder," June 10, 1947, ABA-LON.
16. Camillus Snyder, C.F.A., "Search for Novitiate House in Irish Free State," ABA-LON.
17. Ibid.
18. Ibid.
19. Ibid.
20. Ibid.
21. Ibid.
22. Ibid.
23. Christopher Lynch, C.F.A., "Ecce quam bonum," *Alexiana*, 1949, p. 52.
24. "Brother Camillus to all the Brothers of the Immaculate Conception Province" (undated, ca. February 1948), ABA-LON.
25. Ibid.
26. Lynch, p. 52.
27. Oral interview, Christopher J. Kauffman and Brother Edmund Kelly, June 15, 1975.
28. Lynch, p. 52.
29. Ibid.
30. Ibid., p. 46.
31. Ibid.
32. Ibid., pp. 47–48.
33. Ibid.
34. Lynch, "Ecce quam bonum," p. 52.

35. Ibid.
36. "Minutes of the Provincial Council," Aug. 23, 1951, ABA-LON.
37. Ibid.
38. "Minutes of the General Chapter, 1952," General Chapter File, ABA-EGV.
39. Ibid.
40. Ibid.
41. Wiegers, p. 326.
42. Ibid., pp. 326–328.
43. Ibid., p. 328.
44. Julian Ford, "A Report on Administrative Problems in Our Hospital," September 1951, Gregory Isenhart's private file.
45. Ibid., p. 1.
44. Ibid., p. 2.
45. Ibid., p. 3.
46. Ibid.
47. Ibid.
48. Ibid., p. 6.
49. Ibid.
50. Ibid.
51. Ibid.
52. Ibid., p. 7.
53. Ibid.
54. Ibid.
55. Ibid.
56. Pater Anthony Wessel, "Memorandum on Education," Generalate File, p. 1, ABA-EGV.
57. Ibid.
58. Ibid., p. 2.
59. Ibid.
60. Ibid.
61. Ibid.
62. "Report of the Resolution Adopted at the Provincial Chapter," Jan. 25, 1952, p. 1, Provincial Chapter File, ABA-EGV.
63. Cf. *Alexiana*, 1948, pp. 50–66, 84–100.
64. Ibid., pp. 50–66.
65. Ibid.
66. Ibid.
67. *Alexiana*, 1950, p. 138.
68. *St. Alexius Kalendar, Alexian Brothers Yearbook*, vol. XIII (1953), p. 50.
69. Ibid., p. 51.
70. *Alexiana*, 1950, p. 116.
71. Ibid., p. 129.
72. Wiegers, p. 318.
73. Ibid., p. 281.
74. Ibid., pp. 281–282.
75. "Pater Anthony Wessel to All the Brothers of the Congregation," July 19, 1951, Mission File, ABA-SM.
76. Ibid.
77. "Brother Regis Apel to Pater Anthony Wessel," Oct. 21, 1951, Mission File, ABA-SM.
78. Ibid.
79. Ibid.

80. "Pater Anthony Wessel to all the Brothers of the Congregation," Feb. 20, 1952, Mission File, ABA-SM.

81. Ibid.

82. "Brother Francis X. Joeger to Pater Ludolf Sattler," Jan. 9, 1953, Mission File, ABA-SM.

83. Ibid.

84. Ibid.

85. "Pater Ludolf Sattler to the Brothers of the Immaculate Conception Province," Feb. 12, 1954, Mission File, ABA-SM.

86. Ibid.

87. Ibid.

88. "Minutes of the Provincial Council," May 3, 1953, Provincial Council Minute Book, Current File, ABA-EGV.

89. Ibid.

90. Ibid.

91. "Diary of Events," BT-5, Box 1, Folder 1, ABA-SM.

92. "Provincial Council Minutes," Oct. 9, 1958, Provincial Council Minute Book, Current File, ABA-EGV.

93. Oral interview, Christopher J. Kauffman and Brother Augustine Lohman, July 21, 1977.

94. Felix Bettendorf, C.F.A., "San Jose Project," p. 1., SJ-5, Box 1, Folder 11, ABA-SM.

95. Ibid., p. 6.

96. Ibid., pp. 6–7.

97. Ibid., p. 7.

98. Ibid., pp. 19–21.

99. Ibid., p. 21.

100. Cf. ST-1, Box 1, Folder 2, ABA-SM.

101. Cf. "Provincial Council Minutes."

102. Newspaper cuttings, History File, Alexian Brothers Hospital, Elizabeth, New Jersey.

103. "Brother Reginald Gleasure to Brother Arthur Sanford," Nov. 21, 1961, Current File, ABA-EGV.

104. Ibid.

105. Newspaper cuttings.

106. "Provincial Council Minutes," Nov. 14, 1961, Current File, ABA-EGV.

107. Ibid.

108. Ibid., Jan. 1, 1963.

109. Oral interviews, Christopher J. Kauffman and various Brothers, June 1974 to July 1977.

110. Ibid.

111. Newspaper cuttings, Newspaper File, Public Relations Office, Alexian Brothers Medical Center, Elk Grove Village, Illinois.

112. Ibid.

113. Ibid.

114. Maurice Wilson, C.F.A., "Legacy from Men of Vision," *The Alexian* (Winter 1966–1967), vol. II, no. 4, p. 17.

115. Ibid.

116. Ibid., pp. 17–18.

117. Ibid., p. 21.

118. Gregory Isenhart, C.F.A., "History," Inventory, p. 4, SL-1, ABA-SM.

119. Ibid.

120. Oral interviews, Christopher J. Kauffman and various Brothers, June 1974 to July 1977.

121. Gregory Isenhart, C.F.A., "History," Inventory, p. 4, SL-1, ABA-SM.

122. Ibid.

123. Ibid., p. 3, 0-1, ABA-SM.

124. Newspaper cuttings, 0-9, Box 2, ABA-SM.

125. "Brother Arthur Sanford to Brother Herman Joseph Berkes," Oct. 23, 1963, Current File, ABA-EGV.

126. Ibid.

127. Ibid.

128. Newspaper cuttings, 0-9, Box 2, ABA-SM.

129. Oral interviews, Christopher J. Kauffman and various Brothers, June 1974 to July 1977.

130. Newspaper cuttings, History File, Alexian Brothers Hospital, Elizabeth, New Jersey.

131. Ibid.

132. Ibid.

133. Oral interviews, Christopher J. Kauffman and various Brothers, June 1974 to July 1977.

134. "Provincial Council Minutes," May 3, 1955, Provincial Council Minute Book, ABA-EGV.

135. Ibid.

136. Oral interviews, Christopher J. Kauffman and various Brothers, June 1974 to July 1977.

137. "600 Jahre Alexianerbrüder in Aachen," *Kirchenzeitung für das Bistum Aachen*, April 22, 1951, vol. 6, no. 16, pp. 6–7.

138. *St. Alexius Calendar*, 1964, p. 69.

139. Ibid.

140. John Montjoy, "The Alexian Brothers," *What's on in London*, Oct. 14, 1960, p. 33.

141. *St. Alexius Calendar*, 1961, p. 90.

142. "Provincial Council Minutes," April 22, 1954, ABA-LON.

143. Ibid., March 2, 1962.

144. Newspaper cuttings, ABA-LON.

145. Provincial Council Minutes, Oct. 28, 1955, ABA-LON.

146. Ibid., June 20, 1956.

147. Ibid., August 7, 1966.

148. "Provincial Council Minutes," Aug. 7, 1966, ABA-LON.

149. Cf. correspondence on the Nigerian Mission, 1966–1967, ABA-LON.

Chapter 15

1. Pater Melchior Wimmer, "Easter Circular Letter to All the Brothers of the Congregation," ABA-EGV.

2. "Minutes of the General Chapter," 1962, General Chapters File, ABA-EGV.

3. Ibid.

4. "On Campus," *The Alexian*, vol. I, no. 3 (Fall 1965), p. 9.

5. "Minutes of the General Chapter," 1962.

6. Ibid.

7. Ibid.

8. Ibid.

9. Ibid.

10. "Brother Herman Joseph Berkes to Brother Gregory Isenhart," Nov. 23, 1965, included in Gregory Isenhart's private file.

11. "Brother Flavian Renaud to All the Brothers of Immaculate Conception Province," Dec. 4, 1965, Isenhart private file.

12. "Alexian Brothers, Province of the Immaculate Conception, Provincial Self-Study," Isenhart private file.

13. Ibid., p. 1.

14. Ibid., p. 2.

15. Ibid.

16. Ibid., p. 3.

17. Ibid., pp. 3–4.

18. "Summary of the Views Expressed in Various Reports from the Study Groups of the Province," Categories I-VI, Isenhart private file.

19. Ibid.

20. "Brother Flavian Renaud to Brother Herman Joseph Berkes," May 22, 1966, GI.

21. Ibid.

22. Ibid., May 24, 1966.

23. "Areas of Experimentation Effected in Mid-June, 1966," Isenhart private file.

24. The contents of this article are described in this letter of Edward J. Stokes, S.J., to Brother Flavian Renaud, March 9, 1967, Isenhart private file.

25. Ibid.

26. "Brother Herman Joseph Berkes to Reverend Edward L. Heston, C.S.C.," March 12, 1967, Isenhart private file.

27. "Reverend Edward L. Heston, C.S.C., to Brother Herman Joseph Berkes," March 19, 1967.

28. "Brother Flavian Renaud to Edward J. Stokes, S.J.," April 7, 1967, and "Brother Flavian Renaud to Reverend Paul M. Boyle, C.P.," April 7, 1967, Isenhart private file.

29. "Brother Herman Joseph Berkes to Brother Flavian Renaud," April 11, 1967, Isenhart private file.

30. Ibid.

31. "To Build and to Plant," Alexian Brothers Provincial Chapter, January 1968, p. 7.

32. Ibid.

33. Ibid., p. 4.

34. Ibid.

35. "Provincial Chapter Newsletters," Jan. 6, 8, 14, 1968, Provincial Newsletter File, ABA-EGV.

36. Ibid.

37. Brother Cletus Howard, "General Chapter, 1968," *The Alexian*, vol. II, no. 2 (Summer 1968), p. 9.

38. Ibid., pp. 7–8.

39. Ibid., p. 8.

40. "Some Points from the Provincial Chapter of the St. Alexius Province, January 1969," Isenhart private file.

41. "Brother Flavian Renaud to All the Brothers of the Immaculate Conception Province," Feb. 26, 1964, Isenhart private file.

42. Ibid.

43. "Proposals of the Provincial Chapter of the Sacred Heart Province January, 1969," Isenhart private file.

44. "General Chapter Newsletter," eighth edition, May 17, 1969, p. 1, Generalate Newsletter File, ABA-EGV.

Notes

45. "General Chapter Newsletter," ninth edition, May 21, 1969, pp. 1–2, Generalate Newsletter File, ABA-EGV.

46. Ibid., p. 1.

47. Ibid.

48. General Chapter Newsletter, eighth edition, May 17, 1969, p. 2, Generalate Newsletter File, ABA-EGV.

49. Proposed Charter and General Statutes, etc., Isenhart private file.

Epilogue

1. "St. Alexius Province," *Generalate Newsletter*, vol, 8, no. 1 (March 1977), p. 2, Generalate Newsletter File, ABA-EGV.

2. Oral interview, Christopher J. Kauffman and Brother Charles Renaud, July 18, 1977.

3. "Provincial Newsletter," July 14, 1969, ABA-EGV.

4. "The Province" (Winter 1970–1971), vol. VI, no. 4, p. 26.

5. "Robert M. Strickland to Brother Charles Renaud," July 22, 1970, Waterboro File, ABA-EGV.

6. "Provincial Circular Letter," May 4, 1973, ABA-EGV.

7. Oral Interviews, Christopher J. Kauffman and various Brothers, July 16–19, 1977.

8. Ibid.

9. "Withdrawal from Boys Town," *Generalate Newsletter*, vol. 9, no. 1, (March 1976), Generalate Newsletter File, ABA-EGV.

10. Oral interviews, Christopher J. Kauffman and various Brothers and Mr. Neil Bennett, July 16–19, 1977.

11. Ibid.

12. The following was gleaned from Brother Maurice Wilson's unedited and unpublished "Diary of Events at Gresham" (located in his personal file) and interviews with Brother Maurice and Mr. Neil Bennett.

13. Circular Letter, "Brother Maurice Wilson to all Alexian Brothers," Nov. 13, 1975, ABA-EGV.

14. "Provincial Council Minutes," August 7, 1969, Provincial Council Minute Book, ABA-LON.

15. "Provincial Newsletter," December 1975, ABA-LON.

16. Ibid., May 1977.

17. Ibid.

18. This historian attended the celebrations.

19. Oral interview, Christopher J. Kauffman and Brother Augustine Lohman, July 21, 1977.

20. "Provincial Council Minutes," Nov. 4, 1972, ABA-LON.

21. Cf. correspondence in the "Belgian Brothers File," Current Files, Generalate Office, Signal Mountain, Tennessee.

22. Ibid.

23. Ibid.

24. Ibid.

25. "The Generalate," *Generalate Newsletter*, vol. 8, no. 3 (September 1975), Generalate Newsletter File, ABA-EGV.

26. Cf. "Belgian Brothers File."

27. "The Generalate," *Generalate Newsletter*, vol. 9, no. 4 (December 1976), Generalate Newsletter File, ABA-EGV.

349

Index

Index

351

Index

353